Human Rights Praxis and for Survival

Asserting a critical sociological perspective, *Human Rights Praxis and the Struggle for Survival* reveals the contested historical processes through which fundamental human needs are constructed as "rights" under international law, and how those rights are confronted by the ruling relations and crises inherent to contemporary global capitalism and the waning American hegemonic world order.

Put simply, the book explores why human rights as a formal legal project has failed to deliver on guaranteeing human survival, let alone universal human dignity. Rather than stopping at critique, the authors propose a specific, materialist intellectual and political agenda for the preservation of collective human survival that can achieve the historically unique notions of common humanity and human emancipation. The authors build on previous work, further developing the sociology of human rights as a distinct field at the intersection of Social Sciences and International Law. They take on several provocative theoretical debates, such as those over connections between racism and capitalism; the existence of a global or "transnational" police state; the control, growth, and exploitation of migrants/migration; and the complex relationship between political repression and various forms of domination.

Human Rights Praxis and the Struggle for Survival offers critical analysis of contemporary politics and options for students, scholars, organizers, and stakeholders to grapple with some of the most pressing social problems of human history.

William T. Armaline is a Professor in the Department of Sociology and Interdisciplinary Social Sciences and founder of the Human Rights Minor Program and Human Rights Institute at San José State University. His formal training and professional experience spans sociology, education, and human rights. Dr Armaline's interests, applied work, and scholarly publications address social problems as they relate to political economy, politics, human rights, racism, critical pedagogy, inequality and youth, mass incarceration, policing, and drug policy reform.

Davita Silfen Glasberg is Professor Emerita of Sociology at the University of Connecticut. She is a past President of Sociologists without Borders. She is also a former Dean of the College of Liberal Arts and Sciences at UConn. Her research and teaching interests focus on human rights, political sociology, political economy, and systemic inequalities, including racism and gendered inequities as well as the intersectionality of these. She has published over a dozen books and dozens of articles in these fields.

Human Rights Praxis and the Struggle for Survival

William T. Armaline and
Davita Silfen Glasberg

NEW YORK AND LONDON

Designed cover image: © Shutterstock/Vincenzo Lullo

First published 2025
by Routledge
605 Third Avenue, New York, NY 10158

and by Routledge
4 Park Square, Milton Park, Abingdon, Oxon OX14 4RN

Routledge is an imprint of the Taylor & Francis Group, an informa business

Library of Congress Cataloging-in-Publication Data
Names: Armaline, William T., author. | Glasberg, Davita Silfen, author.
Title: Human rights praxis and the struggle for survival / William T. Armaline and Davita Silfen Glasberg.
Description: New York, NY : Routledge, 2025. | Includes bibliographical references and index.
Identifiers: LCCN 2024021361 (print) | LCCN 2024021362 (ebook) | ISBN 9781032347318 (hardback) | ISBN 9781032347301 (paperback) | ISBN 9781003323556 (ebook)
Subjects: LCSH: Human rights. | Human rights–Economic aspects. | Capitalism–Social aspects. | Human rights and globalization. | Authoritarianism–Social aspects. | Political participation–United States. | Noncitizens–Social conditions.
Classification: LCC JC571 .A689 2024 (print) | LCC JC571 (ebook) | DDC 323–dc23/eng/20240724
LC record available at https://lccn.loc.gov/2024021361
LC ebook record available at https://lccn.loc.gov/2024021362

ISBN: 978-1-032-34731-8 (hbk)
ISBN: 978-1-032-34730-1 (pbk)
ISBN: 978-1-003-32355-6 (ebk)

DOI: 10.4324/9781003323556

Typeset in Sabon
by Taylor & Francis Books

We offer this book in loving memory of our dear friend, Patrick McGuire.

Contents

List of Abbreviations

ADL	Anti-Defamation League
ADNOC	Abu Dhabi National Oil Company
AFTRA	American Federation of Television and Radio Artists
AI	artificial intelligence
ALEC	American Legislative Exchange Council
ALU	Amazon Labor Union
BIPOC	Black, indigenous, and people of color
BJP	Bharatiya Janata Party
BLM	Black Lives Matter (movement)
CAT	Convention Against Torture
CBP	US Customs and Border Protection Agency
CDC	US Center for Disease Control and Prevention
CEDAW	Convention on the Elimination of All forms of Discrimination Against Women
CEO	chief executive officer
CIA	US Central Intelligence Agency
CIT	computer and information technologies
COP28	28th Conference of the Parties (UN climate talks)
CPJ	Committee to Protect Journalists
CRC	Conventions on the Rights of the Child
CTBT	Comprehensive Nuclear Test Ban Treaty
DACA	Deferred Action for Childhood Arrivals
DHS	US Department of Homeland Security
DOD	Department of Defense (US)
DOJ	US Department of Justice
DPA	Defense Production Act
DRC	Democratic Republic of the Congo
EIA	US Energy Information Administration
EPA	Environmental Protection Agency
EU	European Union
EV	electric vehicle
FBI	US Federal Bureau of Investigations
FDA	US Food and Drug Administration

FISA	The Foreign Intelligence Surveillance Act (1978)
FLOC	Farm Labor Organizing Committee
G7	Group of Seven ("advanced" economies)
GDP	gross domestic product
GER	global economic restructuring
HHS	US Department of Health and Human Services
HRE	human rights enterprise
HRW	Human Rights Watch
IAEA	International Atomic Energy Agency
IBHR	International Bill of Human Rights
ICBM	Intercontinental Ballistic Missile
ICC	International Criminal Court
ICCPR	International Covenant on Civil and Political Rights
ICE	US Immigration and Customs Enforcement Agency
ICERD	International Convention on the Elimination of All Forms of Racial Discrimination
ICESCR	International Covenant on Economic, Social, and Cultural Rights
ICIJ	International Consortium of Investigative Journalists
ICJ	UN International Court of Justice
ICNL	International Center for Not-for-Profit Law
IDF	Israel Defense Forces
IEA	International Energy Agency
IMF	International Monetary Fund
IPCC	Intergovernmental Panel on Climate Change
ISA	ideological state apparatus
LPR	legal permanent residence
LWOP	life without the possibility of parole (carceral sentencing)
MIC	military industrial complex
MNC	multinational corporation
NATO	North Atlantic Treaty Organization
NGO	nongovernmental organization
NLRB	National Labor Relations Board
NRRC	Nuclear Risk Reduction Center
NSA	US National Security Agency
NSEERS	National Security Entry-Exit Registration System
OHCHR	UN Office of the High Commissioner for Human Rights
OPEC	Organization of the Petroleum Exporting Countries
ORR	Office of Refugee Resettlement
OTHS	overlapping threats to human survival
PAC	political action committee
PLO	Palestine Liberation Organization
PPE	personal protective equipment
PRO Act	Protecting the Right to Organize Act
REE	rare earth element

RICO	Racketeer Influenced and Corrupt Organizations Act
RSA	repressive state apparatus
RSF	Rapid Support Forces
RTX	Raytheon (corporation)
SAG	Screen Actors Guild
SAP	structural adjustment program
SMO	social movement organization
SPM	supplemental poverty measure
SVB	Silicon Valley Bank
TCC	transnational capitalist class
TNC	transnational corporation
TNS	transnational State (apparatus)
UAE	The United Arab Emirates
UAW	United Auto Workers
UDHR	Universal Declaration of Human Rights
UE	United Electrical, Radio, and Machine Workers of America
UFCW	United Food and Commercial Workers International Union
UN	United Nations
UNHCR	UN High Commissioner for Refugees
UNRWA	UN Relief and Works Agency
WFP	UN World Food Program
WGA	Writers Guild of America
WTO	World Trade Organization

Introduction

Theory vs. Practice

By the turn of the 21st century scholars often discussed the success of human rights as a legal discourse and liberal project to shape and permeate formal international relations (Donnelly 2010, 2013; Ishay 2008; Charvet and Kaczynska-Nay 2008; Kinley 2009). After all, the two Covenants defining international human rights[1] enjoy near universal ratification and it is routine to hear considerations of human rights impacts or abuses in the discussion of policy and practice at every level of national and international politics, across nearly all issue areas and geographies. Saying nothing of their legitimate universality or cultural relativism,[2] their impact in any specific case, or the interests behind their application in any given circumstance, human rights are woven into the legal framework and lexicon of the current international order under waning US and Western hegemony. In international relations over recent decades, human rights served as "the most broadly endorsed basis for the expression of political legitimacy" and "the chosen conceptual framework for discussing, debating, and attempting to improve the human condition" (Heinze 2011:167). In this sense—at the conceptual level and in terms of formal legal discourse—*human rights most certainly came to exist in theory.*

However, *in practice, human rights are not actually guaranteed almost anywhere in the world.* This is apparent from both casual observation and studies on the impacts of international treaties, including those articulating human rights law. Previous research demonstrated that when states ratify human rights instruments it often does not lead to a "normative" effect on policy or practice in that member state (Hathaway 2002). Further, a recent meta-analysis examining over 250,000 international treaties found that only those covering "international trade and finance" or that otherwise had actionable "enforcement mechanisms" (often absent in human rights law) produced their "intended effects" (Hoffman, Baral, Van Katwyk, et al. 2022). Though we will return to the function of transnational state structures to serve the interests of transnational capital, these data speak to the implications so clear to so many in our communities and classrooms—*that*

DOI: 10.4324/9781003323556-1

international law often falls short in delivering on the substance of human rights and the reality of universal human dignity.

American Exceptionalism

This reality is painfully evident and astonishingly hypocritical in the United States—a primary state power behind the creation of human rights and the international legal system. For instance, the creation of the Universal Declaration of Human Rights (UDHR) famously took place under the direction of first lady Eleanor Roosevelt.[3] More importantly, the civil and political human rights in the International Covenant on Civil and Political Rights (ICCPR) and International Bill (IBHR) are based in large part on the Bill of Rights of the US Constitution, and the US played instrumental roles in the creation of the United Nations and international courts. Yet the United States often scoffs at its own international legal obligations and still refuses to ratify some of the most central and widely established human rights instruments, such as the International Covenant on Economic, Social, and Cultural Rights (ICESCR), the International Convention on the Rights of the Child (CRC), or the Convention to End all forms of Discrimination Against Women (CEDAW). Further, the US helped to establish the International Criminal Court in the Rome Statute of 1998, but stopped short of ratifying the statute out of fears of prosecutions against US military personnel and ideological disagreements with US accountability to international law (HRW 2003). By 2002, the George W. Bush Administration effectively withdrew the US signature, and this began a long effort to undermine ICC impact and jurisdiction regarding US foreign policy, including efforts under multiple administrations to curtail investigations of US war crimes in Afghanistan, and sanctioning ICC prosecutors who tried (Psaledakis and Nichols 2020).

The US stance toward the Court seemed to shift somewhat in December of 2022, when Congress loosened restrictions on the ability of the US to contribute to ICC court proceedings concerning the war in Ukraine (Savage 2023). And though neither the US or the Russian Federation are state parties to the Court, the ICC has been participating in the investigation of war crimes and crimes against humanity in the conflict since March 2022. In March of 2023 chief ICC prosecutor Karim Khan announced the opening of two war crimes investigations concerning the abduction of Ukrainian children and the targeting of civilian infrastructure (Simons 2023). However, when the Biden Administration and Justice Department attempted to provide US intelligence materials to aid in these ICC investigations, they were effectively blocked by the Department of Defense and Secretary of Defense Lloyd Austin III, explicitly to avoid setting any precedent for the prosecution of Americans by the Court (Savage 2023).

Generally speaking, the US has played a central role in creating the international legal system, international courts, and human rights framework while simultaneously arguing that the US is beyond the jurisdiction of international law. This contradictory policy stance is a manifestation of American exceptionalism (Hertel and Libel 2011; Ignatieff 2009), whereby the United States views itself as already embodying the democratic, liberal ideals of international law and thus purports to stand outside of its purview and reach.

In part through this twisted exceptionalism, the domestic and foreign policy of the United States makes a mockery of International and even Constitutional law, including some of the oldest Western notions of "rights" as protections that arguably reach back to the Magna Carta of 1215 (such as rights to life and due process, see also Linebaugh 2009). In our previous book (Armaline, Glasberg, and Purkayastha 2015) we argued that the US targeted assassination program, including the murder of US citizens and children in foreign sovereign countries via remote control without charge or trial, along with the US "advanced interrogation" (torture) and "extra-ordinary rendition" (kidnapping) programs as part of the sprawling war on terror *amounted to an obliteration of non-derogable civil and political human rights protections on the global stage*, not to mention violating international bans on assassinations or UN principles of non-aggression and equal sovereignty. The fact that many of these practices have continued under multiple US administrations without individual or collective accountability to international or national law further illustrates this point.

American exceptionalism is not limited to foreign policy, however. The US repeatedly fails to respect, protect, and fulfill its international legal obligations at home to the detriment of the American people. Consider the following challenges to the human rights to life, due process, an adequate standard of living (including food, water/sanitation, and housing), to health, and to be free from discrimination:

- Police in the US killed more people in 2023 than in any other year on record (averaging over three per day), and continue to kill more people than any other advanced nation in the world—a disproportionate number of them poor and of color (Levin 2024; Jones and Sawyer 2020). Jail and prison conditions in the US are a nightmare, where human rights and Constitutional abuses are made worse by overcrowding, understaffing, the COVID-19 pandemic and other public health crises, and increasing complications caused by climate change and extreme weather events (Blakinger 2022). As a result, violence, injuries, and deaths have skyrocketed—particularly in jails like Rikers Island in New York City where over half of the inmate population has been diagnosed with a mental health condition, where over 90% of the inmates are Black or Latinx, where a startling 19 people died in custody in 2022, where local and international human rights organizations have called for it to be shut down, and where the federal government is threatening to take over the facility entirely (McCann 2022; Ransom and Bromwich 2023).

- Infrastructure conditions in the US have degraded to the point that considerable populations—primarily working-class people and people of color in places like Flint (MI), Oakland (CA), communities of California's central valley, or the Mississippi capital city of Jackson—no longer have reliable access to potable water. In fact, almost a decade after the Flint (Michigan) water crisis story broke as national news in 2014 and nearly $500M in federal funding was distributed to replace lead pipes, boil notices and deadly pollution persist for thousands of households in the city (Mahoney 2022). And researchers continue to document the rising contamination of drinking water in the US. For example, one study of 17,900 water utilities and delivery systems showed that violations of the US Safe Drinking Water Act more than doubled between 1980 and 2015 (Allaire, Haowai, and Lall 2018). Additional studies indicate that 50% of American children have detectable levels of lead (for which there is no "safe" amount in human beings) in their blood—climbing up to 80% in states like Missouri (Kite 2021).
- Problems with infrastructure and pollution are only made more complicated by increasing water scarcity and changing weather patterns on a global scale. A *New York Times* investigation of data from nearly 85,000 monitoring stations over the last century (O'Neill, McCann, Syam, Pesta, and Alteen 2023) found that aquifers in the US are being drained faster than they can be replenished due to better access technologies, a lack of effective regulation, and depleting natural supplies due to climate change. In March of 2023 the United Nations Educational, Scientific, and Cultural Organization (UNESCO) issued a report detailing an "imminent" water crisis evidenced by the fact that 2 billion people do not have access to safe drinking water and 3.6 billion people—nearly half the world—do not have access to safe sanitation (UNESCO 2023). Given supply issues and population projections, by 2030 the demand for fresh water is expected to surpass actual global supplies by 40% (Harvey 2023). Finally, in the face of this national and global crisis, the US Supreme Court continues to rule against the Environmental Protection Agency's (EPA) ability to protect public water resources. In *Sackett v. EPA* the Court ruled against EPA protections over 90 million acres of wetlands essential for fresh water supplies, local ecologies, and protection from extreme weather (Kruzel and Chung 2023).
- The US struggles to keep pace with other (post-)industrial countries when it comes to public health and access to health care. According to a 2022 study (Collins, Haynes, and Masitha 2022) 43% of working age adults in the US have no (10%) or inadequate health care coverage, 46% skip or delay medical care because they cannot afford it, and half reported the inability to pay a $1000 medical bill within 30 days. To make matters worse, approximately 15 million more low-income Americans were removed from Medicaid coverage with the ending of a federal pandemic program in April of 2023 (Ivanova 2023). As a result

of this gap in coverage and the high cost of care, over 100M Americans are strapped with medical debt—the leading cause (41%) of bankruptcy in the US (O'Brien 2022). Debt levels are also driven by the outrageous cost of care in the US. Americans pay the most per capita among wealthy nations in the world, yet, according to a March 2023 poll 70% of Americans believe their health care system fails to meet at least one of their major needs (Ducharme 2023).

- Problems in the US health care system and its inequities were made clear in the COVID-19 pandemic, as the country suffered some of the highest infection and mortality rates in the (post-)industrialized world, disproportionately affecting poor and disenfranchised communities without access to personal protective equipment (PPE), health insurance, available beds in health care facilities, or options for remote work (Poor People's Campaign 2022; see also Pascale 2021). The crushing mortality rate from the COVID pandemic combined with increases in drug overdose deaths, gun-related homicides and suicides, heart disease, strokes, and diabetes such that life expectancy is on a downward trend across demographic categories in the US—dropping an average of 2.8 years from a peak of 78.9 years in 2014, to the equivalent of life expectancy in 1996 (John Hopkins Bloomberg School of Public Health 2022). Gun violence continues to metastasize in the US as a cause of shrinking life expectancy and as a public health disaster, where there's an average of 1–2 mass shootings[4] per day (GVA 2023) and gun-related injury is now the clear leading cause of death for children and adolescents (Goldstick, Cunningham, and Carter 2022).
- Most tellingly, the US is experiencing a maternal and infant mortality crisis, ranking 33rd out of 38 OECD member nations on both of these primary public health measures (United Health Foundation 2021; OECD 2022). New research suggests that this crisis is hitting people without access to resources and Black families regardless of socio-economic status particularly hard (Miller, Kliff, and Buchanan 2023). In addition, "maternity care deserts" are spreading in poor and rural districts throughout the country to the extent that in 2020 approximately "half of rural community hospitals did not provide obstetrics care" (Rabin 2023). Notably, those living in care deserts are three times more likely to die from complications related to pregnancy. Maternal deaths have now risen to their highest levels in 60 years, making the US the most dangerous place to give birth among wealthy nations (Toy 2023). Finally, in this context, the US Supreme Court effectively overturned the federal right to abortion in 2022's *Dobbs v. Jackson Women's Health Organization*, severely curtailing reproductive rights, and setting off political battles in states across the country over access to reproductive health care.
- Despite having the largest national economy, sized at approximately $25T, over 40% of the US population is under the poverty line or low income[5] and have less than $400 in savings (Theoharis 2023; Barnes

2019; IPS 2018). Poverty rates were further exacerbated when several pandemic relief programs ended, causing child poverty to rise from a low of 5.2% while programs were in place in 2021 to 12.4% following their termination in 2023 (Oh 2023). The 50-year period of global economic restructuring and financialization of the global economy since the early 1970's suppressed the wages of American workers, who've seen their real hourly wages rise only 18 cents in that time (Strain 2022). Today working conditions in the US rank near the bottom of all 38 OECD nations in terms of wages, protections, and organizing rights (Henderson 2023), and it's increasingly difficult for workers and their kids to get ahead. The US ranked 27th out of 82 measured countries on the Global Social Mobility Index (WEF 2020), and offers far less social class mobility than other wealthy nations. To this point, a 2023 study demonstrated that inter-generational poverty is four times more entrenched in the US than in Denmark or Germany, and twice as much as in Australia or the UK (Parolin, Schmitt, Esping-Andersen, and Fallesen 2023).[6]

The plight of workers and the un-/under-employed is further evidenced by the facts that one in ten US households are food insecure (USDA 2023), household debt in the US hit a record $17T in the first quarter of 2023 (Wallace 2023), and a homelessness and housing crisis can now be felt in most major metropolitan markets—declared public emergencies in cities across California and New York. Over 75% of homes in the US market are now too expensive for middle income Americans making $75K a year or less (over half of American households) (Sor 2023; US Census 2022a). And over half of renters in the US are "cost-burdened" (meaning they pay more than 30% of their income on rent), with rents rising faster than wage growth in 70% of US markets and home values rising faster than wage growth in over 90% of US markets (US Census 2022b; ATTOM 2023; Sy and Fritz 2024). To the extent housing is available, a full time minimum-wage worker currently cannot rent a "modest one bedroom apartment" in 91% of counties in the US (NLIHC 2022). Thanks to the unaffordability and unavailability of housing in the context of reduced COVID relief benefits, homelessness in the US rose 12% across the board in 2023, to the highest levels recorded since HUD began nationwide counts in 2007 (Thomas 2023).

- Finally, as a shocking indication of deregulation, corporate crime, heightened labor exploitation, and economic hardship, "Child Labor Has Made a Comeback" in the United States (Gerstein 2022). Under US federal law minors can be paid the "youth minimum wage" of $4.25 and there are age carve-outs permitting some agricultural work as young as 12 with parental consent. Beyond federal standards, states create their own rules as to the minimum age, minimum conditions, and maximum work hours for employment in any particular industry. These state policies are regressing as corporations turn to low wage child labor to make up for what they report as post-COVID worker shortages (Lalljee 2023; Barab 2023). For instance, legislation introduced in Iowa allows exceptions for 14–17-year-olds to work in previously prohibited industries (such as meatpacking) if participating in "work-based learning," while shielding businesses from civil liability for any illness/injury/death of employed minors (Eller 2023). Legislation in Minnesota allows 16- and 17-year-olds to work in construction with similar protections for employers, and bills introduced in states such as Ohio extend the potential work hours for minors (Trau 2023). In Arkansas, the 2023 "Youth Hiring Act" (HB 1410) removes the requirements that children under the age of 16 obtain work permits that "require proof of the child's age, a description of the work and work schedule and a parent or legal guardian's written consent" (Vrbin 2023).

A vast majority of this new legislation has been coordinated by a conservative, anti-regulatory advocacy group in Florida called the Foundation for Government Accountability, along with its lobbying arm, the Opportunity Solutions Project (Bogage and Paul 2023). Rather than describe child labor as a fix for some temporary COVID related labor shortage, the group claims that teenagers are in fact a "critical source of labor," and that it should be up to parents to decide if and under what conditions children should work (Bogage and Paul 2023). To mirror this sentiment, when debating the rollback of child labor protections in the Florida legislature in 2023, the bill's author argued, "these are not children, these are 16- and 17-year-olds, these are youth workers" (Jay 2023).

In addition to deregulation at the state level, child labor violations—a form of corporate crime—have steadily increased since 2015 (Barab 2023), spiking 88% between 2019–2023 (Looman 2023), with growth in some of the most hazardous professions. Packers Sanitation Services is a company that contracts with the meatpacking industry to do the incredibly dirty and dangerous job of cleaning their facilities and equipment—including bone saws and skull splitters. In 2022 Packers Sanitation was sued by the US Department of Labor for hiring 31 minors as young as 13 years old in Nebraska and Minnesota (Tumin 2022), many of whom suffered chemical burns and other injuries. Indeed, Packers Sanitation ranked among some of the most dangerous employers, had an abysmal record of severe injury, and an amputation record "five times higher than for US manufacturing overall" (Gerstein 2022). In 2023 Packers Sanitation paid $1.5M in fees for illegally employing another 102 children ages 13–17 across 13 meat processing plants in eight states (US Dept. of Labor 2023)—including in states like Arkansas that have now passed legislation to make it easier to employ the same children *legally*. Such fines are peanuts to a massive industrial cleaning company that made over $460M in profit in 2021 alone. Further, Packers Sanitation is owned by Blackstone Group—the largest private equity firm in the world—whose CEO made $1.3B in pay and dividends in 2021, and whose investments in companies like Packers Sanitation are backed in part by public pension funds (Perez 2023).

These corporate crimes seem to be widespread across industries. In the same time span, the Hyundai corporation was caught employing children under 15 to work in a hazardous metal stamping plant in Alabama, and fast-food giants like Chipotle, Burger King, Dunkin', Wendy's, and Qdoba were sanctioned for considerable child labor violations (Gerstein 2022). The criminal exploitation of child labor extends even further to the rising influx of unaccompanied minors from Central American countries like Guatemala. Approximately 130,000 unaccompanied child migrants came to the US in 2022—three times the rate in 2017 (Dreier and Luce 2023). In a 2023 *New York Times* investigation where reporters spoke to 100 migrant child workers, major corporate brands and retailers including Cheerios, General Motors, J. Crew, Target, and Whole Foods were found exploiting migrant child labor in 20 states across the country, many of whom were in hazardous environments and/or working overnight shifts, some in roles where kids had been previously hurt or killed (Dreier and Luce 2023). Further investigation from *The New York Times* (Dreier 2023) revealed that the federal government and White House Administrations largely ignored reports and warnings of the abuse of child migrants, and even pushed out several Health and Human Services (HHS) employees who went to great lengths to alert the agency of potential trafficking and abuse when placing unaccompanied youth with non-relative sponsors (Dreier 2023). Migrant youth and their advocates rang the alarm as well, as calls to the only HHS hotline for unaccompanied migrants exploded—increasing approximately 1300% over the last five years (Dreier 2023).

*****

Perhaps none of this should be surprising. For instance, the US is joined only by Somalia in not having ratified the Convention on the Rights of the Child (CRC), and has a well-documented history of exploiting child labor across industries, particularly before the Fair Labor Standards Act of 1938. The point here is that one cannot argue that the US is "exceptional" in its rights-protection, or that international human rights standards are succeeding in general if, for example, child labor is "making a comeback," public water systems and other critical infrastructure are failing, economic and health precarity define life for an increasing majority, and the criminal legal system continues to be one of the deadliest and most discriminatory of those under measurement.

The international and domestic implications of American exceptionalism illustrate the failures of human rights law to be realized in practice, given: 1) The sheer wealth and power of the US government as also reflected in the American economy—that is, the material ability of the US to respect, protect, and fulfill international legal obligations; 2) The central historical role of the US in creating human rights law, the United Nations, and the post WWII "rule-based international order"; and 3) The numerous policy decisions by the US government that seem to nullify any semblance of this international rule of law—whether in committing the crime of aggression and other war crimes in Iraq (Kramer, Michalowski, and Rothe 2005), unleashing international targeted assassination and torture programs in the broader "war(s) on terror" (Armaline, Glasberg, and Purkayastha 2015), by systematically detaining, restricting, or banning asylum seekers at the southern border—particularly for refugees from the global South (Hesson 2023), or by providing material and political support for Israeli war crimes against Palestinian civilians in the occupied territories (Amnesty International 2022; Segal 2023; CCR 2023).

The Bigger Test: Overlapping Threats to Human Survival

Perhaps the most troubling shortcoming of international law is the seeming inability to reliably bend the arc of human history toward species survival, let alone universal rights practice.[7] The first stated objective of the United Nations Charter, to "save succeeding generations from the scourge of war"—primarily through the principles of non-aggression and "sovereign equality"—continues to face considerable challenges to say the least.[8] Illegal wars of powerful Security Council member states such as the US/UK invasion of Iraq in 2003, the Russian invasion of Ukraine in 2022, and US/EU backed Israeli military operations in the occupied territories have amounted to a bonanza of international war crimes and crimes against humanity, threaten to spiral out into greater regional conflicts, and are leaving humanitarian and environmental catastrophe in their wake. To wit, ongoing humanitarian disasters fueled by conflict in impoverished nations like Yemen, Sudan, or the Democratic Republic of the Congo (DRC) continue to destabilize impoverished and indebted countries in the global South. All of these developments demonstrate the immense challenges confronting formal international efforts toward global peace and security.

Even worse, the threat of nuclear conflict is once again a terrifying reality, exemplified by the Russian invasion of Ukraine that quickly escalated into a broader stand-off between Russia and NATO, where NATO is expanding membership and NATO countries are supplying increasing amounts of military and other aid to Ukraine, and where Russia—the nation with the largest nuclear weapons stockpile—suspended its participation in the last major remaining nuclear arms treaty (New START) (Sullivan 2023) and positioned nuclear weapons in a foreign country (Belarus) for the first time since the fall of the USSR in 1991 (Faulconbridge 2023). A trend toward cold war style military and diplomatic competition is at play between the United States and the People's Republic of China—now the clear geopolitical rival for US control of the Eurasian "world island" (McCoy 2017, 2021)—with potential flash points abound. Specifically, tensions are on the rise between China, Western powers, and their allies in the Pacific (such as Japan or South Korea) over the future of Taiwan and trade and military dominance of the Taiwan Strait and East China Sea, however complicated by the interconnection of great and regional state powers by way of transnational financialized capital. Unfortunately, humanity was already looking down the nuclear barrel, so to speak.

The Bulletin of the Atomic Scientists released a stunning report in January of 2020, announcing that the world was closer than ever to nuclear apocalypse—closer than was the case in 1953 after the USSR and US tested the first thermonuclear weapons. The report stated plainly that, "humanity continues to face two simultaneous existential dangers—nuclear war and climate change" (Mecklin 2020). But these dangers are not mutually exclusive. Social and physical scientists have so far laid out what we call *overlapping threats to collective human survival* (OTHS)—namely those of climate change and weapons[9] proliferation—that most certainly and immediately threaten the survival of humans and thousands of other species on Earth (Parenti 2011; Klein 2014, 2019; Chomsky and Pollin 2020; Ellsberg 2018). These are "overlapping threats" in that they don't coincidentally coexist as phenomena—they are intertwined in such a way to exacerbate one another, increasing the chances of omnicidal crises, and demanding solutions that are appropriately sophisticated to address their relationship(s).

The potentially catastrophic militarization of the world, including both the unthinkable destructive potential of nuclear arsenals and the general routinization of violence and surveillance in everyday life (Pandey 2005) can be understood in relation to a global police state (Robinson 2020) emerging as capitalists and state governments strain to confront political economic and ecological crises of their own creation, with the sprawling US military at its center. This growing militarization of the world, including a return to nuclear arms development, must be understood in the context of capitalism as a global or "transnational" (Robinson 2018) "institutionalized social order" (Fraser 2022) facing a variety of internal and external crises. We will return to these points in greater detail in the following chapters, however it is important here to note that this hyper militarization is potentially catastrophic for human rights and the perpetuation of human civilization in three ways: 1) As a direct threat posed by devastating conflict, including but not limited to nuclear war as geopolitical tensions rise, the world is flooded with weapons, and forced migration (also from climate change impacts) explodes; 2) As a significant source of greenhouse gas emissions and other pollutants, driving climate change and ecological destruction (Crawford 2022; Belcher, Bigger, Neimark, and Kennelly 2019); and 3) As a coercive tool to suppress social movements seeking to confront OTHS (Robinson 2020, 2022a, 2022b), to the extent they are perceived to challenge dominant systems and relations of rule.

Similarly, climate change and related forms of ecological destruction from human activity (such as pollution) pose first a direct threat—perhaps the most certain threat to human and other species survival in the history of human civilization. This was clearly indicated by the Sixth Assessment

Report of the Intergovernmental Panel on Climate Change (IPCC 2021) finding that: 1) No matter what is done, near-surface atmospheric temperatures are now likely to rise 1.5 degrees Celsius higher than pre-industrial levels, have already risen 1.1 degrees, and are on track for 2.1–3.5 degrees rise given current policies and trajectories (Climate Action Tracker 2021; Tollefson 2021); 2) Though a rise of 1.5 degrees will cause considerable challenges affecting billions of people worldwide—dangerous heat waves, severe patterns of drought and flooding, massive wildfires, loss of human habitat due to heat and ocean level rise (especially in the global South) and the loss of life at the poles, coral reefs, and other delicate ecosystems—all of these consequences had materialized by the record breaking summer of 2023, and a rise of 2 degrees or more would present fundamental challenges to organized human civilization in the near future; 3) In order to preserve human and many other species by halting warming at 1.5 degrees, the world must reach "net zero" carbon emissions by 2050.

Combined with other forms of ecological decline, climate change is already causing what is now considered the 6th mass extinction event, marking what is often dubbed the "Anthropocene" for being the only geological period primarily influenced by human activity. In fact, in 2011 researchers found that this extinction event was likely already underway, and on track to wipe out 75% of animal species within the next 300 years (Barnosky, Matzke, Tomiya, et al. 2011). Research has generally confirmed this trend since. For instance, the Living Planet Index (2022) found that wildlife populations of over 5,230 measured species had declined by an average of 69% worldwide between 1970 and 2018. Another study in 2023 (Finn, Grattarola, and Pincheira-Donoso) found that half of the world's species are in a state of decline due entirely to the habitat destruction and other consequences of human activity. The authors offer a grim assessment:

> In contrast with previous mass extinction events … the Anthropocene extinction crisis is undergoing a rapid biodiversity imbalance, with levels of declines (a symptom of extinction) greatly exceeding levels of increases (a symptom of ecological expansion and potentially of evolution) for all groups … global biodiversity is entering a mass extinction, with ecosystem heterogeneity and functioning, biodiversity persistence, and human well-being under increasing threat.
>
> (Finn, Grattarola, and Pincheira-Donoso 2023)

This extinction crisis is also expressed and illustrated through new data on what scientists have called the "planetary boundaries" of Earth's ecosystems—such as that of atmospheric carbon dioxide levels or biodiversity loss—that if exceeded, create inhospitable conditions for human and other species. Specifically, the planetary boundary framework delineates the biophysical and biochemical systems and processes known to regulate the state of the planet within ranges that are historically known and scientifically likely to maintain Earth system stability and life-support systems conductive to the human welfare and societal development experienced during the Holocene.

(Richardson, Steffen, Lucht, et al. 2023)

By 2010 researchers (Foley, Daily, Howarth, Vaccari, et al. 2010) identified nine of these intertwined systems along with their appropriate boundaries, and by 2023 researchers were able to quantify each of these respective boundaries to offer the first real assessment on the status of each system (Richardson, Steffen, Lucht, et al. 2023). This data now suggests that six of the nine planetary boundaries have been exceeded for systems that had otherwise been relatively stable and hospitable to human life for approximately 10,000 years, providing more quantitative evidence of the Anthropocene's arrival.

In addition to this direct threat to human and other life, climate change clearly exacerbates chances of war and other devastating forms of violent conflict—including the use of nuclear weapons and other weapons of mass destruction (Parenti 2011, Chomsky and Pollin 2020), as social and political systems are strained under resource shortages, increased migration, and catastrophic weather events (increasing in frequency and destructive power). Together, the potential of disastrous conflict in an increasingly militarized world and the devastating impacts of climate change and ecological destruction comprise the most certain, overlapping, existential threats to human beings and many other species.

It should be an uncontroversial argument to suggest that efforts to realize universal human rights practice should first ensure the survival of human civilization by addressing its overlapping threats. While it seems obvious that human rights are meaningless in the context of human and other mass extinctions, the strategic implications of this realization are apparently less so. From this vantage point, our work continues to pose the following questions: *Why does the international legal system continue to fall short on ensuring the survival of human civilization, let alone the achievement of universal human dignity? How can critical sociologists collaborate with human rights scholars, students, advocates, journalists, and stakeholders to understand and reckon with that reality?*

A Critical Sociology of Human Rights, The Human Rights Enterprise, and Human Rights Praxis

Over the last 15 years we've joined other scholars in developing the *critical sociology of human rights* as a discipline and theoretical lens through which to understand the process whereby human rights are defined and their substance is realized—or not—in the lives and communities of actual human beings.[10] A critical sociology of human rights should be differentiated from previous, dominant fields of human rights scholarship. While it is unnecessary to go into a detailed history of the various approaches to human rights here as we have in prior works,[11] Canadian sociologist and human rights historian Dominique Clement offers a useful summary (2016:3):

Legal scholars and political scientists have long dominated the study of human rights around the world. Over the past decade, however, that has begun to change…. A historical-sociological approach to human rights can offer unique insights into what is perhaps the most profound social, political, and legal phenomenon of the past century. Legal scholars are likely to focus on the judiciability of rights. Sociologists, for their part, tend to be skeptical of a legal approach to rights. This is not to say that rights are not intimately tied to the law. Of course they are. Rather, from a sociological point of view, human rights derive from society rather than from an abstracted pre-social individual. Law matters only insofar as it inhibits or facilitates the realization of rights in practice.

Beyond these differentiations with law, philosophy, or political science, specifically critical sociological approaches have a common origin in Marxist and other critical (e.g., neo-Marxist, anarchist, feminist, anti-racist, and scholarship from the global South) theories reflecting a tendency toward structural analyses of power. That said, the critical sociology of human rights should be understood as a unique theoretical approach to the topic with at least five defining characteristics (Armaline, Glasberg, and Purkayastha 2015:10–11):

a   Law and legal discourse are seen as socially constructed and understood as an expression and source of institutionalized power;
b   The state and other formal bodies of institutionalized authority, such as the United Nations or International Monetary Fund, are approached critically and are fully conceptualized in appropriate structural context(s);
c   Civil, political, economic, social, and cultural rights are seen as inextricably linked (rather than exclusive categories of rights from which states can successfully pick and choose);
d   Sociologists, if public intellectuals, are presumably concerned with formal human rights regimes and international law—or human rights scholarship for that matter—to the extent that they tend to inhibit or facilitate human rights practice, however substantively defined;
e   Sociologists share the historical perspective that human rights as a concept and practice are ultimately the product of social movements and social struggle.

Critical sociologists have a critical-constructivist view of "law" and "policy" that also demands a thorough defining of the state in real geopolitical and political economic contexts. In this frame, human rights struggles are examined as power struggles, and Nation-states and other transnational state structures are viewed as anything but neutral arbiters.

To illustrate, the "right to food" is only relevant in a society where some have this necessary access to resource and others do not—describing a particular power relationship that is also bound up in the material relations of that society. To effectively achieve the substance of this right—where everyone would have access to food—inevitably requires changing these relations. Legal regimes and forms of legal discourse are necessarily wrapped up in these same social relations, and cannot be conceptualized as providing outside solutions to them. Rather than "abstract principles," sociologists see human rights as conditions requiring particular social and material relations and a "type of social practice" (Clement 2016:7).

In the effort to develop and apply this critical sociological perspective to an understanding of human rights scholarship, law, and advocacy/activism, we developed the human rights enterprise (HRE) as a concept describing the complex ongoing historical process through which human rights are defined and realized in the world (Armaline, Glasberg, and Purkayastha 2011, 2015). In an analysis of this process, we find that the greatest threats to human rights practice tend to be rooted in the accumulation interests of capital and the actions of states that are instrumentally influenced by capitalists and structurally bound by the capitalist system in interaction with other social systems such as racism or patriarchy that are integral to the reinforcement and reproduction of capital accumulation processes. At the same time, international law constructs states—reasonably from the perspective of international relations—as the primary parties responsible for making the human rights protections and guarantees articulated in treaties real in the lives of people. Thus, our scholarship asserts that a significant weakness in the ability of international human rights instruments to realize their intended substance is the ultimate reliance on a member states' ability and willingness to consistently prioritize human rights protections over that of capital accumulation and other interests of ruling elites. Other than the occasional chiding speech or toothless declaration, international law has not (and cannot, absent paired, coherent social movements) address the systemic forces—namely those from the global capitalist system—that most threaten human rights, constrain state actions to protect human rights, and as we will continue to argue, drive overlapping threats to human survival (OTHS).

To explain this concept in greater detail, the HRE refers to:

> The process through which human rights are defined and realized, including but not limited to the legal instruments and regimes often authored by international elites. The human rights enterprise includes both legal, statist approaches to defining and achieving human rights through agreements among duty-bearing states, and social movement approaches that manifest as social struggles over power, resources, and political voice. The human rights enterprise offers a way to

conceptualize human rights as a terrain of social struggle rather than a static, contingent legal construct. In an examination of human rights as a terrain of social struggle, the contradictory role of states becomes more clear: while states are the primary duty bearers under international law, social movements most responsible for realizing human rights – from the civil rights movement to modern anti-globalization, anti-war, environmental, and anti-capitalist movements – almost always form against or in spite of the states (and often partnered private interests) charged with rights protection.

(Armaline, Glasberg, & Purkayastha 2015:14; see also Peck 2011)

The HRE demonstrates the centrality of social struggle and movements from below in formal and informal processes of defining and realizing human rights. We join others in noting the roots of human rights concepts—like civil and political rights—in revolutionary historical periods and theoretical bodies of thought, such as the bourgeois revolutions and political theories capping the late period of Western enlightenment (Ishay 2008). In other words, it should not be controversial to suggest that human rights have always, in fact, been rooted in social struggle. Research continues to show that grassroots organizing, direct action, and in some cases open rebellion by networks of non-governmental (NGO), Social Movement (SMO) and other community stakeholder organizations have historically been most successful in achieving human, civil, or other rights practice in lasting, meaningful ways (Clement 2011, 2016; Singh 2009; Ishay 2008; Molyneux and Razavi 2002; Baxi 2002).

While they can and should protect various liberties in the context of state authority, the formal establishment of "rights" alone does not necessarily ensure fundamental human dignity in practice. The critical sociology of human rights takes aim at the structured inequalities and systems of exploitation without which many rights protections would be irrelevant. This is because, again, human rights struggles are often better understood as power struggles, where the state—and thus any modern rights regime—is bound by its structural and instrumental connections to capitalism and to social systems such as racism or patriarchy. Efforts to understand and realize human rights—what we define as human rights praxis—are in themselves power struggles against these larger systems, structured inequalities, and associated state actions/polices as major impediments to the universal enjoyment of basic human dignity. Human rights praxis (Armaline, Glasberg, and Purkayastha 2015) is a concept to guide scholarly efforts to realize universal rights, where all people enjoy basic human dignity and the potential for a collective human future. It requires a reflexive relationship between scholars and stakeholders in the effort to understand and address shared social problems and structured inequalities that seed and translate into human rights and other humanitarian crises. Finally, forms of praxis traditionally refer to something beyond informed practice—but rather to the collective, reflexive development of effectively counter hegemonic forms of thought and action.

In sum, as an historical theoretical frame, a critical sociology of human rights and concepts like the HRE help to reveal why human rights as a liberal project fails to deliver on the promise of human survival, let alone human rights practice for so many around the world. In the context of OTHS we must return to our assertion that, "human rights praxis is a revolutionary praxis—where ensuring universal, dignified human survival is confronted by the hegemonic forces of capital and increasingly coercive states like the US" (Armaline, Glasberg, and Purkayastha 2015:171).

What is to Come

This book seeks to extend our argument to its ultimate conclusions, first (Chapter 1: The Foreground Material Relations of Capitalist Society, Human Rights, and Crises of State Legitimacy) revisiting our point that global capitalism and the role of states in that system ultimately undermine human rights practice and the sustainability of human civilization, with an application of Nancy Fraser's (2019, 2022; see also Fraser and Jaeggi 2018) theoretical model of capitalism as a global "institutionalized social order." Her provocative theoretical model is exceedingly helpful in that it describes both the foregrounded, internal material relations of capitalism as an economic system, along with its necessary "background" relations that create the "conditions of possibility" necessary for the continuation of capital accumulation (Chapter 2: Contradiction, Crisis, and Overlapping Threats to Human Survival: The Background Relations of Capitalist Society). It presents capitalism as a "type of society" rather than simply an economic mode of production (Fraser 2022). Doing so provides the opportunity to observe the "non-accidental structural imbrication" (Fraser 2022) of capital accumulation with its necessary preconditions of patriarchal heteronormative forms of social reproduction, a sustainable ecology to provide the natural resources necessary for capital accumulation and life itself, forms of expropriation (see also Harvey 2005, 2018) through racism, colonization, and imperial expansion, and forms of state political structures necessary to regulate and maintain capital markets, provide necessary infrastructure for capital accumulation, and provide the repressive and ideological state apparatuses necessary to discipline labor and the broader public.

This theoretical framework helps to pierce through what can become exhausting primacy debates around the relationship between capital accumulation and social systems like patriarchy, racism, or heterosexism. The framework of foreground and background relations, particularly in describing the relations between accumulation and reproduction, and between exploitation and expropriation (including but not limited to systemic racism) created by Fraser (2022) and employed in the framework presented here (Chapters 1 and 2) is informed by the work of critical feminists,[12] Black Marxist intellectuals,[13] scholars conceptualizing what is sometimes called "racial capitalism,"[14] and the continued work of critical contemporary scholars of race and racism[15] who have sought to understand the relationships between capitalism and social systems like patriarchy or systemic racism in their complexity. It seeks to go beyond common conceptions of "intersectionality"[16] in an attempt to map precisely where, how, and why capitalism as a mode of production interacts with other social systems. These social systems manifest themselves at different levels: as global regimes, as dominant processes within Nation-states, and as particular local configurations. As Gargi Bhattacharya and her colleagues have argued (Bhattacharya, Gabriel, and Small 2002; Bhattacharya 2018), these systems have autonomous dynamics and are the forces that shape the other systems—they have areas of overlap and exclusivity simultaneously inhabiting and shaping one another. In agreement, Fraser describes the relationship between capitalism and its necessary conditions of possibility—and even *between* conditions of possibility (imagine, for instance, environmental racism occurring at the convergence of expropriation and ecology) as "symbiotic" and "co-constitutive" (Fraser 2022; Fraser and Jaeggi 2018), with areas of overlap and exclusivity.

Fraser's model is most useful to us here, however, in locating various forms and sources of crisis that define the current era of financialized global capitalism. First, there are traditional "internal" forms of crisis long discussed by Marxists as capitalism's fundamental economic contradictions. Most important among them is the tendency of the general rate of profit to fall in a crisis of overproduction, or what might now also be called an overaccumulation crisis (Robinson 2018, 2020), where in order to avoid stagnation, capital must go to greater and greater lengths to find or create—often through destruction and violence—new sources of profitable investment. Second, "external" forms of crisis occur due to the tendency for capitalism and capitalists to "cannibalize" (Fraser 2022) the very background conditions required for capital accumulation. The problems of infant and maternal mortality noted earlier in this chapter, for instance, serve as a partial illustration of the cannibalization of the capacity for social reproduction in the US.

Two points are most important with regard to crises for the arguments made in this book: First, the unwillingness or inability of state governments to act according to international human rights law can be found primarily as a result of legitimation crises (Fraser 2019; Robinson 2022a) that occur due to states' structural and instrumental ties to capital (see Chapter 1). Even the wealthiest, most powerful states find themselves stuck between the need to provide rights-protective governance on behalf of their constituent publics in such a way to be deemed legitimate in their authority, and the structural and instrumental pressures to maximize national and transnational capital accumulation at what seem to be literally any cost—including war and ecological devastation. Second, at times, internal or external crises can and have now morphed into general crises (Fraser 2022) where multiple crises converge to destabilize the entire social order and potentially the conditions necessary for human civilization itself (see Chapter 2). It is precisely these forms of general crisis that drive and manifest as OTHS.

Many social and physical scientists were already in relative agreement that alternatives to the current capitalist system should be vigorously developed and pursued to give human civilization the best shot at survival, let alone the chance to flourish in the face of climate change or nuclear conflict (Klein 2014, 2019; Chomsky and Pollin 2020; Mecklin 2020; Aronoff, Battistoni, Cohen, and Riofrancos 2019). However, none have employed an explicit theoretical model to articulate the specific connections between capitalism, its necessary background conditions, and the conditions necessary for human survival with the required sophistication and clarity.

We put forward a theoretical model here to illustrate how the capitalist system and the role of states like the US—through its central position in the global police and military state and global finance—undermine the prospects for human rights practice and for the survival of human civilization through driving OTHS. We join others in arguing that OTHS largely stem from the global capitalist system (Klein 2014, 2019; Aronoff, Battistoni, Cohen, and Riofrancos 2019; Chomsky and Pollin 2020) and the global police state emerging as an essential mechanism of rule and investment for a transnational capitalist class facing economic (accumulation) and ecological crises (Robinson 2018, 2020; Chomsky and Waterstone 2021; Aronoff 2021; Crawford 2022). The reality of these implications is of no surprise to indigenous communities and those in the global South on the front lines of climate destruction, or to those suffering through the devastating consequences of war. Our hope and assertion here is that a systematic, theoretically consistent framework will help to reveal precisely how and why the greatest threats to universal human rights practice, especially OTHS, are rooted in the accumulation drive, contradictions, and crises inherent in the foreground and background relations of capitalist society.

Further, we write this book from the perspective of scholars primarily located in the US, who arguably share the greatest opportunity and responsibility to address the substance and impacts of US policies and practices. Even in an increasingly multi-polar world, the US plays a special role as a global power relative to capitalism as an institutionalized social order and the global police state. The US is unique (though not alone) in its ability to command resources to serve capital and dominant "national interests" via resource extraction, colonization, war, overt and covert foreign intervention, or predatory finance/trade/sanction. As US hegemony continues to wane in the face of internal decline and geopolitical competition from China and the other BRICS nations, the US seems to be doubling down on its role as a primary coercive arm of global corporate and finance capital and on its use of military might as a remaining projection of strength for capital interests tied to American empire (see also Chomsky and Prashad 2022). This is a very dangerous and potentially volatile situation, and any discussion of human rights praxis from scholars in the US should recognize its role, and the particular ability and responsibility of those in the US to affect change. The US and broader global police and military state essentially play three roles in relation to the capitalist social order: 1) To coerce and discipline labor while protecting the property of owners as part of the "repressive state apparatus" (Althusser 2001 [1971]); 2) Through "accumulation by dispossession" (Harvey 2005, 2018) and for policing the historically racialized lines between exploitable and expropriable populations in that process; but also 3) As a site of investment and speculation itself through the increasingly privatized (and arguably, unaccountable) military industrial complex—what Robinson (2020, 2022a, 2022b) calls "militarized accumulation," including "accumulation by repression" and the opportunities for privatization and capital investment created in the destruction of warfare—what Naomi Klein (2010; see also Loewenstein 2015) described as "disaster capitalism."

To explore this role of the US (Chapter 3: Confronting the Global Police State) we develop and apply William Robinson's (2020) concept of the global police state as expressed through the criminal legal system (including the prison industrial complex), transnational military industrial complex, and emergent complex to detain, control, and exploit migrant populations (Samaddar 2016). In doing so, we locate the US police and military state—or repressive state apparatus (Althusser 2001 [1971]; Cazenave 2018)—as central to the broader global police state formed in the service of global capital, and discuss the uniquely racist, patriarchal features of the global police state manifested in settler colonial Nation-states like the US in a context of shifting international geopolitics and repeated migration crises (see also Chapter 5). Through exploration of this final point, we will help to illustrate the co-constitutive relationship between capital accumulation and racialized and/or (neo-)colonial forms of expropriation.

All of that said, it is not enough for us to focus exclusively on the repressive state apparatus as the only mechanism of domination or social control through states. In 2015 we suggested that the rise of corporate owning class power, coupled with their increasing "rights," reach, and political influence, would be accompanied by aggressive attempts to suppress rights and political power for the vast majority in the US—workers and the unemployed, women, immigrants, people of color, and indigenous communities. The years since have delivered on this prediction in a number of ways, most obvious in the historic overturning of federal rights to abortion and other related reproductive care in the United States with the 2022 *Dobbs v. Jackson Women's Health Organization*. Witness, too, the continued disproportionate coercion and disenfranchisement of Black, brown, and poor people in the deadly US criminal legal system that, whether looking at police violence, prison and jail conditions, or the repression of social movements, amounts to an ongoing human rights disaster and deterioration of civil and political rights for the American public.

In contrast, the political influence of corporations, banks, and the owning class in the US has grown predictably since the Citizens United case (Evers-

Hillstrom, Arke, and Robinson 2019; Lao 2019; Shiribman 2020). The increased influence of corporate power continues to be seen in its ability to impact policy—such as the massive tax cuts of 2017, but also in its unaccountability to state power demonstrated in cases concerning the use of slave labor (Hurley 2021), revelations concerning corporate and owning class tax evasion (ICIJ 2017, 2021), and the ability for fossil fuel and other companies to retaliate against those who successfully beat them in court (Milman 2021). The unabated rise in the size and power of transnational corporations and banks, and the steady concentration of capital in fewer and fewer hands, has been accompanied by efforts to disenfranchise marginalized populations that echo Jim Crow in language and effect(s) (Berman 2016, 2017; Levinson-King 2020).

Owning class power in the US is achieved and exercised in great part through what Althusser (2001 [1971]) called the "political ideological apparatus" of the capitalist state, and capital accumulation depends on the existence of political state structures as a background condition of possibility to create, maintain, and regulate capital markets (among other things). State repressive and ideological apparatuses work in concert with one another, providing hegemonic and coercive options to protect market interests and suppress dissent through inevitable crises. Analyzing the tumultuous US 2020 election cycle and the barrage of voter suppression bills appearing in the years since, we return to this examination of rampant political disenfranchisement with a particular focus on voter suppression and gerrymandering (Chapter 4: Political Human Rights: Voter Suppression and "Undermining Democracy" in the US). Political disenfranchisement deprives people of participation in the political process while ensuring the interests of the owning class through the creation or prevention of particular policies, political candidates, or political movements. The 2020 presidential election season and its aftermath presented a number of glaring indications that disenfranchisement is still fundamental to American electoral politics, including constant challenges to mail-in ballots (even after elections were certified in states), removal of post office drop boxes, installation of fake ballot drop boxes around city streets, vote nullification schemes, and the encouragement of voter intimidation through the deployment of "poll watchers" to patrol public polling sites.

The formal police state, or repressive state apparatus, does not act alone for purposes of coercive or hegemonic social control. Domination via the political ideological state apparatus also acts to stifle dissent in service to transnational capital. As with American policing, attempts at political domination often reflect the systemic racism and ideologies of white supremacy unique to the US and other settler colonial states. Human rights praxis in the US must include strategies to counter attempts at political disenfranchisement while building an inclusive and politically effective, democratic eco-socialist movement to unwind OTHS and defang the global police state.[17]

Questions of political enfranchisement—in the US and all over the world—are complicated. The UN predicts (McAuliffe and Khadria 2020) increases in human migration resulting from a mix of rising conflicts, resource and care needs in parts of the aging worlds, climate change, and a global economic system relegating more and more people to increasingly precarious labor and living conditions (Apostolidis 2019; Chacko and Price 2020; Jordan 2017). In fact, by 2023 over 110 million people were forcefully displaced from their homes—up from 90 million in 2021 (UN News 2022; UNHCR 2023). Of these, between 62.5 (UNHCR 2023) and 73 million (IDMC 2023) were internally displaced (within national boundaries)—an increase of up to 20% since 2021 (IDMC 2023). Most of the rise of internal and external displacements were notably due to climate change related natural disasters (such as flooding, droughts, tropical storms) and armed conflicts (such as in Yemen, Syria, Sudan, Israel, or Ukraine).

The status and experiences of migrants provide a lens into assessing the actual universality of human rights and the growing processes of politically, socially, and economically disenfranchising migrants who would have been able to claim some types of political, social, economic or cultural rights during previous phases in the 20th century. Further, the case of migrants starkly reveals the dynamic balance powerful states like the US maintain between economic needs for cheap labor—including care labor—and history of reluctance of migrant dependent states to grant political rights to migrants.

Our critical approach (Chapter 5: Migrants, Legitimated Instability, and Human Rights) reveals that many kinds of migrants can be arrayed on a continuum ranging from a) people who are allowed to cross nation-state boundaries to settle long term and seek economic opportunities, or join family members; to b) temporary migrants, refugees, or internally displaced persons; to c) people who are trafficked through force, fraud, and/or coercion (Purkayastha 2018a). Given the tricky balance attempted by states and the diversity of migrant experiences, we take some time to examine the extent to which migrants "have" human rights in a meaningful sense in contemporary capitalist society, and how the role of states relative to the owning class and global police state drive their disenfranchisement. Specifically, we outline the UN conventions that guide migrant rights, and migrant compacts—the UN Compact for Migration and Kolkata Declaration (which has resonance among many countries in the global South), with a particular focus on the United States. Our focus reveals the increased migration of women, children, and those with contingency/temporary permits as 21st century trends in the US. These trends are accompanied by private companies seeking to profit from building empires of detention for the global police state, while criminalizing and denying the rights of migrants and their families.[18] Here again we see the global police state serving as a repressive force to surveille and discipline labor, and as a source of direct investment. The operation of migrant detention centers—which in recent years is eroding the distinction between immigrants and refugees and asylum seekers—

illustrate a coming together of national governments and the transnational state (TNS) (Robinson 2018, 2020) (e.g., the UN, International Monetary Fund, World Bank, WTO, etc.) to foster profit making agendas (Frelick, Kysel, Podkul 2016; Musalo and Lee 2016). We end this discussion by looking at the emergent structures and actors that sustain and wield power to control the movement of people and the contours of their lives prior to, during, and after migration (Purkayastha 2018a).

The book closes (Chapter 6: Conclusion) with a warning that as global capitalism falls deeper into crisis, and states are less able to maintain order through hegemonic consent, the US and broader global police state now engage in a sort of necropolitics (Mbembe 2019), where the death and suffering of millions of climate, economic, conflict, and pandemic refugees along with those otherwise dispossessed by a capitalist society in crisis (like the 2+ million incarcerated or over half million homeless population in the US) can be justified through racial/ethnic nationalism, criminalization, and the construction of national security interests. Such expansive necropolitics can be achieved through simple neglect and inaction, as well as direct state or paramilitary violence. The global police state functions to suppress and exclude those labeled dangerous or disposable, and to provide opportunities for the owning class to invest in systems of surveillance, coercion, and control—as is already the case (Robinson 2020; Cazenave 2018; Vitale 2017; Singh 2017; Zuboff 2019; Harcourt 2018; Schrader 2019).

The precedents for a necropolitical nightmare certainly seem abundant: the normalization of mass public death for the sake of uninterrupted capital accumulation during the COVID-19 pandemic; brutal violence and state terror waged against growing migrant populations like those travelling the deadly Darién Gap and other routes in Latin America to the US and Canada, North African migrants crossing the Mediterranean for Europe, or any number of major internal and external forced migrations across the Asian continent due to climate change and instability (see also Purkayastha 2023); the unwillingness and inability for the UN and the international political class to prevent bloodshed in the Israeli-Palestinian conflict, despite overwhelming international public support for peace and diplomacy; the general indifference shown by powerful nations to those vulnerable to natural disasters and social breakdown, exemplified by US treatment of neighboring Haiti or Puerto Rico (also a US territory/commonwealth with US citizens); and the general failure of wealthy nations to make good on their pledges to help save those populations most at risk from climate destruction.[19]

Human rights praxis in the US must prioritize building a democratic, ecosocialist movement in solidarity with others around the world through union, political, and community organizing. This can and should be done through participation in building a militant, diverse, international labor movement among exploited wage workers and expropriated populations of migrants, domestic workers, and indentured peoples. This arguably involves the rekindling of international anti-racist, anti-imperial, and anti-capitalist solidarity much like the templates established by social movement leaders and scholars such as W.E.B. DuBois, Malcolm X, or their international contemporaries of the 20th century (Anderson 2003; Horne 2008), and the creation of new solidarities born from current contexts. It is critical that solidarity be built 1) at the level of civil society between organizations directly representing public interest rather than between powerful state or economic actors alone; and 2) in contrast to the dominant, prescriptive, pedantic historical model of Western humanitarianism that has tended to act as an extension of hegemonic power rather than of uncorrupted human comradery or mutual aid.[20]

Second, human rights praxis in the US must look to confront, dismantle, and repurpose the global police state—transforming the coercive arm of capital to civil and international corps built on the promise of mutual aid rather than mutual destruction. The pursuits of US global military domination must be abandoned, and its repressive state apparatus (RSA) (Althusser 2001 [1971]) reduced to the function of self-defense, shifting investment and energies to holistic, overlapping solutions to OTHS. Finally, we will contribute to collective visions of democratic eco-socialism, suggesting that despite Marxist critiques of liberal rights as a concept or approach (that we clearly share), eco-socialism is compatible with and should absolutely be accompanied by a human rights framework that provides the concept of universal humanity (non-discriminatory) and the necessary tapestry of rights protections (civil, political, social, economic, cultural) for all to enjoy the freedom and material abundance made possible by collective planning and both indigenous knowledge and modern productive technologies.[21]

Overall, this book illustrates the tension between what we define as effective human rights praxis and the powerful imperatives of contemporary capitalist society that 1) make it such that states, including the US are unable or unwilling to meet their international legal obligations, and 2) form the primary structural barriers to universal human rights practice and the survival of organized human civilization. In this concluding chapter, we argue that democratic forms of eco-socialism *and* interconnected human rights will be necessary for a majority of the world's people to build lives that are secure from constant violence, hunger, deprivation, surveillance, and displacement. Thus, human rights praxis is about examining and confronting the systems, institutions, and processes that directly interfere with or otherwise threaten the establishment of universal human security, dignity, and survival.

Notes

1 International Human Rights are articulated through the International Bill of Human Rights, consisting of the original Universal Declaration of Human Rights as an aspirational document of agreement and "the Covenants"—the International Covenant on Civil and Political Rights (ICCPR) and on Economic, Social,

and Cultural Rights (ICESCR)—that codify rights protections through international treaty, established by the Vienna Convention on the Law of Treaties established in 1969 (Goodhart 2009).

2 It is important to note the position of anti-colonial scholars (Purkayastha 2020, 2018a, 2018b) and cultural relativists who argue that the history of international law is as much one of Western colonial imposition as a democratic process of consensus building. While some like Donnelly suggest that overwhelming consensus provides the foundation for the universality of the current "UDHR Model" for human rights in international law, scholars like Makau Mutua describe the process of creating the model as one of "global universalization without cultural legitimation" (2016:18). Further, when we apply the phrase "universal human rights practice" throughout this book, it is meant literally—in the sense that everyone enjoys the benefit of human rights protections regardless of distinction. This might be achieved through the traditional international human rights instruments or through a greater constellation of human rights practices throughout the world. This larger constellation of human rights practices—not simply those according to formal, legal human rights instruments—should be represented in any description of the human rights enterprise.

3 Roosevelt actually took issue with many aspects of the treaty for which she's often credited. But credit is also due to the organizing and resistance of Black Americans and colonized people all over the world to bring pressure to bear on the drafting and deliberation of the treaty (Anderson 2003). Our point here is that formal human rights law was ushered in under formal US leadership and hegemonic power.

4 Mass shootings are defined by the Gun Violence Archive as incidents where at least four people are shot (injured or killed).

5 Defined as under 200% of the Supplemental Poverty Measure (SPM) that measures both pre-tax income and access to public aid and benefits.

6 Interestingly, the authors also find that, "The US disadvantage is not channeled through family background, mediators, neighborhood effects, or racial/ethnic discrimination. Instead, the US has comparatively weak tax/transfer insurance effects and a more severe residual poverty penalty. Should the US adopt the tax/transfer insurance effects of peer countries, its intergenerational poverty persistence would decline by more than one-third" (Parolin, Schmitt, Esping-Andersen, and Fallesen 2023:1).

7 This is not to suggest that the UN and formal international system, or human rights instruments are of no utility or relevance—we will argue the opposite for an international community with relatively little time to develop broad models for effective cooperation and coordination. But we must reckon with the fact that our current global course seems unable to avoid the most frightful disasters, and seek critical theoretical models that might light a more sensible path.

8 See UN Charter Preamble (www.un.org/en/about-us/un-charter/full-text) and Chapter 1 (www.un.org/en/about-us/un-charter/chapter-1).

9 Though nuclear proliferation is a primary threat here, this includes other "weapons of mass destruction"—increasingly sophisticated kinetic, chemical, biological, and cyber weaponry with the capacity to cause considerable destruction, death, and destabilization.

10 For more literature reflecting a critical sociological approach to human rights, please see for example: Stammers 1999; Sjoberg, Gill, and Williams 2001; Blau and Moncada 2005; Freeman 2011; Blau and Frezzo 2012; Brunsma, Smith, and Gran 2012; Clement 2016; Armaline and Glasberg 2009; Armaline, Glasberg, and Purkayastha 2011, 2015.

11 For a more detailed discussion of the critical sociology of human rights and its differentiation from dominant fields, see Armaline, Glasberg, and Purkayastha (2015:4–15).

12 See, for example, Zaretsky 1986, Laslett and Brenner 1989, Folbre 2002, Vogel 2013, Bhattacharya 2017, and Ferguson 2019.

13 See, for example, James (2023 [1938]), DuBois (1998 [1938]), Williams (2021 [1944]), Cox (2018 [1948]), Rodney (1981), Davis (1983), Marable (1983), and Kelly (2015 [1990]).

14 See the classic works of Robinson (1983) and Kelly (2015 [1990]).

15 See, for example, Cazenave (2016, 2018), Bonilla-Silva (1996, 2001, 2003), Feagin and Ducey (2019), Omi and Winant (2014 [1986]), Ransby 2018, Taylor (2021a, 2021b), Dawson (2013), Gilmore (2007).

16 See, for example, Collins 1999, Crenshaw 2017, Collins and Bilge 2020. We would argue that much more is needed to definitively articulate the reasons behind, specific nature, and strategic implications of the connections between capitalism and various social systems. Engaging in that effort here, we also assert that capitalism as a mode of production is fundamentally different from social systems based on the social construction of race, gender, or sexuality respectively, and should not be equivocated in discussions of their "intersection" or relative primacy in context.

17 Consider, for example, the scientific, political/diplomatic, and sheer logistical task of unwinding US nuclear weapons programs to prevent nuclear war or disasters. This requires political control of a considerable institutional apparatus only arguably found via the state. The same can be said for the institutional requirements for any speedy transitions to eco-socialism. In this sense we will also place ourselves in debates on the socialist left concerning the romanticism of so-called "revolution" and the short- and long-term future of the state.

18 This trend is further complicated as the US is also in need of migrants to fulfil many crucial tasks such as elder care work, which are increasingly fulfilled by female migrants from Asia, Latin America, and Africa.

19 This would largely be through a recently established "loss and damage fund" and other forms of climate finance. Though the fund was agreed to during 2022 COP negotiations in Egypt, most nations have not made good on their pledges and China is not participating in part due to contestations around their status as a "developing" country (Plumer, Friedman, Bearak, and Gross 2022).

20 See Roth, Purkayastha, and Denskus (2024) for a thorough critique of the Western humanitarian model.

21 Here we are referring to Marx's original argument that capitalism provided the technological ability to create conditions of material abundance, yet that abundance was consolidated into the hands and control of the bourgeoisie. Further, the advancement of ever faster, more powerful computer science and informational technologies allow more possibilities for planned economies and market alternatives. However, we also recognize, as did Neo-Marxists from the Frankfurt School, that advanced technologies have become the mechanisms of domination themselves, and that the deployment and control of these technologies would need to be democratized and shift away from their current uses (e.g., extraction, data mining, and surveillance) to serve more emancipatory goals.

References

Allaire, M., W. Haowai and U. Lall. 2018. "National Trends in Drinking Water Quality Violations." *PNAS*, 115 (9): 2078–2083. https://doi.org/10.1073/pnas.1719805115

Althusser, Louis. 2001 [1971]. "Ideology and Ideological State Apparatuses: Notes Towards an Investigation." In *Lenin and Philosophy and Other Essays*, pp. 85–126, edited by L. Althusser. New York: Monthly Review Press.

Amnesty International. 2022. "Israel's Apartheid Against Palestinians: Cruel System of Domination and Crime Against Humanity." *Amnesty International*, February 1. Retrieved on 09/12/23 from www.amnesty.org/en/documents/mde15/5141/2022/en/

Anderson, Carol. 2003. *Eyes Off the Prize: The United Nations and the African American Struggle for Human Rights, 1944–1955*. Cambridge, MA: Cambridge University Press.

Apostolidis, P. 2019. *The Fight for Time: Migrant Day Laborers and the Politics of Precarity*. New York, NY: Oxford University Press.

Armaline, William and Davita Silfen Glasberg. 2009. "What Will States Really Do for Us? The Human Rights Enterprise and Pressure from Below." *Societies Without Borders* 4 (3): 430–451.

Armaline, William, Davita Silfen Glasberg and Bandana Purkayastha. 2011. *Human Rights in our own Backyard: Injustice and Resistance in the US*. Philadelphia, PA: University of Pennsylvania Press.

Armaline, William, Davita Silfen Glasberg and Bandana Purkayastha. 2015. *The Human Rights Enterprise: Political Sociology, State Power and Social Movements*. London: Polity Press.

Aronoff, Kate. 2021. *Overheated*. New York: Bold Type Books.

Aronoff, Kate, A. Battistoni, D.A. Cohen and T. Riofrancos. 2019. *A Planet to Win: Why We Need a Green New Deal*. New York: Verso Books.

ATTOM. 2023. "Renting More Affordable than Homeownership Across Most of the Nation in 2023" (press release and report). Retrieved on 02/08/23 from www.attomdata.com/news/most-recent/attom-2023-rental-affordability-report/

Barab, Jordan. 2023. "Labor Shortages? How About More Child Labor?" *Confined Space*. Retrieved 02/16/23 from https://jordanbarab.com/confinedspace/2023/02/15/labor-shortages-how-about-more-child-labor/

Barnes, Shailly Gupta. 2019. "Explaining the 140 Million: Breaking Down the Numbers Behind the Moral Budget." *Kairos Center*, June 26. Retrieved on 02/08/23 from https://kairoscenter.org/explaining-the-140-million/

Barnosky, Anthony, N. Matzke, S. Tomiya, et al. 2011. "Has Earth's Sixth Mass Extinction Already Arrived?" *Nature*, 471: 51–57.

Baxi, Upendra. 2002. *The Future of Human Rights*. New Delhi: Oxford.

Belcher, Oliver, P. Bigger, B. Neimark and C. Kennelly. 2019. "Hidden Carbon Costs of the 'Every-Where War': Logistics, Geopolitical Ecology, and the Carbon Bootprint of the US Military." *Transactions of the Institute of British Geographers*. doi:10.1111/tran.12319

Berman, Ari. 2016. *Give Us the Ballot: The Modern Struggle for Voting Rights in America*. New York: Picador.

Berman, Ari. 2017. "American Democracy is Now Under Siege by Both Cyber-Espionage and GOP Voter Suppression," *The Nation*, July 12. Retrieved 11/01/20 from www.thenation.com/article/archive/american-democracy-is-now-under-siege-by-both-cyber-espionage-and-gop-voter-suppression/

Bhattacharya, Gargi. 2018. *Rethinking Racial Capitalism, Questions of Reproduction and Survival*. London: Rowman & Littlefield.

Bhattacharya, Gargi, J. Gabriel and S. Small. 2002. *Race and Power, Globalized Racisms in the Twenty-First Century*. London: Routledge.

Bhattacharya, Tithi (Ed.). 2017. *Social Reproduction Theory: Remapping Class, Recentering Oppression*. London: Pluto Books.

Blakinger, Keri. 2022. "Why So Many Jails Are in a "State of Complete Meltdown." *The Marshall Project*. Retrieved 02/08/23 from www.themarshallproject.org/2022/11/04/why-so-many-jails-are-in-a-state-of-complete-meltdown

Blau, Judith and A. Moncada. 2005. *Human Rights*. New York: Rowman & Littlefield.

Blau, Judith and Mark Frezzo. 2012. *Sociology and Human Rights*. New York: Sage.

Bogage, Jacob and M. L. Paul. 2023. "The Conservative Campaign to Rewrite Child Labor Laws." *The Washington Post*, April 23. Retrieved 04/23/23 from www.washingtonpost.com/business/2023/04/23/child-labor-lobbying-fga/

Bonilla-Silva, Eduardo. 1996. "Rethinking Racism: Toward a Structural Interpretation." *American Sociological Review* 62: 465–480.

Bonilla-Silva, Eduardo. 2001. *White Supremacy and Racism in the Post-Civil Rights Era*. Boulder, CO: Lynne Rienner.

Bonilla-Silva, Eduardo. 2003. *Racism Without Racists: Color-Blind Racism and the Persistence of Racial Inequality in the US*. New York: Rowman & Littlefield.

Brunsma, David, K. I. Smith and B. Gran (Eds). 2012. *Sociology for Human Rights: Approaches for Applying Theories and Methods*. New York: Routledge.

Cazenave, N. 2016. *Conceptualizing Racism: Breaking the Chains of Racially Accommodative Language*. Lanham, MD: Rowman & Littlefield.

Cazenave, N. 2018. *Killing African Americans: Police and Vigilante Violence as a Racial Control Mechanism*. New York: Routledge.

Center for Constitutional Rights (CCR). 2023. "United States Complicity and Failure to Prevent the Israeli Government's Unfolding Genocide of Palestinians." *CCR*, November 13. Retrieved 11/14/23 from https://ccrjustice.org/stop-the-genocide

Chacko, E. and M. Price. 2020. "(Un)settled Sojourners in Cities: The Scalar and Temporal Dimensions of Migrant Precarity." *Journal of Ethnic and Migration Studies*, doi:10.1080/1369183X.2020.1731060

Charvet, J. and E. Kaczynska-Nay. 2008. *The Liberal Project and Human Rights: The Theory and Practice of a New World Order*. New York: Cambridge U. Press.

Chomsky, N. and M. Waterstone. 2021. *Consequences of Capitalism*. Chicago, IL: Haymarket Books.

Chomsky, Noam and R. Pollin. 2020. *Climate Crisis and the Global Green New Deal: The Political Economy of Saving the Planet*. New York: Verso Books.

Chomsky, Noam and V. Prashad. 2022. *The Withdrawal: Iraq, Libya, Afghanistan, and the Fragility of US Power*. New York, NY: New Press.

Clement, D. 2011. "A Sociology of Human Rights: Rights Through a Social Movement Lens." *Canadian Review of Sociology*. https://doi.org/10.1111/j.1755-618X.2011.01258.x

Clement, D. 2016. *Human Rights in Canada: A History*. Waterloo, Canada: Wilfrid Laurier University Press.

Climate Action Tracker. 2021. "*Evaluation Methodology for National Net Zero Targets.*" Retrieved 08/24/21 https://climateactiontracker.org/publications/evaluation-methodology-for-national-net-zero-targets/

Collins, P. H. 1999. *Black Feminist Thought: Knowledge, Consciousness, and the Politics of Empowerment* (2nd edition). New York: Routledge.

Collins, P. H. and S. Bilge. 2020. *Intersectionality*. London: Polity Press.

Collins, S., L. Haynes and R. Masitha. 2022. "The State of US Health Insurance in 2022: Findings from the Commonwealth Fund Biennial Health Insurance Survey." *The Commonwealth Fund*. Retrieved 02/08/23 from www.commonwealthfund.org/p

ublications/issue-briefs/2022/sep/state-us-health-insurance-2022-biennial-survey#:~:
text=Forty%2Dthree%20percent%20of%20working,to%20health%20care%20
(23%25)

Cox, Oliver Cromwell. 2018 [1948]. *Caste Class and Race: A Study of Social Dynamics*. London: Forgotten Books.

Crawford, Neta. 2022. *The Pentagon, Climate Change, and War: Charting the Rise and Fall of US Military Emissions*. Cambridge, MA: MIT Press.

Crenshaw, Kimberle W. (Ed.). 2017. *On Intersectionality: Essential Writings*. New York: The New Press.

Davis, Angela. 1983. *Women, Race, and Class*. New York: Vintage Books.

Dawson, Michael. 2013. *Blacks In and Out of the Left*. Cambridge, MA: Harvard University Press.

Donnelly, J. 2010. *International Human Rights*. Boulder, CO: Westview Press.

Donnelly, J. 2013. *Universal Human Rights in Theory and Practice* (3rd edition). Ithaca, NY: Cornell University Press.

Dreier, Hannah. 2023. "US Was Warned of Migrant Child Labor, but 'Didn't Want to Hear It.'" *The New York Times*, April 17. Retrieved 04/17/23 from www. nytimes.com/2023/04/17/us/politics/migrant-child-labor-biden.html?smtyp=cur& smid=tw-nytimes

Dreier, Hannah and K. Luce. 2023. "Alone and Exploited, Migrant Children Work Brutal Jobs Across the US." *The New York Times*, February 25. Retrieved 02/25/ 23 from www.nytimes.com/2023/02/25/us/unaccompanied-migrant-child-worker s-exploitation.html?smid=tw-nytimes&smtyp=cur

DuBois, W.E.B. 1998 [1938]. *Black Reconstruction in America: 1860–1880*. New York: The Free Press.

Ducharme, Jamie. 2023. "Exclusive: More Than 70% of Americans Feel Failed by the Health Care System." *Time Magazine*, May 16. Retrieved 05/16/23 from https:// time.com/6279937/us-health-care-system-attitudes/

Eller, Donnelle. 2023. "The Good and the Bad That Would Bring Big Changes to Labor Laws." *Des Moines Register*, February 6. Retrieved 03/21/23 from www. desmoinesregister.com/story/money/business/2023/02/06/key-points-of-bill-to-cha nge-iowa-child-labor-law/69870761007/

Ellsberg, Daniel. 2018. *The Doomsday Machine: Confessions of a Nuclear War Planner*. New York: Bloomsbury Publishing.

Evers-Hillstrom, Karl, R. Arke and L. Robinson. 2019. "A Look at the Impact of Citizens United on its 9th Anniversary." OpenSecrets.org. Retrieved 11/01/20 from www.opensecrets.org/news/2019/01/citizens-united/

Faulconbridge, Guy. 2023. "Russia Moves Ahead with Deployment of Tactical Nukes in Belarus." *Reuters*, May 25. Retrieved 06/01/23 from www.reuters.com/ business/aerospace-defense/russia-belarus-sign-document-tactical-nuclear-weapon- deployment-belarus-2023-05-25/

Feagin, Joe and Kimberly Ducey. 2019. *Racist America: Roots, Current Realities, and Future Reparations* (4th edition). New York: Routledge.

Ferguson, Susan. 2019. *Women and Work: Feminism, Labor, and Social Reproduction*. London: Pluto Books.

Finn, Catherine, F. Grattarola and D. Pincheira-Donoso. 2023. "More Losers Than Winners: Investigating Anthropocene Defaunation Through the Diversity of Population Trends." *Biological Reviews*. https://doi.org/10.1111/brv.12974

Folbre, Nancy. 2002. *The Invisible Heart*. New York: The New Press.

Foley, Jonathan, G. Daily, R. Howarth, D. Vaccari, et al. 2010. "Boundaries for a Healthy Planet." *Scientific American*. Retrieved 09/18/23 from www.scientificam erican.com/article/boundaries-for-a-healthy-planet/

Fraser, Nancy. 2019. *The Old is Dying and the New Cannot Be Born*. New York: Verso.

Fraser, Nancy. 2022. *Cannibal Capitalism: How Our System is Devouring Democracy, Care, and the Planet—and What We Can Do About It*. London: Verso.

Fraser, Nancy and R. Jaeggi (B. Milstein Ed.). 2018. *Capitalism: A Conversation in Critical Theory*. Cambridge: Polity Press.

Freeman, Michael. 2011. *Human Rights* (2nd edition). New York: Polity Press.

Frelick, Bill, I. Kysel and J. Podkul. 2016. "The Impact of Externalization of Migrant Controls on the Rights of Asylum Seekers and Other Migrants." *Journal on Migration and Human Security*, 4 (4): 190–220.

Gerstein, Terri. 2022. "Child Labor Has Made a Comeback." *Slate*. Retrieved 02/09/23 from https://slate.com/business/2022/11/packers-sanitation-child-labor-departm ent-hyundai-chipotle.html

Gilmore, Ruth Wilson. 2007. *Golden Gulag: Prisons, Surplus, Crisis, and Opposition in Globalizing California*. Berkeley, CA: University of California Press.

Goldstick, J., R. Cunningham and P. Carter. 2022. "Current Causes of Death in Children and Adolescents in the United States." *The New England Journal of Medicine*, 386: 1955–1956. doi:10.1056/NEJMc2201761

Goodhart, M. 2009. *Human Rights: Politics and Practice*. Oxford: Oxford University Press.

Gun Violence Archive (GVA). 2023. *Past Summary Ledgers (2022)*. Retrieved on 02/08/23 from www.gunviolencearchive.org/past-tolls

Harcourt, Bernard. 2018. *The Counterrevolution: How Our Government Went to War Against its Own Citizens*. New York: Basic Books.

Harvey, D. 2005. *The New Imperialism* (revised edition). New York: Oxford University Press.

Harvey, D. 2018. *Marx, Capital, and the Madness of Economic Reason*. New York: Oxford University Press.

Harvey, Fiona. 2023. Global Fresh Water Demand Will Outstrip Supply by 40% by 2030, Say Experts. *The Guardian*, March 16. Retrieved 03/20/23 from www.theguardian. com/environment/2023/mar/17/global-fresh-water-demand-outstrip-supply-by-2030

Hathaway, Oona. 2002. "Do Human Rights Treaties Make a Difference." *The Yale Law Journal* 111 (8): 1935–2042.

Heinze, E. 2011. "Human Rights Contested, Triumphant, and Hegemonic." *International Studies Review* 13 (1): 167–173.

Henderson, Kaitlyn. 2023. "Where Hard Work Doesn't Pay Off." *Oxfam Research*. Retrieved 06/15/23 from www.oxfamamerica.org/explore/research-publications/ where-hard-work-doesnt-pay-off/

Hertel, S. and Libel, K. 2011. *Human Rights in the United States: Beyond Exceptionalism*. Cambridge: Cambridge University Press.

Hesson, Ted. 2023. "Biden Administration Unveils Broad Asylum Restrictions at US–Mexico Border." *Reuters*, February 22. Retrieved 02/22/23 from www.reuters.com/ world/us/biden-roll-out-new-asylum-restrictions-us-mexico-border-sources-2023-02-21/

Hoffman, Steven, P. Baral, S. R. Van Katwyk, et al. 2022. "International Treaties Have Mostly Failed to Produce Their Intended Effects." *Proc National Academy of Sciences USA*, 119 (32). doi:10.1073/pnas.2122854119

Horne, Gerald. 2008. *African Americans and India*. Philadelphia, PA: Temple University Press.

Human Rights Watch (HRW). 2003. *World Report 2003*. Retrieved 02/08/23 from www.hrw.org/legacy/wr2k3/issues1.html

Hurley, L. 2021. "US Supreme Court Rules for Nestle, Cargill Over Slavery Lawsuit." *Reuters*, June 17. Retrieved 09/01/21 from www.reuters.com/business/us-sup reme-court-rules-nestle-cargill-over-slavery-lawsuit-2021-06-17/

Ignatieff, M. 2009. *American Exceptionalism and Human Rights*. Princeton, NJ: Princeton University Press.

Institute for Policy Studies (IPS). 2018. "The War on the Poor." Retrieved on 02/09/23 from https://ips-dc.org/supplemental-poverty-measure/

Intergovernmental Panel on Climate Change (IPCC). 2021. "AR 6 Climate Change 2021: The Physical Science Basis (Sixth Assessment Report)." Retrieved 08/24/21 from www.ipcc.ch/report/ar6/wg1/#SPM

Internal Displacement Monitoring Centre (IDMC). 2023. *2023 Global Report on Internal Displacement*. Retrieved on 05/10/23 from www.internal-displacement. org/global-report/grid2023/

International Consortium of Investigative Journalists (ICIJ). 2017. "Offshore Trove Exposes Trump-Russia links and Piggy Banks of the Wealthiest One Percent." *ICIJ*, November 5. Retrieved 09/01/21 from www.icij.org/investigations/paradis e-papers/paradise-papers-exposes-donald-trump-russia-links-and-piggy-banks-of-th e-wealthiest-1-percent/

International Consortium of Investigative Journalists (ICIJ). 2021. "Five Years Later, Panama Papers Still Having a Big Impact." *ICIJ*, April 3. Retrieved 09/01/21 from www.icij.org/investigations/panama-papers/five-years-later-panama-papers-still-ha ving-a-big-impact/

Ishay, M. R. 2008. *The History of Human Rights: From Ancient Times to the Globalization Era*. Berkeley, CA: University of California Press.

Ivanova, Irina. 2023. "Millions of Americans are About to Lose Medicaid Coverage. Here's What to Know." *CBS News Money Watch*, March 31. Retrieved 03/31/23 from www.cbsnews.com/news/medicaid-cliff-millions-of-americans-lose-coverage-cbs-news-explains/

James, C.L.R. 2023 [1938]. *The Black Jacobins: Toussaint L'Ouverture and the San Domingo Revolution*. New York: Vintage Books.

Jay, Charles. 2023. "As Migrants Flee, Florida GOP Pushes to Ease Child Labor Laws to Deal with Shortage of Workers." *Daily Kos*, December 18. Retrieved 12/30/23 from www.dailykos.com/stories/2023/12/18/2211980/-As-migrants-flee-Florida-GOP-pushes-to-ease-child-labor-laws-to-deal-with-shortage-of-workers

John Hopkins Bloomberg School of Public Health. 2022. *Reversing the Decline: 10 Ideas to Improve Life Expectancy*. Retrieved 02/08/23 from https://publichealth. jhu.edu/2022/life-expectancy-is-declining-in-the-us#:~:text=In%202021%2C%20a n%20American%20was,for%20Disease%20Control%20and%20Prevention

Jones, A. and W. Sawyer. 2020. "Not Just 'A Few Bad Apples': US Police Kill Civilians at Much Higher Rates Than Other Countries." *Prison Policy Initiative*, June 5. Retrieved 02/08/23 from www.prisonpolicy.org/blog/2020/06/05/policekillings/

Jordan, L. 2017. "Introduction: Understanding Migrants' Economic Precarity in Global Cities." *Urban Geography* 38 (10): 1455–1458.

Kelly, Robin D. G. 2015 [1990]. *Hammer and Hoe: Alabama Communists During the Great Depression*. Chapel Hill, NC: University of North Carolina Press.

Kinley, D. 2009. *Civilizing Globalization: Human Rights and the Global Economy.* New York: Cambridge University Press.

Kite, Allison. 2021. "Study: More Than 80% of Missouri, 60% of Kansas Kids Have Lead in Their Blood." *Missouri Independent*, September 30. Retrieved 05/01/23 from https://missouriindependent.com/2021/09/30/study-more-than-80-of-missour i-60-of-kansas-kids-have-lead-in-their-blood/

Klein, Naomi. 2010. *The Shock Doctrine: The Rise of Disaster Capitalism.* New York: Metropolitan Books.

Klein, Naomi. 2014. *This Changes Everything: Capitalism vs. the Climate.* New York: Simon & Schuster.

Klein, Naomi. 2019. *On Fire: The (Burning) Case for a Green New Deal.* New York: Simon & Schuster.

Kramer, R., R. Michalowski and D. Rothe. 2005. "'The Supreme International Crime': How the US War in Iraq Threatens the Rule of Law." *Social Justice*, 32 (2): 52–81. www.jstor.org/stable/29768307

Kruzel, John and C. Chung. 2023. "US Supreme Court Rules Against EPA in Wetlands Regulation Challenge." *Reuters*, May 25. Retrieved 05/25/23 from www.reuters.com/ legal/us-supreme-court-rules-against-epa-wetlands-regulation-challenge-2023-05-25/

Lalljee, Jason. 2023. "Instead of Paying Adults More, Some States Might Let Companies Hire Kids as Young as 14 to Fill the Labor Shortage." *Insider*, February 13. Retrieved 02/09/23 from www.businessinsider.com/fair-labor-standards-act-hir ing-child-laws-worker-shortage-iowa-minnesota-2023-2

Lao, Tim. 2019. "The Citizens United Decision Explained." Brennan Center for Justice. Retrieved 11/01/20 from www.brennancenter.org/our-work/research-rep orts/citizens-united-explained

Laslett, Barbara and Johanna Brenner. 1989. "Gender and Social Reproduction: Historical Perspectives." *Annual Review of Sociology* 15: 381–404. www.jstor.org/ stable/2083231

Levin, S. 2024. "2023 Saw Record Killings by US Police. Who is Most Affected?" *The Guardian*, January 8. Retrieved 01/08/24 from www.theguardian.com/us-news/ 2024/jan/08/2023-us-police-violence-increase-record-deadliest-year-decade

Levinson-King, Robin. 2020. "US Election 2020: Why it Can Be Hard to Vote in the US." *BBC News*. Retrieved 11/01/20 from www.bbc.com/news/election-us-2020-54240651

Linebaugh, Peter. 2009. *The Magna Carta Manifesto: Liberties and Commons for All*. Oakland, CA: University of California Press.

Living Planet Index. 2022. "Living Planet Report 2022." Retrieved on 02/20/23 from www.livingplanetindex.org/latest_results

Loewenstein, Antony. 2015. *Disaster Capitalism: Making a Killing Out of Catastrophe*. New York: Verso.

Looman, Jessica. 2023. "Wage and Hour Division: Working to Keep Kids Safe." *US Department of Labor*, October 19. Retrieved 10/19/23 from https://blog.dol.gov/ 2023/10/19/wage-and-hour-division-working-to-keep-kids-safe

Mahoney, Adam. 2022. "Eight Years Later, Flint's Water Crisis Rages On." *Capital B*. Retrieved 02/08/23 from https://capitalbnews.org/flint-michigan-epa-audit-lead-wa ter-crisis/

Marable, Manning. 1983. *How Capitalism Underdeveloped Black America*. Boston, MA: South End Press.

Mbembe, Achille. 2019. *Necropolitics*. Durham, NC: Duke University Press.

McAuliffe, Marie and B. Khadria. 2020. "World Migration Report 2020." United Nations, International Organization for Migration. Retrieved 11/15/20 from www.un.org/sites/un2.un.org/files/wmr_2020.pdf

McCann, Sam. 2022. "Locking Up People with Health Conditions Doesn't Make Anyone Safer." *Vera Institute*. Retrieved 02/09/23 from www.vera.org/news/locking-up-people-with-mental-health-conditions-doesnt-make-anyone-safer#:~:text=Rikers%20Island%20is%20facing%20a,46%20percent%20the%20year%20before

McCoy, Alfred. 2017. *In the Shadows of the American Century: The Rise and Decline of US Global Power*. Chicago, IL: Haymarket Books.

McCoy, Alfred. 2021. *To Govern the Globe: World Orders and Catastrophic Change*. Chicago, IL: Haymarket Books.

Mecklin, John (Ed.) and the Bulletin of the Atomic Scientists. 2020. "Closer Than Ever: It is 100 Seconds to Midnight." *Bulletin of the Atomic Scientists*. Retrieved 11/01/20 from https://thebulletin.org/doomsday-clock/current-time/

Miller, C., S. Kliff and L. Buchanan. 2023. "Childbirth is Deadlier for Black Families Even When They're Rich, Expansive Study Finds." *The New York Times*, February 12. Retrieved on 02/12/23 from www.nytimes.com/interactive/2023/02/12/upshot/child-maternal-mortality-rich-poor.html

Milman, O. 2021. "Lawyer Steven Donzinger Found Guilty of Withholding Evidence in Chevron Case." *The Guardian*, July 26. Retrieved 09/01/21 from www.theguardian.com/business/2021/jul/26/lawyer-steven-donziger-guilty-chevron

Molyneux, Maxine and Shahra Razavi (Eds). 2002. *Gender Justice, Development, and Rights*. UNRISD. New York: Oxford University Press.

Musalo, Karen and Eunice Lee. 2017. "Seeking a Rational Approach to a Regional Refugee Crisis: Lessons from the Summer 2014 'Surge' of Central American Women and Children at the US-Mexico Border." *JMHS*, 5 (1): 137–179.

Mutua, M. 2016. *Human Rights Standards: Hegemony, Law, and Politics*. New York: SUNY Press.

National Low Income Housing Coalition (NLIHC). 2022. "Out of Reach: The High Cost of Housing." Retrieved 02/20/23 from https://nlihc.org/oor

O'Brien, S. 2022. "100 Million Adults Have Health-Care Debt – And 12% of Them Owe $10,000 or More." *CNBC*, June 22. Retrieved 02/08/23 from www.cnbc.com/2022/06/22/100-million-adults-have-health-care-debt-and-some-owe-10000-or-more.html

O'Neill, Claire, M. McCann. Syam (producers), J. Pesta and D. Alteen (editors). 2023. "America is Using Up its Groundwater Like There's No Tomorrow." *The New York Times*, August 29. Retrieved 08/29/23 from www.nytimes.com/interactive/2023/08/28/climate/groundwater-drying-climate-change.html?smid=nytcore-ios-share&referringSource=articleShare

OECD. 2022. "Maternal Mortality Rates Worldwide in 2019, by County (per 100,000 live births)" (Graph). *Statista*, January 25. Retrieved 02/08/23 from www.statista.com/statistics/1240400/maternal-mortality-rates-worldwide-by-country/

Oh, Inae. 2023. "In One Year, Child Poverty in the United States More Than Doubled." *Mother Jones*, September 12. Retrieved 09/12/23 from www.motherjones.com/politics/2023/09/child-poverty-rate-child-tax-credit/

Omi, Michael and Howard Winant. 2014 [1986]. *Racial Formation in the United States* (3rd edition). New York, NY: Routledge.

Pandey, Gyanendra. 2005. *Routine Violence: Nations, Fragments, Histories*. Palo Alto, CA: Stanford University Press.

Parenti, C. 2011. *Tropic of Chaos*. New York: Nation Books.

Parolin, Z., R. P. Schmitt, G. Esping-Andersen and P. Fallesen. 2023. "The Intergenerational Persistence of Poverty in High-Income Countries." *OSFPrePrints*. https://doi.org/10.31219/osf.io/tb3qz

Pascal, Celine M. 2021. *Living on the Edge: When Hard Times Become a Way of Life*. Cambridge, MA: Polity Press.

Peck, James. 2011. *Ideal Illusions: How the US Government Co-Opted Human Rights*. New York: Metropolitan Books.

Perez, Andrew. 2023. "Workers are Funding Private Equity's Child Labor Exploitation." *The Lever*, March 10. Retrieved on 03/12/23 from www.levernews.com/workers-are-funding-private-equitys-child-labor-exploitation/?utm_source=news letter-email&utm_medium=link&utm_campaign=newsletter-article

Plumer, Brad, L. Friedman, M. Bearak and J. Gross. 2022. "In a First, Rich Countries Agree to Pay for Climate Damages in Poor Nations." *The New York Times*, November 19. Retrieved on 03/01/23 from www.nytimes.com/2022/11/19/climate/un-climate-damage-cop27.html

Poor People's Campaign. 2022. "A Poor People's Pandemic Report: Mapping the Intersections of Poverty, Race, and COVID-19." Retrieved on 02/08/23 from www.poorpeoplescampaign.org/pandemic-report/

Psaledakis, D. and M. Nichols. 2020. "US Blacklists ICC Prosecutor over Afghanistan War Crimes Probe." *Reuters*, September 15. Retrieved 02/08/23 from www.reuters.com/article/usa-icc-sanctions-int/u-s-blacklists-icc-prosecutor-over-afgha nistan-war-crimes-probe-idUSKBN25T2EB

Purkayastha, Bandana. 2018a. "Migration, Migrants, and Human Security." *Current Sociology*, 66 (2): 167–191.

Purkayastha, Bandana. 2018b. "Gender and Human Rights." In *Handbook of the Sociology of Gender*, edited by B. Risman and W. Scarborough. New York: Springer.

Purkayastha, Bandana. 2020. "From Suffrage to Substantive Human Rights: The Unfinished Journey for Racial Minority Women." *Western New England Law Journal*, 42 (3): 119–138.

Purkayastha, Bandana. 2023. "Distancing as Governance." In *On the Margins of Protection*, edited by Paula Banerjee. Kolkata: Orient Black Swan.

Rabin, Roni Caryn. 2023. "Rural Hospitals are Shuttering Their Maternity Units." *The New York Times*, February 26. Retrieved 02/26/23 from www.nytimes.com/2023/02/26/health/rural-hospitals-pregnancy-childbirth.html?campaign_id=9&em c=edit_nn_20230227&instance_id=86393&nl=the-morning&regi_id=138697150& segment_id=126395&te=1&user_id=1ceda8aa3bbd02cbe08de642e72d8593

Ransby, Barbara. 2018. *Making All Black Lives Matter: Reimagining Freedom in the 21st Century*. Oakland, CA: University of California Press.

Ransom, J. and J. Bromwich. 2023. "Tracking Deaths in New York City's Jail System." *The New York Times*, February 4. Retrieved 02/08/23 from www.nytimes.com/article/rikers-deaths-jail.html

Richardson, Katherine, W. Steffen, W. Lucht, J. Bendtsen, et al. 2023. "Earth Beyond Six of Nine Planetary Boundaries." *Science Advances*, 9 (37). doi:10.1126/sciadv.adh2458

Robinson, C. 1983. *Black Marxism: The Making of the Black Radical Tradition*. London: Zed Press.

Robinson, William. 2018. *Into the Tempest: Essays on the New Global Capitalism*. Chicago, IL: Haymarket Books.

Robinson, William. 2020. *The Global Police State*. London: Pluto Press.

Robinson, William. 2022a. *Global Civil War: Capitalism Post-Pandemic*. Oakland, CA: PM Press.

Robinson, William. 2022b. *Can Global Capitalism Endure?* Atlanta, GA: Clarity Press.

Rodney, Walter. 2018 [1981]. *How Europe Underdeveloped Africa*. New York: Verso Books.

Roth, Silke, B. Purkayastha and T. Denskus. 2024. *Humanitarianism and Inequality*. Northampton, MA: Edward Elgar Publishing.

Samaddar, Ranabir. 2016. *A Post-Colonial Enquiry Into Europe's Debt and Migration Crisis*. New York: Springer.

Savage, Charlie. 2023. "Pentagon Blocks Sharing Evidence of Possible War Crimes with Hague Court." *The New York Times*, March 8. Retrieved on 03/10/23 from www.nytimes.com/2023/03/08/us/politics/pentagon-war-crimes-hague.html

Schrader, Stuart. 2019. *Badges without Borders: How Global Counterinsurgency Transformed American Policing*. Oakland, CA: University of California Press.

Segal, Raz. 2023. "A Textbook Case for Genocide." *Jewish Currents*, October 13. Retrieved 10/13/23 from https://jewishcurrents.org/a-textbook-case-of-genocide

Shiribman, David. 2020. "Ten Years On, Citizens United Ruling Has Changed US Politics—But Not in the Way Many Feared," *Los Angeles Times*, January 12. Retrieved 11/01/20 from www.latimes.com/world-nation/story/2020-01-12/citizens-united-ruling-anniversary-how-it-changed-american-politics

Simons, Marlise. 2023. "International Court to Open War Crimes Cases Against Russia, Officials Say." *The New York Times*, March 13. Retrieved on 03/13/23 from www.nytimes.com/2023/03/13/world/europe/icc-war-crimes-russia-ukraine.html

Singh, Nikhil Pal. 2017. *Race and America's Long War*. Oakland, CA: University of California Press.

Singh, Ujjal (Ed.). 2009. *Human Rights and Peace: Ideas, Laws, Institutions, and Movements*. New Delhi: Sage.

Sjoberg, Gideon, E. Gill, and N. Williams. 2001. "A Sociology of Human Rights." *Social Problems*, 48 (1): 11–47.

Sor, Jennifer. 2023. "Housing Has Become So Unaffordable that Over 75% of Homes on the Market Are Too Expensive for Middle Income Buyers." *Business Insider India*, July 12. Retrieved 07/15/23 from www.businessinsider.in/stock-market/news/housing-has-become-so-unaffordable-that-over-75-of-homes-on-the-market-are-too-expensive-for-middle-income-buyers/articleshow/100943695.cms#:~:text=The%20US%20housing%20market%20is,middle%20income%20buyers%20the%20hardest.

Stammers, Neil. 1999. "Social Movements and the Social Construction of Human Rights." *Human Rights Quarterly* 21 (4): 980–1008.

Strain, Michael. 2022. "Have Wages Stagnated for Decades in the US?" American Enterprise Institute. Retrieved on 02/08/23 from www.aei.org/articles/have-wages-stagnated-for-decades-in-the-us/#:~:text=A%20startling%20fact%20is%20that,is%20correctly%20interpreted%20as%20stagnant

Sullivan, Helen. 2023. "What Is the New Start Nuclear Treaty and What Are the Risks of Russia Suspending It?" *The Guardian*, February 21. Retrieved 02/23/23 from www.theguardian.com/world/2023/feb/22/what-is-the-new-start-nuclear-arms-treaty-and-what-are-the-risks-if-russia-vladimir-putin-suspends-it

Sy, Stephanie and Mike Fritz. 2024. "Half of American Renters Pay More than 30% of Income on Housing, Study Shows." *PBS Newshour*, February 8. Retrieved 02/

10/24 from www.pbs.org/newshour/show/half-of-american-renters-pay-more-tha
n-30-of-income-on-housing-study-shows

Taylor, Keeanga Yamahtta. 2021a. *From #BlackLivesMatter to Black Liberation* (2nd edition). Chicago, IL: Haymarket Books.

Taylor, Keeanga Yamahtta. 2021b. *Race for Profit: How Banks and the Real Estate Industry Undermined Black Homeownership*. Chapel Hill, NC: University of North Carolina Press.

Theoharis, Liz. 2023. "Making it in a Poor World." *Tom Dispatch*. Retrieved on 02/08/23 from https://tomdispatch.com/poverty-amid-plenty/

Thomas, Danielle. 2023. "Homelessness in US Surges to Highest-Recorded Level." *The Hill*, December 15. Retrieved 12/16/23 from https://thehill.com/homenews/a dministration/4363103-homelessness-sours-highest-recorded-level/

Tollefson, Jeff. 2021. "IPCC Climate Report: Earth is Warmer Than it's Been in 125,000 Years." *Nature*, August 9. Retrieved 02/20/23 from www.nature.com/arti cles/d41586-021-02179-1

Toy, Sarah. 2023. "US Maternal Mortality Hits Highest Levels since 1965." *The Wall Street Journal*, March 16. Retrieved on 03/16/23 from www.wsj.com/articles/ u-s-maternal-mortality-hits-highest-level-since-1965-f9829776

Trau, Morgan. 2023. "Bill to Extend Working Hours for Ohio Teens Reintroduced by Lawmakers." *Ohio Capital Journal*. Retrieved 02/09/23 from https://ohiocapitaljournal. com/2023/02/07/bill-to-extend-working-hours-for-ohio-teens-reintroduced-by-lawmakers/

Tumin, Remy. 2022. "Labor Department Finds 31 Children Cleaning Meatpacking Plants." *The New York Times*. Retrieved 02/09/23 from www.nytimes.com/2022/ 11/11/business/child-labor-meatpacking-plants.html

United Health Foundation. 2021. *America's Health Rankings Annual Report 2021*. Retrieved on 02/08/23 from www.americashealthrankings.org/learn/reports/2021-a nnual-report/international-comparison

UNESCO. 2023. *UN World Water Development Report*. Retrieved on 03/25/23 from www.unesco.org/reports/wwdr/2023/en

United Nations News. 2022. "2022 Year in Review: 100 Million Displaced, 'A Record That Should Never Have Been Set.'" *UN News*, December 26. Retrieved on 05/01/23 from https://news.un.org/en/story/2022/12/1131957

United States Census Bureau. 2022a. "Percentage Distribution of Household Income in the US in 2021 (graph)." *Statista*. Retrieved 07/15/23 from www.statista.com/sta tistics/203183/percentage-distribution-of-household-income-in-the-us/

United States Census Bureau. 2022b. "More Than 19 Million Renters Burdened by Housing Costs." Retrieved on 02/08/23 from www.census.gov/newsroom/press-re leases/2022/renters-burdened-by-housing-costs.html

United States Department of Agriculture (USDA). 2023. "Food Security Status of US Households in 2021" (Graph). Retrieved on 02/08/23 from www.ers.usda.gov/topics/ food-nutrition-assistance/food-security-in-the-u-s/key-statistics-graphics/#foodsecure

US Department of Labor. 2023. "More Than 100 Children Illegally Employed in Hazardous Jobs, Federal Investigation Finds; Food Sanitation Contractor Pays $1.5M in Penalties." Retrieved 02/16/23 from www.dol.gov/newsroom/releases/ whd/whd20230217-1

Vitale, Alex. 2017. *The End of Policing*. New York: Verso Books.

Vogel, Lisa. 2013. *Marxism and the Oppression of Women*. Boston, MA: Brill.

Vrbin, Tess. 2023. Arkansas Bill to Remove Work Permit Requirement to Children Under 16 Goes to Sanders' Desk. *Louisiana Illuminator*, March 4. Retrieved 03/06/

23 from https://lailluminator.com/2023/03/04/arkansas-bill-to-remove-work-permit-requirement-for-children-under-16-goes-to-sanders-desk/

Wallace, Alicia. 2023. "Americans' Debt Surpasses $17 Trillion for the First Time." *CNN*, May 15. Retrieved 05/15/23 from www.cnn.com/2023/05/15/economy/household-debt-credit-q1/index.html

Williams, Eric. 2021 [1944]. *Capitalism and Slavery* (3rd edition). Chapel Hill, NC: University of North Carolina Press.

World Economic Forum (WEF). 2020. "Global Social Mobility Index 2020: Why Economies Benefit from Fixing Inequality." *World Economic Forum*. Retrieved 03/23/23 from www.weforum.org/publications/global-social-mobility-index-2020-why-economies-benefit-from-fixing-inequality/.

Zaretsky, Eli. 1986. *Capitalism, the Family, and Personal Life*. London: Pluto Press.

Zinn, Maxine Baca and Bonnie Thornton Dill. 1996. "Theorizing Difference from Multiracial Feminism." *Feminist Studies*, 66 (2): 321–331.

Zuboff, Shoshana. 2019. *The Age of Surveillance Capitalism: The Fight for a Human Future at the New Frontier of Power*. New York: Public Affairs.

1 The Foreground Material Relations of Capitalist Society, Human Rights, and Crises of State Legitimacy

Over the last fifteen years, one of our overarching goals has been to offer critical sociological perspectives on the limitations and potentials of human rights as a body of law, form of discourse, conceptual framework, and "social practice" (Clement 2016). Doing so has required building an appropriate theoretical framework or analytical lens that places international law, the state, and the ongoing power struggles to define and realize human rights within certain socio-historical and structural contexts. Specifically, this framework must be fit to analyze the human rights enterprise and envision effective human rights praxis in relation to the forces of capitalism, geopolitics, and perhaps most importantly, the OTHS created by such forces and structural conditions. We attempt to articulate this framework over the course of Chapters 1 and 2 on the "foreground" and "background" relations of "capitalism as an institutionalized social order" (Fraser 2022).

Briefly in review of our previous work on this topic, we've argued (Armaline, Glasberg, and Purkayastha 2011, 2015) that many of the most prevalent, systematic, and devastating human rights abuses are often caused by: 1) The short-term accumulation interests of corporate and finance capital, often out of a competitive necessity to "externalize" any and all costs and risks of their activities to other firms, the state, or—most often—the public, wherever and however possible (see also Bakan 2004; TEEB 2013);[1] and 2) The actions or inaction of states that are instrumentally captured by blocks of capital and structurally constrained by their position relative to the global capitalist system and what will be discussed here as the "background relations" or "conditions of possibility" necessary for capital accumulation—including social systems like racism or patriarchy and the violent geopolitical relations of empire and (neo)colonialism. Finally, an analysis of the human rights enterprise, or the contested historical process through which human rights are defined and realized (or not) in the lives of actual people and communities, reveals that 1) human rights struggles are best understood as power struggles, and that 2) these struggles are almost always waged against or in spite of the state charged with rights protections in the first place.[2]

DOI: 10.4324/9781003323556-2

Indeed, formal international human rights law constructs states as the primary guarantors responsible for realizing the human rights obligations articulated through human rights instruments, assuming the willingness and ability of state parties to choose the provision of universal human rights practice—including when in real or perceived conflict with capital accumulation or other interests of elites. The central role of states has much to do with the fact that international law and the UN Charter were all legitimated through treaties between sovereign Nation-states formed under a Western liberal political order since the World Wars of the 20th century. Regardless of origin, a critical sociological analysis of the human rights enterprise demonstrates that this misunderstanding of the state—as sufficiently unfettered by capital and other structural forces to "respect, protect, and fulfill" the rights articulated in human rights instruments—is a fundamental limitation of international human rights law, and points to capitalism and its background relations as the primary impediments to universal human rights practice and primary drivers of OTHS. It also illustrates that to the extent human rights come to be ensured through state policy/practice or other means of community power or mutual aid, this is almost always the result of actual social struggles and movements that navigate and shift relations of power.

Taking all of that into account, critical sociologists and human rights scholars have so far failed to apply an appropriately sophisticated conceptualization of capitalism relative to the state, other social systems and conditions inextricably linked to capital accumulation, and the various threats to universal human dignity and survival. In this and the following chapter, we sketch such a model for the purposes of critical human rights scholarship, centrally employing Nancy Fraser's (2022; see also Fraser and Jaeggi 2018) conceptualization of capitalism as a resilient, yet crises stricken "institutionalized social order," William Robinson's (2004, 2014, 2018a, 2020, 2022a, 2022b) concepts of the transnational corporation (TNC), transnational state (TNS), transnational capitalist class (TCC), and global police state, and the insights of scholars such as Alfred McCoy (2017, 2021) who shed light on the geopolitical forces and philosophies of human rights at play in the historical transition of global "world orders."

Constructing this theoretical framework first represents a step in conceptually rethinking and mapping contemporary capitalism and its historical development. Specifically:

- It avoids defining capitalism or the state in an overly deterministic "base—superstructure orthodoxy," where capitalism is seen primarily as an economic system, with an economic base or mode of production from which all other aspects of social and political life (Mosquera 2021) are believed to emerge.
- It helps move critical sociology beyond primacy debates around the relationships between capitalism as an economic system and, for instance, social systems like racism or patriarchy. This is done through

a conceptualization of capitalism as an institutionalized social order that includes both the "foreground" material relations of capitalism as an economic system or mode of production, and the "background" relations that provide the "conditions of possibility" for capital accumulation (Fraser 2022).

- It identifies unique characteristics of capitalism in its current historical form, such as the emergence of a transnational capitalist class who own and manage the world's most powerful transnational corporations and financial firms (Robinson 2018a, 2022a), and of a global police state (Robinson 2020, 2022a, 2022b) as a source of capital accumulation and mechanism for disciplining exploited ("free," wage) and expropriated ("dependent," enslaved or otherwise subjugated) labor.
- It considers the role of geopolitical competition in the global expansion of capital, the provision of expropriated forms of capital, the development of the critical technologies (primarily related to energy) that essentially spur and literally fuel each new phase of capitalism, and in providing the requisite international structure(s) and hegemony for global trade and capital flows. Further, this allows one to consider contemporary imperial competition in relation to capitalist crises and OTHS. As we will argue, one key to universal human dignity and the survival of human civilization will not depend on "who wins" these contests so much as our collective ability to escape the pattern of imperial competition altogether in favor of new international material and political relations of cooperation and mutual aid.

In addition to advancing some important theoretical tools, the framework constructed here will be applied to address the first guiding question of this book: *Why does the international legal system continue to fall short on ensuring the survival of human civilization, let alone the achievement of universal human dignity?* Specifically, this framework allows us to locate the inability or unwillingness of states to choose human rights protections when in conflict with the interests of capital accumulation and powerful elites in the legitimacy crises that seem to constrain all state parties. This constraint on the actions of states should also be seen as a defining characteristic of the current era of global capitalism. Second, (see Chapter 2) it allows us to locate the greatest overlapping threats to human survival and human rights practice in the exploitation and expropriation at the heart of capitalist society, and in its tendencies toward general crisis and the "cannibalization" (Fraser 2022) of its conditions of possibility.

The Foreground Relations of Capitalism as an Institutionalized Global Social Order

According to the scholarship of philosopher, feminist, and critical theorist Nancy Fraser, (2016, 2019, 2022; Fraser and Jaeggi 2018), rather than a type of economic system, capitalism is better understood as a "type of society" that reflects both the "foreground" material relations of class that Marx describes as defining any particular mode of production, and the seemingly non-economic "background" relations that provide the necessary "conditions of possibility" for capital accumulation. As a whole, these foreground and background relations comprise what Fraser (2022) calls capitalism as an "institutionalized social order."

The foreground of this social order reflects the specifically capitalist mode of production commonly understood from Marx's *Capital Vol. I.* In Fraser's (2022) read of *Capital,* there are four important features to capitalism's economic foreground:

- It differs from previous modes of production in its defining material, or class relations that are largely reduced from prior epochs to a single conflict between the bourgeoisie (owners/employers) and proletariat (workers/producers). This material relation originates in the expanded conception of private property through the closing of the public commons characteristic to feudalism (Linebaugh 2014), and capitalists' capture[3] of land and other forms of capital (natural/raw materials, industrial machines/factories, finance, and so forth) that together comprise what Marx (2004 [1867]) called the means of production. In Marx's framework, class is defined relative to the control of the means of production and these various forms of capital. The owning class is powerful not simply because they're rich, but because they've captured and monopolize the means of production—the literal ability to produce the goods and services that everyone in society depends on to meet their material needs. The working class is defined by the fact that, absent access to capital and the means of production, they must rent themselves—or in Marx's more romantic accounts of alienation,[4] sell their distinctly human creative productive capacities to a capitalist in return for a wage in order to survive.
- This market of independent, exploitable workers is the second defining characteristic of capitalism as a mode of production—what Fraser (2022:4) calls "doubly free labor." In the first sense, wage workers are relatively independent in that they're free to enter into contract with employers of their choice. In comparison, the labor of feudal serfs, indentured servants of all sorts, domestic and other care workers (often women and children), or various forms of slaves (often racialized populations) is "unfree or dependent, unacknowledged or unremunerated" (Fraser 2022:4). Second, as noted above, and unlike landed peasants or feudal serfs, wage labor is also "free" from access to the necessary means of production and natural resources previously available through public and ancestral commons.
- A third feature of capitalism's economic foreground regards the notion of self-expanding value. Fraser (2022:4) describes this "peculiar" feature as the system's "objective systemic thrust"—for capitalists to

accumulate, and through competition concentrate more and more capital. Value is "self-expanding" through the process of labor exploitation (and as we will find later, expropriation) where all value is created by labor, but the surplus value created by that labor is reaped by the capitalist alone, and translated into forms of profit when the produced commodities are brought to market. Capitalists then reinvest a significant amount of that surplus value back into their enterprises as new capital for the purposes of accumulating even more surplus in following cycles of production. Capitalists are driven to expand the realm of commodities (while also depending on non-commodified resources and labor, as we will find shortly), and to scour the globe for new cheap labor markets to meet their accumulation interests in competition with other capitalists. Here one should note the way that both workers and owners become wrapped up in this "objective" thrust that locks them into a material relation of exploitation, competing interests, and conflict.

- The fourth and final feature that Fraser's model draws from Marx are the specific roles that markets play in capitalist society. First, in capitalism, markets are used in order to distribute the means of production and labor required as inputs for the production process. This requires a "free" market of exploitable wage labor previously described, and the means of production must be commodified and made subject to market forces. Second, and perhaps most importantly, the collective surplus, or abundance made uniquely possible by capitalism's new technologies of mass production and the labor of workers to produce new forms of value in the production process is syphoned off by the owning class and otherwise (re-)distributed through markets rather than some other guiding logic or principle, such as that of democratic public decision-making or respect for international social and economic human rights standards. While capitalism made it possible for human societies to produce incredible abundance, rather than distributing it such that all people could escape the need to toil for daily survival, capitalism concentrates that abundance in the hands of a small bourgeoisie.

Empirically speaking, the upward concentration of wealth and capital on the global scale is readily apparent, and was supercharged through the COVID-19 pandemic. Since 2020 the wealthiest 1% in the world hoarded nearly two thirds of all new wealth—twice that of the remaining 99%. The wealthiest 10% holds 76% of global wealth, earns 52% of all income, and cause 48% of global carbon emissions through their activities and voracious consumption (World Inequality Lab 2022). Global billionaires, whose ranks have doubled in the last 10 years, are now increasing their collective fortunes by $2.7B per day and the wealthiest 81 among them own more than the bottom 50% of the global population combined (Christensen, Hallum, Maitland, Parrinello, and Putaturo 2023). The collective net worth of the approximately 2600 total billionaires in 2022 ($12.2T) would represent the third largest Gross Domestic

Product (GDP) in the world if they were a country, after the US ($25T) and China ($18.3T). In fact, they're worth more than the GDPs of the next three nations (Japan – $4.3T, Germany – $4T – India $3.5T) combined, that represent a population of over 1.63 billion people (Koop 2022; Routley 2022). Finally, according to the most recent analysis by Oxfam International (2024), the holdings of the wealthiest five men in the world increased by 114% since 2020 at a rate of $14 million per hour, making it likely that the first individual trillionaire will emerge in the next decade. To demonstrate their institutionalized economic power beyond sheer wealth, billionaires run or act as the principal shareholder for seven of the ten largest corporations in the world (Oxfam 2024).

This extreme concentration at the top is being met with immiseration below. According to the World Bank's (2022) Poverty and Shared Prosperity Report, efforts long touted by the global business community and their friends in government to end extreme poverty by 2030 will likely fail, given in part to the unequal impacts of the global COVID-19 pandemic, climate change, corporate price hikes, and the disruption of important supply chains from the Ukrainian and other conflicts. In fact, more people (70M) fell into extreme poverty in 2020 than in any year since monitoring began 30 years prior, bringing the 2020 total to a staggering 719 million people earning under $2.15 per day.[5] Additionally, by 2023 the number of people facing acute food insecurity worldwide rose to 333M, an increase of over 200M people since before the COVID-19 pandemic (WFP 2024). According to the UN World Food Program (WFP) this amounts to a "global food crisis," driven primarily by the spread of conflict and mass violence (70% of those going hungry have been affected by war) and by the implications of climate change on food supplies. Here we see one of many instances where the overlapping threats of mass conflict and climate change drive some of the greatest threats to survival among significantly large, vulnerable populations.

Such extreme and intensifying inequality stands starkly counter to the resource distribution necessary to establish the universal, dignified material conditions (rights to food, housing, health care, and so forth) demanded by human rights instruments, and arguably prevents the distribution and investment of resources that will be needed to address the direct and indirect implications of climate change and ecological destruction as OTHS. Moreover, *astronomical wealth disparity is not a coincidental outcome, but a fundamental feature of contemporary capitalist society.*

Capitalism is fueled by the creation and maintenance of desperation, where the massive concentrated wealth of the owning class demands and results from the political repression and economic precarity of the majority. Desperation is further maintained through the background relations of capitalist society, where social systems like patriarchy and systemic racism can disempower, disenfranchise, destabilize, or entirely destroy[6] peoples and their communities while complicating any attempts toward working class consciousness and political solidarity.

Capitalism was born out of violence and theft, and has always been defined by the distinctly exploitive material relation between owners and workers. States emerged throughout this process, shaped in the service of mercantile, then national, and then transnational capital; forging, interpreting, and administering law overwhelmingly in favor of capital accumulation interests over principles of (for instance) civil or human rights when in conflict—conceptions of which changed over time and across imperial world orders (McCoy 2021). Capitalism proves to be at odds with the substance of contemporary human rights due to the exploitation and, as we will discuss in Chapter 2, expropriation of human labor and lives that are central to the process of capital accumulation. Capitalism also confronts the legal framework of international human rights law, in that capital bends the state to its accumulation interests at the cost of international human rights obligations and other priorities—even at the cost of legitimacy in the eyes of the greater public.

What Stage of Capitalism is This?: Regimes of Accumulation

There is agreement among many critical scholars that the historical development of capitalism as an economic system can be understood over the course of four approximate historical periods, each with its own defining characteristics. Fraser (2022) aptly refers to these historical periods as "regimes of accumulation." She notes that each regime is determined by foregrounded struggles over "commodity production and the distribution of surplus" (Fraser 2022:21). That is, by the class struggles over control of the means of production in society and over the surplus, or abundance created by the production process. In addition, each regime of accumulation is determined co-constitutively by boundary struggles (Fraser 2022:21) over the background relations and conditions necessary for capital accumulation, such as viable forms of social reproduction, racism and racialized forms of accumulation, or the ecological and natural resources needed for the production process and the sustaining of life on the planet. While it is beyond the scope of this book to give a detailed history of the foreground and background relations of capitalism as an institutionalized social order, the following provides Fraser (2022) and Robinson's (2018a) perspectives on the historical development of capitalist society and the defining characteristics of each regime of accumulation. Second, this section will illustrate how each regime of accumulation intertwines with and is defined by systemic racism as a social system that will later be described as the primary source of expropriated capital—a background condition for any regime of capital accumulation. Third, while previous eras will be covered in brief, this section will provide a more thorough description of the current regime of accumulation (transnational financialized capitalism) and contemporary systemic racism.

Mercantile Capitalism

The first regime of accumulation is commonly referred to as "mercantile capitalism," referencing the pre-capitalist mercantile trade that would rise in the long, bloody transition away from feudalism in the empires of Europe across the 16th, 17th, and 18th centuries. This is also the period of what Marx (2004) called primitive accumulation that occurred in the "rosy dawn"[7] of capitalist development. Primitive accumulation refers to the violent process through which land and other publicly shared resources or "commons" were "closed," or taken from feudal serfs in Europe, creating a "landless proletariat" (Harvey 2005) out of former peasants that would now have to rent themselves as wage laborers to survive, and commodifying formerly public lands and resources for the new private capital markets (Linebaugh 2014). This process included the often genocidal taking, stealing, or expropriation of land and resources from indigenous populations through competitive colonial expansion of European empires into the Western Hemisphere, Africa (including the establishment of the Trans-Atlantic Slave trade), Asia, and the Pacific. According to Fraser (2022:34–35), "expropriation works by *confiscating* human capacities and natural resources and *conscripting* them into the circuits of capital accumulation." In this last sense (conscription into circuits of capital accumulation), expropriation differs from pre-capitalist forms of plunder. This early expropriation was inextricably tied to the historical construction of race as a modern concept (Smedley and Smedley, 2012) and the emergence of racism as a fully coherent social system (Wilson 1996; Feagin and Ducey 2019) in the same period of conquest and enslavement in the Americas, providing a massive amount of new private capital for the budding bourgeoisie and emerging bourgeois states, including new forms of expropriated (e.g., chattel slave or colonized) labor that was, again, "unfree or dependent, unacknowledged or unremunerated" (Fraser 2022:4). Here Fraser (2022) reads Marx in agreement with Rosa Luxemburg (1968) and David Harvey (2005), arguing that from capital's inception, forms of expropriation have been required in order to create, expand, and undergird forms of labor exploitation and the broader regime of accumulation.

Liberal-Colonial or Classical Competitive Capitalism

The second period of "liberal-colonial" (Fraser 2022) or "classical competitive" (Robinson 2018a) capitalism is marked by the mass productive technologies made available by the industrial revolution, the rise of the modern bourgeoisie and bourgeois state following the American and French Revolutions, and the establishment of formal colonial systems creating formal sectors of free, exploitable, typically white labor and expropriated racialized and/or colonized labor. In the US, this would align historically with the Jim Crow system of debt peonage and white racial backlash against the post-civil war reconstruction period in the form of vigilante violence (including the emergence of the Ku Klux Klan and their systematic use of lynching and other forms of terrorism) and extreme social sanctions (e.g., "black codes") providing for what W.E.B. DuBois (1998 [1903]) called the psychological "wages of whiteness" that helped to separate white wage workers from racialized, expropriated labor in daily life (Wilson 1996; Feagin and Ducey 2019; Blackmon 2008). It would also mark the completion of Western expansion in the expropriation of indigenous and Mexican lands in North America and the US claim to colonial domination of the Western Hemisphere on behalf of US capital interests through the Monroe Doctrine of 1823, while competing European empires continued to colonize swaths of the African and Asian continents.

State Managed or Corporate Monopoly Capitalism

The third period of "state-managed" (Fraser 2022), or "corporate," or "monopoly" (Robinson 2018a) capitalism spanning from the late 19th to the late 20th century is marked by several important characteristics:

- First, it's characterized by the global domination of Nation-states, and a "world economy" of trade and finance in an "integrated international market." That is, the economy was comprised of "circuits of accumulation"[8] (Robinson 2018a) or what Marx called "circuits of capital" that operated at the national level in competition with other nations. This in part resulted in two world wars, and then the creation of the first international systems of diplomacy in the League of Nations and United Nations that would create what we refer to as the liberal "rule based international order," including the creation of international humanitarian and human rights law.
- Second, this period is marked by the establishment of the modern industrial corporation that would emerge in the late 19th century. In the US, corporations would gain many of the rights of people under the Constitution[9] through a questionable interpretation of the 14th Amendment—intended to extend equality under the law to former slaves, but used by corporate lawyers to argue the rights of incorporated businesses (Bakan 2004). The corporate model would quickly become the dominant institutional business form in the world economy.
- Third, during and following the world wars, the Keynesian welfare state model flourished in the West, where capitalist states took more active roles in regulating the activities of industry (think of the Food and Drug Administration, for example), and providing resources to offset the damage of capitalist crises (such as the New Deal in response to the Great Depression) and potential of spreading revolutions against the capitalist system at the nation-state level.
- Fourth, there was an emergence of "socialist alternatives" (Robinson 2018a) in the form of revolutions that would form the USSR, The

Peoples Republic of China, and other (aligned and nonaligned) socialist regimes across the formerly colonized world. These revolutions were inspired by socialist, communist, anti-colonial, and anarchist theories of the time, from the West and from all over the shifting colonial landscape.

- Finally, the period of "state-managed" or "corporate-competitive" capitalism reflects the distinct era of systemic racism in the US and much of the West marked by legal segregation and a racially segmented labor market (Wilson 1996; Feagin and Ducey 2019) that would exist following the *Plessy v. Ferguson* decision in 1896 until the Civil Rights Acts of 1965 and 1968. Though still an explicit, legally segregated labor market working through an approach of exclusion, formal segregation created, for the first time in Fraser's view, the opening for a hybridization or mixing of exploitation and expropriation within an historical regime of accumulation. She explains, "In state-managed capitalism, therefore, exploitation no longer appeared so separate from expropriation. Rather, the two exes became internally articulated in racialized industrial labor, on the one hand, and in compromised postcolonial citizenship, on the other" (Fraser 2022:45).

The Current Regime: Transnational Financialized Capitalism

The current period, spanning the decades since the 1970s, is referred to as *Global* (Fraser 2022) or *Transnational* (Robinson 2018a) *Financialized Capitalism*. It is crucial for the theoretical model put forth here to understand several defining characteristics of our age, particularly in identifying various forms of crises and contradictions that, as we argue, lay behind the greatest threats to universal human rights practice and OTHS.

A Transnational or Global System

Where state-managed, monopoly capitalism was defined by a "world" or "international" economy of competing circuits of accumulation largely contained within Nation-states, our current period is defined by a fully integrated "global" or "transnational" system reflecting transnational circuits of accumulation. This change occurred through a process of economic globalization from above, or global economic restructuring (GER) that occurred in the late 20th century, made possible by the development of digital information technology and digitization,[10] modern computing, and the creation of the world wide web or internet (Robinson 2018a, 2022b).[11] Globalization also included creating transnational supply chains and the outsourcing of the productive and (later) service capacities to the developing world, the "opening" of Nation-states like China to transnational capital investment, and the break-up and privatization of the former USSR. The US would remain for a time as the global political hegemon in a temporarily unipolar world, and establish itself as the far-and-away dominant military power in terms of spending, scale, and global reach.

Globalized production has come to be dominated by transnational corporations (TNCs). TNCs are generally defined as firms that have headquarters in multiple countries, rather than being headquartered and centrally managed in a single country with subsidiaries elsewhere, as is the case for Multinational Corporations (MNC). Robinson (2018a:60–61) notes of the TNC's role and rise,

> the ability of TNCs to plan, organize, coordinate, and control activities across countries makes them central agents of globalization. The number of TNCs increased from 7,000 in 1970 to 104,000 by 2010 … and their sales climbed from $2.5 trillion in 1982 to $36.7 trillion in 2015. As of 2013, nearly 900,000 affiliates of TNCs produced goods and services estimated at $34T, which represented 45% of the entire world economic output.

The ownership, location, distribution of capital, and distribution of surplus value from TNCs cannot be reasonably defined within single Nation-states, many of which are now dwarfed by corporate behemoths.

Apple, for example, became the world's first $1T corporation in 2018, ballooned to another record-setting market capitalization of $3T in January of 2023, and held around $2.8T by the summer of that year. Apple's market cap is higher than the GDPs of entire nations like Canada ($1.99T), South Korea ($1.81T), Russia ($1.78T), or Brazil ($1.61T) (World Bank 2023b). While nominally an American company incorporated and headquartered in California, Apple has 41 other international headquarters and corporate offices around the world, including in Shanghai and Munich. In 2016 Apple agreed to invest $275B in its operations in China, where a great deal of Apple products are manufactured, and where Apple generates a fifth of its annual revenue (Newman 2023). At the same time, Apple is trying to diversify its global supply chains by moving 25% of iPhone production to India, and had so far shifted 7%, or $7B in iPhones by April of 2023 (Phartiyal 2023).

For needed raw materials like cobalt—a battery ingredient for electronic vehicles and other high-tech products—Apple joins many other corporations in sourcing from industrial and so-called "artisanal" mines in the southern Katanga region of the Democratic Republic of Congo (DRC], where over 130 armed militia groups contest for control of land and minerals. Mass violence, destabilization, and famine are widespread, such that 8 million people are in urgent need of assistance, 26 million are hungry, 35,000 mostly women and girls have sought treatment and services for sexual assault (Lederer 2023). In the fall of 2023, UN Humanitarian Office Director Edem Wosornu described conditions on the ground as the worst they had ever seen (Lederer 2023), and the UN International Organization for Migration reported that nearly 7 million people were displaced due to escalating violence (Neysmith 2023). In this desperate context, children formally work or informally salvage in cobalt mines for minuscule payment, often doing the difficult and dangerous job of mining and processing the toxic mineral, sometimes literally by hand or with make-shift tools (Kara 2023; Balu 2023). The lack of any state regulation allows the cobalt mining industry to hyper-exploit workers with abandon and externalize huge environmental costs to the public through mass clearcutting of forests and pollution of air, soil, and clean water sources (Kara 2023).

The area now known as the DRC was the site of Portuguese and genocidal Belgian colonization in the 19th and 20th centuries respectively, and today's regional mining industry should be understood as a neocolonial project of Chinese and other firms who source technology giants like Apple Inc. with raw materials as part of a so-far successful effort since 2009 to dominate global cobalt production. Over 70% of global cobalt production comes from the DRC and they have over half of the estimated global cobalt reserves (8.3 million metric tons) (Kara 2023; US Geological Survey 2023). Though Apple Inc. promises to use only recycled rare/heavy metal resources by 2025 and a carbon neutral supply chain by 2030 (Balu 2023), all of the above demonstrates how the most powerful tech firms still have their feet firmly planted in some of the oldest, most brutal forms of capitalist exploitation and neocolonial expropriation of labor in the sourcing of raw materials. Additionally, it illustrates how Apple Inc. operates across a transnational circuit of accumulation, demonstrated here in terms of production—but also easily demonstrated in terms of global ownership (who owns or is invested in Apple and its subsidiaries?), or marketing and consumption (who buys/uses Apple products?).

Financialization

TNCs like Apple Inc. are very powerful, yet capitalism is no longer dominated primarily by firms in the traditional productive economy. Instead, the most powerful corporate firms join big finance—banks and other asset management firms—in dominating the global economy. This shift occurred through the financialization of the global economy that took place alongside and following economic globalization in the late 20th century, also facilitated by the advances in digital technologies previously mentioned. Just as dominant corporate firms have always required and exhibited close relationships with banks in order to function (Mintz and Schwartz 1985), transnational financial institutions and transnational finance capital emerged alongside transnational corporations and the transnational state apparatus to literally finance the globalization process. In the late 20th century, this included the often-predatory international loans from wealthy nations and firms to the developing, post-colonial and post-Soviet world that created the situations of modern international debt dependency and economic neocolonialism so familiar in recent decades (see Armaline and Glasberg 2009; Robinson 2004, 2014). More recently it would include the trillions of dollars in bailouts and zero interest financing (quantitative easing) given to financial firms deemed "too big to fail" in response to the Great Recession in 2008, and again in the Covid-19 market crash of 2020. Though quantitative easing has since ended with sharp interest rate hikes from the US Federal Reserve in an attempt to curb inflation, the government assisted emergency purchases of failed regional banks like Silicon Valley Bank in the US (Smialek and Rappeport 2023) or of Switzerland's Credit Suisse in 2023 (Thompson 2023)—both of which tanked after the Fed interest rate hikes—demonstrate the continued centrality of and state deference to finance capital.

Second, financialization occurred in great part due to the over-accumulation crisis that haunts the current period of capitalism. While we will return to the subject of crises at the end of Chapter 2, an "over-accumulation crisis" refers to one where wealth has been highly concentrated in the hands of a very few people and firms, and opportunities to re-invest that wealth as capital in the productive economy for a profitable return shrink, creating stagnation and any number of other economic and social problems. To address this issue, capitalists must search for or create new opportunities for profitable investment, and attempt to solve this problem in part through financial speculation (gambling, essentially) and the creation of risky financial instruments, such as the now infamously fraudulent mortgage-backed securities and credit default swaps that imploded and sank the global economy in the Great Recession of 2008. Robinson (2022b:32–33) offers a brief summary of this trend:

> Financialization began in the late twentieth century with the deregulation and liberalization of financial markets worldwide, along with the introduction of computer and information technology into these markets. As national financial systems merged into an increasingly integrated global financial system, transnational finance capital emerged as the hegemonic fraction of capital on a world scale.... Financialization has made it possible to turn the global economy into a giant casino for transnational investors. Declining profitability leads to the shift in investment from expanding the production of commodities to financial speculation.... As a result, the gap between the productive economy of goods and services and fictitious capital has grown to an unfathomable chasm. Fictitious capital refers to money thrown into circulation without any base in commodities or in production.... In 2018, for example, the gross world product or the total value of goods and services produced in the world, stood at some $75 trillion whereas the global derivatives market—a marker of speculative activity—was estimated at a mind boggling $1 quadrillion.

As a reflection of this turn to finance and fictitious capital, banks and other financial asset management firms represent the most powerful ("hegemonic") bloc of capital in the global economy (Robinson 2018a). Of these, researchers in 2018 identified 17 "Global Financial Giants" each holding at least $1T, that collectively managed over $41T in investment funds from wealthy individuals, states, and other firms (Phillips 2018). The largest examples included Blackrock ($9.1T in assets), Vanguard ($8.1T), and Fidelity Management and Research ($3.9T) (SWFI 2023). These Giants operate in nations all over the globe, are heavily cross-invested in each other, and represent the most superconnected[12] firms on Earth—both with other Global Giants and with the major MNCs and TNCs, only 147 of which control about 40% of global wealth (Vitali, Glattfelder, and Battison 2011; Phillips 2018). Their highest priority, as Phillips (2018) points out, is to guarantee a return of at least 3–10% for investors, by any means available. As opportunities for profitable investment dry up in the productive economy, investment activity becomes increasingly risky, predatory, and potentially dangerous for society and the capital accumulation process itself. Fraser (2019:37–38) argues in agreement on this point that financialization is "a deeply predatory and unstable form of social organization that liberates capital accumulation from the very constraints needed to sustain it over time." We will return to the potentially destructive or "cannibalistic" aspects of the system in our discussion of crises, but will now turn to the emergence of a transnational capitalist class or global bourgeoisie as another critical characteristic of the current regime of accumulation.

The Transnational Capitalist Class and Global Power Elite

Conceptually, Robinson (2018a, 2022b) defines the transnational capitalist class [TCC] as "those who own and manage the transnational corporations and financial institutions that drive the global economy" (Robinson 2018a:165). This class formation is transnational in that it's "grounded in global circuits of accumulation, marketing, and finance unbound from particular national territories and because its interests lie in global rather than local accumulation" (Robinson 2018a:165). Thanks to capitalism's objective systemic thrust toward ever expanding capital, the TCC "pursues people and resources all over the world in its insatiable desire for private profit and eternal accumulation" (Sklair 2001:4) according to a relatively shared neoliberal market ideology (more below), including the belief that "continued growth through profit-driven consumerism will by itself eventually solve global poverty, mass inequality, and environmental collapse" (Phillips 2018:25; Sklair 2001).

   That being said, as the emergence of TNCs or transnational finance capital did not mean the end or irrelevance of national level banks and corporate firms in the global economy, the emergence of a TCC does not negate the existence of more localized economic elites or of capitalists whose interests tie more closely with the perceived national interests of a particular state. Rather, the TCC forms out of the creation of transnational circuits of accumulation and a shifting class relation between capitalists and an increasingly precarious global working class that is unique to the current regime of accumulation. Robinson (2022b:57) summarizes that impact:

the heightened structural power achieved by the TCC through globalization and financialization has enabled it to undermine redistributive policies and to impose a new labor regime on the global working class based on flexibilization and precarization, or proletarianization under conditions of permanent insecurity or precariousness.

And the precarity of the global workforce seems only to have increased in recent years. Currently, for example, approximately half of global workers (1.7 billion people) are employed in countries where inflation continues to outpace wages—including for many workers in the United States (Christensen, Hallum, Maitland, Parrinello, and Putaturo 2023; World Bank 2023a). Further, approximately 2 billion workers were employed in the informal economy in 2022 and almost half of the world (47% or 4 billion people) lack any form of social protection through employment or the state, such as social security or health care (ILO 2023). The global labor market is far more precarious for women and young people (aged 15–24), such that "for every economically inactive man there are two such women," unemployment rates among the young are three times that of adults, and over one in five of young people are not in any form of education, employment, or training (ILO 2023:2). Though there has been some marginal progress over the last 3 decades, women workers only claim 34.7% of global income (World Inequality Lab 2022).

Meanwhile, the global super-rich are managing to secure their concentration of wealth and "undermine redistributive policies," often across generations, in part through their ability to navigate, capture, or avoid the regulatory and taxation capacity of Nation-states. Since 2013, the International Consortium of Investigative Journalists (ICIJ)[13] researched and released three significant caches of leaked data, referred to as the Panama Papers, the Paradise Papers, and the Pandora Papers that illustrated the tax avoidance schemes of many of the most wealthy and powerful people in the world, typically using complicated networks of shell companies located in countries with little financial regulation. The Pandora Papers alone included information on 35 world leaders and 300 other public officials (ministers, judges, mayors, military generals, etc.), as well as many of the world's wealthiest billionaires (Guardian Investigations Team 2021). Oxfam International (Christensen, Hallum, Maitland, Parrinello, and Putaturo 2023) points out that for every $1 raised in taxes in the world, only four cents come from taxing forms of wealth, and that half of the world's billionaires live in countries with no form of wealth or inheritance tax, such that a "new aristocracy" is emerging from the realities of capital concentration and the ease at which the owning class escapes taxation. Indeed, the study notes that some of the world's richest people, such as Elon Musk (net worth of $180B in 2023) or Jeff Bezos (net worth of $114B in 2023) paid an effective tax rate of 3.2% and under 1% respectively (Christensen, Hallum, Maitland, Parrinello, and Putaturo 2023).

Within the TCC there is a group that can be identified as the Global Power Elite—the most powerful segment of the global bourgeoisie. Their power is not simply derived from sheer wealth or a monopoly on the means of production, but also through control of society's major bureaucratic institutions (TNCs like Amazon, state agencies like the US Department of Defense, or financial institutions like JP Morgan Chase) that can leverage incredible human and other resources to achieve whatever interests, as we learn from Mills (1956) in his original study of the "power elite" at the early height of American imperial hegemony.

Though some have argued that there is a "superclass" of a few thousand individuals with incredible wealth and access to the decision-making levers of society (Rothkopf 2008), Phillips (2018) identified "389 Global Power Elites as the key managers of concentrated capital, the facilitators of capital growth, and the system's protectors [who] generally know or know of each other—often personally—do business together" (Phillips 2018:29). Further, they "all serve(d) on the board of directors of major capital investment firms or other major corporations and banks" (Phillips 2018:29). This includes approximately 200 individuals who sit on the boards of the Global Giants and manage over $41T in finance capital, such as Jamie Dimon (JP Morgan Chase), Laurence "Larry" Fink (Blackrock), or C.S. Venkatakrishnan (Barclays). A vast majority of these individuals are male (70%), whites of European descent (84%), have advanced degrees from elite private universities, hold citizenship in multiple countries, and live or do regular business in the major financial centers of the world (e.g., New York, London, Singapore, etc.) (Phillips 2018).

For the purposes of conceptualizing the TCC and Global Power Elite one could argue that those running Global Giants would be joined, for example, by those who control the US Federal Reserve and Treasury Department—that for now control the supply of the global currency of exchange in the dollar and the sale of US debt—and those managing other major national reserve banks and sovereign wealth funds around the world. Though integrated somewhat differently with Western elites due to geopolitical factors, one would include those who control the Chinese Communist Party apparatus (namely, Chairman Xi) and massive Chinese banking sector—with the 4 largest banks in the world by total asset value: Industrial and Commercial Bank of China Ltd. ($5.7T), the China Construction Bank Corp. ($5T), the Agricultural Bank of China, and the Bank of China Ltd. ($4.2T) (Khan, Terris, Meggeson, and Taqi 2023). The overarching point here is not to arrive at an exact number or list of names or firms. Rather, it is to describe an evolving but clearly identifiable transnational capitalist class and concentrated Global Power Elite within that class formation who are highly connected through their institutions and social networks, exhibit the ability to coordinate interest and actions, reflect a relatively shared ideology on the centrality of markets and growth (capital expansion/accumulation), and "rule" in the sense that they both share in the monopoly on the means of production and can influence if not completely capture decision-making in politics and government through the control of corporate firms, banks, and state institutions.

To the extent wealth and power is concentrated in the TCC, whose general interests are represented by a Global Power Elite, global power dynamics appear as a form of polyarchy, whereby "a small group actually rules, on behalf of capital, and participation in decision-making by the majority is confined to choosing among competing elites in tightly controlled electoral processes [within nation states]" (Robinson 2018a:18). We will return to the impacts of concentrated capital on democracy and civil/political human rights in Chapter 4, however it is important to point out some general aspects of class domination that help to define our regime of accumulation. To do so, we need to further explore the relationship between transnational capital, Nation-states, and transnational state apparatuses, as well as the hegemonic ideology that informs these relationships.

Neoliberal Ideology

Many Keynesian economic policies in the West were largely replaced throughout the period of global economic restructuring by de-regulatory, so called "free-market," neoliberal approaches that increasingly freed capital from the restraints of the nation-state as part of the globalization process. It is worth reviewing David Harvey's (2007:1–3) definition of neoliberalism in full as the central ideological component of capitalism since global economic restructuring, as it helps to foreshadow the roles of states relative to capital accumulation:

Neoliberalism is ... a theory of political economic practices that proposes that human well-being can best be advanced by liberating individual entrepreneurial freedoms and skills within an institutional framework characterized by strong private property rights, free markets and free trade. The role of the state is to create and preserve the institutional framework appropriate to such practices.... It must ... set up those military, defense, police, and legal structures and functions required to secure private property rights and to guarantee, by force if need be, the proper functioning of markets. Furthermore, if markets do not exist (in areas such as land, water, education, health care, social security, or environmental pollution) then they must be created, by state action if necessary. But beyond these tasks the state should not venture. State interventions in markets (once created) must be kept to a bare minimum because, according to the theory, the state cannot possibly possess enough information to second-guess market signals ... and because powerful interest groups will inevitably distort and bias state interventions (particularly in democracies) for their own benefit.

Neoliberalism demands a state in service of capital interests that provides the infrastructure, minimal regulation, and repressive apparatus to maintain and, if need be, facilitate the expansion of markets—often through violence. Neoliberalism served as the primary logic of economic globalization, and remains as an impressively persistent political economic worldview of elite decision makers, particularly in the West. This is evidenced in France, where under the Presidency of Emmanuel Macron, the government sided with capital and neoliberal economists to raise the retirement age from 62–64 in 2023, despite strikes and protests that repeatedly brought many aspects of French life to a standstill (Parks 2023). The battle over pension reform in France demonstrated the persistence of neoliberal economic policies, while also illustrating the potential for resistance and counter hegemonic alternatives.

Despite the relative ubiquity of the neoliberal model since globalization, several more nuanced ideologies compete for hegemony in the present moment. For instance, the incredible economic success story of China since the 1990s in terms of raw economic growth, technological development, and the monumental achievement of lifting 800 million people out of extreme poverty between approximately 1980–2020 represents a revisionary challenge to the wisdom of Western neoliberalism. Interestingly, a 2022 report by the World Bank, China's Ministry of Finance, and others suggested that China's success in fighting poverty was first from "economic transformation to open new economic opportunities" in the opening of Chinese markets to private capital investment, "the introduction of market incentives," and incremental industrialization and urbanization—that is, in part from participation in neoliberal economic globalization (World Bank and DRC of the State Council 2022). Second, the report argues that significant government subsidy to struggling regions and (later) households, as well as significant public investment in things like education, infrastructure, and agricultural development was critical to improve the material conditions of so many people— suggesting the utility of more state market intervention, direct public investment, and direct redistribution of resources. China's recently slowed, yet continued economic rise as potentially the largest national economy by mid-century is likely to impact the guiding logic of the global economic system, in that their experience with state market intervention and direct domestic and foreign investment represent some successful departures from Western neoliberalism.

Further, in Western states like the US, Fraser (2019) notes that there are different distinguishable forms of neoliberalism in play. The "progressive neoliberalism" exemplified by the Clinton, Obama, and Biden Administrations (e.g., "third wave" corporate democrats) merge corporate capital interests with liberal (not critical or "left") politics of feminism, multiculturalism, environmentalism, and LGBTQ+ rights. Whereas the "reactionary neoliberalism" of the traditional American Republican Party establishment represented in the Reagan, Bush Sr., and Bush Jr. Administrations reflect an economic program centered on "bolstering finance, military production, and extractive energy" (Fraser 2019:16) for the benefit of a small owning class. Rather than the politics of social inclusion, reactionary neoliberalism employs an exclusionary politics along lines of race, class, nationality, sexuality, and gender.

Lastly, as a partial consequence of the massive wealth inequality and economic precarity/destabilization that stemmed from the 2008 Great Recession and COVID-19 pandemic (also featuring a significant market crash in 2020), competing forms of populism have emerged to challenge the traditionally neoliberal ruling parties in the West. According to Fraser (2019), in the US these took the form of "progressive populism" represented by, for example, the 2016 and 2020 Presidential runs of Bernie Sanders, as well as many other Social Democratic candidates for various other political offices. They also took the form of a kind of "reactionary populism" represented in the political discourse of the so called "MAGA," and Christian Nationalist segments of the American right wing, or in the form of similarly successful right-wing movements in Hungary (Orbán), India (Modi), Poland (Duda) or Italy (Meloni). Reactionary populism promises (though so far tends not to deliver) populist approaches to resource distribution in a "hyperreactionary" (Fraser 2019:26) political framework of exclusion that Robinson (2022a:136) calls "twenty first century fascism." Twenty first century fascism is authoritarian, centered around the perceived strength of a single leader, and "involves a fusion of repressive and reactionary state power with a fascist mobilization in civil society" that takes the form of a violent, often patriarchal, "toxic mix of reactionary nationalism and racism" (Robinson 2022a:136–137). Yet, despite the emergence of left and right popular movements in what Fraser (2019) perceives as a "hegemonic crisis" of the global capitalist order, the dominance of neoliberal logic seems to remain, even if only due to the lack of a clearly established alternative. More importantly, one outcome of neoliberal economic globalization has been to position national states and transnational state apparatuses in the devastating service of capital accumulation.

The State and Transnational State Apparatus

While the relative power and sovereignty of the nation-state to the most powerful blocs of capital has transformed dramatically in the current historical period, states have always been essential for capital accumulation and capitalism as an institutionalized social order. Specifically, they're required to provide the monetary policy, currency, and regulation to maintain relative "macroeconomic stability;" the infrastructure necessary for economic activity such as for transportation, education, or communications; and, as we will explore in detail in Chapter 3, a repressive state apparatus for purposes of social control (Robinson 2018a:16) in the effort to protect private property (literally and conceptually) and counter inevitable resistance from the exploited and expropriated.

Robinson (2022a:123) describes the structural relation of states to capital in the spirit of Poulantzas (2014[1978]), asserting that:

> [T]he state is charged with organizing the general conditions of accumulation, for its existence and its legitimacy is dependent on a vibrant economy, that is, upon the reproduction of capitalist production relations, or the capital-labor relation. The state exercises its autonomy from the directives of capitalists as individuals, as groups, or as fractions, but it is not autonomous from those relations.

The work of structural state theorists is crucial here in pointing out that the relation between state and capital is not simply a vulgar one of instrumental capture by economic elites—though that is an ever-present feature via corruption and more often legal avenues (lobbying or campaign finance). But there are also deep structural connections from the mutual evolution of capitalism and the state across the regimes of accumulation previously described. Though the economic and political are formally separated in capitalist society, there is an "underlying unity" of economics and politics (Robinson 2022a), and the state and capital are best understood as "structurally imbricated" (Fraser 2022) with one another.

One defining characteristic of our current regime of accumulation is that it's virtually impossible for any state to stand completely outside of the global capitalist marketplace. In terms of the foregrounded economic relations discussed thus far,[14] national states play crucial roles for the purposes of transnational capital accumulation. Broadly, they serve as "territorially bound juridical units … transformed into transmission belts and filtering devices for the imposition of the transnational agenda" (Robinson 2018a:16). Again, this is not to say that capital interests tied closely to more narrowly defined "national interests" in geopolitical context in any way disappear, or that capitalists operating at any level are completely aligned at all times on all things. Rather, as an increasing trend, "capitalists and elites in each country have captured their respective national states, or at least key ministries in these states, from where they promote the transnational agenda, so that national states become proactive agents of globalization" (Robinson 2018a:16).

However, no single state has the authority or reach to provide the kind of market infrastructure necessary for transnational circuits of accumulation. In order to resolve this problem, global elites developed what Robinson (2014, 2018a) calls "transnational state apparatuses" (TNS) throughout the period of economic globalization, such as the European Union (EU) (1993), the World Trade Organization (WTO) (1995), the G20 (1999) and smaller assemblies like the G7, and "a number of national and transnational regulatory and oversight bodies in the wake of the 2008 global recession—that would allow the global ruling class to take collective action to stabilize the system" (Robinson 2022:66). The TNS allows the TCC "to convert structural power of the global economy into a supranational political authority, to promote an open global economy, impose a uniform set of rules, and develop transnational policy coordination" (Robinson 2022:66). Broadly speaking, we should see the building of this transnational state infrastructure as still very much in process as the transnational economic and geopolitical terrains shift and change. Roughly then, the TNS should be understood as

> a dense network of supranational institutions and relationships that increasingly bypass formal states, and that should be conceived as an emergent transnational state that has not acquired any centralized institutional form, is still very much in formation, and is subject to all sorts of contradictory pressures.
>
> (Robinson 2018a:16)

The shaping of national states and TNS apparatuses by capital creates what Robinson (2022a) and Fraser (2019) both call a "legitimacy crisis" of the state, that results from states favoring the interests of capital accumulation over governance in the interest of the public—including many forms of rights protection. What does this relationship between national states, the TNS, and transnational capital tell us about the ability of states to achieve other kinds of goals or functions, such as those obligated under international human rights law?

Legitimacy Crises of the Contemporary State

Robinson (2022b:70) describes the legitimacy crisis of the state as a "contradiction between the need to promote trans-national capital accumulation in its territory in competition with other states and its need to achieve internal political legitimacy and stabilize the domestic social order." Capital accumulation typically requires states to provide financial incentives to companies while disciplining workers, and national states are put into competitive positions to attract private investment in this regard. Robinson (2022b:70) continues on this point:

> Attracting trans-national corporate and financial investment to the national territory requires providing capital with investment incentives, such as labor discipline and low wages, a lax regulatory environment, tax concessions, investment subsidies, and so on. The result is rising inequality, impoverishment, and insecurity for the working and popular classes, precisely the conditions that throw states into crises of legitimacy, destabilize national political systems, and jeopardize elite control.

Competition for capital investment can put incredible downward pressure on the lives and livelihoods of working people—directly threatening economic and social human rights. It can constrain democracy and democratic decision-making in state governance—directly threatening political and civil human rights, and often results in forms of ecological destruction due to lax regulation. Most importantly, *the structural imbrication of the state to capital and the resulting legitimacy crisis that follows explains how states consistently prove unable or unwilling to fulfill their obligations to international human rights law.* States are structured to facilitate national and transnational circuits of accumulation, and subject to the instrumental influence of an increasingly powerful TCC such that capital interests dominate those of rights protection and other governing priorities—even to the point where the public legitimacy and functional abilities of the state are put in jeopardy.

Fraser (2022b:119) agrees that the most powerful blocks of corporate and finance capital now discipline the state rather than the other way around, and similarly describes the crisis as resulting from a contradiction "between the imperatives of capital accumulation and the maintenance of the public powers on which accumulation also relies." Not only does Fraser recognize the legitimacy problem for states in service of capital, but the particularly cannibalistic relationship that capital forms with the state infrastructures that it needs to maintain circuits of accumulation. For instance, privatization, tax cuts, and deregulation in the interests of capital can result in the hollowing out of the state, leaving a less capable, stable infrastructure for sustained accumulation. This is the reality that poorer nations experienced throughout economic globalization, as the structural adjustment programs (SAPs) applied in the maintenance of international debts demanded anti-democratic, neoliberal economic reforms all over the developing world in order to attract capital investment. In fact, nations like Argentina—once a laboratory for neoliberal economists from the University of Chicago and Western capital interests (Klein 2010)—continue to suffer from the impacts of neoliberal deregulation, privatization, and international debt. In 2023 Argentina struggled to service a $44 billion debt to the IMF, experienced a blinding annual inflation rate of 109% while the Argentine peso dropped to a record low exchange rate of 500/$1, and the country grappled with the impacts of climate change in the form of extreme drought (Lo Bianco and Nessi 2023). International debt and the legitimacy crises that follow are once again ballooning due in part to the financial impacts of climate change and ecological destruction in poorer nations. Half of the global population now lives in a country where the government must spend more on servicing the interest on their international debt than on education, health, and other "essential" public investments (UN Global Crisis Response Group 2023).

The hollowing out of public resources and state capacity is also arguably happening in wealthy, so-called "core" industrial nations like the US. Such a picture of American institutional decline was painted in the previous chapter, and Americans have met this reality with distrust. According to Gallop (Jones 2022), faith in major American institutions (such as Congress, public schools, or forms of news media) is at the lowest point since measures began in 1979, with all three major branches of government ranking at (Congress) or near (the Presidency and Supreme Court) the bottom of the list. These poll numbers are consistent with an emergent crisis of state legitimacy, where people's belief in the capability or legitimate authority of the state fades. The hollowing out or cannibalization of political state structures in the short-term interests of capital accumulation—whether through privatization, regulatory capture, tax reform, or corruption—contributes to the legitimacy crisis by objectively limiting state capacities to effectively govern in the eyes and interests of the general public.

Contemporary Systemic Racism

Finally, global financialized capitalism corresponds uncoincidentally with contemporary systemic racism, or systemic racism of the post-civil rights era, beginning in the early 1970's following the civil rights acts of the 1960's in the US at the onset of global economic restructuring. Racism is a social system in the sense that patriarchy is a social system—one of power relations based on the socially constructed categories of race or gender, respectively. A macro step up from Feagin's (and Carmichael and Hamilton (1967)) concept of institutional racism (1977), systemic racism is a "highly organized system of 'race' justified oppression" that manifests in and through society's "interrelated major institutions of economics, politics, education, family, and religion" (Cazenave 2018:55; see also Cazenave 2016; Feagin 2006:6). In describing the prior regimes of accumulation, we've so far noted how each has been roughly accompanied by similarly identifiable eras of systemic racism in the US and much of the Western world: conquest and enslavement with primitive accumulation and mercantile capitalism; Jim Crow/debt peonage and colonization with liberal-colonial or classical competitive capitalism; formal segregation/apartheid with state managed or corporate monopoly capitalism; and now contemporary systemic racism with transnational financialized capitalism. Each one of these eras[15] can be identified by their 1) unique, hegemonic ideologies, namely to achieve the (re)construction, ascription, and legitimation of racial categories through the racialization process and historically contingent racial state projects (Omi and Winant 2014 [1986]); 2) mechanisms for coercive social control, required in the face of ever-present resistance and crisis; and 3) political economic or material manifestations, largely shaped by the system's structural imbrication with the foregrounded economic relations of capitalist society.

Ideologically, contemporary systemic racism is characterized by what is now relatively well known as "colorblind" ideology, prevalent in formal policy discourse following the civil rights acts of the 1960s and establishment of actionable anti-discrimination law in the US. A colorblind ideology asserts that a) racism does not, or no longer exists; b) to the extent racial inequalities exist, they are due to individual traits or structural factors other than racism; c) to the extent racism still exists, it is merely a form of inter-personal bigotry that can, should, and for the most part has been solved through "colorblind" practice and thought (Bonilla-Silva 1996, 2001; Brewer and Heitzeg 2008). While there are legitimate arguments for the deconstruction of racial categories altogether as inherently hierarchical and discriminatory since their inception, these should not be mistaken for col-orblindness. Colorblind ideology is insidious in denying the existence of racism (rather than consciously deconstructing and confronting race as a political act), where in prior eras the social and legal supremacy of whites and subjugation of other racial groups was a matter of overt policy. In doing so, blame and burden for resulting inequalities are placed on oppressed populations and individuals of color.

One example of colorblind ideology in current US law would be the rul-ings (*Fair Admissions v. Harvard College* and *Students for Fair Admissions v. the University of North Carolina*) by the Supreme Court in 2023 to end race-based admissions or "affirmative action" for colleges and universities. In the presentation of these cases, Justices in the Majority argued that Asian-American and White students were effectively discriminated against by affirmative action programs in what they described as the "zero sum" game of college admissions, and that those students "do not shoulder the debts of their ancestors" (Montague 2023). In dissent, Justice Sotomayor called the rulings "a superficial rule of race-blindness on the nation," asserting that "ignoring racial inequality will not make it disappear" (Mon-tague 2023). The Majority's rulings reflect a neoliberal colorblindness in arguing that racism can be reduced to the actions of one's ancestors (and thus no longer exists as a social system), and that ending race-based admis-sions would achieve a more ideal system based on individual merit. Yet, the Court allowed lineage (vs. merit) based, so-called "legacy" admissions—overwhelmingly favoring Whites and elites, especially in the most presti-gious institutions such as those attended by all Supreme Court Justices—to continue unabated. Further, the Court expressly allowed race-based admis-sions to continue in all military academies and recruitment, prompting Jus-tice Ketanji Brown Jackson to decry the Majority conclusion that, "racial diversity in higher education is only worth potentially preserving insofar as it might be needed to prepare Black Americans and other underrepresented minorities for success in the bunker, not the boardroom" (Hussain 2023).

To be abundantly clear, "diversifying boardrooms" is a superficial goal reflecting a cynical, manifestly played out, and arguably failed strategy of countering racism, patriarchy, or capitalism in any meaningful way. The racial diversification of owning and ruling elites is not an appropriate mea-sure of successful anti-racist, let alone anti-capitalist praxis. Further, there are reasonable criticisms of affirmative action admissions programs—of their tendency to most benefit White women (Leo Moore 2022; Parker 2021) rather than students of color, their failure to consider socio-economic status and the barriers faced by even high performing poor students (Giancola and

Kahlenberg 2016), or even that they dilute important merit-based aspects of college admissions (given sufficient evidence) as the Majority seemed to claim. But the Court's decisions do not reflect a consistent dedication to merit-based admissions to American educational institutions. They do reflect a broader pattern—what the Center for Constitutional Rights (2023) calls an "obsession with colorblindness"—that was also made evident in the 2013 *Shelby v. Holder* decision, where the Court struck down a key component of the Voting Rights Act, essentially arguing that racial discrimination was no longer a sufficient enough problem to justify the federal procedural protections that had previously guarded against discriminatory election law. Predictably, as will be made clear in Chapter 4, efforts to disenfranchise poor voters and voters of color emerged since, and have intensified in recent election cycles.

The dominance of colorblind ideology in formal discourse following the civil rights acts of the late 1960's does not negate the existence of overtly racist ideology, overt acts of racial terror, or overt expressions of white supremacy. This is readily apparent in the US, where in 2020 the Southern Poverty Law Center (SPLC) (2020) reported a 55% increase in white nationalist organizations throughout the Trump Administration (2016–2020), following a sizable increase throughout the Obama Administrations (2008–2016). Though this number has declined since 2021, data suggests that a more concentrated group of white nationalist and other so-called "hate groups" have focused and increased their attention toward public demonstrations, public propaganda, and control or disruption of local decision-making (ADL Center on Extremism 2023b). In 2018 there were 1,214 recorded public demonstrations, but by 2022 demonstrations and incidents of "white supremacist propaganda" had increased by over five and a half times to 6,751 (ADL Center on Extremism 2023b).

In addition, linked to a broader epidemic of gun violence and mass shootings, the number of mass murders by "extremists" in the US since 2020 is already at least 3 times higher than in any decade since the 1970s, and in 2022, "right-wing extremists committed every ideologically driven mass killing identified in the US with an 'unusually high' proportion perpetuated by white supremacists" (Saric 2023; ADL Center on Extremism 2023a). This most notably included the case of a 19-year-old self-styled white supremacist who purposefully drove over 200 miles to a Tops supermarket in a predominantly Black Buffalo neighborhood and gunned down 13 people, 11 of whom were Black, ten of whom lost their lives. It remains the deadliest shooting in the city's history, and is reminiscent of the 2015 murder of nine members of the historic Emanuel African Methodist Episcopal Church in South Carolina by a 21-year-old white supremacist who claimed to act out of a fear that "Blacks were taking over the world" (Num and Collins 2015).

Violent terrorism against Black and other populations of color at the hands of so-called "lone wolves" or paramilitary organizations like the Ku Klux Klan since the Civil War Reconstruction period represent forms of extra-legal coercion. However, the state has always been the primary agent or legitimating force in the social control and repression of racialized populations in the US and greater West. While in previous eras this would have been represented by legal, overt regimes of slavery, indigenous genocide/theft/removal, debt peonage, and apartheid, in the contemporary era coercive forms of social control are primarily achieved through the criminal legal system. Absent the overt racial discourse of previous eras, today's state repressive apparatus employs seemingly race neutral (colorblind) approaches to public safety that target, surveille, sanction, and kill people of color—African American, Latinx, and indigenous populations in particular—at consistently disparate rates (Alexander 2020). For instance, 38% of those incarcerated in the US are African American, yet they only make up 12% of the US population (Sawyer and Wagner 2023). Though this is an improvement from the height of the wars on drugs and crime, it remains a significant overrepresentation. Despite the efforts of the #BlackLivesMatter movement to confront racist police violence, culminating in the massive public protests in the summer of 2020, fatal encounters with police in the US have steadily increased each year. Though a majority of those fatally shot by police are White, Black Americans are fatally shot by police at a rate (5.8 per million) over twice that of Whites (2.3) and Hispanics (2.5) according to data collected between 2015 and May of 2023 (*Washington Post* 2023).

Chapter 3 will explore the role of the US and broader global police state in the repression of labor, racialized populations, and those deemed superfluous or dangerous to the status quo in greater detail. For now, it's sufficient to suggest that the state repressive apparatus (surveillance, policing, incarceration) and extra-legal forms of terrorism (intimidation, lynching, vigilante killings, mass shootings) together represent the "operational mechanisms" (Cazenave 2018:123) of coercive social control for contemporary systemic racism as a social system. These mechanisms can destabilize Black and other communities of color, while also providing the coercive tools to surveille and repress resistance in the case of hegemonic breakdown.

Though the civil rights acts of the 1960's and related legal reforms curbed overt forms of racial exclusion in American institutions, considerable economic inequalities persist along racial lines in the US. Census (2023) data from 2022 reveals that Blacks and Hispanics continue to account for a disproportionate percentage of those in poverty—by 1.7 and 1.5 times their percentage of the general population respectively, in comparison to Whites (0.7 times) and Asians (0.8 times). This gap between White and Black or Hispanic poverty rates improved considerably since 1965 but has remained relatively constant since 2000. According to the US Treasury (Bowdler and Harris 2022), median household incomes for Blacks ($46K) and Hispanics ($55K) trailed that of their White ($75K) and Asian ($95K) counterparts in 2020, and this earnings gap has remained virtually unchanged since 1970. The persistence of the earnings gap is one contribution to racial wealth disparities. In fact, the first continuous study of racial wealth inequality in the

US from Census data and tax records reaching back to 1860 (Derenoncourt, Kim, Kuhn, and Schularick 2022) found that the "White-to-Black per-capita wealth ratio" was 6 to 1 in 2019, and that the White to Black wealth gap was virtually the same in 2020 as in 1950.[16] Wealth disparities are just as apparent in the ownership of investment capital, where White Americans still dominate many markets and own over 89% of all stocks, worth about $28.17T (Daly 2023). In terms of home ownership, Black households continue to have the lowest homeownership rate in the country at 41.7%, which is 30% lower than for White households (Hermann 2023).

Illustrated by Keeanga Yamahtta Taylor's research (2021b), housing discrimination and predatory behavior in the lending and real estate industries continued as a significant feature of systemic racism in the US well after the civil rights acts of the 1960's, deeply impacting the political economic and geographic stability of Black households and communities. The attempts to expand homeownership in the 1990's and 2000's during the run up to the Great Recession of 2008 offers an example of this persistence, but also the persistence of systemic racism's political economic or material realities in the colorblind era. In terms of political economy, contemporary systemic racism is distinct from all previous eras in being the first to reflect an economy operating by way of selective (racial) inclusion rather than by forms of partial (legal segregation) or complete (colonization or enslavement) exclusion.

In the 1990's and 2000's the federal government, banking (mortgages), and real estate industries were encouraging American consumers to purchase homes as the traditional ticket into the asset holding middle class. However, much of this expansion of home ownership was done by offering working class households and households of color previously excluded from much of the housing market by segregation or cost (or both) seemingly attractive "zero money down" or (initially) low payment mortgages that turned out to be highly predatory in nature and completely unstable forms of debt (e.g., subprime mortgages). All of this was fueled by a feeding frenzy for what were in fact fraudulent[17] mortgage-backed securities—financial products created out of mortgages that allowed investors to speculate (gamble) on their value. In this case capital's search for a return on their investment dollar in the context of shrinking opportunities in the productive economy drove the creation of increasingly predatory loans in order to feed the demand for increasingly risky (and again, often fraudulent) forms of fictitious capital.

On the consumption side, an aggressive mortgage industry was part of a larger economy running on consumer debt of all sorts, since work and pay in the new US service sector economy was increasingly precarious in comparison to the unionized production jobs that had since been outsourced through global economic restructuring (Fraser 2022). This dependency on debt is only more severe today as the crises of capital heighten—total heighten. Total household debt in the US surpassed $17 trillion in the first quarter of 2023, breaking all previous records and revealing a precipitous rise since the COVID-19 pandemic (Federal Reserve Bank of New York

2023). On the production/finance side, capitalists seeking return on investment facilitated "the proliferation of highly inventive but dicey 'financial products,' which fatten investors and cannibalize citizen-workers of every color, but especially racialized borrowers" (Fraser 2016).

In the end, it all came crashing down in the most severe crisis of capital since the Great Depression. Though we go into greater detail on how the global Great Recession came to pass in our previous (2015) book, our points here are that 1) Black households and other households of color were among those explicitly targeted for predatory, sub-prime mortgages in the voracious attempt for capital to bring more and more chips into the Wall Street casino; and 2) Black households paid some of the biggest prices for this selective inclusion into the legally integrated housing market. Between 2005 and 2009 the median net worth of White households sank by 17%, while median Black household wealth dropped a startling 53% and the Black-White homeownership gap increased (Tippett, Jones-DeWeever, Rockeymoore, Hamilton, and Darity 2014). This is largely because Black borrowers were so heavily targeted for predatory loans. In fact, by 2000 in the middle of the feeding frenzy, Black borrowers were five times more likely to (re)finance in the subprime market, and these disparities remained even after controlling for income or credit scores. As a result, by 2010 Black and Latinx households were 45% and 47% (respectively) more likely than White households to face foreclosure (Burd-Sharps and Rasch 2015) in the depths of the crisis.

The political economics of contemporary systemic racism operate through a form of selective inclusion into the (foregrounded) neoliberal capitalist economy. The targeting of Black and Latinx households for predatory mortgages is a perfect demonstration of such inclusion on the terms and in the interest of banks and investment firms. While it is important to note the persistence of structural racial inequalities in the US and wider Western world, this does not necessarily mean that "the color line" is always the most significant in determining, let alone solving material inequality in contemporary society. In fact, if one breaks down Black and White US household wealth into deciles (10% increments), rather than look only at the mean or median wealth measures,

> what you find is that nearly all White wealth is owned by the top 10 percent of White households just as nearly all Black wealth is owned by the top 10 percent of Black households… [and] the disparity between the top deciles in each race drives over three-fourths of the racial wealth gap.
>
> (Bruenig 2020)

The implications of this are strategically important. First, it further problematizes the assumption that Blackness represents a unified "lived experience," let alone politics, that papers over important class conflicts internal to Black and other racialized populations. On that point Taylor

(2023; see also Gates 2016; Younge 2007) reminds us that "the greatest transformation in Black life in the past 50 years has been class polarization *among* black families." Second, the greatest gulf in material realities is not between a majority of working White families and working families of color, but between everyday people of all backgrounds and economic elites. This suggests the strategic potential of diverse class consciousness and solidarity in the face of systemic racism and capital accumulation, to which we will return in the concluding chapter.

For now, simply demonstrating systemic racism's recent transformations into a system of selective inclusion serves as an illustration of the capacity for social systems like racism or patriarchy to change and shift. They do so in part as contested terrains shaped by resistance, but also as part of the background relations of capitalist society that Fraser (2022) argues are co-constitutively connected to one another and to capitalism's foregrounded material relations. In the following chapter, we will explore these background relations, their connections to one another and to the material relations of capitalist society, their inherent contradictions, and the resultant forms of crisis that both define capitalist society and manifest as the greatest threats to human rights and survival.

Notes

1 The 2013 Economics of Ecosystems and Biodiversity Business Coalition (TEEB for Business) report that the highest 100 corporate environmental externalities (such as air or water pollution) transfer approximately $7.3T of cost into the laps of the global public.
2 See also Tsutsui, Whitlinger, and Lim (2012:368): "International human rights laws emerged as settlements between civil society actors, who mobilize collectively to establish human rights as a guiding principle of the international community, and state actors, most of whom resist the pressure from civil society to reform."
3 This capture often occurred first through the violent process of primitive accumulation, to which we will soon return.
4 Here we are referring to Marx's notion of alienation from ones' "species being" that appears in his (1988 [1844]) *Economic and Philosophic Manuscripts of 1844*. Though this should be differentiated with how Marx continues to develop the notion of alienation in his later works, we find his earlier concept more qualitatively rich and appropriate to describe the precarity and personal sacrifice inherent in contemporary wage labor.
5 Approximately 60% (389M) of those living in extreme poverty are in Sub-Saharan Africa, a region notably in the crosshairs of both climate change and imperial competition (World Bank 2022).
6 Consider the cases of indigenous genocide and forced migration or the trend of femicide in the Americas over the last several centuries.
7 Marx clearly recognizes (1) the conquest of indigenous populations and what we will call forms of expropriation as part of this initial process of primitive accumulation, (2) the central role of state violence in that process, and (3) how the process plays out also according to geopolitical or imperial competition. He writes (Marx 2004 [1867]:915), "The discovery of gold and silver in America, the extirpation, enslavement and entombment in mines of the aboriginal population,

the beginning of the conquest and looting of the East Indies, the turning of Africa into a warren for the commercial hunting of black-skins, signaled the rosy dawn of the era of capitalist production. These idyllic proceedings are the chief moments of primitive accumulation…. These methods depend in part on brute force, e.g., the colonial system. But, they all employ the power of the state, the concentrated and organized force of society, to hasten, hot-house fashion, the process of transformation of the feudal mode of production into the capitalist mode, and to shorten the transition. Force is the midwife of every old society pregnant with a new one. It is itself an economic power."

8 Robinson (2018:55) defines a "circuit of accumulation" as, "the process by which the production of a good or a service is first planned and financed (by capitalists), followed by attaining and then mixing together the component parts (labor, raw materials, buildings and machinery, and so on) in production sequences, and then by the marketing of the final product. At the end of this process the capitalist recovers his initial capital outlay as well as profit and has thus 'accumulated' capital. This is what Karl Marx referred to as the 'circuit of capital.'"

9 Most importantly, in addition to the benefit of limited liability where business owners are protected by an intermediary Board of Directors, these rights included that of free speech, to sue and be sued, to buy and own/trade stock, and so forth.

10 See Robinson (2014, 2018, 2022a, 2022b) for a detailed definition of globalization, "digitization," and financialization as three defining features of the current regime of accumulation. Digitization broadly refers to the ability to transfer, communicate, analyze, and commodify nearly all information digitally at increasing scale and speed.

11 For more on this process, the resulting relationship between states and capital, and the inability or unwillingness of states to abide by their obligations to human rights instruments, please see Armaline and Glasberg (2009).

12 These connections are through "interlocking directorates" between the world's major banks, corporations, and insurance companies. Interlocking directorates generally refer to the overlapping board membership between banks, corporations, and insurance companies that allow for a certain amount of political economic coordination, and help to establish a powerful elite of owners and managers who make many of the most consequential economic decisions in capitalist society. See Mintz and Schwartz (1985) for the groundbreaking sociological study of interlocking directorates and the "power structure" of the American business community.

13 For more on these and other investigations from the ICIJ, see: www.icij.org/investigations/

14 There are additional, overlapping roles relative to other social systems and the "background relations" of capitalist society. Much of this will be explored in Chapters 3, 4, and 5.

15 Though many scholars employ a similar historical framework in the sociology of race and racism, we are borrowing originally from Carter Wilson (1996), though with slightly altered and simplified language also in line with the framework offered by Feagin and Ducey (2019).

16 Interestingly, the study demonstrated that the time of greatest racial wealth equality between Blacks and Whites in the US was during the brief post-Civil War Reconstruction period.

17 Part of the mortgage-backed securities scam was for ratings agencies to puroposefully inflate the scores of financial products that in fact contained highly unstable sub-prime mortgages that were unlikely to be repaid. Many of the financial products based on these bad mortgages were fraudulently sold to individuals, public pension funds, and Nation-states like Greece as highly rated (A, A +) "safe" investments, even while the brokers and firms selling the products were actively betting against their performance (and the interests of their clients).

References

Alexander, Michelle. 2020. *The New Jim Crow*. New York: The New Press.

Anti-Defamation League (ADL) Center on Extremism. 2023a. "Murder and Extremism in the United States in 2022." *ADL*. Retrieved on 06/01/23 from www.adl. org/resources/report/murder-and-extremism-united-states-2022

Anti-Defamation League (ADL) Center on Extremism. 2023b. "White Supremacist Propaganda Soars to All-Time High in 2022." *ADL*. Retrieved on 06/01/23 from www. adl.org/resources/report/white-supremacist-propaganda-soars-all-time-high-2022

Armaline, William and Davita Silfen Glasberg. 2009. "What Will States Really Do for Us? The Human Rights Enterprise and Pressure from Below." *Societies Without Borders* 4 (3): 430–451.

Armaline, William, Davita Silfen Glasberg and Bandana Purkayastha. 2011. *Human Rights in our Own Backyard: Injustice and Resistance in the US*. Philadelphia, PA: University of Pennsylvania Press.

Armaline, William, Davita Silfen Glasberg and Bandana Purkayastha. 2015. *The Human Rights Enterprise: Political Sociology, State Power and Social Movements*. London: Polity Press.

Bakan, Joel. 2004. *The Corporation: The Pathological Pursuit of Profit and Power*. New York: Free Press.

Balu, Nivedita. 2023. "Apple to Use Only Recycled Cobalt in Batteries by 2025." *Reuters*, April 13. Retrieved on 06/15/23 from www.reuters.com/technology/apple-use-100-recycled-cobalt-batteries-by-2025-2023-04-13/#:~:text=Most%20cobalt%20is%20produced%20as,a%20year%20earlier%2C%20Apple%20said

Blackmon, Douglas. 2008. *Slavery by Another Name: The Re-Enslavement of Black Americans from the Civil War to World War II*. New York: Doubleday.

Bonilla-Silva, Eduardo. 1996. "Rethinking Racism: Toward a Structural Interpretation." *American Sociological Review* 62: 465–480.

Bonilla-Silva, Eduardo. 2001. *White Supremacy and Racism in the Post-Civil Rights Era*. Boulder, CO: Lynne Rienner.

Bowdler, Janis and Benjamin Harris. 2022. "Racial Inequality in the United States." *US Department of the Treasury*, July 1. Retrieved 06/15/23 from https://home.treasury. gov/news/featured-stories/racial-inequality-in-the-united-states#:~:text=These%20earnings%20differences%20have%20changed,Black%20and%20Hispanic%20families%2C%20respectively

Brewer, Rose and Nancy A. Heitzeg. 2008. "The Racialization of Crime and Punishment: Criminal Justice, Color-Blind Racism, and the Political Economy of the Prison Industrial Complex." *American Behavioral Scientist* 51 (5): 625–643.

Bruenig, Matt. 2020. "The Racial Wealth Gap Is About the Upper Classes." *Jacobin*, July 5. Retrieved 05/15/23 from https://jacobin.com/2020/07/racial-wealth-gap-redistribution

Burd-Sharps, Sarah and Rebecca Rasch. 2015. "Impact of the US Housing Crisis on the Racial Wealth Gap Across Generations." *American Civil Liberties Union*. Retrieved 06/01/23 from www.aclu.org/wp-content/uploads/legal-documents/discrimlend_final.pdf

Carmichael, Stokely and Charles Hamilton. 1967. *Black Power: The Politics of Liberation in America*. New York: Vintage Books.

Cazenave, N. 2016. *Conceptualizing Racism: Breaking the Chains of Racially Accommodative Language*. Lanham, MD: Rowman & Littlefield.

Cazenave, N. 2018. *Killing African Americans: Police and Vigilante Violence as a Racial Control Mechanism.* New York: Routledge.

Center for Constitutional Rights (CCR). 2023. "Center for Constitutional Rights Denounces the Supreme Court's Gutting of Affirmative Action." *CCR*, June 23. Retrieved 10/01/23 from https://ccrjustice.org/home/press-center/press-releases/center-constitutional-rights-denounces-supreme-court-s-gutting

Christensen, Martin-Brehm, C. Hallum, A. Maitland, Q. Parrinello and C. Putaturo. 2023. "Survival of the Richest: How We Must Tax the Super-Rich Now to Fight Inequality." *Oxfam International.* Retrieved 02/15/23 from www.oxfam.org/en/research/survival-richest

Clement, D. 2016. *Human Rights in Canada: A History.* Waterloo, Canada: Wilfrid Laurier University Press.

Daly, Lyle. 2023. "How Many Americans Own Stock? About 150 Million—But the Wealthiest 1% Own More Than Half." *The Motley Fool.* Retrieved 02/15/23 from www.fool.com/research/how-many-americans-own-stock/#:~:text=While%20over%20half%20of%20American,of%20stocks%2C%20worth%20%2416.76%20trillion

Derenoncourt, Ellora, C.H. Kim, M. Kuhn, M. Schularick. 2022. "Wealth of Two Nations: The US Racial Wealth Gap, 1860–2020." *National Bureau of Economic Research*, Working Paper 30101. Retrieved 02/15/23 from www.nber.org/papers/w30101

DuBois, W.E.B. 1998 [1938]. *Black Reconstruction in America: 1860–1880.* New York: The Free Press.

Feagin, Joe. 1977. "Indirect Institutionalized Discrimination: A Typology and Policy Analysis." *American Politics Quarterly* 5 (1): 177–220.

Feagin, Joe. 2006. *Systemic Racism: A Theory of Oppression.* New York: Routledge.

Feagin, Joe and Kimberly Ducey. 2019. *Racist America: Roots, Current Realities, and Future Reparations* (4th edition). New York: Routledge.

Federal Reserve Bank of New York (press release). 2023. "Total Household Debt Reaches $17.05 Trillion in Q1 2023; Mortgage Loan Growth Slows." *Federal Reserve Bank of New York*, May 15. Retrieved 06/01/23 from www.newyorkfed.org/newsevents/news/research/2023/20230515

Fraser, Nancy. 2016. Expropriation and Exploitation in Racialized Capitalism: A Reply to Michael Dawson. *Critical Historical Studies* 3 (1): 163–178. https://doi.org/10.1086/685814

Fraser, Nancy. 2019. *The Old is Dying and the New Cannot Be Born.* New York: Verso.

Fraser, Nancy. 2022. *Cannibal Capitalism: How Our System is Devouring Democracy, Care, and the Planet—and What We Can Do About It.* London: Verso.

Fraser, Nancy and R. Jaeggi (B. Milstein Ed.). 2018. *Capitalism: A Conversation in Critical Theory.* Cambridge: Polity Press.

Gates, Henry L. Jr. 2016. "Black American and the Class Divide." *The New York Times*, February 1. Retrieved on 09/01/23 from www.nytimes.com/2016/02/07/education/edlife/black-america-and-the-class-divide.html

Giancola, Jennifer and Richard Kahlenberg. 2016. "True Merit: Ensuring Our Brightest Students Have Access to Our Best Colleges and Universities." *Jack Kent Cooke Foundation.* Retrieved 07/07/23 from www.jkcf.org/research/true-merit-ensuring-our-brightest-students-have-access-to-our-best-colleges-and-universities/

Guardian Investigatons Team. 2021. "Pandora Papers: Biggest Ever Leak of Offshore Data Exposes Financial Secrets of the Rich and Powerful." *The Guardian*, October 3. Retrieved 02/15/23 from www.theguardian.com/news/2021/oct/03/pandora-papers-biggest-ever-leak-of-offshore-data-exposes-financial-secrets-of-rich-and-powerful

Harvey, D. 2005. *The New Imperialism* (revised edition). New York: Oxford University Press.

Harvey, D. 2007. *A Brief History of Neoliberalism*. New York: Oxford University Press.

Harvey, D. 2018. *Marx, Capital, and the Madness of Economic Reason*. New York: Oxford University Press.

Hermann, Alexander. 2023. "In Nearly Every State, People of Color are Less Likely to Own Homes Compared to White Households." *Joint Center for Housing Studies of Harvard University*, February 8. Retrieved 06/01/23 from www.jchs.harva rd.edu/blog/nearly-every-state-people-color-are-less-likely-own-homes-compared-white-households#:~:text=However%2C%20the%20racial%20homeownership%20gap,points%20lower%20than%20white%20households

Hussain, Murtaza. 2023. "Supreme Court: Affirmative Action is OK—If the Students are Getting Sent to Die in Wars." *The Intercept*, June 29. Retrieved on 06/30/23 from https://theintercept.com/2023/06/29/supreme-court-affirmative-action-milita ry-academy/?utm_medium=email&utm_source=The%20Intercept%20Newsletter

International Labor Organization (ILO). 2023. World Employment and Social Outlook: Trends 2023. *ILO*. Retrieved 05/01/23 from www.ilo.org/global/research/global-reports/weso/WCMS_865332/lang–en/index.htm

Jones, Jeffrey. 2022. "Confidence in US Institutions Down; Average at New Low." *Gallup News*, April 5. Retrieved 05/01/23 from https://news.gallup.com/poll/394283/confidence-institutions-down-average-new-low.aspx

Kara, Siddharth. 2023. *Cobalt Red: How the Blood of the Congo Powers Our Lives*. New York: St. Martin's Press.

Khan, Zia, H. Terris, B. Meggeson and M. Taqi. 2023. "The World's 100 Largest Banks, 2023." *S&P Market Intelligence*, April 26. Retrieved 05/01/23 from www.spglobal. com/marketintelligence/en/news-insights/research/the-world-s-100-largest-banks-2023

Klein, Naomi. 2010. *The Shock Doctrine: The Rise of Disaster Capitalism*. New York: Metropolitan Books.

Koop, Avery. 2022. "Top Heavy: Countries by Share of the Global Economy." *Visual Capitalist*, December 29. Retrieved 02/15/23 from www.visualcapitalist. com/countries-by-share-of-global-economy/

Lederer, Edith. 2023. "An Alarming Humanitarian Crisis and Sexual Violence Wrack Eastern Congo, UN Official Says." *ABC News*, September 5. Retrieved 09/07/23 from https://abcnews.go.com/US/wireStory/alarming-humanitarian-crisis-massive-sexual-violence-conflict-wracked-102949839#:~:text=UNITED%20NATIONS%20%2D%2D%20The%20humanitarian,official%20said%20Tuesday

Leo Moore, Wendy. 2022. "Affirmative Action Benefits White Women Most." *Teen Vogue*, March 30. Retrieved 07/05/23 from www.teenvogue.com/story/affirma tive-action-who-benefits

Linebaugh, Peter. 2014. *Stop Thief! The Commons, Enclosures, and Resistance*. Oakland, CA: PM Press.

Lo Bianco, Miguel and Hernan Nessi. 2023. "Argentina Inflation Smashes Past Every Forecast to Hit 109%." *Reuters*, May 12. Retrieved on 05/20/23 from www.reuters.com/world/americas/country-beggars-argentines-reel-104-inflation-keeps-rising-2023-05-12/

Luxemburg, Rosa. 1968. *The Accumulation of Capital*. New York: Monthly Review Press.

Marx, Karl. 1988 [1844]. *Economic and Philosophic Manuscripts of 1844 and the Communist Manifesto* (trans. Martin Milligan). New York: Prometheus Books.

Marx, Karl. 2004 [1867]. *Capital* Vol. I. (trans. Ben Fowkes). London: Penguin Press.

McCoy, Alfred. 2017. *In the Shadows of the American Century: The Rise and Decline of US Global Power.* Chicago, IL: Haymarket Books.

McCoy, Alfred. 2021. *To Govern the Globe: World Orders and Catastrophic Change.* Chicago, IL: Haymarket Books.

Mills, C. W. 1956. *The Power Elite.* New York: Oxford University Press.

Mintz, Beth and M. Schwartz. 1985. *The Power and Structure of American Business.* Chicago: University of Chicago Press.

Montague, Zach. 2023. "Inside the Courtroom, Justices Exchanged Divergent Views of the Ruling." *The New York Times*, June 29. Retrieved 06/30/23 from www.nytimes.com/live/2023/06/29/us/affirmative-action-supreme-court

Mosquera, Martin. 2021. "Nancy Fraser: 'Cannibal Capitalism' Is on Our Horizon (Interview with Nancy Fraser)." *Jacobin.* Retrieved 02/01/23 from https://jacobin.com/2021/09/nancy-fraser-cannibal-capitalism-interview

Newman, Jay. 2023. "Apple is a Chinese Company." *Financial Times*, May 2. Retrieved on 05/02/23 from www.ft.com/content/bf8e3846-2421-4f91-becf-2dfe39ec9941

Neysmith, Elettra. 2023. "DR Congo Violence Forces 7m From Their Homes – UN." *BBC News*, October 31. Retrieved 11/04/23 from www.bbc.com/news/topics/cvenzmgylgwt/democratic-republic-of-congo

Num, Russ and Jeffrey Collins. 2015. "White Gunman Caught in Killing of 9 in Historically Black Church." *AP*, June 18. Retrieved 06/01/23 from https://apnews.com/article/politics-south-carolina-religion-charleston-arrests-8747b77ae03a426e864f042454cab603

Omi, Michael and Howard Winant. 2014 [1986]. *Racial Formation in the United States* (3rd edition). New York: Routledge.

Oxfam International. 2024. "Wealth of Five Richest Men Doubles Since 2020 as Five Billion People Made Poorer in 'Decade of Division,' says Oxfam." *Oxfam International*, January 15. Retrieved 02/10/24 from www.oxfam.org/en/press-releases/wealth-five-richest-men-doubles-2020-five-billion-people-made-poorer-decade-division

Parker, Kim. 2021. "What's Behind the Growing Gap Between Men and Women in College Completion?" *Pew Research Center*, November 8. Retrieved 05/01/23 from www.pewresearch.org/short-reads/2021/11/08/whats-behind-the-growing-gap-between-men-and-women-in-college-completion/

Parks, Miles. 2023. "Despite Fierce Protests, France Has Raised Retirement Age From 62–64." *NPR*, April 15. Retrieved 05/01/23 from www.npr.org/2023/04/15/1170246219/despite-fierce-protests-france-has-raised-the-retirement-age-from-62-to-64#:~:text=Despite%20fierce%20protests%2C%20France%20has,from%202062%20to%2064%20%3A%20NPR&text=Press-,Despite%20fierce%20protests%2C%20France%20has%20raised%20the%20retirement%20age%20from,France%20from%2062%20to%2064

Phartiyal, Sankalp. 2023. "Apple India iPhone Output Soars to $7 Billion in China Shift." *Bloomberg*, April 12. Retrieved 05/01/23 from www.bloomberg.com/news/articles/2023-04-13/apple-triples-india-iphone-output-to-7-billion-in-china-shift#xj4y7vzkg

Phillips, Peter. 2018. *Giants: The Global Power Elite.* New York: Seven Stories Press.

Poulantzas, Nicos. 2014 [1978]. *State, Power, Socialism.* New York: Verso Books.

Robinson, William. 2004. *A Theory of Global Capitalism: Production, Class, and the State in a Transnational World.* Baltimore, MD: Johns Hopkins Press.

Robinson, William. 2014. *Global Capitalism and the Crisis of Humanity.* New York: Cambridge University Press.

Robinson, William. 2018a. *Into the Tempest: Essays on the New Global Capitalism.* Chicago, IL: Haymarket Books.

Robinson, William. 2018b. "Debating the Precariat: An Exchange on the Essay, 'The Precariat: Today's Transformative Class?'" *Great Transition Initiative [GTI]*. Retrieved on 07/01/23 from https://greattransition.org/roundtable/precariat-william -robinson

Robinson, William. 2020. *The Global Police State.* London, England: Pluto Press.

Robinson, William. 2022a. *Global Civil War: Capitalism Post-Pandemic.* Oakland, CA: PM Press.

Robinson, William. 2022b. *Can Global Capitalism Endure?* Atlanta, GA: Clarity Press.

Rothkopf, David. 2008. *Superclass: The Global Power Elite and the World They are Making.* New York: Farrar, Straus and Giroux.

Routley, Nick. 2022. "Charted: The World's Most Populous Countries (1973–2023)." *Visual Capitalist*, October 11. Retrieved on 02/15/23 from www.visualcapitalist. com/most-populous-countries-over-50-years/

Saric, Ivana. 2023. "All US Extremist Mass Killings in 2022 Linked to Far Right, Report Says." *Axios*, February 23. Retrieved on 06/01/23 from www.axios.com/ 2023/02/23/mass-killings-extremism-adl-report-2022

Sawyer, Wendy and Peter Wagner. 2023. "Mass Incarceration: The Whole Pie 2023." *Prison Policy Institute.* Retrieved 06/15/23 from www.prisonpolicy.org/reports/p ie2023.html#bigpicture

Sklair, Leslie. 2001. *The Transnational Capitalist Class.* Oxford, UK: Blackwell.

Smedley, Audrey and Brian Smedley. 2012. *Race in North America: Origin and Evolution of a Worldview.* New York: Routledge.

Smialek, Jeanna and Alan Rappeport. 2023. "Was This a Bailout? Skeptics Descend on Silicon Valley Bank Response." *The New York Times*, March 13. Retrieved 05/01/ 23 from www.nytimes.com/2023/03/13/business/economy/svb-bailout-questions.html

Southern Poverty Law Center (SPLC). 2020. "The Year in Hate and Extremism 2019. Southern Poverty Law Center Intelligence Project." Retrieved 06/01/23 from www. splcenter.org/year-hate-and-extremism-2019

Sovereign Wealth Fund Institute (SWFI). 2023. "Top 100 Asset Manager: Managers by Managed AUM." *SWFI*. Retrieved 05/20/23 from www.swfinstitute.org/ fund-manager-rankings/asset-manager

Taylor, Keeanga Yamahtta. 2023. "Black Class Matters: Class Conflict Undermines Assumptions About Political Solidarity." *Hammer and Hope* 2. https://hammera ndhope.org/article/black-america-2020-protests

The Economics of Ecosystems and Biodiversity Business Coalition (TEEB for Business). 2013. "Natural Capital at Risk – The Top 100 Externalities of Business." Retrieved 05/01/23 from http://sdg.iisd.org/news/teeb-for-business-lists-100-top -environmental-externalities/

Thompson, Mark. 2023. "UBS is Buying Credit Suisse in Bid to Halt Banking Crisis." *CNN*, March 20. Retrieved 05/01/23 from www.cnn.com/2023/03/19/business/cred it-suisse-ubs-rescue/index.html

Tippett, Rebecca, A. Jones-DeWeever, M. Rockeymoore, D. Hamilton and W. Darity. 2014. "Beyond Broke: Why Closing the Racial Wealth Gap is a Priority for National Economic Security." *Center for Global Policy Solutions.* Retrieved 06/01/ 23 from http://globalpolicysolutions.org/report/beyond-broke/

Tsutsui, K., C. Whitlinger and A. Lim. 2012. "International Human Rights Law and Social Movements: States' Resistance and Civil Society's Insistence." *Annual Review of Law and Social Science* 8: 367–396.

UN Global Crisis Response Group. 2023. "A World of Debt: A Growing Burden to Global Prosperity." *United Nations.* Retrieved 07/13/23 from https://unctad.org/world-of-debt

US Census Bureau (press release). 2023. "National Poverty in America Awareness Month: January 2023." *US Census Bureau.* Retrieved 06/01/23 from www.census.gov/newsroom/stories/poverty-awareness-month.html

US Geological Survey. 2023. "Reserves of Cobalt Worldwide in 2022, by Country (in Metric Tons) [graph]." *Statista.* Retrieved 06/01/23 from www.statista.com/statistics/264930/global-cobalt-reserves/#:~:text=The%20Democratic%20Republic%20of%20the,metric%20tons%20as%20of%202022

Vitali, Stefania, J. Glattfelder and S. Battison. 2011. "The Network of Global Corporate Control." *PLOS One.* https://doi.org/10.1371/journal.pone.0025995.

Washington Post. 2023. "Rate of Fatal Police Shootings in the United States from 2015 to May 2023, by Ethnicity." *Statista.* Retrieved 06/15/23 from www.statista.com/statistics/1123070/police-shootings-rate-ethnicity-us/

Wilson, Carter. 1996. *Racism: From Slavery to Advanced Capitalism.* Thousand Oaks, CA: Sage Publications.

World Bank. 2022. "Poverty and Shared Prosperity 2022: Correcting Course." *World Bank,* Washington, DC. License: Creative Commons Attribution CC BY 3.0 IGO. Retrieved 01/20/23 from www.worldbank.org/en/publication/poverty-and-shared-prosperity

World Bank. 2023a. "Labor Force, Total (table)." *The World Bank.* Retrieved 05/01/23 from https://data.worldbank.org/indicator/SL.TLF.TOTL.IN

World Bank. 2023b. "GDP (current US$)." Retrieved 05/15/23 from https://data.worldbank.org/indicator/NY.GDP.MKTP.CD?most_recent_value_desc=true

World Bank and the Development Research Center of the State Council, the People's Republic of China. 2022. "Four Decades of Poverty Reduction in China: Drivers, Insights for the World, and the Way Ahead." *World Bank.* doi:10.1596/978-1-4648-1877-6

World Food Program (WFP). 2024. "A Global Food Crisis." *WFP.* Retrieved 02/20/24 from www.wfp.org/global-hunger-crisis

World Inequality Lab. 2022. "World Inequality Report [WIR] 2022." *World Inequality Lab.* Retrieved 05/01/23 from https://wir2022.wid.world/

Younge, Gary. 2007. "'We Used to Think There Was a Black Community' (interview w/ Angela Davis)". *The Guardian,* November 8. Retrieved 09/01/23 from www.theguardian.com/world/2007/nov/08/usa.gender

2 Contradiction, Crisis, and Overlapping Threats to Human Survival

The Background Relations of Capitalist Society

In addition to its foreground class or material relations, capitalism as an institutionalized social order is comprised of at least four "background relations" that create the "conditions of possibility" for capital accumulation in any particular regime or historical period (Fraser 2022; Fraser and Jaeggi 2018). These conditions and relations can be summarized as follows:

1 Forms of social reproduction to sustain society across generations, reflecting certain gendered (patriarchal) and sexual (heteronormative) relations;
2 State political structures necessary to regulate and maintain capital markets, provide necessary infrastructure for capital accumulation, and provide the repressive and ideological state apparatuses necessary to discipline labor and the broader public—reflecting a particular relation between politics and the economy, and particular ruling relations under state authority;
3 A sustainable ecology to provide the natural resources necessary for capital accumulation and life itself, reflecting a certain (objectified, commodified) relation between capital accumulation and the living planet;
4 Forms of expropriation, primarily through systemic racism and (neo)colonial/imperial relations that both supplement and facilitate the foregrounded exploitative relation of wage labor.

Before providing further description, it is useful to articulate the interconnections between background and foreground relations of capitalism as an institutionalized social order to demonstrate the model's appropriate sophistication. Background relations should be understood as deeply connected to one another and to the foreground material relations of capitalist society. Fraser (2022) describes the nature of these relationships as a form of "non-accidental structural imbrication," meaning that they're interconnected and institutionalized, and their reproduction cannot be reduced to individual agency or mere discourse. Second, it means that each connection is not epiphenomenal, but "co-constitutive" (Fraser 2022) and historically contingent. Background and foreground relations are best understood as "symbiotic" (Fraser 2022) in that they don't coincidentally overlap, but come to depend

DOI: 10.4324/9781003323556-3

on each other to exist—driving and shaping one another as they evolve together over time.

Simultaneously, each background and foreground relation has mutually exclusive terrains of existence where they operate in partial autonomy from the others. Fraser (2022:21) explains that, for example,

> even as these 'non-economic' orders make commodity production possible, they are not reducible to that enabling function. Far from being wholly exhausted by, or entirely subservient to, the dynamics of accumulation, each of these hidden abodes harbors distinctive ontologies of social practice and normative ideals.

To wit, feminist scholars (Federici, 2004, 2018) have pointed out that patriarchal systems pre-dated even the earliest forms of mercantile capitalism and continue to exist in forms of institutionalized social practices, such as interpersonal and structural violence against women, that have and could perpetuate independent of, for instance, capital accumulation or systemic racism.

In dialectical fashion, both the foreground relations and background relations of capitalist society should be understood as the manifestation and embodiment of class and boundary struggles over the nature of those relations and the resulting conditions. Each regime of accumulation ultimately emerges from these historically situated class and boundary struggles and the relations and conditions they (re)produce. It is crucial to note for purposes of praxis that boundary struggles are potentially but not automatically effective in challenging capitalist society through some coincidental, ever-present intersection with capital accumulation. Instead, Fraser (2022:26) notes that the "emancipatory potential" of boundary struggles "would consist in their capacity to envision new configurations, not 'merely' of economy, but also of the relation of economy to society, nature, and polity."

Arguably one example of a boundary struggle exhibiting both emancipatory potential and apparent limitations of this kind is the Black Lives Matter (BLM) movement that arrived in two phases in response to police and vigilante murders of unarmed Black Americans. The movement began after the vigilante killing of 17-year-old Trayvon Martin in Florida in 2012, and exploded in 2014 following viral police killings of those like 18-year-old Michael Brown in Ferguson, MO, 12-year-old Tamir Rice in Cleveland, OH, and 47-year-old Eric Garner in New York City. This first phase of the movement followed a general pattern where massive public demonstrations took place in each respective city to demand investigations and indictments in the face of inaction from public officials. In cases where there was some attempt to investigate or charge law enforcement officers, it was typically only after protesters demanded action in the streets, offering an interesting counterpoint to those who argue against aggressive public demonstration as effective praxis (see Ciccariello-Maher 2015 for the counterpoint at length).

The BLM movement grew as much in reaction to law enforcement responses to peaceful protests as to the individual police murders streaming across a quickly growing social media landscape. Videos played all over the world of a militarized law enforcement response to what began as a peaceful vigil for slain teenager Michael Brown in Ferguson, Missouri, showing small town police in full military armor and armored vehicles, assaulting those in the street with "less than lethal" crowd control weapons, threatening unarmed journalists and community members exercising their rights with assault and high caliber sniper rifles as if in a war zone. Amnesty International (2014) described the militarized response as having a "chilling effect" on Constitutional and human rights, and the story quickly became an embarrassment for the Obama Administration who ordered a DOJ (2015) investigation of the Ferguson Police Department, finding that they had long targeted working class Black residents with abuse, harassment, and—fitting for financialized capitalism—saddling Black residents with predatory forms of legal debt from an inability to pay fines for minor infractions such as jaywalking.

In addition to solidarity protests in global cities, the BLM movement quickly entered the arena of international law and politics. Young organizers like those from Chicago's "We Charge Genocide" employed the discourse of human rights law (as did their organizational namesake in 1951) and brought the movement's calls to end racist police violence to the 2014 review of the US under the Convention Against Torture (CAT) in Geneva, in the first ever public protest in such proceedings (Berlatsky 2014; Hansford and Jagannath 2015). Organizers from Ferguson and other cities began corresponding and organizing with Palestinian rights organizations to resist the considerably interconnected American and Israeli police and military states (Bailey 2015). As a temporary but considerable policy win, the Obama Administration was pressured to limit the transfer of certain military equipment to local law enforcement under the federal 1033 program (the Trump Administration reversed this order under then Attorney General Jeff Sessions) (Goldman 2017).

The BLM movement in its first phase took the form of a series of grassroots protests in direct, immediate response to the police murders of unarmed Black youth and adults. It rhymed with the American civil rights movements of the previous two centuries, where the police and vigilante murders of young Black Americans like Emmett Till in 1955 (and the purposeful public display of his body by his mother) were often the sparks to expanded organizing campaigns and purposeful rebellion. It also represents a form of human rights praxis and the human rights enterprise in motion, where grassroots stakeholders were first struggling to (re)define human rights in asserting the value of Black life. Second, they were gripped in a power struggle to realize those rights—for equal protection under the law as well as the rights to life and due process (let alone to be free from discrimination). Evident in every account from protests of this era, as was the case for the 20th century civil rights movement before it, and as will be made clear in the continued surveillance and repression of those who protest the American police state in Chapter 3, these struggles were waged in spite or against the state responsible for rights protection. Further, the BLM movement demonstrates a specific kind of power struggle—in this case two overlapping boundary struggles (vs. class struggle) over the background relations of expropriation (against systemic racism and neocolonialism), and over the relations of economy and political state structures in determining the power and role of the repressive state apparatus (police and prisons) to coerce Black people and other people of color.

What might be recognized as BLM's second phase emerged in 2020, in the wake of viral police murders of 46-year-old George Floyd in Minneapolis, MN and 26-year-old Breonna Taylor in Louisville, KY (among too many others). Similarly, public protests demanded investigations and legal accountability for those responsible for the murders, but these demands were joined by growing calls for institutional changes that ranged from policing reforms, to the full or partial "defunding" of police, to police and prison abolition. By this time the movement had grown in its original grassroots form, but also much more into the networks of non-profit organizations and political party interests. By the summer of 2020, BLM's second phase erupted into what may have been the largest public protests in US history—with an estimated 15 to 26 million people participating in May and June of 2020—noting that protests also broke out in cities around the world in response to both American and distinct local forms of racism and police violence (Buchanan, Bui, and Patel 2020). Donations flowed into non-profit organizations like the Black Lives Matter Global Action Network, who reported over $42M in assets in the 2021–22 FY (Morrison 2023). Public protests reflected a much more diverse cross section of the general public despite the onset of a terrifying pandemic, and managed to reach a fever pitch in cities like Minneapolis where the 3rd Precinct police headquarters were burned to the ground on June 28th 2020 (Birnstengel 2022). However, though two thirds of all adults in the US "strongly" or "somewhat" supported the BLM movement at the height of the protests, that support dropped to barely over half (51%) by 2023 (Hatfield 2023).

A full analysis of the movement and its impacts is beyond the scope of this illustration. Suffice it to say that BLM produced invaluable tools, organizations, networks, resources, and strategies for anti-racist and anti-colonial boundary struggles (Ransby 2018). Some of these struggles yielded reforms in places like Minneapolis, where 3 years after the murder of George Floyd the police department began a reorganization following investigations from the Minnesota Department of Human Rights revealing racist and abusive policing practices by Minneapolis PD (Babineau and Lopez 2023).[1] It is too early to say whether the kind of reforms proposed in Minneapolis and other municipalities will have an impact on the deadliness or racial disparities of policing in the US. What we can say is that the largest movement in US history fell short of fundamentally challenging the use of traditional policing and incarceration in American society. But this is a high bar to measure the success of such a movement, and it serves as an indication of the power invested in the repressive state apparatus as much as it indicates any strategic shortcoming—and these certainly exist—of those invested in the BLM movement. Exactly three years out from the protests, reporter Jamiles Lartey from the Marshall project offered a summary (2023):

> States have passed hundreds of reform bills, and a number of cities have rolled out alternative response programs for mental health calls that would have historically have been handled by police alone. But the overall footprint and funding of police remains roughly unchallenged. In addition, congress has failed to pass comprehensive police reform, and elements of the Biden Administration's policing executive order are long overdue.

An honest assessment of the BLM movement would have to record the failure to significantly shift resources from traditional forms of policing and incarceration to non-carceral alternatives (Manthey, Esposito, and Hernandez 2022; Liebhaber 2023), or to significantly impact the number of people being killed by police (Levin 2024). For the purposes of the conversation of class and boundary struggles offered here, one might note that despite the potential of the BLM movement to merge with a vaguely left-populist, democratic socialist movement manifested in part by the 2016 and 2020 Bernie Sanders campaigns and the early sparks of a re-emergent and notably diverse labor movement in the US—that did not happen on the whole.

In fact, no clear, consistent, coherent, collective, widespread political project emerged from the two movements that remain—rather there were a series of demands, manifestos, and policy targets from a spectrum of grassroots and not-so-grassroots organizations, politicians and political party affiliates, and any number of movement celebrities, only sometimes in line with one another and not always produced by those on the ground in social movements with the actual power to demand or enact reform. The last point was ultimately born out in the inability of the BLM movement to reduce racist police violence or displace traditional policing and incarceration in the US, or for the left-populist/democratic socialist movement to achieve its stated electoral (e.g., Sanders campaigns) or policy (e.g., Medicare for All) goals. Still, this moment in history was an opportunity for effective praxis informed by an analysis of the structural imbrication of material and boundary relations—for a multi-racial and multi-generational struggle against systemic racism, the repressive state apparatus, and class war from above.

The following sections offer a brief summary of each set of background relations and resulting conditions of possibility to better describe their interrelation to one another and to capital accumulation. With regard to this interrelation, Fraser (2022) argues that in each regime of accumulation there is a tendency for the background conditions of possibility to be "cannibalized" in the accumulation process, causing what will be described in the final section of this chapter as an "external crisis" in capitalist society, just as there are "internal crises" to capital accumulation that have been discussed by critical scholars since the 19th century. Where internal crises result from the inherent economic contradictions of capital accumulation, external crises emerge from "intra-realm contradictions" (Fraser 2022:118) that arise between the drive for capital accumulation and the ability for background relations to create the conditions of possibility for capitalism to perpetuate. Moreover, each of these internal and external crises manifest as fundamental challenges to human rights practice, and when internal and/or external crises reach their heightened extremes, they become a "general crisis," and potentially manifest as an OTHS. In this respect capitalism is "a veritable dynamo of self-destabilization [that] periodically perpetuates crises while routinely eating away at the basis of our existence" (Fraser 2022:xv), and represents the greatest, most persistent threat to achieving universal human dignity.

Social Reproduction

Critical feminists[2] have long revealed the many ways in which forms of social reproduction are prerequisite to production and capital accumulation. Fraser (2022:9) defines social reproduction as

> the forms of provisioning, caregiving, and interaction that produce and sustain human beings and social bonds.... Central here is the work of birthing and socializing the young, building communities, producing and reproducing shared meanings, affective dispositions, and horizons of value that underpin social cooperation.

In a Marxist framework, having and raising kids, caring for the elderly, ill, or differently abled, or socializing and educating new generations are all forms of labor in that they produce value, primarily through the physical reproduction of a sufficiently healthy, trained human workforce. However, reproductive labor is often subject to expropriation—not remunerated for a wage, or extremely devalued in the labor market. This is achieved largely through the patriarchal gendering and racialization of reproductive labor all over the world, in order for it to be expropriated and devalued in the accumulation process. To describe it as a relation, "capitalist societies separate social reproduction from economic production, associating the first with women, and obscuring its importance and worth" (Fraser 2022:57), even though capitalism depends on reproductive labor to function. This is reflected in current data showing that women and girls worldwide do three fourths of all unpaid care work, representing over $10.8 trillion of free labor to the global economy per year (Lawson, Butt, Harvey, et al. 2020).

In the current period, reproduction as a condition of possibility for capitalism is being cannibalized in the accumulation process. Finance capital is currently authorized to "discipline states and publics in the immediate interests of private investors, not least by demanding public disinvestment from social reproduction" (Fraser 2022:68). This translates into less public investment into, for example, education, child care, elder care, social security, or public health systems. These vital resources are privatized or disappear entirely in a context where more and more households are dual income by obligation, and workers are subject to the precarious jobs of the neoliberal era with less and less available time and money for care work of all types. A "care gap" is created as a result, and,

> to fill the care gap, the regime imports migrant workers from poorer to richer countries. Typically it is racialized.... Far from filling the care gap, the net effect is to displace it—from richer to poorer families, from the Global North to the Global South.
>
> (Fraser 2022:70)

Feminist scholars have also referred to this tendency in conceptualizing the "third shift" (Gerstel 2000) and the specific role played by Black women and typically racialized women from the global South to earn a wage for their household (exploited labor), provide (expropriated, unpaid) domestic labor in their own households and communities, and provide (exploited/expropriated) care work in service of privileged households and institutions to fill the care gap created by the material relations of transnational capitalism.

The signs of capital devouring forms of social reproduction are all around us. Again, despite being the wealthiest country in the world, spending more per capita on health care than any other nation in the world, and having unrivaled access to medical technology and innovations for those who can afford it, the US is the most dangerous of all (38) "high income" countries to give birth, especially for the poor and for Black women (Gunja, Gumas, and Williams 2023). In fact, the high and racially disparate rate of maternal mortality is a statistical trend across the entire Western Hemisphere. A 2023 study by the UN Population Fund (2023:4) found that maternal deaths across the Americas for "Afrodescendent" women were "alarmingly high" in both absolute and relative (to non-Hispanic White) terms, due to "structural racism and sexism" that exists (as we would expect from the theoretical model offered here) across income levels and nationalities.

Global birth rates are also on the decline, and it cannot be explained by the massive death toll of the COVID-19 pandemic alone. In 2000 the global fertility rate was 2.7 births per woman, where today the rate is 2.3 and falling—barely above the "replacement rate" (2.1) to keep pace with global deaths (*The Economist* 2023). This includes the 15 countries with the largest GDP, namely China and India that together represent over a third of the global population, and represents the first population growth reversal of this magnitude since the Black

Death (*The Economist* 2023).[3] Slowing birthrates are mixing with aging workforces such that by 2050, 40% of the population in places like the EU, China, and Japan will be over the age of 65 (Leatherby 2023).

While this may create relative economic opportunity for nations with such overwhelmingly young workforces, it highlights a coming onslaught for elder care needs in wealthy and less wealthy nations alike. It puts an economic strain on countries and younger workers to provide for pensions and social security programs for seniors lucky enough to still have them in the neoliberal era that continues to see a push to privatize health care and retirement systems. By 2050 wealthy nations will have less than 2 workers between the age of 20 and 65 for every worker over the age of 65 (the ratio is over 3/1 in 2023), which will put even greater economic strains on social security and health care systems (*The Economist* 2023). Indeed, the social security system in the US currently faces insolvency by 2033 (Horsley 2023) absent any changes to the program. Even if access to public benefits like social security are shored up (and they absolutely should be), the economic future looks grim for aging members of the American working class. In the US, about half of those between the ages of 55 and 65 have no retirement savings (Shamlian and Cutrona 2023), 1 in 3 adults over the age of 65 are "economically insecure" (making less than 200% of the federal poverty line) (NCOA 2023), and over 80% of households with elder adults (47 million households) are "financially struggling" and at risk of "economic insecurity" (Basel, Silberman, Tavares, Cohen, and Wylie 2023). In sum, the care gap is evident in wealthy nations like the US at both ends of the life course, and will have increasingly destabilizing economic and social effects without significant changes in economic policy.

The care gap resulting from financialized global capitalism can also be viewed through the insufficient resourcing of public schools and day care in the US. Child care is largely privatized in the US, and the availability and quality of care depend on a family's ability to pay and live within reach of available agencies or individual care givers. In the first two years of the COVID pandemic, 20,000 child care centers were permanently shuttered in the US. Those that stayed in business are still struggling to hire enough professional caregivers, and were still 40,000 staff short of pre-2020 levels in 2023 (Bhattarai 2023). As a partial result, the industry has been unable to meet the current need for child care, and would have to expand capacity by approximately 3.6 million child care "slots" to satisfy demand (Bhattarai 2023). Making matters worse, the end of federal funding designed to stem the loss of child care resources during the COVID pandemic could mean that an additional 70,000 child care programs disappear, impacting care for another 3.2 million kids and their families (Bhattarai 2023).

Public education in the US shows similar signs of decline. In states like Tennessee, over half of all public school facilities have been rated as being in less than "good" (poor, unsatisfactory, or fair) physical condition, with many districts battling aging infrastructures, climate change impacts, and funding challenges from efforts to privatize education in the state through the charter or "school choice" movement (Thomhave 2022). In 2022 the American Society of Civil Engineers gave public school facilities in the US an overall grade of D+, noting that the average public school building is approximately 50 years old (ASCE 2021). The performance of American public school students also seems to be in decline, where for example, average reading and math scores for 13-year-olds in 2022 were the lowest seen in decades (Carrillo 2023). Further, chronic absenteeism (missing more than 10% of the school year) among students in the US doubled to 28% between the 2018–19 and 2021–22 academic years (MacGillis 2024). Equally concerning, school administrators estimated that half of all public school students in the US were at least one year behind grade level in at least one academic subject at the start of the 2022–23 school year (NCES 2022). While some of the performance gap can be attributed to disruptions to in-person schooling during the COVID-19 pandemic, downward trends were already at play and suggest more to the story. In fact, a pre-pandemic study from The Century Foundation (2020) looked at links between public school funding and student performance and estimated that over 2/3rds of school districts have a "funding gap," where bringing student test scores to average rates would require additional public investment. The study finds that low income schools and schools serving a majority Black or Latinx student population are most likely to have such funding gaps, and that it would require an additional investment of $150B per year to close them (TCF 2020).

Finally, the return of child labor in the US represents a stunning example of capitalism cannibalizing social reproduction. Predictably, young workers are already losing their lives in the legal and illegal turn by American corporations to child labor in some of the most dangerous and unforgiving environments. At the end of June 2023, a 16-year-old boy was killed in an industrial sawmill accident while working legally under expanded child labor laws at Florence Hardwoods in northern Wisconsin (Yang 2023). Two weeks later, in July of 2023, a 16-year-old boy who immigrated from Guatemala died from injuries sustained while cleaning equipment at the Mar-Jac Poultry plant in Hattiesburg, Mississippi, after he was employed illegally by the company (Stancil 2023). Whether in the American meatpacking industry or in the artisan mines of the Congo, children are absolutely on the menu for exploitation and expropriation in the short-term accumulation interests of big capital.

State Political Structures

Each regime of accumulation can be defined in part by the background relations between the economy and state political structures. One unique feature of capitalism relative to previous modes of production, such as feudalism, is the formal (institutional, legal) separation of economy and politics (i.e., private and public). However, while they do remain separate and distinct, they also form a unity of sorts from their structural imbrication that developed since capital's birth. We've already discussed how capitalists depend on states and other political state structures, now including transnational state apparatuses, in order to provide the monetary policy, currency, and regulation to maintain macroeconomic stability; the infrastructure necessary for economic activity such as for transportation, education, or communications; and a repressive state apparatus for purposes of social control in the attempt to protect private property and counter inevitable resistance. We've also noted how the state plays a particular role in the other background relations of capitalist society, for instance in legitimating the ideological frameworks and providing the primary social control components for contemporary systemic racism—part of the background relations of expropriation described below.

In the transition to financialized global capitalism, rather than states protecting the long-term stability and broader interests of capital (such as under Keynesianism), and gaining significant regulatory and other controls on corporations and banks as they had in the prior regime, this relationship switched somewhat under a neoliberal model. Specifically,

> central banks and global financial institutions have replaced states as the arbiters of an increasingly globalized economy… [and] it is largely through debt that capital now cannibalizes labor, disciplines states, transfers value from periphery to core, and sucks wealth from society and nature.
>
> (Fraser 2022:128)

Indeed, we've covered the rise and domination of corporate, but especially finance capital over the state, and the legitimacy crisis that arises for the contemporary state under the pressures to govern in the interest of national and transnational capital accumulation. Recount also that financialized debt has been used as a way to both float markets to avoid crisis in the case of skyrocketing consumer debt, and to discipline and enmesh national states through international debt dependency since global economic restructuring.

This relation between economy and political state structures in the current regime yields certain ruling relations under state authority. Whether illustrated by voter suppression and disenfranchisement in the US (ACLU 2021), the suspension of judicial powers in Israel (McKernan 2023), or the removal of term limits for Chairman Xi in China (Isachenkov and Tong-Hyung 2023), states are responding to legitimacy and other crises with increasingly authoritarian or anti-democratic politics, and in some cases forms of 21st century fascism—reflected for example in many of the right-wing parties in Europe and the Americas, in Israel (Amnesty International 2022b), and in the case of Hindu nationalism in India. Further, the growing concentration of wealth and political power in the hands of the TCC and its Global Power Elite manifests as polyarchy rather than representative or direct forms of democracy at the national and transnational levels. This is a result of the tendency for capital—and the power that comes along with monopolizing capital—to be concentrated into the hands of a small owning class through the accumulation process. The structural imbrication of the state to the process of capital accumulation limits the extent to which states can govern in the expressed interest of the public, even in formally democratic systems. To these points, Fraser (2022:122) asserts that an analysis of the background relation between (capitalist) economy and state political structures across regimes reveals that, "by virtue of its inherent structure, then, capitalism is fundamentally anti-democratic."

And just as with forms of reproduction, there is a tendency for the conditions of possibility yielded from state political structures to be hollowed out or cannibalized in the seeking of short-term accumulation in the current regime. Fraser (2022:122) provides a simple summary of how this tends to play out, particularly in the US:

> The trouble is that capital, by its very nature, tries to have it both ways. On the one hand, it free loads [off] of public power, availing itself of the legal regimes, repressive forces, infrastructures, and regulatory agencies that are indispensable to accumulation. At the same time, the thirst for profit periodically tempts some fractions of the capitalist class to rebel against public power to bad-mouth it as inferior to markets, and to scheme to weaken it. In such cases, when short-term interests trump long-term survival, capital once again threatens to destroy the very political conditions of its own possibility.

This tendency can take several forms. The first and most obvious is through efforts by the TCC and powerful firms to reduce their taxes, effectively defunding the state. This can be done through the kind of tax avoidance previously discussed, where the TCC has been extremely effective. It can also be done through using their financial leverage over policy makers to simply push for tax cuts. In fact, according to the Center for American Progress (Kogen 2023), tax cuts for "the wealthy and profitable corporations" enacted in the GW Bush Administration tax cuts of 2001 and 2003, their extension under the Obama Administration in 2010 and 2012, and under the Trump Administration in 2017, "added $10 trillion to the [national] debt since their enactment and are responsible for 57 percent of the increase in the debt ratio since 2001." The unyielding growth of the US federal debt and legislators' inabilities to address it have now resulted in the first ever ratings agency downgrades of US Treasury bonds—once after a debt deal showdown in 2011 and similarly again in 2023.

Another way capital cannibalizes political state structures is through the process of privatization, where capitalists seek to commodify and control public goods and services. Generally speaking, the private sector has been extremely successful in shifting previously public goods and services from the state to private control. In the US, "there are now 2.6 times as many government contractors as there are government employees" (Cohen and Mikaelian 2021:21). But privatization needs to be understood beyond the "outsourcing of a good or service to a private company" (Cohen and Mikaelian 2021:4). It is as much a "transfer of power" from the general public to "unelected, unaccountable, and inscrutable corporations and their executives" (Cohen and Mikaelian 2021:4). Privatization operates as a "political strategy" for big capital and its organic intellectuals in the think tanks and consulting firms to "tap into the $7 trillion of public revenue (which swelled to $9 trillion during the COVID crisis) spent by local, state, and federal government agencies each year and carve out a piece (sometimes a very large piece) for themselves" (Cohen and Mikaelian 2021:21).

Privatization surrenders public goods and services to private interests, transfers power from the public to relatively unaccountable corporate firms (often with disastrous human rights implications), and is one way through which capital cannibalizes its conditions of possibility. All of this is apparent in the ongoing national (US) and global struggle over water privatization. Access to safe drinking water and sanitation was declared an explicit human right in a 2015 UN General Assembly resolution (UNGA 2015), and had previously been understood as a human right under ICESCR Article 11 (the right to an adequate standard of living). However, as Cohen and Mikaelian (2021) point out in their research of water privatization, the provision of water to the masses through public water systems has existed since antiquity, and this was more often than not out of a sense of shared moral obligation, and in response to the need to improve public health and avoid what would eventually be understood as water borne illness. In the US by as early as 1900, 82% of the 50 largest cities had their own public water works, and by the New Deal era public water works had expanded to over 20,000 systems serving communities big and small. However, federal funding of water and sanitation systems in the US has remained relatively flat for decades and local municipalities have struggled to afford the costs of maintaining and replacing water systems. For instance, local spending on these systems dropped 22% in the years following the Great Recession of 2008, as municipal revenues cratered from the economic crisis (Cohen and Mikaelian 2021).

Corporations seeking to commodify and capture as much of the public water supply as possible have pushed back on the notion of water as a right or public good. Nestle—a transnational corporate giant with over 2000 brands of beverages and other edible goods for people and pets—is commonly among the top three sellers of bottled water in the world. Nestle CEO Peter Brabeck asserted that it was "extreme" to suggest that "as a human being you should have a right to water," and that it should be treated as other commodified "foodstuffs" and distributed through the market (Cohen and Mikaelian 2021:54). In 2015, as the UN General Assembly articulated the human right to water and sanitation, and California residents were suffering under a brutal drought and public water restrictions, Nestle was bottling municipal water supplies to sell it as "spring water" on the private market (Cohen and Mikaelian 2021:54; Bacher 2015; Forbes 2015).

Corporations have also sought to exploit the desperation of municipalities to deliver water and sanitation services under conditions of austerity. In Apple Valley, California, a small town northeast of Los Angeles, Park Water—a private firm owned by the powerful Carlyle Group—was contracted to run water and sanitation services. In the 13 years prior to the drought of 2015, Park Water raised rates on Apple Valley by 68%, and attempted another 30% hike in the middle of a statewide drought (Cohen and Mikaelian 2021:61; Starkman 2015). This amounted to prices 50–100% higher than in neighboring public water systems, and while providing Park Water and Carlyle Group boosts in profit, did not deliver superior services or a share of the windfall with Apple Valley residents.

The neglect, privatization, and general degradation of public water and sanitation systems in the US is an example of how the relation of economy to political state structures is one of cannibalization. In the context of shrinking national and global fresh water supplies due to climate change and pollution, water systems in the US leak over 6 billion gallons of water a day (enough to fill 9,000 swimming pools) across over 2.2 million miles of typically underground pipes (ASCE 2021). Poor infrastructure is most devastating for the most marginalized American communities. In 2017, UN Special Rapporteur on Extreme Poverty and Human Rights, Philip Alston toured rural Black communities in Alabama including places like Lowndes County, where he reported that "raw sewage flows from homes exposed PVC pipes and into open trenches and pits," and residents were suffering from poverty related diseases like hookworm, rarely found in wealthy countries (EJI 2017).

The degradation of these public systems, and the inability to provide water and sanitation as an obvious condition of possibility for capital accumulation and the general functioning of society, at a certain point becomes a big problem for capital and for the legitimacy of the state. For their part, the US Congress and the Biden Administration recognized the scale of these problems and pledged $50B to repairing and updating public water and sanitation systems across the US through the Infrastructure Investment and Jobs Act of 2022. While this is the largest such investment in recent history, the American Society of Civil Engineers (2020) estimated in 2020 that the annual national funding gap for water infrastructure in 2019 alone was $81B, and that the gap will grow to a staggering $136B by 2029. It is clear that more public investment in water, sanitation, and other basic infrastructure will be needed for the US to endure the strains put on water supplies by climate change, and that water privatization has not been a terribly useful solution for communities suffering in the gap.

Finally, capital cannibalizes state political structures through aggressive deregulation and forms of regulatory capture. Deregulation refers to where capital interests pressure the state to weaken or eliminate state regulatory powers. Regulatory capture involves the creation of "revolving doors" between regulatory agencies and the industry firms they are directed to regulate, such that the decision makers in state agencies have backgrounds or ties to the firms and industries under the scrutiny of regulators.

Perhaps one of the best examples of both of these at work would be the successful efforts of the banking industry and their representatives then serving as official advisors to the Clinton Administration (Roberts 2014) to overturn the Depression era Glass-Steagall Act by passing the Financial Services Modernization Act in 1999. This policy change allowed for the retroactive merger of Citigroup and Travelers Group and unleashed "a wave of Wall Street consolidation that was later blamed for forcing taxpayers to spend billions bailing out the enlarged banks after the sub-prime mortgage crisis" (Roberts 2014). Out of an effort to maximize their power, size, and short-term profitability (through allowing banks to make speculative investments), national and transnational finance capital deregulated the banking industry to the point of destabilization and eventual crisis in the Great Recession and the largest bank failures in all of US history. Demonstrating the persistence of this trend, the second largest bank failure in US history was that of Silicon Valley Bank (SVB) in 2023, that collapsed under a bank run that revealed mismanagement and insufficient capital holdings. The bank failed because SVB had successfully lobbied since 2010 to not be held to the regulatory and oversight standards (that would have demanded, for example, higher capital requirements) put in place under "Dodd-Frank" and other regulatory legislation meant to avoid another financial crisis (Burns and Rock 2023). Finance capital, in the search for higher and faster returns through increasingly risky investments and speculation, has repeatedly sought to undermine the ability for the state to regulate their activities. While perhaps profitable at first, the long-term impact of this trend is to remove important safeguards that provide long-term stability for capital accumulation, and, as in the case of SVB, big problems are often soon to follow. Though the cannibalization of state political structures can certainly be destabilizing, the voracious consumption and destruction of the natural environment in the capital accumulation process presents more fundamental challenges to human rights and human survival.

Sustainable Ecology

As it is with forms of reproduction, capital accumulation is dependent on the functioning of natural ecosystems to provide the raw materials needed for production and to provide the conditions of possibility for sustaining human and other forms of life over generations. However, capitalism "harbors a deep seated ecological contradiction" (Fraser 2022:78) where the objective thrust toward constant, endless accumulation and concentration of capital is confronted by a finite supply of natural planetary resources that are actually devalued and assumed without limit in the accumulation process.[4] Fraser (2022:82) explains,

On the one hand, the system's economy is constitutively dependent on nature, both as a tap for production's inputs and as a sink for disposing its waste. At the same time, capitalist society institutes a stark division between the two "realms"—constructing economy as a field of creative human action that generates value, while positioning nature as a realm on stuff, devoid of value, but infinitely self-replenishing and generally available to be processed in commodity production.

The relation between capitalist economy and natural ecosystems is one of "extraction" ("tap") and "externalization" ("sink") where, out of competitive obligation, capitalists[5] 1) seek to source their raw materials (form of "inputs") as quickly and cheaply as possible[6] while 2) externalizing as many of the costs of resource extraction and the production process to other parties (the public, the state, or other firms) and the ecosphere on which everything depends (pollution, over-harvesting of animal and plant stocks, habitat destruction). Such a relation tends toward crisis when the practices of extraction and externalization cannibalize and destroy the ecological conditions of possibility for production and for life itself in the accumulation process.

This relation and tendency toward crisis runs through all regimes of accumulation, each of which can be understood to some extent by the raw materials needed to fuel production and, as will be discussed shortly, imperial world orders. For instance, in pre-capitalist society and mercantile capitalism through the 17th century, production was fueled primarily by the physical labor, "somatic" (McNeill 2001) or "muscle" (Fraser 2022) power of human beings (exploited and expropriated labor) and domesticated animals (horses, oxen, etc.), and the "mastery of the winds" (e.g. Dutch/English transportation by sail and use of the windmill), Liberal-Colonial or Classical Competitive Capitalism of the 18th and 19th centuries would be the first "exosomatic" regime (McNeill 2001), or the first to "take carbonized solar energy from beneath the crust of the Earth and convert it to mechanical energy *outside of living bodies*" (Fraser 2022:96) through the burning of coal as a base fuel for transportation (rail, steam ships), early industrial production, and finally for the production of electricity by the end of the period. Monopoly capitalism of the 20th century would change dramatically from discoveries like that of the combustion engine and (petro-)chemical engineering that would make wide use of oil as the new key exosomatic source of energy powering production.

Now, transnational financialized capitalism is marked by a continued dependence on fossil fuels amidst a race to new "green" and alternative energy sources. This includes the scramble for heavy metals needed for battery and other high-tech industries previously discussed in the case of Apple Inc. and cobalt mines in the DRC. In that case, as part of a transnational circuit of accumulation, mining companies are extracting cobalt and other mineral resources at minimal cost through extreme forms of labor exploitation and expropriation to supply tech firms, while externalizing the environmental (deforestation, habitat destruction, water/soil/air pollution) and social (poverty, illness, death/injury, community and political destabilization) costs to the public, state, and local ecosystems. One result is the short-term, profitable sourcing of heavy metals for big tech and other industrial production (such as for electric vehicles (EVs)), but the looting of mineral resources and externalized costs of extraction devastate impacted communities and the natural environment as well.

The long-term ecological costs of capitalist production, particularly since the industrial revolution and the move to exosomatic modes of energy production are now abundantly evident in the forms of human induced climate change and ecological destruction that must be understood together as an OTHS. As will be discussed in the final section of this chapter on crises, the ecological contradiction fundamental to capitalism emerges in the current period as a "general crisis" that threatens to end organized human civilization along with thousands of other species and natural habitats (Fraser 2022). For now, it is sufficient to illustrate that climate change and ecological destruction are overwhelmingly a result of capitalism's defining ecological contradiction. As a manifestation of the cannibalistic relation of capital to ecology, capitalists and their associates in government collaborate to extract more and more natural resources as cheaply as possible while externalizing the costs of extraction and production wherever, however they can.

Viewed through the theoretical lens presented here, climate change and ecological destruction absolutely involves consumption, but is primarily driven by production—that is, by circuits of accumulation ultimately dominated by the TCC. This is not to say that consumption is irrelevant by any means, particularly when one thinks about problems with pollution and waste, or when thinking about the unequal distribution and use of finite natural resources. Calls for wealthy nations to pay their fair share in financing climate change solutions are legitimate, given their consumption and expropriation of natural resources from indigenous lands the world over and especially in the global South—communities who now face some of the most extreme, immediate, existential threats of climate change. It is also legitimate to point out considerable disparities in emissions related to individual consumption. To no surprise, these disparities match those of wealth, where the consumption of the richest 1% accounts for 16% of total global consumption—more emissions than the poorest two thirds (5 billion people) of the world combined—and the richest 10% account for over 50% of global emissions (Khalfan, Nilsson Lewis, Aguilar, et al. 2023). According to current statistics, it would take 1500 years for someone in the global majority to produce a carbon footprint on par with a billionaire (Khalfan, Nilsson Lewis, Aguilar, et al. 2023). However, this does not mean that consumption—even of the world's wealthiest—is what drives climate change and ecological destruction. Nor does it mean that simply convincing people to change their consumption habits is a viable strategy to avoid climate disaster. But producers and the politicians in their pockets have a material interest in pushing such narratives.

Fossil fuel companies have spent significant time and money shifting blame and attention for greenhouse gas emissions to the consuming public. According to research on oil company advertising (Supran and Oreskes 2021; see also Huber 2022), British Petroleum (BP) spent millions first popularizing the term "carbon footprint" in the early 2000s, and in 2019 launched an individual carbon footprint calculator online. Similarly, ExxonMobil advertising systematically constructed consumers as the drivers of climate change rather than producers, who were cast as simply doing their jobs in service to the public (Supran and Oreskes 2021).

These approaches reflect "consumer sovereignty theory," and are flawed in ignoring the material relation at the heart of production. As Huber (2022:13) explains,

> consumer sovereignty assumes that producers are captive to the demands of consumers, indeed that they are simply responding to the latter—rather than what is in fact the case: production constrains consumption choices ... power over the economy is not diffuse, but concentrated in the hands of those who control productive resources.

Here we return to classic Marx, where power is derived primarily from a monopoly on the means of production, and the owning class who control the means of production direct the production process, in part through instrumental influence over and structural imbrication with the national and transnational state. Applying a Marxist framework then, it becomes clear that surviving climate change will require wresting control of productive resources (the means of production) from the TCC and freeing precious ecosystems from the ravages of capital accumulation. Because of the productive material relation central to capitalism and the ecological contradiction inherent in capitalist society, so many critical scholars insist that, "Capitalism ... represents the sociohistorical driver of climate change, and hence the core institutionalized dynamic that must be dismantled in order to stop it" (Fraser 2022:78).

Data makes it relatively clear that fossil fuel and other related industries (such as in the military industrial complex) are responsible for the lion's share of historical and projected emissions, and that the fossil fuel industry has worked incredibly hard to mask their culpability to the public and to prevent movements away from fossil fuels. Over half of all greenhouse gas emissions since the industrial revolution have been emitted since 1988 (Frumhoff 2014)—in the period of global economic restructuring and transnational financialized capitalism. Over 70% of the emissions since 1988 have been caused by the activities of 100 private corporations and (petro)state entities (e.g., Saudi Arabia's Aramco) (Riley 2017). Even in the face of countless studies, conferences, agreements, declarations, and other diplomatic efforts on the international legal stage to address the problem, "CO2 emissions from energy and industry have increased by 60% since the UN Convention on Climate Change was signed in 1992" (IEA 2021).

All the while, fossil fuel companies understood the danger of extracting and burning fossil fuels at ever increasing rates. In 1977 Exxon senior scientist James Black reported that "there is general scientific agreement that the most likely manner in which mankind is influencing the global climate is through carbon dioxide release from the burning of fossil fuels." A year later he predicted that doubling atmospheric CO2 levels would increase average global temperatures by two or three degrees Celsius, which is on par with current estimates from the scientific community (Hall 2015). Fossil fuel companies not only knew their industry's success could mean devastating results for the entire living planet, but they spent billions of dollars over decades to publicly deny that inescapable reality—let alone their responsibility for it (Holden 2020).

There is little reason to be hopeful for the market's invisible hand to nudge the fossil fuel industry into the kind of expedited, large scale energy transition required to reach global emissions reduction targets. Though there are signs of constraints on demand ahead, profits in the fossil fuel industry are impressive to say the least. The International Energy Agency (IEA) estimates that the global oil and gas industry made $4T in 2022, up from an average of $1.5T in recent years (Adomaitis 2023). Despite their profitability, industry players received approximately $11M in state subsidies every minute in 2020 ($5.9T total) according to an IMF report (Parry, Black, and Vernon 2021) that decried the fact that fossil fuel prices did not reflect their true cost to the environment and public health, and that taxpayers commonly covered the bill. Without considerable reform these subsidies are projected to rise to $6.4T by 2025, and the continued public and private investment in fossil fuels conflicts with the need to immediately invest in clean energy sources. According to the IEA (2021), to reach net zero emissions by 2050, "annual clean energy investment worldwide will need to more than triple by 2030 to around $4 trillion." Overall, the level of profit and public subsidy in the fossil fuel industry illustrates their power and political influence, along with the fact that market incentives exist for continued extraction, and that states will tend to act in the interest of capital—even in the face of global catastrophe.

Efforts to expand fossil fuel exploration and extraction further illustrates the intrenchment of state and corporate power in the industry. In 2021, the IEA reported that in order to reach global "net-zero" emissions by 2050, the sale of all new combustion engine passenger vehicles must stop by 2035, all unabated coal and power plants must be phased out by 2040, and that after 2021 no new coal power plants or fossil fuel extraction projects could be approved for development. In 2023, the UN finally made an explicit call to "phase out all unabated fossil fuels," with a reminder that greenhouse gas emissions will have to peak by 2025, leaving only 25 years to reach net zero and hold global warming at 1.5 degrees (Harvey 2021, 2023). Despite these abundantly clear, dire warnings, and though US based fossil fuel firms are wildly profitable, and though the US is already the biggest producer and consumer of oil and gas in the world, the Biden Administration continued to approve of new fossil fuel exploration and extraction like the controversial $80B Willow Oil project, allowing ConocoPhillips to pull from an oil reserve roughly the size of the state of Indiana on public and indigenous land (*Al Jazeera* 2023). In fact, in its first two years the Biden Administration approved 6,430 permits for oil and gas drilling on federal lands (Center for Biological Diversity 2023), despite a 2020 campaign promise that there would be "no more drilling on federal lands, period" (Stevens 2023).

The pathological trend toward continued fossil fuel exploration and extraction is transnational. The UK announced that it will approve 100 new licenses for oil and gas exploration in the North Sea in order to "become more energy independent" (Ravikumar and Singleton 2023). China is claiming to be on a path to carbon neutrality by 2060, but is leaning heavily on coal for energy production throughout its transition, and expects to have rising emissions as a result that may not peak until 2030 (Hung 2022). Moreover, thanks to climate change disruptions like increasing droughts and heat waves, China has been forced at times to rely on the dirty fuel to meet rising energy demands (Kemp 2023). Perhaps most importantly, the expansion of fossil fuel extraction has been underwritten by transnational finance capital. The major financial firms from the US and China have joined other transnational finance capital in investing over $3.2T in fossil fuel industry expansion in the global South since the Paris Climate Accords in 2015 (Noor 2023), calling into question whether current economic or geopolitical trends are leaning toward a survivable energy transition.

These trends are reflected in assessments being made by transnational firms like ExxonMobil (2023), predicting that rather than meeting net zero targets, by 2050 increasing energy demands and lagging affordable green alternatives will mean still meeting over half of global energy needs with fossil fuels. This, of course, will produce more greenhouse gas emissions. To wit, the same report projects that as a result of continued fossil fuel dependence, global emissions would only drop by approximately 25% by 2050, ensuring catastrophic warming beyond 2 degrees Celsius. Given the previous accuracy of industry scientists (though not always shared with the public), it would be a mistake to chalk up such reports to corporate wish casting and political manipulation. Instead, this is a clear demonstration of the psychopathic objective thrust toward capital accumulation that motivates corporate and financial firms, and the danger of depending on market forces for the kind of energy transition that human survival demands.

The accumulation interests of certain segments of transnational capital align with geopolitical interests ("energy independence" for example) in such a way that drives fossil fuel consumption while cannibalizing and destroying the ecological conditions of possibility for accumulation and human life. As we will argue throughout this book, to overcome OTHS and have any shot at the realization of universal human rights practice, the world will need to escape the unyielding accumulation drive of capitalism and the traps of continued imperial competition. For this, we must turn to the final background relation of capitalism as an institutionalized social order: that between labor exploitation and the expropriation of labor and other forms of capital through systemic racism, (neo)colonialism, and imperial conquest.

Exploitation vs. Expropriation: Racism, (Neo)Colonialism, and Imperial World Orders

The final background relation of capitalist society is that between the exploitation of "free" wage labor and the expropriation of unfree, dependent, or enslaved labor and other expropriated forms of capital. Expropriation first appears in the violent process of primitive accumulation, but can later be found as a process of confiscation and conscription (Fraser 2022) across all regimes of accumulation that provides conditions of possibility for the exploitation of labor. Further, not unlike the relationship between capital and the state, the historical relation between exploitation and expropriation—which includes but is not limited to the relationship between capitalism and systemic racism—is symbiotic, co-constitutive, and "nonaccidental" (Fraser 2016).

The relationship between capitalism and racism has been a topic of vigorous debate and controversy in scholarly disciplines and political movements for over a century. The theoretical framework put forth here and by Fraser (2016, 2022) are informed by the work of Black Marxist intellectuals,[7] attempts to conceptualize what is sometimes called "racial capitalism,"[8] and the continued work contemporary critical scholars of race and racism[9] who have sought to understand this relationship in its complexity. Demonstrated in the writing and speeches of those like Frantz Fanon, Fred Hampton, Paul Robeson, Angela Davis, and many others, this is a tradition born of struggle meant as a form of revolutionary anti-racist, anti-imperial, and anti-capitalist praxis. Though it is beyond the scope of this book to explore the canon in detail,[10] it guides our understanding of systemic racism as relatively exclusive from and yet deeply, purposefully, structurally imbricated with capital accumulation.

Specifically, we've so far described how each regime of accumulation was non-accidentally correspondent with a distinct era of systemic racism, composed of an ideological framework to construct and justify the ascription of racial identities and meanings, modes of social control to address inevitable resistance, and a political economic manifestation that overwhelmingly reflects an historically specific structural imbrication to capital accumulation. Here we join Fraser (2016, 2022) in locating systemic racism as the primary mechanism (along with nationalism, (neo)colonialism, and competitive imperial conquest) for distinguishing expropriable labor and resources and justifying their confiscation and conscription into circuits of capital accumulation. That is, we see that systemic racism has so far been central to the expropriation—the violent theft and dispossession—that is an ever-present condition of possibility for capital accumulation, and a fundamental threat to universal human rights practice. The later point should be obvious given the epically brutal world histories of the chattel slave trade and colonial imperialism, and in that all human rights instruments include a broad anti-discriminatory clause, in that even the United States has signed and ratified the International Convention on the Elimination of All Forms of Racial Discrimination (ICERD), and in that the very notion of cultural human rights and the right to self-determination are in part a direct reflection of anti-colonial struggles throughout the late 19th and 20th centuries. Less obvious are the specific conditions of possibility that expropriation offers capital accumulation.

Expropriation first provides a way to undercut the price of "free" labor for producers, and thus raise the rate of exploitation while "restoring profitability and navigating crisis" (Fraser 2016). The expropriation of resources such as land, oil, water, or minerals and of human labor provides cheap inputs for accumulation, but also cheap goods, services, and resources (such as land or domestic servants) for wage laborers. In sum, following the establishment of capital and free labor itself through primitive accumulation, expropriation then serves to stave off internal crises and the "tendency of the rate of profit to fall" (Fraser 2016) through providing a direct source of free or low-cost capital that is confiscated and conscripted into the accumulation process, and through applying downward pressure on the cost of exploitable labor, or wages. Expropriation undercuts wages directly, by providing an even cheaper alternative source of human labor for owners, and indirectly by subsidizing the lives of exploited workers and allowing for lower prevailing wages in the free labor market. It is worth quoting Fraser (2022:34–35) here at length to describe how expropriation manifests as an integral form of "accumulation by other means":

Dispensing with the contractual relation through which capital purchases "labor power" in exchange for wages, expropriation works by *confiscating* capacities and resources and *conscripting* them into capital's circuits of self-expansion. The confiscation may be blatant and violent, as in New World slavery—or it may be veiled by a cloak of commerce, as in the predatory loans and debt foreclosures of the present era. The expropriated subjects may be rural or indigenous communities in the capitalist periphery—or they may be members of subject or subordinated groups in the capitalist core. They may end up as exploited proletarians, if they're lucky—or, if not, as paupers, slum dwellers, sharecroppers, "natives," or slaves, subjects of ongoing expropriation outside the wage nexus. The confiscated assets may be labor, land, animals, tools, mineral or energy deposits—but also human beings, their sexual and reproductive capacities, their children and bodily organs. The conscription of these assets into capital's circuits may be direct, involving immediate conversion into value—as, again, in slavery; or it may be mediated and indirect, as in the unwaged labor of family members in semi-proletarianized households. What is essential, however, is that the commandeered capacities get incorporated into the value-expanding process that defines capital.

Gendered forms of racism and (ethno)nationalism combine to relegate those worthy of "free" wage work and the legal rights of full citizenship from those who, along with their lands and resources, are subject to expropriation. In conversation with Michael Dawson, Fraser (2016) describes this as a form of "political subjectification," or "the codification by public powers of the status hierarchies that distinguish citizens from subjects, nationals from aliens, entitled workers from dependent scroungers." It should be noted that the distinction of exploitable and expropriable labor through political subjectification along lines of race, ethnicity, or citizenship status has other impacts—among them are barriers to solidarity and collective power of all workers in the struggle against capital and empire.[11] We will return to this point in the final chapter, but note here again that the material and background relations of capital reflect contested terrains of class and boundary struggles.

As Fraser notes in her description of expropriated labor above and we discussed in Chapter 1, contemporary systemic racism differs from previous eras in that it is a more covert system of selective inclusion rather than the overt racial exclusion that defined previous periods. Though systemic racism remains a powerful mechanism of expropriation in capitalist society, the selective inclusion of transnational financialized capitalism corresponds with a blurring of the lines between expropriable and exploitable labor that were previously clear and exclusive through distinctions of race, ethnicity, and nationality. Fraser (2016) describes this change:

> In place of the earlier, sharp divide between expropriable subjects and exploitable citizen-workers, there appears a continuum. At one end lies the growing mass of defenseless expropriable subjects; at the other, the dwindling ranks of protected exploited citizen-workers. At the center sits a figure, already glimpsed in the previous era, but now generalized: the *expropriable-and-exploitable citizen-worker,* formally free but acutely vulnerable. No longer restricted to peripheral populations and racial minorities, this hybrid figure is becoming the norm in much of the historic core.

The emergence of the expropriable-and-exploitable citizen-worker closely matches what scholars like William Robinson (2018) describe as the increasingly precarious nature of wage work around the world. These jobs are typically by contract, part-time (often "gig" or "on call" work), absent health and other benefits, temporary, outsourced, informal, non-unionized, un-/deregulated, and as a result often potentially harmful or dangerous. Rather than a new class of some sort (the "precariat"), Robinson (2018) describes how the condition of increasing precariousness is being "generalized to all sorts of work… imposed on increasing numbers of the global working class in the face of capitalist globalization and the transition underway for several decades now from Fordist to flexible accumulation."

While Fraser (2022) does not use the language of cannibalization to describe this background relation, we intend to pursue this in an extension of her framework. Specifically, we would assert that to the extent cannibalization appears in the background relation between exploitation and expropriation, it appears as a devouring of the classically "free" wage worker, leaving an increasingly vulnerable, insecure global "expropriable-and-exploitable" subject. In Chapter 4 we will discuss our ongoing argument that the human and other (e.g., Constitutional) rights of citizens shrink in the face of expanding corporate rights and political influence. Then, in Chapter 5 we will turn to the terrifying precarity of those swept up in the global migration crisis, and the potentials of a necropolitical nightmare in a period of "general" or "epochal" crisis. Indeed, the increasing precarity of the global worker is also the result of an unfolding migration crisis resulting from a cruel nexus of climate change impacts, war, and the "global enclosures" that have dislocated those in the global South in the decades since economic restructuring (Robinson 2022b:58). Migrants make up another population whose time, labor, bodies, and property can be treated as forfeit and expropriable, and migration will continue to expand from the process of transnational capital accumulation and impacts of OTHS.

The separation of exploitable and expropriable labor, as well as the ideological justifications for expropriation have historically been achieved through systemic racism, but also through forms of nationalism that tend to weaponize citizenship and construction of the other in geopolitical pursuits and dominant ideological constructions of national interest. The process of expropriation itself operates through the ideological, political economic, and social control components of systemic racism, and through the related "war making" (Singh 2017) and conquest so inherent in settler colonialism and neocolonialism (of the past and today) and central to imperial competition.

Regimes of Accumulation, Imperial Geopolitics, and World Orders

In agreement with Robinson and many other critical scholars (see world systems analysis, for example), Fraser asserts that, "capitalism's political order is inherently geopolitical" (Fraser 2016). Geopolitics refer to strategic methods "for the management of empire through the use of geography (air, land, and sea) to maximize military and economic advantage" (McCoy 2021:19). In the context of capitalism as an institutionalized social order, maximizing military and economic advantage means harnessing the structurally imbricated powers, drives, and interests of capitalism and political state structures. From capitalism's "rosy dawn," the military and economic expansion of empire has tended to coincide with the processes of primitive accumulation and expropriation that provide the conditions of possibility for the expansion and concentration of capital. For instance, the genocidal western expansion of the US, like the establishment of any settler-colonial nation, simultaneously served to maximize the growing military and economic power and influence for the emergent US empire while confiscating and conscripting various forms of capital into the accumulation process, enriching capitalists, land owning elites, and many of the conquerors in their service.

Still, the relationship between capital and the geopolitics of imperial competition should not be reduced to the provision of expropriated capital. The structuring of trade and international relations has also been achieved through the order and infrastructure imposed by empire. Capitalists have traditionally depended on "the organizational and military capacities of a succession of global hegemons, each of which has undertaken to (re)shape an international environment conducive to sustained and ever-expanding accumulation within a multistate system" (Fraser 2016). A "global hegemon," refers to an empire of a certain sort—one that emerges at the head of what McCoy (2017, 2021) calls a "world order."

Empires predate and certainly persist since the establishment of the modern nation-state, and refer to the most macro, "unstable, even volatile forms of governance that often exhibit contradictory attributes—they are constant yet changing, idealistic but barbaric, and powerful yet fragile" (McCoy 2021:18). After the birth of the modern nation-state, empires have taken shape through colonial and neocolonial arrangements, considerably structured according to racist colonial hierarchies (Fanon 2000 [1952], 2021 [1961]) and distinctions between the so-called civilizing forces of colonization and the subaltern, colonized other (Said 1979).

In the last five centuries the world has seen the rise and fall of approximately ninety identifiable empires, but only three have emerged as global hegemons of global world orders in over half a millennium dominated by the West (McCoy 2021). World orders are "deeply rooted, resilient global systems created by a convergence of economic, ideological, and geopolitical forces" (McCoy 2021:9). They are formally reflected in "broad agreements about relations" between nations and "entwine themselves in the cultures, commerce, and values of countless societies," influencing "the languages people speak, the laws that order their lives, and the ways they work, worship, and play" (McCoy 2021:9). Each world order can be distinguished by their imperial hegemon, and by what McCoy (2021:14) argues are three defining attributes: "the principle of sovereignty that delineated each state's territorial boundaries, the concept of human rights that governed all peoples within those boundaries, and a distinctive form of energy that drove the economy sustaining it all." In line with how critical sociologists understand the human rights enterprise, human rights concepts or frameworks were not built-in features of these world orders or of the geopolitical strategies of their imperial hegemons. Instead, "each global hegemon, it its time, visited some sort of outrage upon humanity inspiring reformers to articulate higher standards for human rights and liberties" (McCoy 2021:11). Human rights appear out of an attempt to resist and respond to the horrors of imperial rule, the machinations of which are virtually inseparable from the accumulation of capital through exploitation and expropriation. After their construction or revision, the realization of human rights remained a contested terrain, often eventually contradicted by the state hegemon of the period.

Not unlike modes of production, each world order is born of catastrophe and change. World orders arise out of the simultaneous conditions of a "massively destructive cataclysm" with widespread, "major social change" (McCoy 2021:9). In an attempt to summarize here, the three world orders according to McCoy (2021) can be understood as follows:

The first world order to span the globe was that of the *Iberian Age,* beginning in 1496 under the imperial hegemony of Spain and Portugal. The Iberian Age emerged from the devastation of the Black Death that killed over 60% of the populations of Europe and China, and the social changes that would mark the slow, violent end of the feudal mode of production and institutionalized social order. Imperial hegemony of the period was based on Iberian control of major ports and transportation choke points all over the increasingly connected world, thanks to new sea faring and navigational advancements, and through the harnessing of somatic/muscle power and wind power (in the case of sailing vessels). The Iberian world order provided the infrastructure for and corresponded with the pre-capitalist, mercantile, and early liberal-colonial regimes of accumulation. Further, in the so-called "age of exploration," this first world order included the creation and legitimation of racial categories for the purposes of expropriation—particularly indigenous nations subject to conquest, Africans brought into what would become the North Atlantic slave trade, and "White" colonizers who in reality were deeply divided by centuries of war, but constructed as a unified, superior "race" to justify and facilitate their employment of conquest, colonization, and enslavement. This was achieved through papal bulls (declarations from the Catholic Church) and the Treaty of Tordesillas (1494) that, together, "forged history's first global order by imposing a religious segregation between Christians and 'pagans' that would persist for another three hundred years" (McCoy 2021:10) and delineated what populations could be subject to the theft, dispossession, and enslavement at the hands of European powers. The Iberian world order reflected what might be considered an expansive conception of imperial sovereignty, and a narrow conception of human rights that legitimated conquest and enslavement (McCoy 2021). However, this yielded a global debate over the foundations and practices of slavery that would eventually lead to notions of universal humanity that appear in the writings of dissenters[12] and abolitionists, and that would re-appear in the debates of enlightenment thinkers and the bourgeois (English, American, and French) revolutions of the late enlightenment period.

The second world order, or *British Imperial Era* would arise under early Dutch and then primarily British hegemony, following the devastating impacts of the Napoleonic wars (1815), noting that Europe had already been embroiled in decades of revolution, conflict, and upheaval at the end of the 18th century. The British Imperial Era would be shaped by the widespread impacts of the industrial revolution and the take-off of industrial production along with new information/communication technologies and modes of transport. British imperial power was based in the domination of coal as the key source of energy fueling industrial capitalism in the liberal-colonial and early state managed regimes of capital accumulation, military domination of the seas, and through the formal colonization of the Americas, Africa, and Asian "orient." British imperial hegemony employed a limited conception of imperial sovereignty that included aspects of "informal empire" made up of "client states that remained nominally independent while still opening themselves to (British) trade and diplomatic leadership" (McCoy 2021:140), but also included formal colonies where legal and (quasi)scientific racial categorization was used to legitimate brutal expropriation of labor and resources. Indeed, the British Imperial Era uncoincidentally corresponded with the era of systemic racism defined by racial debt peonage, formal segregation, and apartheid so central to colonization and other racialized forms of expropriation. These colonial relations were formalized under the Congress of Vienna in 1815 to divvy up Europe after the Napoleonic wars under British dominance and the Berlin Congress of 1885 to divvy up the African Continent among European colonial empires. Colonization and imperial expansion were legitimated by and couched in a contradictory vision of human rights. In the 19th century, the British Empire aimed to end the global slave trade and the distinctions between Christian and "pagan" or "savage" that previously provided the religious and legal foundations for African enslavement and the genocidal expropriation of indigenous lives and land. These efforts were generally successful, but paled in comparison to the nearly continuous resistance of the enslaved and abolitionists who gave their lives for liberation over several centuries. But this did not spell the end of racialized expropriation. Instead, the British and other Western powers employed the day's racial pseudo-science to legitimate "slavery by another name" (Blackmon 2008) through (internal) apartheid and (external) formal colonization.

American global hegemony—the third and so far remaining world order—arose from the devastation of two World Wars as the last global superpower left standing and new hegemon, despite the bi-polar cold war split between East and West that would shape the following decades. The US would use this position to lead the creation of the global financial system (in the Bretton Woods Conference of 1944), the United Nations (in the UN Conference on International Organization in 1945), and the liberal "rule based international order" of which formal human rights law became a part. While the first half of this period corresponded with the state managed regime of capital accumulation and the twilight of formal segregation/apartheid (by then directly confronted by a mounting civil rights movement in the US and anti-colonial movements elsewhere), the second half, marked by global economic restructuring, uncoincidentally corresponds with the regime of transnational financialized capitalism and contemporary systemic racism previously discussed in great detail.

This new international order reflected a conception of nation-state (vs. imperial) sovereignty, articulated through the UN and international law, and was organized as a community of sovereign, internationally recognized Nation-states "governed as equals under the rule of law" (McCoy 2021:194). This new legal framework included the assertion of identifiable, individual human rights applicable to a universal human standard (non-discriminatory and inalienable), articulated primarily through the International Bill of Human Rights (IBHR), under the foundation of consensus (see also Donnelly 2013). However, as our work points out, the US has acted and presented itself as "exceptional" with regard to international legal obligations, and US policy and practice have done as much to undermine human rights in the world as realize them. US imperial power has depended so far on unfettered access to oil as the key source of energy, and the "duality" of unmatched military might and dominant influence over the international order embodied by the UN and other TNS structures. However, the US repeatedly violates and undermines that international order (and human rights), particularly but not exclusively through overt and covert foreign military intervention and through serving as the biggest arms dealer in the world that arms some of the most oppressive regimes.

Though human rights as an exclusive body of law did not exist until the period of American hegemony, each world order reflected an evolving conception of human rights that emerged from contestations over the reach and rules of empire, most evident in international debate over the practices of slavery and colonization. Thanks in great part to the wildly hypocritical nature of American exceptionalism with regard to its own "rules based international order," and due to the defiance of other powerful states and private firms in the pursuits of accumulation and geopolitical gain, human rights remain a contested terrain even after their full legal codification.

But the US led order is shifting. It is hard at this point not to agree with McCoy (2017) and other analysts (Chomsky and Prashad 2022) that US hegemony has waned in the face of its own missteps and the increasing wealth and influence of China and what are known as the BRICS (Brazil, Russia, India, China, South Africa) nations.[13] The US price tag for the disastrous wars on terror (in Afghanistan, Iraq, Pakistan, Syria, and many other locations) is estimated at $8 trillion (Crawford 2021), and their record of failure and blowback demonstrated the fallibility of US military power. Costly wars abroad were coupled with round after round of tax cuts for corporations and the owning class such that US national debt grew to the highest in the world (Duggal 2023) at approximately $32 trillion. And servicing that debt is now one of the biggest annual government expenses at approximately $663 billion in 2023 (Guida and Goodman 2023). This comes at great opportunity cost to the public, as annual debt servicing is far more than federal spending on elementary and secondary education, disaster relief, agriculture, science and space programs, foreign aid, and environmental protections combined (Desilver 2023).

In the same years that the US put several wars on the proverbial credit card, China went from a minor economic player to the major producer and "workshop of the world," (McCoy 2023b) now claiming over 18% of global GDP (World Economics 2023). This allowed them to sock away an impressive $4 trillion in foreign reserves (McCoy 2023a, 2023b) that instead of spending on military adventurism was spent on the building of soft power. This includes the trillion dollar "Belt and Road Initiative"—a megaproject of infrastructure, diplomacy, and trade to connect the Eurasian landmass as a "unified market stretching 6,000 miles from the North Sea to the South China Sea, eventually encompassing 70% of all humanity, and effectively fusing Europe and Asia into a single economic continent" (McCoy 2023b). As part of these efforts China now owns or operates terminals in over 90 international commercial ports (Kardon and Leutert 2023) that it helped to finance, build, or both, and seeks to expand this influence through providing infrastructure loans to over 148 countries, helping to make China the largest lender in the world (McCoy 2023a).

China has been successful in translating increased economic influence to diplomatic influence as they lay the groundwork for Belt and Road, which involves navigating a number of long-standing rivalries. For instance, China was able to broker a return of diplomatic relations between geopolitical opponents Saudi Arabia and Iran while landing a $400 billion infrastructure deal with Iran and agreeing to make Saudi Arabia their chief supplier of oil—for which the Saudis have considered payments in Chinese yuan rather than the dollar (McCoy 2023a; Said and Kalin 2023). This is coupled with a similar arrangement with fossil fuel exporter Russia, for whom China is their biggest customer, where China is paying for a majority of Russian oil and other goods in Chinese yuan instead of the dollar (Tan 2023). And China's not the only nation on the come up.

China has been joined by the other BRICS nations. In fact, for the first time in 2023, total economic output of the BRICS nations surpassed that of the G7 (O'Kane 2023). Out of a response to US use of economic sanctions, and to the wildly destabilizing impacts of the US driven Great Recession of 2008 and of US Federal Reserve interest rate changes on foreign markets and currencies, members of BRICS have openly discussed creating digital or other currency alternatives to trade in the dollar (Shekhar 2023; Guistra 2023). In addition, BRICS nations created the New Development Bank and Contingent Reserve Arrangement to provide alternatives for the global South to the World Bank and International Monetary Fund (IMF) respectively. They've also encouraged trading in local currencies to cut dependence on dollar-based exchange and strengthen BRICS currencies (O'Kane 2023). All of this activity represents an expansion of the transnational state apparatus beyond the UN, Bretton Woods institutions, World Trade Organization, and other transnational political state structures formed under US/ Western hegemony.

Whether it also signifies a shift from American hegemony as described to a Chinese-led or otherwise "multi-polar" world order remains an open question and subject of heated debate. China's economic rise has been complicated by a problem with skyrocketing internal debt, where local governments and their affiliates and real estate development firms are in the hole for trillions of dollars, and several major real estate developers have defaulted on their loans (Bradsher 2023). This has placed more pressure on China to collect on its extensive loans to other countries amidst rising interest rates that have made it increasingly difficult for the more impoverished debtor nations to pay (Bradsher 2023). Repayment is a serious concern given that by some estimates over half of China's loans are to "borrowers in financial distress," up from 5% of their portfolio in 2010 (Bradsher 2023). Not completely unlike the international debt dependency of global economic restructuring, there is now an evolving financialized power relationship between Chinese banks and many recipients of Chinese investment.

Whether the New Development Bank or CRA reflect any significant departure from the predatory, ecologically and socially destructive nature of international development finance established in the Washington consensus is up for debate. Both the New Development Bank and the CRA allied with the World Bank in their creation (Bond 2023; World Bank 2016). That being said, the New Development Bank proposes lending without the kinds of structural adjustment programs that forced debtor nations into austerity under the Bretton Woods institutions. It is arguably too early to tell whether these efforts to disrupt the previous cycles of debt dependency will succeed (Prashad 2023), or if they will improve the quality of life for everyday people in debtor nations (Bond 2023). However, given the next-level repressive authoritarianism of the group's recently invited members like Saudi Arabia or Egypt, there should frankly be few fantasies that the group is operating according to some shared benevolent, higher ideals (such as that of anti-imperialism or resource redistribution) other than appeasing the objective thrust of accumulation and pursuing perceived geopolitical interests.[14]

And all the hype and online currency scams aside, global de-dollarization may or may not be on the immediate horizon either. While it's true that the dollar's share of global reserve currencies dropped from 71% in 2000 to 58% in 2022, data suggests that the decline may be due to countries diversifying into smaller currencies rather than a single replacement, while the dollar still overwhelmingly dominates as the standard in, for instance, foreign currency exchange transactions (Krugman 2023), and no serious competitor to the dollar exists as a global standard. On this point the US Federal Reserve predicts that "diminution of the dollar's status seems unlikely in the near term" (Bertaut, von Beschwitz, and Curcuru 2023). Finally, control of the reserve currency alone will not decide the fate of imperial hegemons. It also depends on control of critical new technologies and energy sources like in previous imperial world orders and regimes of accumulation.

McCoy (2021) and Robinson (2022a, 2022b) agree that geopolitics will be heavily influenced by a race to control the nascent next generation of information and green energy technologies, such as quantum computing, artificial intelligence (AI), and increasingly advanced battery design—what Robinson (2020, 2022a, 2022b) and others call the technologies of a "fourth industrial revolution." The extractive competition for minerals and other 21st century strategic resources are already a part of this race. And as multiple great powers and petrostates demonstrate—including the US, China, Russia, the UK, Saudi Arabia, India, and many others, this race and market-based energy transition is being run so much on fossil fuels that emissions targets for a survivable climate are unlikely to be met. The structurally imbricated drives toward capital accumulation and geopolitical competition—what might be vaguely conceptualized as the global "free market"—ensure rather than avoid climate catastrophe *no matter who wins the race.*

Additionally, geopolitical competition and the shifting of imperial world orders commonly manifests in overt and covert forms of war and conflict. The Ukrainian conflict has become a grinding stalemate of trench warfare in an ongoing nightmare for soldiers and civilians. It is in part a proxy war between US led NATO countries and Russia over the aggressive expansion of NATO (and NATO military forces) closer and closer to Russian borders (Marcetic 2022; Sachs 2023). But the brutal and obviously illegal Russian invasion is also arguably driven by a crisis of legitimacy for the Russian ruling elite (Democracy Now 2023; Smith 2023). Simultaneously, the US and US allies continue to trade diplomatic and dangerous military jabs with China over control of trade routes in the South China Sea, and over the status of Taiwan—a critical supplier of advanced microchips and other valuable technologies to the West.

The so-called "new cold war" (Achcar 2023) between the US and a moderately aligned China and Russia should be understood relative to transnational financialized capitalism and state legitimacy crisis. All states are struggling somewhat to maintain their legitimacy at home in the face of economic and other challenges brought on by a global economic crisis of capital (overaccumulation, below) and complicating factors like the COVID-19 pandemic. There are some inherent dangers here, where the trappings of twenty-first century fascism and military belligerence can, and have become attractive to states experiencing legitimacy crisis and real institutional decline. Robinson (2022b:70) notes that "international frictions escalate as states, in their efforts to retain legitimacy, seek to sublimate social and political tensions and to keep the social order from fractioning. This may involve channeling internal tensions toward scapegoated communities, such as migrants or refugees, or toward an external enemy."

Historian Greg Grandin (2019) provides a detailed account of the tendency to externalize these tensions in the US, particularly as the settler colonial nation confronts imperial decline and runs out of expropriable labor and capital on its western or imperial "frontier," previously used as both pressure release valve and material supplement (e.g., free real estate) during legitimacy crises. In such conditions, as will be discussed in the following chapter, the US has a unique interest in solving internal tensions through militarism, in that the US economy relies much more on "militarized accumulation" (Robinson 2020) than do nations like China, and in that the US position as global hegemon is in part based on the maintenance of approximately 750 military bases in 80 countries spanning the globe (McBrien 2023) and encircling the Eurasian world island. As the economic and diplomatic hegemonic dominance of the US wanes, the US could become an increasingly belligerent force in the world (directly, and indirectly through arms sales and financing foreign militaries), deeply invested at the center of a "global police state" (Chomsky and Prashad 2022; Robinson 2020).

It is beyond our abilities and the scope of this book to make any specific predictions on the fate of American hegemony or of a future world order under Chinese or some alternative form of multi-lateral international relations. Such predictions may be beside the point in that the world may not survive a competitive transition to a Chinese or any new imperial order in the way that history has so far guided. Unlike the calamities that shaped the transitions of previous world orders, and unlike the prior internal and external crises of capital that shaped each regime of accumulation, the potential crises confronting the current regime of accumulation and global world order manifest as existential, OTHS. Surviving climate change will require unprecedented levels of global cooperation and mutual aid that in too many ways fundamentally contradict with the related pursuits of capital accumulation and imperial (geopolitical) competitive interests. Escaping the dangers of apocalyptic nuclear conflict will require abandoning great power competition in favor of disarmament and diplomacy between the peoples of those nations.

A System of Crisis and Contradiction

One of the contributions of Marxist theory is the recognition that capitalism is a system bound for and defined by contradictions and resulting crises. For the purposes of the theoretical framework offered here, we should understand the distinctions between internal, external, and general (Fraser 2022) or epochal (Robinson 2022b) forms of crisis. An internal crisis should be understood as one that arises from the contradictions inherent in the fore-grounded material relations of capitalism as a global institutionalized social order. The central internal crisis of capitalism appears first in the market as what Marx and Marxists describe as a crisis of overproduction, where productive efficiency increases due to advances in technology (such as automation) and reduced labor costs (such as through globalization and precaritization), yet the consumer population is too immiserated from low wages and unemployment to create sufficient demand for products, leaving smaller and smaller returns on investment in the productive economy, even while surplus continues to consolidate.

What appears as overproduction in the market then transforms into a broader crisis of overaccumulation, appearing in economic shocks like the Great Recession (Robinson 2020). Previously mentioned, Robinson (2022b:28) describes overaccumulation as a global structural crisis where, "enormous amounts of capital (profits) are built up but investors cannot find productive outlet to unload the accumulated surplus." Stagnation follows when the bourgeois and powerful firms stack profits as wealth, but that wealth no longer converts to (expanding) capital in the accumulation process. *One should not confuse the accumulation of wealth with the continued accumulation and circulation of capital.* Overaccumulation is a crisis that can temporarily create the former but threatens the latter. Robinson notes (2022b:30, see also *The Economist* 2020) that between the Great Recession of 2008 and 2020, "the rate of profit has fallen while the mass of profit has risen (an increase in the mass of profit and an increase in the rate of profit are not one and the same). The total cash held in reserves of the world's 2000 biggest non-financial corporations increased from \$6.6T in 2010 to \$14.2T in 2020—considerably more than foreign exchange reserves of the world's central governments—as the global economy stagnated."

According to Robinson (2022b), overaccumulation originates in the tendency discussed by Marxists of the overarching rate of profit to fall in late capitalist society.[15] In these conditions, capitalists must search high and low for profitable investment—including the creation of risky forms of speculation and fictitious capital and opportunities for expropriation (such as for neocolonialism) to make up for the lack of profitable investment options in the productive economy. Phillips (2018:30) joins Robinson in the observation that capital has been "centralized" and "overaccumulated" such that three options remain for capital investment: "risky financial speculation, wars and war preparation, and the privatization of public institutions." We've already detailed the extents to which transnational capital has been thoroughly financialized, evident in the size and scale of financial firms, the financial sector, and forms of fictitious capital. We've also discussed the cannibalization of political state structures that appears in part as an aggressive privatization of the public sphere. In the following chapter we will explore "militarized accumulation" (Robinson 2020) where war preparation, war fighting, and the clean-up and re-building that take place after conflicts (a form of disaster capitalism (Klein 2010)) serve as some of the last reliably profitable investments.

Internal crises can be seriously destabilizing in their moments of rupture, as was the case in the Great Recession. In their most extreme, they can signal change in the regime of accumulation, as capitalism is forced to reckon with or synthesize the consequences of its internal contradictions. External crises can be especially destructive as well. This is because background relations provide not only the conditions of possibility for capital accumulation, but for the reproduction of human life.

An external crisis stems from a contradiction in the background relations of capitalism as an institutionalized social order. One example would be the contradictory relationship between capital accumulation and reproduction, where forms of biological and social reproduction are absolutely necessary for capital accumulation (and human life/civilization), yet these forms of reproduction are cannibalized in the accumulation process. An external crisis of reproduction appears, manifesting in the US as the "care gap," falling life expectancies, widespread use of child labor, and abysmal maternal and infant mortality rates. Another external crisis would be the legitimacy crisis of the state, where the cannibalization of political state structures and the undermining of state power by the TCC in pursuit of short-term profit results in curtailing the ability and motivation of states to govern in the public interest—including the provision of human rights protections when in conflict with the real or perceived interests of transnational capital. For the purposes of our work, *the fact that so many states are so often unable or unwilling to abide by international human rights obligations can be explained by the existence and exacerbation of such crises of legitimacy.*

Most concerning to us, and for the entire human rights enterprise, is the fact that external crises can combine and mutate into what can be called a general (Fraser 2022) or epochal (Robinson 2022b) crisis. An epochal crisis refers to the combination of internal and external crises that can spawn a new mode of production and type of society entirely, such as in the transition between feudalism and capitalism. A general crisis refers to when a single crisis or combination of crises come(s) to pose a significant threat to the conditions of possibility for human life—that is, they come to pose an overlapping threat to human survival (OTHS).

This is most clear in the cannibalization, pollution, and destruction behind climate change, habitat destruction, and the 6th mass extinction event in the planet's history. The contradictions inherent in the background relations between economy and ecology have advanced to the point of general crisis, and the gravity of this crisis no longer requires data to be felt. July of 2023 was the hottest month in all of recorded history (Hausfather 2023), and perhaps in the last 120,000 years (Thompson 2023). Heat records are being shattered all over the world by several degrees, causing deaths like the 62K people who passed in a European heatwave in 2022 (Ramirez 2023) and contributing to wildfires like those across Canada that burned forest acreage equal to the size of the state of Georgia (Ebbs, Jacobo, Manzo, and Peck 2023), or the fire on the Hawaiian island of Maui that took over 1000 lives and destroyed the town of Lahaina in the summer of 2023 (Brock and Helsel 2023). In the same months ocean temperatures reached that of a hot tub in the Florida Keys (Prociv 2023), also causing widespread death ("bleaching") across coral reefs (NOAA 2023) and massive die offs of fish due to the temperature's effects on oceanic oxygen levels (Weise 2023). The same heat waves disoriented South American countries that recorded record *winter* temperatures over 40 degrees Celsius (104 degrees Fahrenheit) in Bolivia, Paraguay, and Brazil (Livingston 2023).

Rising temperatures are already altering the geography of habitable environments for humans and other species. One percent of the world's land area is now so hot to be intolerable for human survival, but this will grow to 20% by 2070. In fact, over 600 million people live outside of the "environmental niche" (based on a combination of measures like temperature and precipitation) that can best support organized human life, and these numbers are expected to grow to 2 billion by 2030 and 3.7 billion by 2090 (Lenton, Xu, Abrams, Ghadiali, et al. 2023). Beyond heat, island and other coastal habitat (for humans and many other species) continues to shrink and change from sea level rise and destructive weather events. Over 300 million people, most of them in China, Bangladesh, India, Vietnam, Indonesia, and Thailand, will be subject to regular flooding events by 2050 even if net zero emissions are achieved (Kulp and Strauss 2019). This includes many island nations, for whom sea level rise is an immediate existential threat (Jackson 2022; Fletcher, Boyd, Neal, and Tice 2010).

As a result of rapidly changing habitat conditions, "climate driven migration could easily eclipse even the largest estimates as enormous segments of the earth's population seek safe havens" (Lustgarten 2023). It is already the case, according to the UN High Commissioner for Refugees (Grandi 2021), that 90% of refugees and 70% of internally displaced people are from "countries on the front lines of climate change."

The combination of factors like exploding (internal and external) migration and dwindling natural resources like potable water has already proven to drive political instability, conflict, and war. For instance, studies suggest this is the case across much of the African Continent for herding and farming communities (a majority of people in the region) (Parenti 2011; Nunn and McGuirk 2021). But this seems to be a universal trend. A meta-analysis in 2015 found that changes in temperature and precipitation associated with climate change increased the chances for violence and conflict in both wealthy and impoverished countries. Specifically, the study estimated that for every 1 degree Celsius of average surface temperature increase, the chances of interpersonal violence rise by 2.4% and the chances of conflict between groups (riots/unrest, ethnic/tribal clashes, civil war, etc.) increase by 11.3% (Burke, Hsiang, and Miguel 2015). UN experts have for some time recognized the complicated but undeniable relationship between climate change and conflict (UNCC 2022), and point to the increasing precariousness and vulnerability of populations struggling under conditions of intensifying drought/flood cycles, sea level rise, more destructive and frequent extreme weather events, disrupted food supplies and famine, and forced migration as a primary source of conflict and political instability in the world.

An overlapping general crisis and threat to human survival is that of war and nuclear apocalypse as a result of the structurally imbricated drives of capital accumulation and geopolitical competition, and out of attempts by states to manage crises of legitimacy that emerge from such pursuits. Arising similarly as an external crisis, this time of expropriation, the imbricated drives toward capital accumulation (including investments in militarized accumulation and the global police state to stave overaccumulation crisis), and to provide expropriated labor and capital through forms of neocolonial imperialism increase the chances of war between heavily armed, even nuclear powers. The situation is made only more dangerous as states like the US rely more heavily on the business of war, surveillance, and suppression to solve its external crises of legitimacy and assert Western military dominance in the face of waning economic and diplomatic hegemony.

That said, one should not confuse our current period with the crises of capital that led up to the world wars of the 20th century. Our geopolitical context is comparatively complicated by the development of transnational capital and the actual interconnection and interpenetration (in terms of capital investment, trade, and global supply chains), of national economies such that a complete "decoupling" of, for instance, China and other BRICS nations from the West is difficult to imagine. Still, the sum effect of the internal crisis of overaccumulation, with the external crises of state legitimacy, ecological destruction, and imperial competition is to push the world to the brink. UN Secretary General Antonio Guterres claimed in 2022 that the world faced nuclear threats unseen since "the height of the Cold War" (Lederer 2022). In fact, current conditions may be worse. Citing the dangers emanating from the War in Ukraine (including explicit nuclear threats by Russian leadership), the prediction that China's nuclear arsenal could grow to five times its current size and rival that of the US and Russia by 2035, continued nuclear missile development by North Korea, the failure to renegotiate the Iranian nuclear deal, and so-called "nuclear modernization" programs in India, the US, China, and Russia, the Bulletin of the Atomic Scientists (Mecklin 2023) have moved their "doomsday clock" to 90 seconds to midnight—indicating that *this is now the closest the world has ever been to nuclear annihilation.*

Notes

1 For instance, between 2017 and 2020 78% of those stopped and searched (in or out of a vehicle) by Minneapolis PD were Black, though Black residents represent only 19% of the local population (Babineau and Lopez 2023).

2 See, for example, Zaretsky 1986, Laslett and Brenner 1989, Folbre 2002, Vogel 2013, Bhattacharya 2017, and Ferguson 2019.

3 This is likely the result of many factors including rising middle-class populations in places like China and India and increasing access to reproductive health care in the global South.

4 Foster (2015) offers a helpful summary: "[Marx] insisted that nature and labor together constituted the dual sources of all wealth. By incorporating only labor (or human services) into economic value calculations, capitalism ensured that the ecological and social costs of production would be excluded from the bottom line. Indeed, classical liberal political economy, Marx argued, treated the natural conditions of production (raw materials, energy, the fertility of the soil, etc.) as 'free gifts of nature' to capital. He based his critique on open-system thermodynamics, in which production is constrained by a solar budget and by limited supplies of fossil fuels—referred to by Engels as 'past solar heat,' which was being systematically 'squandered.'"

5 This would include formal state or state partnered capital, as the nationalized fossil fuel giants. In these cases, firms may be more flexible in their potential responses to the competitive market due to state backing and, in some cases, state market intervention.

6 Noted in the next section, this was and still is typically achieved through imperial and (neo)colonial forms of expropriation.

7 See, for example, James (2023 [1938]), DuBois (1998 [1938]), Williams (2021 [1944]), Cox (2018 [1948]), Rodney (2018), Davis (1983), Marable (1983), and Kelly (2015 [1990]).

8 See the classic works of Robinson (1983) and Kelly (2015 [1990]).

9 See, for example, Cazenave (2016, 2018), Bonilla-Silva (1996, 2001, 2003), Feagin and Ducey (2019), Omi and Winant (2014 [1986]), Ransby (2018), Taylor (2021a, 2021b), Dawson (2013), Gilmore (2007).

10 See Fraser (2016) and related works for an informative exchange between Nancy Fraser and Michael Dawson on how this tradition could or should inform contemporary critical scholarship and critical politics.

11 To this point, Keeanga Yamahtta Taylor (2021a:206) suggests, "Capitalism used racism to justify plunder, conquest, and slavery, but as Karl Marx pointed out, it would also come to use racism to divide and rule—to pit one section of the working class against another and, in so doing, blunt the class consciousness of all."

12 McCoy (2021:68) quotes the Spanish reformer from the 16th century, Fray Bartolome de las Casas (Phelan 1969): "All the peoples of the world are humans and there is only one definition of all humans... that is that they are rational.... Thus, all the races of humankind are as one."

13 BRICS is an evolving diplomatic and trading block between many of what are now some of the most wealthy and populous nations, many from the formerly colonized world. In 2023 BRICS extended invitations to Argentina, Saudi Arabia, Iran, Ethiopia, Egypt, and the U.A.E. in the first ever expansion of the group (Erlanger, Pierson, and Chutel 2023).

14 Saudi Arabia joins the US as one of the most egregious state actors in the world when it comes to human rights and global security. Saudi Arabia remains under monarchial rule, where 81 people were executed in a single day in 2022 (Amnesty International 2022b) and their US-assisted war and blockade against Yemen yielded an ongoing humanitarian disaster of epic proportions. US ally Egypt has been under the military and then political rule of Abdel Fattah el-Sisi following a coup in 2013. Since then, Egypt has subjected 60k+ political prisoners to indefinite detention and systematic torture, including the denial of medical care (Yee 2022).

15 Robinson makes the empirical argument for this tendency: "The decline in the average rate of profit in the post WWII period has been widely documented. According to the Financial Times, it stood at about fifteen percent in the post-WWII period, dropped by the end of the 1980s to ten percent and continued to

decline, to six percent in 2017 ... one report after another has confirmed the long-term secular decline in profitability, notwithstanding short-term fluctuations, and along with it, the steady decline since 1970 in the growth of the net stock of capital (a proxy for productive investment) in the rich countries of the Organization for Economic Cooperation and Development (Robinson 2022b:28–29; see also Roberts 2016).

References

Achcar, Gilbert. 2023. *The New Cold War: The United States, Russia, and China from Kosovo to Ukraine.* London: Westbourne Press.

Adomaitis, Nerijus. 2023. "Oil and Gas Industry Earned $4 Trillion Last Year, Says IEA Chief." *Reuters*, February 14. Retrieved 07/10/23 from www.reuters.com/busi ness/energy/oil-gas-industry-earned-4-trillion-last-year-says-iea-chief-2023-02-14/

Al Jazeera. 2023. "Willow Oil Drilling Project in Alaska: Here's What to Know." *Al Jazeera*, March 14. Retrieved 07/10/23 from www.aljazeera.com/news/2023/3/14/ controversial-alaska-oil-drilling-heres-what-you-need-to-know

American Civil Liberties Union (ACLU). 2021. "Block the Vote: How Politicians are Trying to Block Voters from the Ballot Box." *ACLU*, August 17. Retrieved 07/01/23 from www.aclu.org/news/civil-liberties/block-the-vote-voter-suppression-in-2020

American Society of Civil Engineers (ASCE). 2020. "The Economic Benefits of Investing in Water Infrastructure: How a Failure to Act Would Affect the US Economic Recovery." *ASCE.* Retrieved 07/15/23 from www.asce.org/publications-and-news/civil-engineer ing-source/society-news/article/2020/08/26/chronic-underinvestment-in-americas-water-infrastructure-puts-the-economy-at-risk

American Society of Civil Engineers (ASCE). 2021. "A Comprehensive Assessment of America's Infrastructure: 2021 Report Card for America's Infrastructure." *ASCE.* Retrieved on 06/15/23 from https://infrastructurereportcard.org/

Amnesty International. 2014. "On the Streets of America: Human Rights Abuses in Ferguson." *Amnesty International*, October 23. Retrieved 06/15/23 from www.am nestyusa.org/reports/on-the-streets-of-america-human-rights-abuses-in-ferguson/

Amnesty International. 2022a. "Amnesty International Global Report: Death Sentences and Executions 2022." *Amnesty International.* Retrieved 07/15/23 from www.amnesty.org/en/documents/act50/6548/2023/en/

Amnesty International. 2022b. "Israel's Apartheid Against Palestinians: Cruel System of Domination and Crime Against Humanity." *Amnesty International.* Retrieved 07/15/23 from www.amnesty.org/en/documents/mde15/5141/2022/en/

Babineau, Andi and David Lopez. 2023. "Minneapolis Agrees to Policing Plan Overhaul Forged After George Floyd's Killing." *CNN*, April 1. Retrieved 06/01/2023 from www.cnn.com/2023/03/31/us/minneapolis-police-reform-george-floyd/index.html

Bacher, Dan. 2015. "Activists 'Shut Down' Nestle Water Bottling Plant in Sacramento." *Truthout*, March 31. Retrieved 07/15/23 from https://truthout.org/articles/activists-shut-down-nestle-water-bottling-plant-in-sacramento/#:~:text=Environmental%20a nd%20human%20rights%20activists%2C%20holding%20plastic%20%E2%80% 9Ctorches%E2%80%9D%20and,company's%20operations%20for%20the%20day

Bailey, Kristian Davis. 2015. "Black-Palestinian Solidarity in the Ferguson-Gaza Era." *American Quarterly*, 67 (4): 1017–1026. www.jstor.org/stable/43822935

Basel, Rocki, S. Silberman, J. Tavares, M. Cohen and M. Wylie. 2023. "The 80%: The Continued Toll of Financial Insecurity in Retirement." *NCOA*, April 10.

Retrieved 07/01/23 from https://ncoa.org/article/addressing-the-nations-retirem
ent-crisis-the-80-percent-financially-struggling

Berlatsky, Noah. 2014. "At the United Nations, Chicago Activists Protest Police
Brutality." *The Atlantic*, November 17. Retrieved 06/15/23 from www.theatlantic.
com/national/archive/2014/11/we-charge-genocide-movement-chicago-un/382843/

Bertaut, Carol, Bastian von Beschwitz and Stephanie Curcuru. 2023. "'The International Role of the US Dollar' Post-COVID Edition." *FEDS Notes*, June 23.
Retrieved 07/07/2023 from www.federalreserve.gov/econres/notes/feds-notes/the-in
ternational-role-of-the-us-dollar-post-covid-edition-20230623.html

Bhattacharya, Tithi (Ed.). 2017. *Social Reproduction Theory: Remapping Class,
Recentering Oppression*. London: Pluto Books.

Bhattarai, Abha. 2023. "Child Care is About to Get More Expensive, as Federal
Funds Dry Up." *The Washington Post*, September 5. Retrieved 09/05/23 from
www.washingtonpost.com/business/2023/09/05/child-care-cliff-day-care/

Birnstengel, Grace. 2022. "2 Years After it Burned, No Clear Path Forward for
Minneapolis 3rd Precinct Site." *Minnesota Public Radio (MPR)*, May 28. Retrieved
06/15/23 from www.mprnews.org/story/2022/05/27/2-years-after-it-burned-no-clea
r-path-forward-for-minneapolis-3rd-precinct-site

Blackmon, Douglas. 2008. *Slavery by Another Name: The Re-Enslavement of Black
Americans from the Civil War to World War II*. New York, NY: Doubleday.

Bond, Patrick. 2023. "The BRICS Johannesburg Summit's Hype, Hope, and Help-
lessness." *Counterpunch*, August 18. Retrieved 08/18/23 from www.counterpunch.
org/2023/08/18/the-brics-johannesburg-summits-hype-hope-and-helplessness/

Bonilla-Silva, Eduardo. 1996. "Rethinking Racism: Toward a Structural Interpretation." *American Sociological Review* 62: 465–480.

Bonilla-Silva, Eduardo. 2001. *White Supremacy and Racism in the Post-Civil Rights
Era*. Boulder, CO: Lynne Rienner.

Bonilla-Silva, Eduardo. 2003. *Racism Without Racists: Color-Blind Racism and the
Persistence of Racial Inequality in the US*. New York: Rowman & Littlefield.

Bradsher, Keith. 2023. "Why China Has a Giant Pile of Debt." *The New York
Times*, July 8. Retrieved 07/10/23 from www.nytimes.com/2023/07/08/business/
china-debt-explained.html?smid=nytcore-ios-share&referringSource=articleShare

Brock, Sam and Phil Helsel. 2023. "List of Possible Unaccounted for After Maui Fire
Now 1,000 to 1,100." *NBC News*, August 22. Retrieved on 07/01/23 from www.
nbcnews.com/news/us-news/list-possible-unaccounted-maui-fire-now-1000-1100-rcna
101332

Buchanan, Larry, Q. Bui and J. K. Patel. 2020. "Black Lives Matter May Be the Largest
Movement in US History." *The New York Times*, July 3. Retrieved 05/15/23 from
www.nytimes.com/interactive/2020/07/03/us/george-floyd-protests-crowd-size.html

Burke, Marshall, S. Hsiang and E. Miguel. 2015. "Climate and Conflict." *Annual
Review of Economics* 7: 577–617. https://doi.org/10.1146/annurev-econom
ics-080614-115430

Burns, Rebecca and Julia Rock. 2023. "Silicon Valley Bank Said It Was Too Small to
Need Regulation. Now it's 'Too Big to Fail.'" *The Guardian*, March 17. Retrieved
07/01/23 from www.theguardian.com/commentisfree/2023/mar/17/silicon-valley-ba
nk-bailout-dodd-frank-regulation-opinion

Carrillo, Sequoia. 2023. "US Reading and Math Scores Drop to Lowest Level in
Decades." *NPR*, June 21. Retrieved on 07/01/23 from www.npr.org/2023/06/21/
1183445544/u-s-reading-and-math-scores-drop-to-lowest-level-in-decades

Cazenave, N. 2016. *Conceptualizing Racism: Breaking the Chains of Racially Accommodative Language.* Lanham, MD: Rowman & Littlefield.

Cazenave, N. 2018. *Killing African Americans: Police and Vigilante Violence as a Racial Control Mechanism.* New York: Routledge.

Center for Biological Diversity. 2023. "Biden Oil and Gas Proposal Marks Massive Climate Failure." *Center for Biological Diversity*, July 20. Retrieved 07/25/23 from https://biologicaldiversity.org/w/news/press-releases/biden-oil-and-gas-proposal-ma rks-massive-climate-failure-2023-07-20/

Chomsky, Noam and V. Prashad. 2022. *The Withdrawal: Iraq, Libya, Afghanistan, and the Fragility of US Power.* New York: New Press.

Ciccariello-Maher, George. 2015. "Riots Work: Wolf Blitzer and Washington Post Completely Missed the Real Lesson from Baltimore." *Salon*, May 4. Retrieved 05/15/23 from www.salon.com/2015/05/04/riots_work_wolf_blitzer_and_the_washing ton_post_completely_missed_the_real_lesson_from_baltimore/

Cohen, Donald and Allen Mikaelian. 2021. *The Privatization of Everything: How the Plunder of Public Goods Transformed America and How We Can Fight Back.* New York: The New Press.

Cox, Oliver Cromwell. 2018 [1948]. *Caste, Class and Race: A Study of Social Dynamics.* London: Forgotten Books.

Crawford, Neta. 2021. "The US Budgetary Costs of the Post-9/11 Wars." *Watson Institute (Brown University) Costs of War Project.* Retrieved 07/01/23 from https://watson.brown.edu/costsofwar/figures/2021/BudgetaryCosts

Crawford, Neta. 2022. *The Pentagon, Climate Change, and War: Charting the Rise and Fall of US Military Emissions.* Cambridge, MA: MIT Press.

Davis, Angela. 1983. *Women, Race, and Class.* New York: Vintage Books.

Dawson, Michael. 2013. *Blacks In and Out of the Left.* Cambridge, MA: Harvard University Press.

Democracy Now. 2023. "Ukrainian and Russian Activists on How Putin's War Emboldens 'Authoritarian Forces' Around the World." *Democracy Now*, September 7. Retrieved 09/07/23 from www.democracynow.org/2023/9/7/hanna_pere khoda_ilya_budraitskis_ukraine_russia

Desilver, Drew. 2023. "5 Facts About the US National Debt." *Pew Research Center*, February 14. Retrieved 07/10/23 from www.pewresearch.org/short-reads/2023/02/14/facts-about-the-us-national-debt/

Donnelly, Jack. 2013. *Universal Human Rights in Theory and Action.* Ithaca, NY: Cornell University Press.

DuBois, W.E.B. 1998 [1938]. *Black Reconstruction in America: 1860–1880.* New York: The Free Press.

Duggal, Hanna. 2023. "How Does US Debt Rank Compared with the Rest of the World?" *Al Jazeera*, May 31. Retrieved 07/22/23 from www.aljazeera.com/econom y/2023/5/31/infographic-how-does-us-debt-rank-compared-world

Ebbs, Stephanie, J. Jacobo, D. Manzo and D. Peck. 2023. "Canada's Unprecedented Wildfires Could Soon Get Worse, Experts Say." *ABC News*, August 22. Retrieved 08/22/23 from https://abcnews.go.com/International/canadas-unprecedented-fire-season-worse-experts/story?id=102426195#:~:text=As%20of%20Tuesday%2C%20more%20than,Forest%20Fire%20Centre%20(CIFFC)

Equal Justice Initiative (EJI). 2017. "United Nations Poverty Investigation Finds Shocking Conditions in Alabama." *Equal Justice Initiative*, December 15. Retrieved

07/01/23 from www.americanprogress.org/article/tax-cuts-are-primarily-responsi ble-for-the-increasing-debt-ratio/

Erlanger, Steven, D. Pierson and L. Chutel. 2023. "Iran, Saudi Arabia, and Egypt Join Emerging Nations Group." *The New York Times*, August 24. Retrieved 08/ 24/23 from www.nytimes.com/2023/08/24/world/europe/brics-expansion-xi-lula. html?smid=nytcore-ios-share&referringSource=articleShare

ExxonMobil. 2023. "ExxonMobil Global Outlook: Our View to 2050" (Executive Summary). *ExxonMobil*. Retrieved on 08/29/23 from https://corporate.exxonmobil.com/ -/media/global/files/global-outlook/2023/2023-global-outlook-executive-summary.pdf

Fanon, Frantz. 2000 [1952]. *Black Skin, White Masks*. New York: Grove Press.

Fanon, Frantz. 2021 [1961]. *The Wretched of the Earth*. New York: Grove Press.

Feagin, Joe and Kimberly Ducey. 2019. *Racist America: Roots, Current Realities, and Future Reparations* (4th edition). New York: Routledge.

Federici, Sylvia. 2004. *Caliban and the Witch: Women, the Body, and Primitive Accumulation*. Brooklyn, NY: Autonomedia.

Federici, Sylvia. 2018. *Witches, Witch Hunting, and Women*. Oakland, CA: PM Press.

Ferguson, Susan. 2019. *Women and Work: Feminism, Labor, and Social Reproduction*. London: Pluto Books.

Fletcher, Charles, R. Boyd, W. Neal and V. Tice. 2010. *Living on the Shores of Hawaii: Natural Hazards, the Environment, and our Communities*. Honolulu, HI: Univ. of Hawaii Press.

Folbre, Nancy. 2002. *The Invisible Heart*. New York: The New Press.

Forbes. 2015. "Majority Against Nestle California Water Bottling." *Forbes*, May 11. Retrieved 07/15/23 from www.forbes.com/sites/brandindex/2015/05/11/majority-a gainst-nestle-california-water-bottling-2/?sh=ffd2abd630dd

Foster, John Bellamy. 2015. "Marxism and Ecology: Common Fonts of a Great Transition." *Monthly Review*. Retrieved 07/01/23 from https://monthlyreview.org/ 2015/12/01/marxism-and-ecology/#en15

Fraser, Nancy. 2016. Expropriation and Exploitation in Racialized Capitalism: A Reply to Michael Dawson. *Critical Historical Studies* 3 (1): 163–178. https://doi. org/10.1086/685814

Fraser, Nancy. 2019. *The Old is Dying and the New Cannot Be Born*. New York: Verso.

Fraser, Nancy. 2022. *Cannibal Capitalism: How Our System is Devouring Democracy, Care, and the Planet—and What We Can Do About It*. London: Verso.

Fraser, Nancy and R. Jaeggi (B. Milstein Ed.). 2018. *Capitalism: A Conversation in Critical Theory*. Cambridge: Polity Press.

Frumhoff, Peter. 2014. "Global Warming Fact: More Than Half of All Industrial CO_2 Pollution Has Been Emitted Since 1988." *Union of Concerned Scientists, The Equation*, December 15. Retrieved 07/10/23 from https://blog.ucsusa.org/peter-frumhoff/ global-warming-fact-co2-emissions-since-1988-764/#:~:text=This%20brings%20the %20total%20industrial,have%20released%20just%20since%201988

Gerstel, Naomi. 2000. "The Third Shift: Gender and Care Work Outside the Home." *Qualitative Sociology*, 23 (4): 467–483. doi:10.1023/A:1005530909739

Gilmore, Ruth Wilson. 2007. *Golden Gulag: Prisons, Surplus, Crisis, and Opposition in Globalizing California*. Berkeley, CA: University of California Press.

Goldman, Adam. 2017. "Trump Reverses Restrictions on Military Hardware for Police." *The New York Times*, August 28. Retrieved 06/15/23 from www.nytimes.com/2017/08/28/us/politics/trump-police-military-surplus-equipment.html

Grandi, Filippo. 2021. "Climate Change is an Emergency for Everyone, Everywhere." *UNHCR*, November 9. Retrieved on 07/15/23 from www.unhcr.org/news/stories/climate-change-emergency-everyone-everywhere#:~:text=But%20for%20millions%20of%20people,lines%20of%20the%20climate%20emergency

Grandin, Greg. 2019. *The End of the Myth: From the Frontier to the Border Wall in the Mind of America*. New York: Metropolitan Books.

Guida, Victoria and Jasper Goodman. 2023. "Growing Interest in US Debt." *Politico*, October 3. Retrieved 10/03/23 from www.politico.com/newsletters/morning-money/2023/10/03/growing-interest-in-u-s-debt-00119592#:~:text=If%20that%20bears%20out%2C%20that's,on%20Budget%20and%20Policy%20Priorities

Guistra, Frank. 2023. "De-Dollarization: Not a Matter of If, but When." *Responsible Statecraft*, May 3. Retrieved 07/20/23 from https://responsiblestatecraft.org/2023/05/03/de-dollarization-not-a-matter-of-if-but-when/

Gunja, Munira, E. Gumas and R. Williams II. 2023. "US Health Care from a Global Perspective, 2022: Accelerating Spending, Worsening Outcomes." *The Commonwealth Fund*, January 31. Retrieved 07/01/23 from www.commonwealthfund.org/publications/issue-briefs/2023/jan/us-health-care-global-perspective-2022

Hall, Shannon. 2015. "Exxon Knew About Climate Change Almost 40 Years Ago." *Scientific American*, October 26. Retrieved 07/01/23 from www.scientificamerican.com/article/exxon-knew-about-climate-change-almost-40-years-ago/

Hansford, Justin and Meena Jagannath. 2015. "Ferguson to Geneva: Using the Human Rights Framework to Push Forward a Vision for Racial Justice in the United States After Ferguson." *Hastings Race and Poverty Law Journal*, 12 (2): 121–154.

Harvey, Fiona. 2021. "No New Oil, Gas, or Coal Development if World is to Reach Net Zero by 2050, Says World Energy Body." *The Guardian*, May 18. Retrieved 07/01/23 from www.theguardian.com/environment/2021/may/18/no-new-investment-in-fossil-fuels-demands-top-energy-economist

Harvey, Fiona. 2023. "'A Critical Moment': UN Warns World Will Miss Climate Targets Unless Fossil Fuels Phased Out." *The Guardian*, September 8. Retrieved 09/08/23 from www.theguardian.com/environment/2023/sep/08/un-report-calls-for-phasing-out-of-fossil-fuels-as-paris-climate-goals-being-missed

Hatfield, Jenn. 2023. "8 Facts About Black Lives Matter." *Pew Research Center*, July 12. Retrieved 07/15/23 from www.pewresearch.org/short-reads/2023/07/12/8-facts-about-black-lives-matter/

Hausfather, Zeke. 2023. "State of the Climate: 2023 Now Likely Hottest Year on Record After Extreme Summer." *Carbon Brief*, July 26. Retrieved 08/10/23 from www.carbonbrief.org/state-of-the-climate-2023-now-likely-hottest-year-on-record-after-extreme-summer/

Holden, Emily. 2020. "How the Oil Industry has Spent Billions to Control the Climate Change Conversation." *The Guardian*, January 8. Retrieved 06/15/23 from www.theguardian.com/business/2020/jan/08/oil-companies-climate-crisis-pr-spending

Horsley, Scott. 2023. "Social Security is Now Expected to Run Short of Cash by 2033." *NPR*, March 31. Retrieved 07/01/23 from www.npr.org/2023/03/31/1167378958/social-security-medicare-entitlement-programs-budget#:~:text=News letters-,Social%20Security%20is%20now%20expected%20to%20run%20short%20of%20cash,out%20of%20cash%20by%202031

Huber, Matthew. 2022. *Climate Change as Class War: Building Socialism on a Warming Planet.* New York: Verso Books.

Hung, Shih Yu. 2022. "Coal to Power China's Energy Transition." *Forbes,* April 26. Retrieved 07/10/23 from www.forbes.com/sites/thebakersinstitute/2022/04/26/coal-to-power-chinas-energy-transition/?sh=3a2e49621b9e

International Energy Agency (IEA). 2021. "Net Zero by 2050: A Roadmap for the Global Energy Sector." *IEA.* Retrieved 06/15/23 from www.iea.org/reports/net-zero-by-2050

Isachenkov, Vladimir and Kim Tong-Hyung. 2023. "Xi Awarded 3rd Term as China's President, Extending Rule." *AP,* March 10. Retrieved 07/15/23 from https://apnews.com/article/xi-jinping-china-president-vote-5e6230d8c881dc17b11a781e832accd1

Jackson, Lagipoiva C. 2022. "Amid Rising Seas, Island Nations Push for Legal Protection." *PBS News Hour,* September 30. Retrieved 07/13/23 from www.pbs.org/newshour/world/amid-rising-seas-island-nations-push-for-legal-protection

James, C.L.R. 2023 [1938]. *The Black Jacobins: Toussaint L'Ouverture and the San Domingo Revolution.* New York: Vintage Books.

Kardon, Isaac and Wendy Leutert. 2023. "China's Port Power: The Maritime Network Sustaining Global Military Reach." *Foreign Affairs,* May 22. Retrieved 07/10/23 from www.foreignaffairs.com/united-states/chinas-port-power#:~:text=Chinese%20companies%20now%20own%20or,global%20operations%20of%20the%20PLA

Kelly, Robin D. G. 2015 [1990]. *Hammer and Hoe: Alabama Communists During the Great Depression.* Chapel Hill, NC: University of North Carolina Press.

Kemp, John. 2023. "Column: Beset by Drought, China Turned to Coal to Keep the Lights On." *Reuters,* July 21. Retrieved 07/25/23 from www.reuters.com/business/energy/beset-by-drought-china-turned-coal-keep-lights-kemp-2023-07-21/#:~:text=LONDON%2C%20July%2021%20(Reuters),power%20in%20the%20southern%20provinces

Khalfan, Ashfaq, A. Nilsson Lewis, C. Aguilar, et. al. 2023. "Climate Equality: A Planet for the 99%." *Oxfam International,* November 20. Retrieved 11/20/23 from https://policy-practice.oxfam.org/resources/climate-equality-a-planet-for-the-99-621551/

Klein, Naomi. 2010. *The Shock Doctrine: The Rise of Disaster Capitalism.* New York: Metropolitan Books.

Kogen, Bobby. 2023. "Tax Cuts are Primarily Responsible for the Increasing Debt Ratio." *Center for American Progress,* March 27. Retrieved 07/01/23 from www.americanprogress.org/article/tax-cuts-are-primarily-responsible-for-the-increasing-debt-ratio/

Krugman, Paul. 2023. "Wonking Out: De-Dollarization Debunked." *The New York Times,* July 7. Retrieved 07/10/23 from www.nytimes.com/2023/07/07/opinion/dollar-strength-reserve-currency.html?smid=nytcore-ios-share&referringSource=articleShare

Kulp, Scott and B. Strauss. 2019. "New Elevation Data Triple Estimates of Global Vulnerability to Sea-Level Rise and Coastal Flooding." *Nature Communications* 10 (4844). https://doi.org/10.1038/s41467-019-12808-z

Lartey, Jamiles. 2023. "Three Years After George Floyd's Murder, Police Reforms are Slow Paced." *The Marshall Project,* June 3. Retrieved 06/15/23 from www.themarshallproject.org/2023/06/03/george-floyd-police-reform

Laslett, Barbara and Johanna Brenner. 1989. "Gender and Social Reproduction: Historical Perspectives." *Annual Review of Sociology* 15: 381–404. www.jstor.org/stable/2083231

Lawson, Max, A. Butt, R. Harvey, et al. 2020. "Time to Care: Unpaid and Underpaid Care Work and the Global Inequality Crisis." *Oxfam International*, January 20. Retrieved 06/01/23 from www.oxfam.org/en/research/time-care

Leatherby, Lauren. 2023. "How a Vast Demographic Shift Will Reshape the World." *The New York Times*, July 16. Retrieved 07/16/23 from www.nytimes.com/interactive/2023/07/16/world/world-demographics.html

Lederer, Edith. 2022. "UN Chief Warns World is One Step from 'Nuclear Annihilation.'" *Associated Press*, August 1. Retrieved 07/20/23 from https://apnews.com/article/russia-ukraine-covid-health-antonio-guterres-2871563e530f9a676d7884b3e2d871c3

Lenton, Timothy, C. Xu, J. Abrams, A. Ghadiali, et al. 2023. "Quantifying the Human Cost of Global Warming." *Nature Sustainability*. https://doi.org/10.1038/s41893-023-01132-6

Levin, S. 2024. "2023 Saw Record Killings by US Police. Who is Most Affected?" Retrieved 01/08/24 from www.theguardian.com/us-news/2024/jan/08/2023-us-police-violence-increase-record-deadliest-year-decade

Liebhaber, Lauren. 2023. "How Spending on Public Safety and Policing has Changed Over the Last 40 Years." *Digital Journal*, May 31. Retrieved 06/15/23 from www.digitaljournal.com/world/how-spending-on-public-safety-and-policing-has-changed-over-the-last-40-years/article

Livingston, Ian. 2023. "Heat Records are Being Smashed in Multiple Parts of the Globe." *The Washington Post*, August 24. Retrieved 08/25/23 from www.washingtonpost.com/weather/2023/08/24/global-heat-records-europe-asia-south-america/

Lustgarten, Abraham. 2023. "Climate Crisis is on Track to Push One-Third of Humanity Out of its Most Livable Environment." *ProPublica*, June 6. Retrieved 07/10/23 from www.propublica.org/article/climate-crisis-niche-migration-environment-population?taid=64d96080b029ae000127e290&utm_campaign=trueanthem&utm_medium=social&utm_source=twitter

MacGillis, Alec. 2024. "Skipping School: America's Hidden Education Crisis." *ProPublica*, January 8. Retrieved 01/08/24 from www.propublica.org/article/school-absenteeism-truancy-education-students?campaign_id=9&emc=edit_nn_20240109&instance_id=112054&nl=the-morning&regi_id=138697150&segment_id=154673&te=1&user_id=1ceda8aa3bbd02cbe08de642e72d8593

Manthey, Grace, F. Esposito and Amanda Hernandez. 2022. "Despite 'Defunding' Claims, Police Funding has Increased in Many US Cities." *ABC News*, October 16. Retrieved 06/15/23 from https://abcnews.go.com/US/defunding-claims-police-funding-increased-us-cities/story?id=91511971

Marable, Manning. 1983. *How Capitalism Underdeveloped Black America*. Boston, MA: South End Press.

Marcetic, Branko. 2022. "NATO Expansion and the Origins of Russia's Invasion of Ukraine." *Responsible Statecraft*, November 18. Retrieved 07/15/23 from https://responsiblestatecraft.org/2022/11/18/nato-expansion-and-the-origins-of-russias-invasion-of-ukraine//

McBrien, Tyler. 2023. "Why the US Should Close its Overseas Military Bases." *Foreign Policy*, May 16. Retrieved 07/01/23 from https://foreignpolicy.com/2023/05/16/military-defense-overseas-bases-united-states-force-posture/

McCoy, Alfred. 2017. *In the Shadows of the American Century: The Rise and Decline of US Global Power*. Chicago, IL: Haymarket Books.

McCoy, Alfred. 2021. *To Govern the Globe: World Orders and Catastrophic Change*. Chicago, IL: Haymarket Books.

McCoy, Alfred. 2023a. "The Rise of China (and the Fall of the US?): Tectonic Eruptions in Eurasia Erode America's Global Power." *TomDispatch*, April 27. Retrieved 07/01/23 from https://tomdispatch.com/the-rise-of-china-and-the-fall-of-the-u-s/

McCoy, Alfred. 2023b. "Peace for Ukraine Courtesy of China: Another Step in Beijing's Rise to Global Power." *TomDispatch*, June 13. Retrieved 07/01/23 from https://tomdispatch.com/peace-for-ukraine-courtesy-of-china/

McKernan, Bethan. 2023. "Israeli Parliament votes in Netanyahu's Controversial Supreme Court Changes." *The Guardian*, July 24. Retrieved 07/27/23 from www.theguardian.com/world/2023/jul/24/israeli-parliament-votes-in-netanyahu controversial-supreme-court-changes

McNeill, J. R. 2001. *Something New Under the Sun: An Environmental History of the Twentieth-Century World*. New York: W.W. Norton.

Mecklin, John. 2023. "A Time of Unprecedented Danger: It is 90 Seconds to Midnight." *Bulletin of the Atomic Scientists*, January 24. Retrieved 07/10/23 from https://the bulletin.org/doomsday-clock/current-time/nuclear-risk/

Morrison, Aaron. 2023. "New Black Lives Matter Tax Documents Show Foundation is Tightening its Belt, has $30M in Assets." *AP*, May 26. Retrieved 07/01/23 from https://ap news.com/article/black-lives-matter-donations-george-floyd-protests-ddcf0d21d130a5d4 6256aa6c5d145ea7

National Center for Educational Statistics (NCES). 2022. "Administrators Report Roughly Half of Public School Students Began 2022–23 School Year Behind Grade Level in At Least One Academic Subject." *NCES*, February 9. Retrieved 06/01/23 from https://nces.ed.gov/whatsnew/press_releases/2_09_2023.asp

National Council on Aging (NCOA). 2023. "Get the Facts on Economic Security for Seniors." *NCOA*, June 7. Retrieved 07/01/23 from https://ncoa.org/article/get-the-facts-on-economic-security-for-seniors

National Oceanic and Atmospheric Administration (NOAA). 2023. "Extreme Ocean Temperatures Are Affecting Florida's Coral Reef." *NOAA*, August 16. Retrieved 08/18/23 from www.nesdis.noaa.gov/news/extreme-ocean-temperatures-are-affecting-floridas-coral-reef#:~:text=On%20Thursday%2C%20August%2017%2C%202023, Florida%20Keys%20National%20Marine%20Sanctuary

Noor, Dharna. 2023. "Banks Pouring Trillions to Fossil Fuel Expansion in Global South, Report Finds." *The Guardian*, September 4. Retrieved 09/04/23 from www. theguardian.com/us-news/2023/sep/04/banks-pour-trillions-fossil-fuel-expansion-global-south-report-says

Nunn, Nathan and Eoin McGuirk. 2021. "How Climate Shocks Trigger Inter-Group Conflicts: Evidence from Africa's Transhumant Pastoralists." *VoxDev*, April 30. Retrieved 07/15/23 from https://voxdev.org/topic/energy-environment/how-clima te-shocks-trigger-inter-group-conflicts-evidence-africa-s-seasonal-migrants

O'Kane, Caitlin. 2023. "What is BRICS? Group of World Leaders that Considered Making a New Currency Meet to Discuss Economy." *CBS News*, August 21. Retrieved 08/21/23 from www.cbsnews.com/news/what-is-brics-group-of-worl d-leaders-that-considered-making-a-new-currency-meet-to-discuss-economy/

Omi, Michael and Howard Winant. 2014 [1986]. *Racial Formation in the United States* (3rd edition). New York, NY: Routledge.

Parenti, C. 2011. *Tropic of Chaos*. New York: Nation Books.

Parry, Ian, Simon Black and Nate Vernon. 2021. "Still Not Getting Energy Prices Right: A Global and Country Update on Fossil Fuel Subsidies." *International Monetary Fund* (IMF). Retrieved 07/01/23 from www.imf.org/en/Publications/WP/Issues/2021/09/23/Still-Not-Getting-Energy-Prices-Right-A-Global-and-Country-Update-of-Fossil-Fuel-Subsidies-466004

Phelan, John. 1969. "The Apologetic History of Fray Bartolome de las Casas." *Hispanic American Historical Review* 49 (1): 94–99.

Phillips, Peter. 2018. *Giants: The Global Power Elite*. New York: Seven Stories Press.

Prashad, Vijay. 2023. "The BRICS Have Changed the Balance of Forces, but They Will Not by Themselves Change the World: The Thirty-Third Newsletter (2023)." *Tricontinental*, August 17. Retrieved 08/17/23 from https://thetricontinental.org/newsletterissue/brics-summit-johannesburg/

Prociv, Kathryn. 2023. "Like a Hot Tub: Water Temperatures Off Florida Soar Over 100 Degrees, Stunning Experts." *NBC News*, July 25. Retrieved 08/01/23 from www.nbcnews.com/news/weather/hot-tub-water-temperatures-florida-soar-100-degrees-stunning-experts-rcna96163

Ramirez, Rachel. 2023. "Nearly 62,000 People Died from Record-Breaking Heat in Europe Last Summer. It's a Lesson for the US Too." *CNN World*, July 14. Retrieved 08/01/23 from www.cnn.com/2023/07/10/world/deadly-europe-heatwave-2022-climate/index.html#:~:text=Follow%20CNN-,Nearly%2062%2C000%20people%20died%20from%20record%2Dbreaking%20heat%20in%20Europe,lesson%20for%20the%20US%2C%20too&text=Paramedics%20help%20a%20patient%20into,Monday%2C%20July%2018%2C%202022

Ransby, Barbara. 2018. *Making All Black Lives Matter: Reimagining Freedom in the 21st Century*. Oakland, CA: University of California Press.

Ravikumar, Sahin and Sharon Singleton. 2023. "Britain Commits to Hundreds of North Sea Oil Gas Licenses." *Reuters*, July 31. Retrieved 07/10/23 from www.reuters.com/business/energy/uk-grant-hundreds-new-north-sea-oil-gas-licences-2023-07-31/

Riley, Tess. 2017. "Just 100 Companies Responsible for 71% of Global Emissions, Study Says." *The Guardian*, July 10. Retrieved 09/15/23 from www.theguardian.com/sustainable-business/2017/jul/10/100-fossil-fuel-companies-investors-responsible-71-global-emissions-cdp-study-climate-change

Roberts, Dan. 2014. "Wall Street Deregulation Pushed by Clinton Advisers, Documents Reveal." *The Guardian*, April 19. Retrieved 07/01/23 from www.theguardian.com/world/2014/apr/19/wall-street-deregulation-clinton-advisers-obama

Roberts, Michael. 2016. *The Long Depression: How it Happened, Why it Happened, and What Happens Next*. Chicago, IL: Haymarket Books.

Robinson, C. 1983. *Black Marxism: The Making of the Black Radical Tradition*. London: Zed Press.

Robinson, William. 2018. "Debating the Precariat: An Exchange on the Essay, 'The Precariat: Today's Transformative Class?'" *Great Transition Initiative (GTI)*. Retrieved on 07/01/23 from https://greattransition.org/roundtable/precariat-william-robinson

Robinson, William. 2020. *The Global Police State*. London, England: Pluto Press.

Robinson, William. 2022a. *Global Civil War: Capitalism Post-Pandemic*. Oakland, CA: PM Press.

Robinson, William. 2022b. *Can Global Capitalism Endure?* Atlanta, GA: Clarity Press.

Rodney, Walter. 2018 [1981]. *How Europe Underdeveloped Africa*. New York: Verso Books.

Sachs, Jeffrey. 2023. "The War in Ukraine Was Provoked—and Why That Matters to Achieve Peace." *Common Dreams*, May 23. Retrieved 08/01/23 from www.comm ondreams.org/opinion/the-war-in-ukraine-was-provoked-and-why-that-matters-if-we-want-peace

Said, Edward. 1979. *Orientalism*. New York: Vintage Books.

Said, Summer and Stephen Kalin. 2023. "Saudi Arabia Considers Accepting Yuan Instead of Dollars for Chinese Oil Sales." *The Wall Street Journal*, March 15. Retrieved 07/10/23 from www.wsj.com/articles/saudi-arabia-considers-acceptin g-yuan-instead-of-dollars-for-chinese-oil-sales-11647351541

Shamlian, Janet and Nic Cutrona. 2023. "Millions of Americans Nearing Retirement Age With No Savings." *CBS Evening News*, March 01. Retrieved 07/01/23 from www.cbsnews.com/news/millions-of-americans-nearing-retirement-age-no-savings/

Shekhar, Vidhu. 2023. "Petro-Yuan or Petro-BRICS: The Need for Better Alternative Reserve Currencies to Break Dollar Dominance." *Forbes India*, March 30. Retrieved 07/17/23 from www.forbesindia.com/article/bharatiya-vidya-bhava n039s-spjimr/petroyuan-or-petrobrics-the-need-for-better-alternative-reserve-curr encies-to-break-dollar-dominance/84063/1

Singh, Nikhil Pal. 2017. *Race and America's Long War*. Oakland, CA: University of California Press.

Smith, Ashley. 2023. "Resisting Russian Imperialism: 2 Socialists—A Ukrainian and a Russian—on Ukraine's Struggle for Self-Determination." *The Nation*, September 7. Retrieved 09/07/23 from www.thenation.com/article/archive/resisting-russian-imperia lism-2-socialists-a-ukrainian-and-a-russian-on-ukraines-struggle-for-self-determination/

Stancil, Kenny. 2023. "GOP Assault on Child Labor Laws Under Fresh Scrutiny After 16-Year-Old Dies at Poultry Plant." *Common Dreams*, July 19. Retrieved 07/20/23 from www.commondreams.org/news/mississippi-poultry-plant-teen-dies

Starkman, Dean. 2015. "Cities and Private Equity Firms Fight Over Ownership of Water Systems." *Los Angeles Times*, October 15. Retrieved 07/15/23 from www.la times.com/business/la-fi-public-private-properties-20151015-story.html

Stevens, Harry. 2023. "Why Biden's Oil Policies Upset Oil Companies and Environmentalists." *The Washington Post*, March 29. Retrieved 07/01/23 from www.wa shingtonpost.com/climate-environment/interactive/2023/biden-oil-drilling-permits-wil low-project/

Supran, Geoffrey and Naomi Oreskes. 2021. "The Forgotten Oil Ads That Told Us Climate Change Was Nothing." *The Guardian*, November 18. Retrieved 07/01/23 from www.theguardian.com/environment/2021/nov/18/the-forgotten-oil-ads-that-tol d-us-climate-change-was-nothing

Tan, Huileng. 2023. "China's Mounting Such a Strong Attack on the Dollar's Dominance that it's Paying for Almost All of its Russian Oil Imports in the Yuan." *Business Insider*, May 11. Retrieved 07/10/23 from www.businessinsider.com/dedolla riztion-china-yuan-russia-oil-imports-sanctions-2023-5#:~:text=China%20has%20ra mped%20up%20the,oil%20and%20coal%20from%20Russia

Taylor, Keeanga Yamahtta. 2021a. *From #BlackLivesMatter to Black Liberation* (2nd edition). Chicago, IL: Haymarket Books.

Taylor, Keeanga Yamahtta. 2021b. *Race for Profit: How Banks and the Real Estate Industry Undermined Black Homeownership*. Chapel Hill, NC: University of North Carolina Press.

The Century Foundation (TCF). 2020. "Closing America's Education Funding Gaps." *The Century Foundation*, July 22. Retrieved 06/15/23 from https://tcf.org/content/report/closing-americas-education-funding/

The Economist (briefing). 2020. "Businesses are Proving Quite Resilient to the Pandemic." *The Economist*, May 16. Retrieved on 04/11/23 from www.economist.com/briefing/2020/05/16/businesses-are-proving-quite-resilient-to-the-pandemic

The Economist [editorial board]. 2023. "Global Fertility Has Collapsed, With Profound Economic Consequences." *The Economist*, June 1. Retrieved 07/01/23 from www.economist.com/leaders/2023/06/01/global-fertility-has-collapsed-with-profound-economic-consequences

Thomhave, Kalena. 2022. "The School Privatization Movement's Latest Scheme to Undermine Public Education." *In These Times*, April 26. Retrieved 06/15/23 from https://inthesetimes.com/article/school-privatization-public-education-vouchers-savings-accounts

Thompson, Andrea. 2023. "July 2023 Is Hottest Month Ever Recorded on Earth." *Scientific American*, July 27. Retrieved 08/01/23 from www.scientificamerican.com/article/july-2023-is-hottest-month-ever-recorded-on-earth/

UN Climate Change (UNFCCC secretariat). 2022. "Conflict and Climate" (interview with UNHCR head Filippo Grandi). *UNCC*, July 12. Retrieved 07/10/23 from https://unfccc.int/blog/conflict-and-climate

US Department of Justice Civil Rights Division. 2015. "Investigation of the Ferguson Police Department." *DOJ*, March 4. Retrieved 07/01/23 from www.justice.gov/sites/default/files/opa/press-releases/attachments/2015/03/04/ferguson_police_department_report.pdf

UN General Assembly (UNGA). 2015. "Resolution Adopted by the General Assembly: 70/169. The Human Rights to Safe Drinking Water and Sanitation." *UNGA*, December 15. Retrieved 07/15/23 from https://digitallibrary.un.org/record/821067

UN Population Fund (UNFPA). 2023. "Maternal Health Analysis of Women and Girls of African Descent in the Americas." *UNFPA*. Retrieved 07/20/23 from www.unfpa.org/publications/maternal-health-analysis-women-and-girls-african-descent-americas

Vogel, Lisa. 2013. *Marxism and the Oppression of Women*. Boston, MA: Brill.

Weise, Elizabeth. 2023. "Rotting Seaweed, Dead Fish, No Sand: Climate Change Threatens to Ruin US Beaches." *USA Today*, June 17. Retrieved on 07/12/23 from www.usatoday.com/story/news/nation/2023/06/17/gross-climate-change-effects-soil-us-beaches-seaweed-dead-fish/70318332007/

Williams, Eric. 2021 [1944]. *Capitalism and Slavery* (3rd edition). Chapel Hill, NC: University of North Carolina Press.

World Bank. 2016. "World Bank Group, New Development Bank Lay Groundwork for Cooperation" [press release]. *The World Bank*, September 9. Retrieved 07/10/23 from www.worldbank.org/en/news/press-release/2016/09/09/world-bank-group-new-development-bank-lay-groundwork-for-cooperation

World Economics. 2023. "China's Share of Global GDP: Percentage Share of Global GDP in 2022." *World Economics*. Retrieved 07/01/23 from www.worldeconomics.com/Share-of-Global-GDP/China.aspx

Yang, Maya. 2023. "Teen Dies in Sawmill Accident as US States Aim to Roll Back Child Labor Laws." *The Guardian*, July 6. Retrieved 07/20/23 from www.theguardian.com/us-news/2023/jul/06/boy-16-dies-sawmill-accident-wisconsin

Yee, Vivian. 2022. "'A Slow Death': Egypt's Political Prisoners Recount Horrific Conditions." *The New York Times*, August 8. Retrieved 07/15/23 from www.nytimes.com/2022/08/08/world/middleeast/egypts-prisons-conditions.html
Zaretsky, Eli. 1986. *Capitalism, the Family, and Personal Life*. London: Pluto Press.

3 Confronting the Global Police State

The potentially catastrophic militarization of the world, including the unthinkable destructive potential of nuclear arsenals, can be understood in relation to a global police state (Robinson 2020). The basis for the global police state emerges as transnational capital, Nation-states, and TNS apparatuses strain to address the internal crisis of overaccumulation and external crises of state legitimacy in a shifting geopolitical environment made more volatile by those efforts. One should think of the global police state as consisting not only of formal state militaries, but "systems of mass incarceration, immigrant detention and deportation, refugee control systems, the construction of border and containment walls, mass surveillance, urban policing, [and] the deployment of paramilitary and private mercenary armies" (Robinson 2020:72). The global police state is not a single, unified institutional entity, but a concept to represent the collective public and private repressive forces in the service of transnational capital that, together, create a condition of ubiquitous global surveillance, ever-ready coercion, and potentially catastrophic military conflict. It appears not only in the sheer growth of military, police, and intelligence agencies, but also in the "militarization of civil society and the crossover between the military and the civilian application of weapons, tracking, security, surveillance, and other systems of control" (Robinson 2020:63), where nearly all of human society is brought within its reach, and any community can become a "battlespace" for its deployment (Robinson 2020).

The global police state did not arrive by accident, but to fill three essential roles on behalf of transnational capital in the current regime of accumulation: 1) As a social control mechanism to coerce and discipline an increasingly precarious and "superfluous" (Robinson 2020, 2022a) global labor force as the "repressive state apparatus" (Althusser 2001 [1971]) of transnational capital; 2) As a mechanism for "accumulation by dispossession" (Harvey 2005, 2018) and for policing the historically racialized lines between exploitable and expropriable populations in that process; and 3) As a site of investment and speculation itself through what Robinson (2020, 2022a, 2022b) calls "militarized accumulation." Toward this end the global police state is heavily privatized, and inseparable from what is now a very

DOI: 10.4324/9781003323556-4

powerful, interconnected "nexus" of transnational finance, the most powerful TNCs in computer and information technologies (CIT), and the military industrial complex (MIC) representing the relationship between states and the private, transnational security industries that supply police, intelligence, military, private mercenary, and paramilitary forces. In playing these roles, the global police state poses direct and indirect threats to human rights and the perpetuation of human civilization.

The existence and growth of the global police state is potentially catastrophic for human rights and survival in three ways: 1) As a direct threat posed by devastating conflict, including but not limited to nuclear war, as geopolitical tensions increase, the world is flooded with weapons, and forced migration (also from climate change impacts) explodes; 2) As a significant source of greenhouse gas emissions and other pollutants, driving climate change and ecological destruction (Crawford 2022, 2019; Belcher, Bigger, Neimark, and Kennelly 2019); and 3) As a coercive tool to suppress social movements seeking to confront OTHS (Robinson 2020, 2022a, 2022b), to the extent they are perceived to challenge dominant systems and relations of rule. To this last point, and as an extension of its role in repressing the global working class, the growth of the global police state contributes to increasingly authoritarian, anti-democratic forms of government, including but not limited to forms of 21st century fascism (Robinson 2020, 2022a, 2022b).

Disciplining the Global Working Class

As previously discussed, the nation-state and other state political structures, including those at the transnational level, are needed not only to maintain and reproduce the foregrounded material relations of labor exploitation, but also to maintain and reproduce many of the background relations of capitalist society, such as those of gendered reproduction or deeply racialized forms of expropriation. The state fills these roles through what Althusser (2001 [1970]) conceptualized as the repressive state apparatus (RSA), manifested in the "laws, the courts, the police, the national guard, and other branches of the military, and the vigilantes whose actions the state sanctions," (Cazenave 2018:190); and the ideological state apparatus (ISA) that hegemonically communicates "a nation's dominant ideologies of who should be treated in what way and why—which are generated and disseminated throughout the culture, including the media, schools, and various government agencies and policies."

Similar to Gramsci and other neo-Marxists, Althusser considered the ISA's ability to establish hegemonic forms of rule as most active in securing "the reproduction specifically of the relations of production," while the RSA provides a "shield" behind which owning and ruling class power is unified and consolidated (Althusser 2001 [1971]). Specifically, for Althusser, the RSA acts by "securing by force (physical or otherwise) the political conditions" necessary for the reproduction of exploitive material relations, the reproduction of the state itself, and to shield and backstop the hegemonic functions of the ISA, especially in the face of resistance (Althusser 2001 [1970]). The repressive and ideological apparatuses of national and transnational state structures work in relative concert with one another, and while the RSA operates primarily through repression and the ISA operates primarily through hegemony (Gramsci 1971), both have some capacity to operate through repression and ideology. Finally, in contrast, the RSA is unified under the state monopoly on the use of force, but the ISA is much more diversified, including an educational apparatus, a political apparatus, and so forth.

A full exploration of neo-Marxist theories of the state is not necessary for the purposes of the theoretical framework applied or arguments put forward in this book. Though the following chapter will explore the political state apparatus (part of the ISA) in the maintenance of capitalist society and as a contested terrain over human rights and species survival, here we only mean to ground the social control and disciplinary functions of the global police state in what critical theorists have understood for some time as the repressive functions and apparatuses of national states. The contemporary RSAs of national states provide the initial conditions of capital accumulation through primitive accumulation and, for that matter, other ongoing forms of gendered, racial, and/or (neo)colonial forms of expropriation. For instance, state RSAs provide the coercive and social control mechanisms necessary for systemic racism and (neo)colonization during what Omi and Winant (2014 [1986]) called the process of "racialization" that constructs, legitimates, and ascribes racial and national identities and in executing racial (often also state) projects that seek to expropriate the land, lives, labor, and resources of racialized and/or colonized peoples. Further, the contemporary RSAs of national states—with powerful military states like the US at its center—now perform the necessarily transnational function of disciplining a global working class.

The transnational imperative for social control grows in the face of breathtaking material inequality, social and political instability, and growing insecurity of the global workforce, who are increasingly subject to forced dislocation, precarious employment, and various forms of often violent expropriation. Specifically, the global working class consists of: a) "doubly-free" wage laborers who are exploited in the creation of surplus value; b) Expropriable-and-exploitable citizen-workers (Fraser 2022), including but not limited to the so-called "global precariat;" and c) deeply insecure populations of migrants, prisoners, coerced/trafficked labor (including some forms of military conscription and sex trafficking), women, children, and "modern day" slaves (Bales 2016) whose lives, labor, land, and property are deemed expropriable. We've already discussed how the state differentiates exploited and expropriated labor over time (according to gender, race, nationality/citizenship, etc.), how in the current period more populations of exploited labor are made subject to expropriation and general precarity, and how the interconnection between exploitation and expropriation is a necessary precondition for accumulation in general. Due to the blurring lines between exploitable and expropriable labor, and in contrast with more orthodox definitions of who is or is not a part of the potentially revolutionary proletariat, we agree with Robinson (2020:47) that "they are … categories of the global working class that are conjoined; they form a unity in their antagonistic relationship to transnational capital." As a strategic implication, we argue that human rights praxis and the broader global movement for democratic eco-socialism of which it must be a part needs to strive for a political unity in class and boundary struggles that reflects the actual structural unity between exploitation and expropriation in the accumulation process.

This is not to gloss over the qualitative differences in the lives of various segments of the global working class, or even within these segments, but to demonstrate the need and grounds for their political solidarity on some level. Fundamentally insecure, expropriable populations are those most subject to severe human rights abuses, whose ranks are growing and will continue to grow as a result of heightening OTHS (climate change and potentially catastrophic levels of conflict), and in contrast to the expanding "rights" and political power (polyarchy) of TNCs, transnational finance capital, and the TCC. They represent what Robinson (2020, 2022a, 2022b) calls a global "surplus" population that tends to, in practice, fall outside of any meaningful rights protections and become subject not only to expropriation by capital, but to surveillance, militarized policing and border security, incarceration, callous neglect or disregard, and downright deadly violence by the global police state. To summarize,

> extreme inequality requires extreme violence and repression, that lend themselves to a global police state and projects of twenty first century fascism…. It is this imperative of social control that in the first instance brings forth a global police state.
>
> (Robinson 2020:41)

Interestingly, Robinson (2020, 2022a, 2022b) also points out that the same revolutionary technologies that render more and more of the global working class "surplus" in the production process and subject to expropriation—such as artificial intelligence (AI), advanced facial recognition/biometric technologies, and robotics—are being employed by the global police state to socially control and to coerce the same population.

Regarding resistance and class conflict, Althusser (Althusser 2001 [1971]) discusses the RSA and ISA in relation to the revolutionary strategies of traditional Marxists who argued that:

> The proletariat must seize State power in order to destroy the existing bourgeois State apparatus and, in a first phase, replace it with a quite different, proletarian, State apparatus, then in later phases set in motion a radical process, that of the destruction of the State.

We will not presume to take on the debate between electoral, state, libertarian, and other socialists on the general strategic visions for socialism or the end of the modern state in this text.[1] Instead, as will be discussed in the concluding chapter, we envision that given the enormity and immediacy of their greatest overlapping threats, human rights and survival should be ensured through a process of diplomacy, denuclearization, and disarmament that includes a redistribution of the resources dedicated to the global police state for the purposes of mitigating the implications of climate change and global instability/insecurity.

In the uncomfortably short term, this will demand something close to capture of national state power in places like the US and of TNS power in the case of the UN by civil society and diverse (i.e., by race, gender, ethnicity, sexuality, nationality, industry, and so forth) working class interests, through a combination of the many means available, focusing on, but not limited to the growth and political mobilization of a *militant international labor movement of the exploited and expropriated global working class*. Such state power and infrastructure are needed to nationalize and wind down fossil fuel industry TNCs, and to reimagine and repurpose the global police state and militaristic approaches to domestic policy and foreign relations, especially in the face of unyielding market incentives to expand both fossil fuel extraction and the global arms trade. Organized labor is one of few existing mechanisms through which state power can be confronted or mobilized, corporate power can be subdued, and democratic solidarity can be (and is being) built across race, ethnicity, nationality, age, gender, sexuality, and industry in tangible, collective, material pursuits. There are many signs of these struggles already underway, and opportunities for human rights scholars, advocates, and stakeholders to contribute to these efforts, especially for those of us in the US with the responsibility and ability to reign in the historically unprecedented (in size, scope, and destructive power) American military and transnational military industrial complex.

Accumulation by Dispossession and Competition for Strategic Resources in the 21st Century

What we have so far discussed as "expropriation" is a concept that extends (Fraser 2022) in part from what critical geographer and Marxist theorist, David Harvey (2005) defined as accumulation by dispossession, or capital accumulation by means of confiscation, "predation, fraud, and violence" that extends well beyond the "original stage" of primitive accumulation. Further, in agreement with Robinson (2018a, 2022a, 2022b) and Fraser (2022), Harvey argues that accumulation by dispossession functions to address, but at best postpones, the heightening global crisis of overaccumulation. Harvey argues convincingly (2005, 2007) that since the period of global economic restructuring, accumulation by dispossession has been achieved both through the weaponization of international debt dependency and through the more straightforward use of state and state sanctioned police, military, and paramilitary violence to confiscate resources and labor, and conscribe them into national and transnational circuits of accumulation. Applying the theoretical model put forward here, accumulation by dispossession should be understood as a process also deeply engaged in the background relations of capitalist society, such as in the social control and systematic dispossession of women, people of color, and those without the recognitions of citizenship. We have so far discussed the role of international debt dependency in establishing and maintaining US hegemonic power since GER (see also Armaline and Glasberg 2009), and in the rising power and influence of China and other BRICS+ nations through direct lending and the establishment of alternative TNS structures of international finance. The global police state also contributes to securing accumulation by dispossession through threat or application of force, particularly as capital and imperial competition intensifies for scarce natural resources such as fresh water, or crucial sources of energy such as fossil fuels or the minerals necessary for green energy alternatives.

Many interstate conflicts in the last several decades have been in large part over the control of and access to oil and other critical fossil fuels (for use by militaries, industry, and consumers). This should be no surprise as oil has been a key energy source of any significant state power since the World Wars. Depending on how one defines the role of oil in the preconditions of war, 25–50% of interstate wars since 1973 have been connected to "oil-related causal mechanisms" (Colgan 2013). Additional data analysis of conflicts between 1970 and 2012 (Chisadza, Clance, Gupta, and Wohar 2023) indicates that the discovery of new oil reserves is a causal factor in both intra- and interstate conflicts. In the case of civil wars or intrastate conflict, the discovery of oil reserves tends to exacerbate already existing economic and ethnic divisions, where

> the rents accrued from such natural resources can provide motivation and opportunities for elite groups to support themselves through expropriation, and lead to exploitation of ethnic minority groups, which can instigate internal conflict between the two groups (for example, oil conflicts in Angola and the Niger Delta).
>
> (Chisadza, Clance, Gupta, and Wohar 2023)

Comparatively, the effect of discovering new sources of oil on interstate conflict is similar, though takes a bit longer depending on geopolitical factors such as, "the location of the resources and the feasibility of engaging in conflict with a neighboring country" (Chisadza, Clance, Gupta, and Wohar 2023; see also Caselli, Morelli, and Rohner 2015).

Big capital and competing imperial powers secure access to oil beyond their borders (or within them, in the case of extraction from protected public or indigenous territories) through trade, economic predation, or direct military forms of conquest and the (neo)colonial relations that follow. These various mechanisms allow for the dispossession of oil and other natural resources from local populations, who are burdened with the human, environmental, and other costs of extraction. The illegal 2003 US and allied invasion of Iraq serves as an instructive historical example of oil and other forms of capital captured through violent dispossession. Though the G.W. Bush Administration claimed the invasion was to "disarm Iraq of weapons of mass destruction, to end Saddam Hussein's support for terrorism, and to free Iraqi people" (Bush 2003), many of these claims were infamously debunked—recalling, for instance, Colin Powell's abhorrent theater at the UN Security Council, full of false claims regarding Iraqi weapons development with a prop vial of anthrax to boot (Schwarz 2018).

Iraq has the 5th largest proven oil reserves and is the 2nd largest oil producer in OPEC behind Saudi Arabia (USEIA 2021). Beyond being part of the neoconservative geopolitical strategy employed at the time to counter the so-called "axis of evil," it became clear that the Iraq invasion of 2003 was part of a larger plan to ensure Western access to regional oil, deny that oil to competitors, and to reduce the power of OPEC to control global supplies by auctioning off Iraqi oil production to US and other international firms (Palast 2005). CENTCOM Commander (2003–2007) General John Abizaid stated plainly in 2008 that the war and broader "dynamics" of US foreign policy in the region were "very much about oil and we can't really deny that" (Pitney 2011). Similar admissions were made in the memoir of former Federal Reserve Secretary Alan Greenspan and by then-Senator, and later Defense Secretary Chuck Hagel, who in 2007 remarked, "people say we're not fighting for oil. Of course we are" (Juhasz 2023).

Whether or not the US gambit for oil was ultimately successful on those terms is debatable. Though several American companies like Haliburton won significant drilling contracts, most of the major oil fields were sold off to the stewardship of European, Russian, Chinese and other firms (Kramer 2011). In fact, Chinese firms are now the most active players in Iraqi energy production, having secured over half of all contracts since 2018 (Crisp 2022). From a geopolitical perspective, the Iraq war is commonly seen as one of the defining blunders of what has become a period of American hegemonic decline. Yet, the US and allied forces—extensions of the repressive state apparatuses of these national states and of the larger global police state—were deployed to dispossess Iraqis of their oil, sovereignty, and other general resources, successfully facilitating the expropriation of those resources to the benefit of transnational capital across what would now be considered the geopolitical spectrum of great powers.

The human costs of dispossession in Iraq were staggering, and the wars on terror of which the Iraq invasion was a part yielded some of the most egregious violations of international human rights law since their inception,[2] and did irreparable damage to the normative impact of human rights protections. Since the illegal US allied invasion in 2003, somewhere between

280,000 and 316,000 Iraqis died as a direct result of violence (Crawford, Lutz, Rubaii, et al. 2023), but many more perished from the invasion and occupation. According to public health surveys of Iraqi households, the civilian death toll from direct violence and from "the collapse of infrastructure and other indirect, but war-related causes" is estimated at over 405,000 (Hagopian, Flaxman, Takaro, et al. 2013). This followed the already devastating impacts of US and UN Security Council sanctions on Iraq. Those sanctions at first prevented the sale of Iraqi oil, but then established the disastrous "oil for food" program that provided little for Iraqis while releasing oil to global markets—resulting in the death of over 1.5 million civilians, over 500,000 of them children, due to malnutrition, disease, and lack of access to basic supplies (GICJ 2017). In a simple and stunning articulation of the choice between international human rights frameworks and the structurally imbricated drives toward capital accumulation and perceived geopolitical gain, when asked about the sanctions in a *60 Minutes* interview by Lesley Stahl, Secretary of State Madeleine Albright claimed that the sacrifice of half a million Iraqi children was "worth it" (Jackson 2022) to achieve stated US interests.

In addition to oil and other fossil fuels, capital accumulation and geopolitical ambitions are now dependent on access to dwindling sources of clean, potable water, and to the minerals needed for high-tech manufacturing, military production, and a green energy transition. The global water crisis described in previous chapters, from which over a quarter of the world (2 billion people) already lack access to fresh water (Lai 2022), is due to industrial and public over-consumption (AghaKouchak, Mirchi, Madani, et al. 2021), the pollution of existing water sources, and the complicated implications of climate change. Specifically, these include the loss of fresh water stores from melting glaciers and the phenomenon of evapotranspiration, where the warming air holds more moisture, causing a transfer of water from the ground to the atmosphere. Accelerating evapotranspiration shrinks available water supplies while increasing the frequency, size, and severity of weather events such as hurricanes/typhoons (Huntington 2006; Skliris et al. 2016). A reducing water supply amidst increasing demand and extreme weather patterns has led to steady increases in water related social instability and conflict. Researchers (Unfried, Kis-Katos, and Poser 2022) point to direct regional disputes over fresh water sources in, for example, the 2020 construction of the Grand Ethiopian Renaissance Dam (between Ethiopia, Sudan, and Egypt), over access to rivers in states across India (Richards and Singh 2002; McQuaid et al. 2017), and between herders and farmers in countries such as Nigeria. They point further to the role of water shortages in exacerbating existing (proxy war) conflicts, such as in the civil war and humanitarian disaster in Yemen, where up to half of the population had not been able to meet "basic water needs" (Suter 2017), or in Syria, where the capture and control of dams and fresh water sources has been a goal of warring factions (Suter 2017; McQuaid et al. 2017).

Adding to existing research on the connections between "climate shocks" and conflict (Parenti 2011; Hsiang et al. 2013; Burke, Hsiang, and Miguel 2015; Harari and La Ferrara 2018), data analysis examining Africa, the Caribbean, and Central America between 2002 and 2017 (Unfried, Kis-Katos, and Poser 2022) revealed a causal link between local conflict and declining water supplies, with those impacts being most severe when punctuated by a shock of some sort—such as a drought or dramatic infrastructure failure. The study found that a single standard deviation decline in local water supplies from drought and an "intensifying water cycle" more than tripled the chances of conflict in that region. The complicated relationship between water scarcity and conflict is also illuminated through the Pacific Institute's Water Conflict Chronology project,[3] documenting approximately 1300 conflicts since 2500 B.C., a vast majority of which occurred only in the last half century (since global economic restructuring), and revolved around agricultural production (70% of global fresh water use goes to agriculture) (Milne 2022; World Bank 2022). According to the project findings, water can act as a "trigger" for conflict between groups in direct dispute over access, and as a "weapon" of conflict, when access is denied to enemy populations, or when key water infrastructure is a "casualty" or "target" in a conflict (Milne 2022).

One of the most obvious examples of water as a weapon can be seen in the ongoing political and military struggles between Israel and Palestinians in the occupied territories. Since the Oslo Accords of 1993, Israel controls over 80% of water reserves in the West Bank (Rahman 2023) and has restricted the flow of water along with all other resources into the Gaza Strip as part of its blockade since 2007. To demonstrate the disparate outcomes in water access, Israelis and Israeli settlers consume a per-capita average of at least 247 liters of water per day, but Palestinians under Israeli military control are only allotted an average of 20 liters per day, per person (Rahman 2023). This amounts to the absolute minimum needed for human survival, and far less than the 50–100 liters per day required by international law to "ensure the full realization" of the human right to water and sanitation without significant public health impacts (UN WSSCC 2015; OHCHR Special Rapporteur on the Human Right to Safe Drinking Water and Sanitation 2023). In addition to household consumption, access to water is critical to supply Palestinian farms and orchards in what is considered their bread basket of the Jordan Valley (Debre 2023).

Beyond controlling the flow of water in the occupied territories, the Israeli government destroyed over 160 "unauthorized Palestinian reservoirs, sewage networks and wells" (Debre 2023) between 2021 and 2023 as part of a wider strategy to destabilize Palestinian water infrastructure and undermine Palestinian means of resisting the forced shortage. In Gaza, one of the most densely populated places in the world, 90–95% of the water supply (from the Coastal Aquifer, contaminated by sewage and seawater) was already unfit for human consumption, and rooftops were littered with water-collection tanks that often ran dry in attempts to offset unequal access to public water supplies and the lack of effective water infrastructure (Amnesty International 2017). Of course, this was before many of those rooftops were reduced to rubble by the Israeli military beginning in October of 2023, thanks in great part to diplomatic support, arms, and economic aid from the US.

As many readers will no doubt be aware, on October 7, 2023, Hamas and other militant groups within Gaza launched an attack on Israeli soldiers and civilians bordering the Gaza Strip, killing approximately 1,200 people[4] and taking approximately 240 hostages in the assault (PBS Newshour 2023). Though Hamas is not a state party to the UN, and there are some provisions in international law for the "right to resist" occupation,[5] the form and content of the attacks violated international law in the targeting and terrorizing of civilians.[6] Beyond the killings and taking of hostages, UN envoy Pramila Patten reported in March of 2023 that there were "reasonable grounds" that sexual assault and rape were used against a so far unidentifiable number of Israeli women and girls in multiple locations targeted in the October 7 attacks, and called on Israel to allow for the Independent International Commission of Inquiry on the Palestinian territories and Israel "to carry out full-fledged investigations into the alleged violations" (Lederer 2024; Fassihi and Kershner 2024). In addition, the UN envoy's investigation—meant to report back to the Secretary General on the weaponization of sexual violence in conflicts around the world—reported on sexual assault and humiliation used against Palestinian women and girls who were taken into custody by the Israeli Defense Forces (IDF) as part of Israel's military response to the October 7 attacks (Fassihi and Kershner 2024; see also Borger 2024).

Israel's broader military response was to unleash a brutal campaign of unyielding, indiscriminate bombardment, amounting to wildly disproportionate, collective punishment against the more than two million civilians of Gaza (half of whom are children), and violent settler expansion in the West Bank[7] (where Hamas does not govern)—all of which qualify as war crimes and crimes against humanity for, among other things, the targeting of civilians and critical civilian infrastructure. By the end of February 2024, over 30,000 Palestinians—two thirds of them women and children—had been killed and over 70,000 injured by Israel's military operation (Al Mughrabi 2024), and 240 Israeli soldiers had been killed during the IDF's ground invasion of Gaza (Fabian 2024). The count of Palestinian civilian casualties is bound to climb, as they do not include the thousands missing, many believed to be buried under the buildings destroyed by the bombings and demolitions that Israel claimed necessary to target a system of underground tunnels created by Hamas. The Israeli bombardment and ground invasion targeted schools, universities, religious sites, hospitals, refugee encampments, and countless residential neighborhoods. Also notable, Israel's military campaign in Gaza has been one of the deadliest in history for journalists, medical workers, and UN staff (Jones 2024; Hassan, Manjra, and London 2024; Cumming-Bruce 2023), for which UN agencies and organizations to protect the lives and rights of journalists have repeatedly called for accountability—so far in vain.

As another strategy employed in Israel's response to the October 7 attacks, and in the most extreme weaponization of water (but also food, medical supplies, and other basic needs) possible, what began as a blockade was turned into a "complete siege" when Israeli Defense Minister Yoav Gallant declared that "no electricity, no food, no water, [and] no fuel" would be allowed into the Gaza Strip, and that Israel was "fighting human animals" and "acting accordingly" (Fabian 2023) in conducting a deadly siege against the entire civilian population. The siege and destruction of Palestinian water and agricultural infrastructure caused massive outbreaks of starvation, preventable disease, and dehydration among the Palestinian civilian population, such that Human Rights Watch (2023b) issued a report in December of 2023 decrying Israel's weaponization of access to food and water as an international war crime.[8] This report was joined by experts from the UN World Food Program (WFP), who in February of 2024 also decried the intentional destruction of food and the severe restriction of humanitarian aid and water resources as international war crimes (Lakhani 2024b) against Gaza's civilian population.

In response to the ongoing humanitarian crisis in Gaza as a result of the conflict, by February of 2024 there were three separate attempts to pass resolutions at the UN Security Council calling for a ceasefire—all of which were vetoed by the US, who continued to provide diplomatic cover for the Israeli government (Nichols 2024). In addition, as the International Court of Justice (ICJ) continued to deliberate an advisory opinion on the Israeli occupation of Palestinian territories (Syed 2024), South Africa brought formal charges of genocide in an ICJ case against Israel in January of 2024 (Bigg and Gupta 2024). Though a ruling on the genocide charge is not likely to come for some time, the Court made an initial ruling that Israel was plausibly committing genocide, and had to take "immediate and effective measures" (Amnesty International 2024) to end the targeting of Palestinian civilians, prohibit and punish public incitements of genocidal acts by members of the Israeli government, and protect Palestinian civilians at risk "by ensuring sufficient humanitarian assistance and enabling basic services" (Amnesty International 2024; Bigg and Gupta 2024). However, as we pen this chapter, Israel has yet to comply with these orders, as observed by international human rights watchdogs including Amnesty International (2024).

All of this said, it is absolutely beyond the scope of this book to provide the long historical contexts necessary for a complete analysis of Israeli-Palestinian relations. We simply wish to make three points here. First, the weaponization of water in the conflict speaks to its role as a critical resource of the 21st century, and the role or functions of the global police state relative to these resources and to expropriation—in this case of Palestinian land, lives, and resources. And the payoff for Israel and transnational capital could be significant. As Robinson and Nguyen (2024) note:

In late October, as Israeli bombardment intensified, Israel set about granting licenses to transnational energy companies for gas and oil exploration off the Mediterranean coast,[9] part of its plan to become a major regional gas producer and energy hub as well as an alternative to Russian gas for Western Europe.

Second, as will be discussed later in the chapter, the Israeli RSA is thoroughly connected to that of the US, EU, and even (through the transnational military industrial complex) to geopolitical rivals of the West such as China, and plays a specific role as part of a global police state. Third, the international legal system has been so far unable to stop the ongoing carnage in Israel, despite overwhelming international pressure demanding peaceful diplomacy, and despite this being a primary function of the United Nations. These conditions have amounted to a legitimacy crisis for the Biden (US) and Netanyahu (Israel) Administrations complicit in the bloodshed, and for the UN and international "rules based order" that has so far been impotent to stop the ongoing carnage (Robinson and Nguyen 2024; Callamard 2024).

Beyond weaponizing water access in acts of war or repression, the global police state works to ensure (in part through forms of dispossession) and reserve (through repression and social control) the world's increasingly finite strategic resources for the purposes of capitalist production and distribution to the most privileged consumer markets. In the bigger, global picture, the pollution and over-consumption of fresh water supplies from big agriculture and other extractive and productive industries is part of the broader cannibalization of the ecological conditions of possibility necessary for capital accumulation and human survival. When water scarcity increases, so does social instability and the chances for conflict and war, and so does the role of water in all conflicts. Moreover, the capture and control of water supplies—and the social control of those without them—for the purposes of capital accumulation and structurally imbricated geopolitical pursuits—falls to the global police state as more and more of the global population is dispossessed of water rights through privatization (such as in the case of Bolivia in the 2000s) and cannibalization.

Securing the Minerals and Rare Earth Elements (REEs) for 21st Century Production

Like water and oil, the global police state can be deployed in the capital and geopolitical competition for the more common and rare-earth elemental ingredients (REEs) needed for high-tech industrial, commercial, and military production. These include minerals like lithium, nickel, and cobalt as base materials for battery storage of all sorts, and minerals like copper and aluminum as critical ingredients for the electrification of energy infrastructures and any "green" energy transition. They also include REEs like germanium (needed for high-speed microchips, night-vision, and satellites), gallium (needed for radar and satellites), or beryllium (needed for targeting and surveillance systems in fighter jets, for example) that despite their short supply are key ingredients for modern military and surveillance technologies. In fact, the US Geological Survey now tracks and lists the minerals "critical to US national, security, economic, infrastructure, and energy needs" (USGS 2022; Bazilian, Holland, and Busby 2023) every three years. In 2022 the list included 50 such minerals (17 are REEs) "essential to the economic or national security of the US and which has a supply chain vulnerable to disruption" (USGS 2022).

Minerals have become a key strategic resource in the current regime of capital accumulation, and for a global energy transition away from fossil fuels because they're paramount to the productive capacity of the most powerful nexus of transnational capital—that of finance, big tech (CIT) TNCs, and the transnational military industrial complex. But in order to obtain these strategic resources, much like the effort to obtain oil, various forms of dispossession—through (neocolonial) forms of "soft" economic power and the leveraging of debt, or of "hard" power in the deployment of state and state sanctioned violence—are used to guarantee supply chains for transnational capital. As previously discussed, primitive accumulation, accumulation by dispossession, and other forms of expropriation have historically been achieved primarily through a structural imbrication between capital accumulation and political state structures that provide the necessary legitimacy (through, for example, claims of humanitarian intervention or pursuit of national security interests) and means (RSA and ISA) for expropriation at scale. However, "both the United States and China are dependent on critical minerals sourced largely from outside their borders… in countries over which they are not sovereign" (Hendrix 2022). Many of these nations are relatively small, poor, and socially unstable, making them vulnerable to both hard and soft approaches to dispossession and expropriation at the hand of transnational finance capital and the global police state in their service.

We have previously discussed the devastating impacts of neocolonial extraction of cobalt in the ravaged DRC, which holds a majority of proven global reserves. Consider also the small West African nation of Guinea that has a quarter of proven global reserves (USGS 2022) and accounts for half of all global exports of bauxite (used in the processing of aluminum) (OEC 2023). According to analysts, this presents a situation where, "the possibility of controlling massive shares of global supplies through direct military intervention or use of extreme diplomatic leverage" (Hendrix 2022) is extremely high, and the lives and human rights of local populations are potentially deemed expendable.

From a human rights standpoint, this increases the dangers and chances of dispossession and other forms of expropriation that could extend to new (neo)colonial international relations and even to that of interstate wars, since, as previously discussed, capital accumulation and forms of (neo)colonial expropriation necessarily play out through the relatively persistent infrastructure and structural scaffolding of competitive imperial geopolitics under identifiable world orders. China currently dominates the geopolitical competition for extracting, processing, and conscribing strategic mineral resources into national and transnational circuits of accumulation through a soft power approach of direct investment and lending practices that—like in the case of the DRC—can materialize in what are arguably neocolonial relations of expropriation. China is invested in a vast global mining and processing network that controls 63% of all REE mining, processes 65% of cobalt supplies, over 66% of aluminum refining and smelting, 80% of lithium refining, and 80% of global graphite production and refining (Hendrix 2022; Runde and Hardman 2023). In contrast, according to analysists, the US "has too little production capacity and possesses too few of the world's reserves to entertain the idea of self-sufficiency" and would need the help of "partners and allies" to secure access to the raw/refined materials and component parts for critical supply chains (Runde and Hardman 2023).

This could happen in a number of ways, including increased economic cooperation and improved trade relations between the US and China, keeping in mind that many American, European, and transnational firms continue to rely on Chinese supplies of raw/refined materials and component parts. However, it could also manifest in increasingly belligerent trade and military relations between nuclear powers. Indeed, international tensions over the fate of Taiwan and the Taiwanese Straight has much to do with the supply of computing components required for modern commercial and military production for all nations, where Taiwan provides over 60% of all and 90% of the most sophisticated semiconductors to global markets (*The Economist* 2023). In October of 2022 the US banned the export of all advanced microchips to China, and has worked to bring microchip manufacturing to the US through the CHIPS and Science Act (*The Economist* 2023). China's begun a push for domestic microchip production as well (aiming for 70% domestic production by 2025), and in July of 2023 banned the export of gallium and germanium—both REEs that are needed for US defense industry supply chains (Eckert 2023).

While these tensions may be cause for concern, the deep interpenetration of Chinese and American capital ownership and global supply chains serves as a complicating factor in great power conflict in the traditional sense. In other words, Chinese and American policy (let alone the lives and investments of Chinese and American members of the TCC) are both heavily framed and driven by the interests of transnational capital (specifically the nexus of finance capital, high-tech TNCs, and the transnational military industrial complex) and the objective thrust of transnational accumulation. This does not eliminate the chances of conflict, given the sometimes unpredictable decisions made to resolve crises of legitimacy and the risks of an arms race, but makes an immediate "decoupling" seem far-fetched. To this point, US Under Secretary for Economic Growth and the Environment, Jose Fernandez insisted in September of 2023 that the US is "perfectly happy to work with [China] and right now we purchase many of the minerals from Chinese companies" (Marlow 2023), noting the need for Chinese supplies to fuel US transition to electric vehicles (EVs).

However, these circumstantial protections do not necessarily extend to comparatively poor sourcing nations—some still reeling from long histories with (neo)colonial expropriation. For instance, there's a competitive push to establish new relations with South American countries like Argentina, Bolivia, and Chile, that together hold approximately half of all proven lithium reserves, or Brazil, with the third largest (tied with Russia) reserves of REEs in the world (Runde and Hardman 2023). But what kind of relations are being (re-)established? Again, China has chosen a path of leveraging direct investment and debt to gain access to resources, having invested over $10 billion in Peru to control all of Peruvian iron and 25% of Peruvian copper production, and partnering in the purchase by Chinese firms of Argentinian lithium mines and lithium carbonite production projects (Runde and Hardman 2023). While these should not be mistaken for somehow altruistic or equitable relations by any means, US trade and political relations with Caribbean, Central, and South American neighbors have been comparatively brutal economic and overt/covert military interventions: in the imperial conquest of Caribbean and Central American (and Pacific Island) nations on behalf of American business interests (such as the United Fruit Company) in the late 19th and early 20th century at the hands of those like later-repentant conqueror Major General Smedley Butler (Katz 2022), the neoliberal experiments and coups in Argentina and Chile at the onset of GED in the 1970s, genocidal and wildly illegal interventions in Guatemala, El Salvador, or Nicaragua in the late cold war era, support for repressive right-wing regimes in nations like Columbia or Brazil, or in current crippling sanctions against those in countries like Venezuela—all leaving multi-generational trails of pain, dislocation, and death that are not easily forgotten.

If history is a guide, the US—on behalf of transnational capital interests—is willing to expropriate necessary resources or ensure access to source materials through projecting military or economic power, noting that economic and trade sanctions are often ultimately backed by military force and that the economic hegemony of the US continues to wane. Further, debt relations between China and source nations could devolve into more predatory neocolonial relations, particularly if internal economic crises continue in China and indebted nations and private sector entities remain unable to pay. For instance, China has been forced to cancel some of its infrastructure projects, raise interest rates, and shift from infrastructure to rescue lending to low- and middle-income debtor nations in the Belt and Road initiative (Bradsher 2023a, 2023b). In any case, whether or not the traditional practices and politics of extraction continue will have massive effects on the human rights and survival of populations in source countries. For example, the mining and refining of lithium and copper require a great deal of fresh water, yet over 50% of lithium production is in countries suffering from "high water stress" (shortage). Similarly, approximately 80% of Chilean copper mines are located in some of its driest regions (IEA 2022).

The global police state serves as the repressive force for disciplining the global working class and dispossessing certain populations of their labor, lives, land, and resources. In doing so, it plays important roles in legitimating and enforcing the evolving distinctions between those subject to "doubly free" wage labor and what seems to be an ever-expanding category of those subject to expropriation. The role of the global police state in the process should be understood as an extension of the traditional role of political state structures to provide the repressive apparatus or social control mechanism for both systemic racism and nationalism.

Policing the Racialized Boundaries of Exploitation and Expropriation

In addition to disciplining the global working class (consisting of exploited and expropriated labor), the global police state helps to define and serves to enforce the legal and political distinctions between doubly free wage labor with the full privileges of citizenship, and those constructed as somehow outside of rights protection and vulnerable to expropriation. For the most part, this is accomplished in two ways: first, in the enforcement of border policies and the greater politics of citizenship and nationality also fundamental to waging war; and second, as the social control component (typically through the criminal legal system) of systemic racism, keeping in mind that the boundaries between those who are full rights holding wage workers and those who are without rights have historically been drawn according to constructions of race and nationality.

One of the defining features of globalization "from above" since global economic restructuring has been the freeing of capital from the traditional constraints of national boundary or identity (see Armaline and Glasberg 2009; Robinson 2018a). Indeed, this was a necessary step in the creation or evolution of transnational capital and transnational circuits of accumulation. But globalization did not signal the end of nation-state borders or conceptions of national citizenship, as this was a freedom reserved only for capital and the TCC. For workers, national borders and distinctions of citizenship were to become militarized and weaponized such that working populations (and their unions) could be atomized and pitted against one another in competition for jobs and other material resources. This is the well-known history of off-shoring American manufacturing since the 1970's that accelerated after "free-trade" agreements like NAFTA in the 1990s, where corporations were given the freedom of movement in search of cheaper labor/production costs (including license to expropriate through the leveraging of international debt dependency and structural adjustment programs in the former Soviet empire and global South) while American workers were left behind and pitted against workers in the global South in competition for employment. Workers and indigenous groups resisted these changes vigorously—in, for example, the armed resistance of indigenous Zapatistas in the Mexican state of Chiapas in the 1990s and 2000s, and the various "anti-globalization" protests to disrupt meetings of the global power elite, such as the "Battle of Seattle" in 1999—but were ultimately unable to prevent such tectonic shifts in the regime of accumulation.

This feature of transnational financialized global capitalism, where capital is relatively free from the constraints of nation-state boundaries but labor is not, requires political state structures to create and enforce the politics of borders and citizenship as part of the disciplining of the global working class. To do so, ISAs create and legitimate border and immigration policies (through politics, media, and education, for example), and RSAs enforce those policies to make them real in the lives of those they're meant to discipline and control (through walls, checkpoints, security forces like US border control, expanding surveillance, intelligence and deportation forces like US Immigration and Customs Enforcement (ICE), and expanding immigrant detention facilities). The militarization and hardening of national borders, and the rightward trend of immigration policies around the world are increasing in the face of exploding migration created by the various internal and external contradictions of capitalist society and their resultant crises. Most important among them are the general crises of climate change and of widespread conflict and social instability.

Some have referred to this trend as one of "militarized global apartheid," where an historically racialized and otherwise hierarchical global labor market from exploitable to expropriable labor is created based on "differential access to mobility" and meaningful (rights holding) access to citizenship (Besteman 2019). Generally speaking, as wealthy and powerful nations in the global North (now arguably including BRICS+ powers such as China and Saudi Arabia) expand "systems of resource plunder" in source nations of the global South, they render those areas ecologically and socially "unsustainable for ordinary life" (Besteman 2019). We have so far discussed this in detail when it comes to the conquest of water, fossil fuels, and other strategic resources of the 21st century. However, in response, rather than developing appropriate, rights protective immigration policies in solidarity with affected populations and in line with international law, wealthy and powerful nations are instead "investing in militarized border regimes" (Besteman 2019) to control, restrict, or completely disregard those thrust headlong into crises of insecurity, migration, and generally increasing precarity among the global working class. These militarized border regimes are part of each state RSA and are connected as part of the global police state engaged in the disciplining of the global working class, including the enforcement of border politics and constructions of nation and citizenship.

To wit, the US has increased funding to its Customs and Border Protection (CBP) and Immigration and Customs Enforcement (ICE) forces every year since 2012, up to an annual price tag of nearly $25 billion by 2024—more than any other federal law enforcement agency (Akkerman 2023). EU spending on border security is also at record highs, and Frontex—the border patrol and coast guard agency for the EU—now receives more funding than any other EU agency (Akkerman 2023). This is recognized by analysts as part of a "worldwide trend" of "enforcement-first immigration policies" (Akkerman 2023) enacted in the face of economic (accumulation), ecological (climate change), and socio-political (such as migration) challenges. These polices have materialized in recent decades in the form of "militarized border technologies and personnel, interdictions at sea, biometric tracking of the mobile, detention centers, holding facilities, and the criminalization of mobility" (Besteman 2019). Researchers point to a "rapid proliferation" of over 74 border and separation walls over the last 20 years in places such as Poland, Turkey, Israel, and along the US-Mexico border, noting that there were less than a dozen such barriers when the Berlin Wall fell in 1989 (Vallet 2022).

We will return to migration crises in Chapter 5, but intend here to articulate the role of the global police state in policing nation-state borders and the politics of citizenship as part of broader functions to discipline and forcefully differentiate segments of the global working class. The global police state enforces ideological and legal notions of citizenship and who is deserving of rights protection and fundamental human dignities. In these ways it helps to designate, isolate, and politically subjugate populations of expropriable partial- or non-citizens in the eyes of structurally imbricated state and capital interests, regardless of international legal obligations to respect certain non-derogable human rights.

The construction (ISA) and enforcement (RSA) of nationalism and "who belongs" or "who counts" in society is a critical element of war and conquest in this way as well. As Singh (Singh 2017: 142) points out, "in race war and colonial war, there can only be one sovereign, and the opponent is not recognized as a political rival but rather viewed as an unjust enemy or a criminal." Once constructed as such, those dehumanized through criminalization and racialization are subject to virtually unbounded violence and theft at the hands of RSAs and the global police state. In the current period, this applies similarly to migrants forced to attempt death defying travel through the Darién Gap or across the Mediterranean Sea—increasingly constructed as criminals and illegal immigrants with little regard for the right of migrants to apply for asylum or receive humane treatment, those undergoing brutal conditions in US jails and prisons, and those in the crosshairs of US and allied "forever wars" against terror in the Middle East and Africa.

Because they are literally part of the same repressive state apparatus, and as demonstrated in the tight relationship between Israeli and US military and law enforcement agencies, it is common for military and police forces, and for "foreign policy and domestic politics" to "develop in a reciprocal relationship and produce mutually reinforcing approaches to managing social conflict" (Singh 2017:8). When it comes to internal or domestic politics, especially for settler colonial states like the US, the criminalization and dehumanization of those subject to expropriation is achieved through the criminal legal system. Recall from Chapter 1 that in the current regime of accumulation, criminal legal systems (part of the RSA) serve as the coercive social control component of both capitalism (such as in the protection of private property) and contemporary systemic racism (such as in the disparate criminal sentencing of Black Americans in the prison boom or surveillance of Muslim Americans following the 9/11 attacks on the US). Critical scholars argue that the primary institutional functions and origins of police in the US "are intimately tied to the management of inequalities of race and class" and "the suppression of workers and the tight surveillance and micromanagement of black and brown lives" (Vitale 2017).

There is an abundance of literature[10] from critical scholars and police/prison abolitionists on the role of criminal law, policing, jails, and forms of civil sanction in the criminalization and repression of populations of color in the US—Black, indigenous, and Latinx communities in particular. Much of this work has received considerable attention since the BLM movement and will not be recounted in detail here. That said, the disproportionate criminalization and sanction of Black, indigenous, and other populations of color (BIPOC) continues to be evident in relevant statistics. Though representing only 13% of the total population, Black Americans account for 38% of those in prison or jails, over 30% of those on probation or parole, and 48% of those serving life sentences (PPI 2023a). The disproportionate criminalization and incarceration of indigenous people in the US is also on the rise. Though representing a fraction of 1% of the US population, indigenous people make up 2.1% of those in jails and prisons and 2.3% of those on supervision or parole (Wang 2021). The number of indigenous people in American jails increased 85% since 2000, and in "Indian country" (native reservation) jail populations increased by 61% in approximately the same time period (between 2000 and 2018) (Wang 2021).

Moreover, as previously mentioned, police killed more people in 2023 than in any previous year in the last decade—continuing a trend of deadly police violence in the US (Levin 2024). According to considerable data by international public health experts, the burden of this state and state sanctioned violence "is known to fall disproportionately on Black, Indigenous, and Hispanic populations" (Sharara, Wool, et al. 2021). For instance, Black Americans are 2.9 times as likely as Whites to be killed in police encounters, such that an estimated 1 in 1000 Black men in the US will die from police violence (Mapping Police Violence 2023; Edwards, Lee, and Esposito 2021). Additional studies of public health data demonstrate that Latinx populations in the US are 1.33 times more likely to be killed by police violence than Whites, and that between 2011 and 2020 the Latinx population in the US grew by 18.3% while the number of them killed by police rose by 61.4% (Contreras 2023).

Those most targeted by police and most subject to incarceration in the US also represent some of the most impoverished, formally uneducated, and otherwise insecure working class people in the country. They are among the growing numbers of precarious "expropirable-and-exploitable citizen workers" (Fraser 2016, 2022) unique to the current regime of accumulation. Long standing critical criminological scholarship, such as Reiman and Leighton's (2023 [1979]) *The Rich Get Richer and the Poor Get Prison,* illustrates the many ways that the US legal system fails to sanction criminally (as opposed to non-, administrative, or civil actions) the wealthy for crimes of great significance to social stability and security (such as in the criminal fraud at the root of the Great Recession in 2008), while it is extremely successful in the criminal sanction of working class and unemployed people, even for crimes that have much smaller individual social impacts (property crime, interpersonal violence, petty drug sales, etc.). Others, such as Loic Wacquant (2009), point to the role of criminal legal systems and the project of mass incarceration in the US to socially control poor populations as neoliberal reform took hold and welfare benefits were drastically cut in the late 20th century.

The trend of criminalizing America's poor continues to be borne out in relevant data. On average, incarcerated people in the US earned annual incomes of $19,650 and $13,890 for men and women respectively at the time of their arrest—41% less than their counterparts of the same age (27–42) (Rabuy and Kopf 2015). Further, 39% of those incarcerated were unemployed within 30 days of their arrest, 42% of those in state prison came from a low income household that received public assistance, and those in state prisons are far more likely to have experienced homelessness than other adults of the same age (Wang, Sawyer, Herring, and Widra 2022). In terms of education, more that 75% of state prisoners, 59% of federal prisoners, and 69% of those in jails do not have a high school diploma or equivalent (Harlow 2003). Approximately 20% of the US prison population are former foster youth (state wards), and about 70% of foster youth are arrested at least once by the time they are 26 years old (Baron 2022). Finally, 43% of those in state prisons, 44% of those in US jails, and between 1/4th and 1/3rd of those shot each year in police encounters have been diagnosed with a mental health disorder (PPI 2023b). To this point, according to Los Angeles County officials, the L.A. County Jail has become "the largest de facto mental health institution in the US" since the "twin towers" facility opened in 1997 (Scauzillo 2023).

Unfortunately, there have not been significant changes in the racial and wealth disparities of American policing and imprisonment in recent years. To make matters worse, the conditions of incarceration have deteriorated considerably such that the human and Constitutional rights of those in the criminal legal system are in constant jeopardy. This is most striking and particularly concerning in a number of US jails, keeping in mind that over 2/3rds of those in jail have not been convicted of a crime and are awaiting trial (Dholakia 2023). Reporting from the Marshall Project describes a "complete meltdown" in jails across the country, pointing to problems with overcrowding, understaffing, abuse and the inability to ensure the safety of inmates or staff, and deteriorating physical conditions as facilities began once again filling to capacity in the wake of the COVID pandemic (Blakinger 2022). They point to cases such as the chaining of mentally ill prisoners to chairs for days at a time in L.A. County Jail, a suit against Southern Regional Jail in West Virginia over urine and semen being found in the food, the "crumbling infrastructure" of Fulton County Jail in Atlanta, GA, and the lack of clean drinking water in facilities like King County Jail in Seattle, WA. (Blakinger 2022).

These reports are joined by sickening case examples of the abuse and neglect of detainees awaiting trial, often ending in death. In 2021, a 29-year-old man suffering an apparent psychotic episode was placed in solitary confinement for three weeks without access to health care or a toilet in the Jackson County Jail (Indiana), and was found dead on the floor of his cell in his own waste, having passed from severe malnutrition (Ganeva 2023). In 2022, 35-year-old Lashawn Thompson, who suffered from schizophrenia, was placed in the psychiatric wing of the Fulton County Jail (Georgia) to await trial for a misdemeanor battery charge. Rather than exercise his Constitutional and human rights to due process, Mr. Thompson was found dead in his cell, having been completely physically infested ("eaten alive") with bedbugs and other insects in a cell so unsanitary that it was "not fit for a deceased animal" according to the family's attorney (Conklin 2023). In 2023, videos smuggled out of L.A. County Jail on a thumb drive revealed "a jail system awash in far more violence and disarray than previously revealed to the public" (Blakinger 2023). The videos showed countless stabbings, beatings, and fights with little response from guards, an inmate attempting suicide, inmates being beaten by guards, and even a detained woman giving birth in the middle of a hallway in a pool of blood on the floor (Blakinger 2023).

In response to the overwhelming evidence of racism, abuse, neglect, and substandard conditions in US carceral facilities, the UN Human Rights Committee called for a complete moratorium of life sentences without the possibility of parole (LWOP) in November of 2023, or what human rights advocates call "death by incarceration" in the US for the first time ever, on claims of racial discrimination and torture in violation of the ICCPR (CCR 2023b). In sum, it is not an exaggeration to suggest that the disparities and conditions of incarceration in the US amount to an ongoing human rights catastrophe with regard to protections under three US ratified instruments: the ICCPR (racial discrimination, torture), CAT (torture), and ICERD (racial discrimination). One's exposure to the carceral system has a great deal to do with whether or not one has the wealth/resources to escape it, and the extent to which one has been dehumanized, made subject to expropriation, and targeted by courts and law enforcement agencies in the overlapping constructions of race, citizenship, and criminality.

Police and other law enforcement agencies are part of the repressive apparatus of state political structures that are required to maintain both the foregrounded material relations and the background relations necessary for the continued accumulation of national and transnational capital. The multifaceted role of police in these regards can be difficult to understand or explain with appropriate sophistication. It is worth considering scholar Keeanga Yamahtta Taylor's (2021:108) definition of American policing to inform our understanding of their role in capitalist society:

> The police function to enforce the rule of the politically powerful and the economic elite: this is why poor and working-class communities are so heavily policed. African Americans are overrepresented among the ranks of the poor and the working class so police overwhelmingly focus on those neighborhoods even as they direct their violence more generally against all working-class people, including whites. But the police also reflect and reinforce the dominant ideology of the state that employs them, which also explains why they are inherently racist and resistant to substantive reform. In other words, if the task of the police is to maintain law and order, then that role takes on a specific meaning in a fundamentally racist society.

Rather than applying ham-fisted class or race reductionism, Taylor describes the central drive of police as an extension of the repressive apparatus of states (political state structures) not only to ensure capital accumulation, but also to preserve the social systems (such as systemic racism or patriarchy) that are inherently but not exclusively ideological (based on the socially constructed categories of race or gender), and essential to or symbiotic with the material relations of production. Taylor's approach is also notable in that it reflects an understanding of racism as a structural or systemic phenomenon that is in no way reducible to the biases or sadism of individual law enforcement officers.

To the extent that law enforcement agencies are meant to solve crimes in the US for the provision of public safety, data suggests that policing and mass incarceration have not been terribly successful in that regard. Mass incarceration in the US has been understood for some time now by scholars as an abject failure in reducing crime or addressing what are very real social problems, like gun violence or sexual assault. The Vera Institute describes this as the "Prison Paradox," where "the impact of incarceration on crime is limited and has been diminishing," and "increased incarceration has no effect on violent crime and may actually lead to higher crime rates when incarceration is concentrated in certain communities" (Stemen 2017). Still, states such as Indiana, Nebraska, Georgia, and Alabama are investing billions of dollars in expanding jail and prison construction despite grappling with high poverty rates and any number of competing budget needs (Gabbatt 2023).

Similar patterns characterize policing in the US. Between 1977 and 2020 state and local funding for police increased from $45 billion to $129 billion (Urban Institute 2023), and following the BLM protests in 2020 calling for defunding of police agencies, a vast majority of cities and counties actually increased the size and budget of police departments (Kummerer 2022; Manthey, Esposito, and Hernandez 2022). These increased investments continue, despite the fact that (for example) homicides decreased by 13% nationwide in 2023—marking the largest single year drop on record, and adding to evidence that the spike in crime rates during COVID were not indicative of broader or more lasting trends (Levin 2024). Massive facilities such as the $67 million so-called "cop city" in Atlanta, GA (Pratt 2023) and what has been called a $44 million "police playground" in San Pablo, CA (Lauer 2023) are being constructed to train law enforcement officers in what is arguably militarized urban counterinsurgency, despite considerable organized public resistance (Lennard 2023). On top of state and local budgets, the Biden Administration's "Safer America Plan" will fund an additional 100,000 police officers across the country (The White House 2022).

Yet, there is little data indicating that such growth in police forces increases public safety or reduces crime. In fact, research looking at the relationship between the size of police departments and crime rates between 1968 and 2013 found that the effect of larger police forces on crime is "negative, small, and not statistically significant," and that, "changing policing strategy is likely to have a greater impact on crime than adding more police" (Lee, Eck, and Corsaro 2016). Moreover, according to researchers, US Law Enforcement agencies "have never successfully solved crimes with any regularity" (Baughman 2021), as illustrated by clearance rates.[11] The clearance rate by law enforcement agencies for all violent crimes tends to be less than 50%, and less than 25% for property crimes (Laufer and Hughes 2021). In actuality, police in the US spend a majority of their time on officer-initiated stops ("proactive policing") and the enforcement of "routine, minor issues" (Kanu 2022; Smith, Graves, Guerrero, Ochoa, and Bitran 2022; Friedman 2021) rather than investigating reported crimes. This includes the deeply racist/classist practice of "stop and frisk" policing that was declared unconstitutional in 2013, but is once again growing at the hands of the NYPD in neighborhoods of color such as in Harlem (26th and 30th precincts), where only 4% of those stopped between 2003–2022 were White (Cleary 2023).

Beyond poor clearance rates, research suggests that at least 1% of those incarcerated for violent crimes and over 4% of those on death row have been wrongly convicted (Rubin 2023; Gross 2017). A stunning exposé by ProPublica (Rubin 2023) found that in Louisiana, where 82% of death sentences have been overturned since 1976 (Baumgartner and Lyman 2016), the 5th Circuit Court of Appeals—through a panel of all White judges—chose to casually disregard at least 5,000 petitions from prisoners who wished to challenge their conviction or sentencing—a vast majority of them Black, many indigent, who had "limited education and struggled to present their arguments in the language of the courts" (Rubin 2023). The scandal remained relatively unknown to the public until the 2023 ProPublica investigation, even though the staff member in charge of denying the petitions shot himself in his office in 2007 over his complicity in the matter, as made clear in a detailed suicide note that he distributed to members of the court.[12]

The problems of police violence or the failure of police in the US effectively to "solve" crimes or significantly impact crime rates have evaded most reform efforts. Despite calls to diversify police forces, provide police better training and professionalization, or develop "trust" in policing (Armaline, Vera Sanchez, and Correia 2014) through community policing and other such programs, there is little reason to believe that these approaches are effective. This is apparent from persistence of relevant statistics and from the fact that all of these reforms have been tried many, many times in the past. As Taylor (2021:118–119) illustrates beautifully in her historical examination of policing in the US, "dramatic changes in composition and professionalization have not had the effect of mitigating the tensions between police and Black communities," noting that, "the explosion of the incarceration of Black men, women, and children took place *after* the years-long effort to 'professionalize' and diversify the police." Liberal reforms to policing and the system of mass incarceration are not effective in these regards primarily because RSAs and the global police state exist in part to politically subjugate and repress those marked for expropriation in the maintenance of accumulation and social systems like systemic racism.

However, racialized populations of color and non-citizens are not the only populations forcefully differentiated as expropriable by the global police state. Women and trans/non-binary people capable of giving birth are also surveilled and criminally sanctioned by RSAs in the maintenance of the background relations of social reproduction. Since the overturning of *Roe v. Wade* by the US Supreme Court and the many statewide abortion bans that now exist across the country, women, trans/non-binary people capable of giving birth, and their friends, family, and associates are increasingly surveilled and some even criminally prosecuted for attempting to end their pregnancies on their own, or for acting as an "accomplice" to someone seeking to do so (Mansoor 2023). But even before the overturning of *Roe*, more and more women had been criminally prosecuted in the US on the basis of their pregnancy or the death of their unborn child. Ironically, this came as a result of "fetal harm" bills that were initially intended to protect pregnant people by making it a crime to harm a fetus (this is the case in at least 38 states in the US) (Baldwin 2022). However, these laws have since been used to criminally weaponize the construction of "fetal personhood" in an attempt to assert independent rights to an unborn fetus, separate from that of the person carrying the pregnancy. According to research by National Advocates for Pregnant Women (NAPW) and Fordham University, between 1973 and 2005 there were approximately 400 "cases where pregnancy, including pregnancy loss, was used in a criminal investigation" (Baldwin 2022). This number quadrupled between 2006 and 2020 to over 1,300 cases, and advocates anticipate that such arrests and prosecutions could rise to include those attempting to find or self-administer reproductive care (Baldwin 2022). In 2024 the Alabama Supreme Court expanded the concept of fetal personhood to include frozen human embryos like those used for in vitro fertilization (IVF), virtually prohibiting such procedures in the state. Perhaps notable, the concurring opinion of Chief Justice Tom Parker in the case (*Burdick-Aysenne v. Center for Reproductive Medicine*) referenced the word "God" 41 times, in what was basically a theological rather than legal or medical position taken by the Court (Mystal 2024).

One case held up by reproductive rights advocates and legal scholars as a possible warning of what is to come is that of Celeste Burgess. Celeste, a 19-year old from Nebraska, was sentenced to three months in jail for "concealing or abandoning a dead body" as a minor (17), after self-administering abortive medication obtained with the help of her mother beyond the 20 week ban in place at the time. Her 42-year-old mother was charged with a felony and sentenced to two years in prison for "aiding an abortion past 20 weeks of gestation and misdemeanor charges of false reporting and concealing human remains" (Hammel 2023). Prosecutors in both cases relied heavily on the private communications (via Facebook and other online platforms) between Celeste and her mother, who apparently discussed their plans to end the pregnancy. Though the Celeste case is an outlier in some respects (only 1% of all abortions in the US occur beyond 20 weeks of gestation (KFF 2019)), it marks a departure from prior norms of the US criminal legal system in three important ways. First, it demonstrates a breaking with prior claims that criminal prosecutions would be aimed at abortion providers rather than pregnant people. Second, it opens the door for aggressive criminal prosecution for those who assist or are "accomplices" in seeking abortions in states such as Nebraska, Texas, or Oklahoma that have included such language in their bans. Third, reproductive rights advocates note the chilling effect of surveilling the communications of pregnant people in that it scares people from seeking reproductive health information online, or from using online applications tracking ovulation, conception, or menstrual cycles for fear of their being surveilled by law enforcement (Baldwin 2022). At the end of the day, women and others capable of child birth in the US are subject to increasing levels of surveillance, intimidation, and coercion in such a way that curtails their lives, rights, and freedoms in comparison to others in society.

The state repression of women and pregnant people is nothing new in the US (Hira 2021; MacKinnon 1991) or in other nations around the world, as another function of the RSA is to police the overwhelmingly patriarchal and heteronormative background relations of social reproduction in the interests of capital accumulation. In the following chapter we will discuss the shrinking of reproductive and other rights for everyday people in the face of expanding corporate "rights" and power. For now, we simply mean to illustrate one of the many ways the RSA and global police state serve forcefully to differentiate expropriable populations, this time in the case of gender and (literal) reproduction.

Beyond enforcing the boundaries between exploitable and expropriable populations in the disciplining of the global working class, states' expanding investment and deployment of surveillance, police, prisons, militarized border security, and migrant detention centers should be understood as a source of capital accumulation via the most powerful nexus of transnational capital. In short, the global police state is big business for transnational capital in search for return on investment in the productive economy, where states and their publics often cut the check.

Militarized Accumulation and Accumulation by Repression

Militarized accumulation refers to when "a global war economy relies on perpetual state-organized war making, social control, and repression," and the "state-organized practices are outsourced to transnational corporate capital, involving the fusion of private accumulation with state militarization in order to sustain the process of capital accumulation" (Robinson 2022b:59). This global war economy encompasses what we have so far referred to as the transnational military industrial complex of state RSAs (military, police, intelligence agencies, border patrol and immigration enforcement, courts, etc.), transnational corporations in the defense and security industries that supply weapons and weapons technologies, and political actors, organizations, and think tanks who determine state policies and budgets. It comprises one third of the largest, most powerful nexus of transnational capital (with transnational finance and the other major transnational CIT firms) as one of the remaining consistent, large-scale sources of profitable investment in a global productive economy stricken by overaccumulation and other crises. Finally, the military industrial complex should not be understood as built on simple conspiracy, but through a confluence of interests that arise in the process of militarized accumulation between RSAs, private firms/contractors, and political actors. Interests evolve around the business of war, but also around the policing and surveillance of the global working class and resistance movements—what Robinson (2020:72) calls "accumulation by repression," and the business of rebuilding in the wake of violence and destruction—what Klein (2010) and Loewenstein (2015) have called "disaster capitalism."

These interests are fed to the extent there's an expanding weapons and security industry and a consistent stream of conflicts, as is currently the case. The market for worldwide border militarization is "worth an estimated US $48 billion in 2022 and on pace to grow to as much as US $81 billion by 2030" (Akkerman 2023). The private security market is projected to grow from $17.5 billion in 2022 to $36 billion by 2028 (Statista Market Insights 2023a), and the global cybersecurity market will expand similarly from $166.2 billion in 2023 to $273.6 billion in 2028 (Statista Market Insights 2023b). Global military spending reached a record high of $2.26 trillion in 2022, up 3.7% over the previous year due in no small part to the war in Ukraine (Tian, Da Silva, Liang, et al. 2023), with 2023 on track to top it. Further, the wars in Ukraine and Israel—among others—have created opportunities for forms of disaster capitalism (Klein 2010, Loewenstein 2015), where in the wake of natural disasters (such as extreme weather events linked to climate change) and wars, capitalists are able to exploit public shock and desperation in order to privatize formerly public resources/ services, avoid government regulation, tax, and other liabilities, and land lucrative contracts in any rebuilding efforts.

Transnational finance capital has already begun to sink its teeth into Ukraine, even while the conflict roils on. In March of 2023 the World Bank (2023) estimated that the reconstruction of Ukraine would cost approximately $411 billion over ten years—no doubt an underestimate given the persistence of hostilities since. So far, private equity giant BlackRock, JPMorgan Chase Bank, and the neoliberal McKinsey consulting firm are advising the Ukrainian government on the creation of a "reconstruction bank" that can be leveraged to attract significant investments from transnational capital (Masters 2023), and BlackRock's Financial Markets Advisory unit is leading the economic plan for Ukrainian reconstruction and recovery (Marcetic 2023). This gives all three transnational firms the first look at potential investment opportunities for themselves and their clients, while deepening existing relationships with the Ukrainian government. For instance, JPMorgan Chase had already helped to raise the $25 billion Ukrainian sovereign debt fund since 2010 and administered a $20 billion debt restructuring plan in 2022 (Masters 2023). Their influences were quickly felt, in that the Ukrainian parliament deregulated urban planning law to the benefit of private developers, weakened the bargaining power of labor unions, and reduced labor protections for a majority of Ukrainian workers by the end of 2022 (Masters 2023). Finally, the Biden Administration's appointment of former Commerce Secretary and billionaire Democratic donor, Penny Pritzker to serve as the US's "special representative for Ukraine's economic recovery" in September of 2023 signaled a desire of the US and transnational capital to ensure the country's recovery would provide opportunity for private investment (Crowley 2023). As the remaining military hegemon and most powerful coercive mechanism at the disposal of transnational capital, the US continues to dominate defense markets while ensuring that the destruction from conflict and crises translates into opportunities for capital accumulation.

The Repressive State Apparatus of the US and the Global Police State

The US commands the most powerful and expansive military force in the history of world orders, and its RSA is at the center of the global police state. The unprecedented reach and destructive power of the US RSA is expressed through an array of approximately 750 military bases across 80 countries (Hussein and Haddad 2021) and countless satellites dotting the night sky, together capable of delivering planetary annihilation from air, land, and sea. It is expressed internally through the ability and willingness to incarcerate nearly 2 million people (with another 800,000 on parole and nearly 3 million people on probation) (Sawyer and Wagner 2023), and through increasing investments into militarized law enforcement agencies, regardless of their ability to solve crimes or improve public safety. In addition to ensuring US hegemony and geopolitical dominance, the massive RSA of the US is at the center of the global police state first, because it is "the most powerful instrument in the arsenal of global capitalism" to protect the interests of transnational investors and repress any political forces that might threaten them or the system itself (Robinson 2020:75).[13] Particularly when viewed as part of a broader network of RSAs connected through treaties (NATO) and other formal security agreements, no other state or imperial power in history compares.

Second, the US is at the center of the global police state in terms of arms production and distribution. The US is by far the world's largest arms dealer, controlling over 40% of global weapons exports in 2022.[14] And US exports are at their highest rate since immediately following the fall of the Soviet Union—up 30% since 2012 (Lipton 2023b). It should be no surprise that arms sold by the US and affiliated weapons firms have not brought peace, stability, and human rights practice in their wake. Even though US policy technically prevents the distribution of arms to countries who would use them to commit international crimes, such regulations have not stopped the US from arming a majority of the world's autocratic regimes, such as the El Sisi regime in Egypt or the Kingdom of Saudi Arabia (Semler 2023). Though some arms are employed for what could be constructed as legitimate defensive purposes, two thirds of conflicts between 2017 and 2021 involved one or more parties that purchased arms from the US (Hartung 2022).

Third, the US is at the center of the global police state as the largest consumer of weapons and weapons technologies, spending more than any other nation on its military and broader RSA. Total spending on military, law enforcement, incarceration, and border/immigration enforcement in the US came to $1.1 trillion in 2023 (Koshgarian, Lusuegro, and Siddique 2023). In terms of internal repression, the US spends approximately $277 billion per year (over $759 million per day) on law enforcement agencies and incarceration. For perspective, this is approximately $25 billion more than Chinese *military* expenditures in 2020 (Semler 2022). And China is second only to the US in military spending. The US has the largest annual military budget by far—projected at $886 billion for 2024 (Center for Arms Control and Non-Proliferation 2023), accounting for over 39% of global spending, and more than the next 10 countries combined in 2022 (Tian, Da Silva, Liang, et al. 2023). This is on top of $14 trillion in Pentagon spending since the start of the war in Afghanistan and broader "war on terror" in 2001, one third to one half of which went to private military contractors. Due to the overwhelming public expenditures on defense and the capture of defense budgets by transnational capital, it is estimated that each US taxpayer contributes over $1,000 per year to defense contractors, while only $270 goes to funding public schools and only $6 goes to funding renewable energy development (Koshgarian, Siddique, and Lusuegro 2023).

Recall that militarized accumulation involves the outsourcing (privatization) of weapons production, logistics, and even war fighting to transnational capital. Nearly a third of US weapons contracts since 2001 went to five of the most dominant transnational firms: Lockheed Martin, Boeing, General Dynamics, Raytheon, and Northrop Grumman (Hartung 2021). The number of weapons contracts and stock values of these and other companies have risen predictably with the onset of wars in Ukraine and Israel, particularly given the US and EU pledges of military aid and the general ambiguity around how or when either conflict could end, or spiral into more protracted conflicts. According to a report by the Financial Times (Pfeifer and Sugiura 2023), the order backlogs of the 15 largest weapons contractors in the world were up 10% in 2022 to the highest point ($777.6 billion) since these statistics have been available, with 2023 on track to surpass it. The report also suggests that "the sustained spending spurred investors' interest in the sector," noting that over the same period the Morgan Stanley (MSCI) financial index for the international weapons industry was up by 25% and the European Stoxx index for aerospace and defense industry stocks was up a whopping 50% (Pfeifer and Sugiura 2023).

Less than a month after Israel declared war on Hamas in response to the Oct. 7th attacks, Raytheon (RTX) and General Dynamics stock prices spiked by over 10% in line with gains across the industry (Perez, Campbell, Warner, and Stockton 2023). RTX CEO Greg Hayes was clear on the benefit to his business and the direction of US defense spending from the two brutal conflicts: "I think really across the entire Raytheon portfolio, you're going to see a benefit of restocking.... On top of what we think is going to be an increase in DOD (Department of Defense) top line" (Perez, Campbell, Warner, and Stockton 2023). In earnings calls with investors, Chairman, President, and CEO of Lockheed Martin, Jim Taiclet, noted what we have so far described as the growth of the global police state in the face of an increasingly complicated and crises stricken global political economic order, commenting that,

> In the longer term there are things that are changing significantly. One is the global threat environment and the geopolitical situations getting more concerning and challenging.... That's refocusing the US and certainly our allies around the world on national defense in an increasing manner.
>
> (Goodkind 2023)

In addition to weapons production, private contractors have taken on an increasing amount of military logistics, security, and war fighting for and with US and allied forces. By 2011, the US employed more private contractors on the ground in Iraq and Afghanistan than actual military personnel. And by 2019 there were 50% more private contractors than military soldiers and administrators fighting and providing logistics in both conflicts (Peltier 2020). The expanding privatization of the US RSA and global police state is also evident from the records of other federal agencies. In fact, there are now more private contractors than government employees who conduct intelligence and other operations for the Central Intelligence Agency (CIA), Department of Homeland Security (DHS), and National Security Agency (NSA) (Peltier 2020). The expanded role of private contractors by the US and other states (such as Russia's employment of the former Wagner Group in the Ukrainian war and in neocolonial interventions on the African Continent) provides opportunity for militarized accumulation, but also provides cover for their employers. The use of private contractors, who do not share the same legal obligations as the state in sharing information with the public, allows for the human and economic costs of conflict to be shrouded such that the number contractors employed, injured, or killed is not transparent, nor is the flow of funding to what is typically a maze of contractors and subcontractors (Peltier 2020).

It is important to note here that the boost in profitability for transnational corporations in the military industrial complex can be relatively short-lived. For example, though Lockheed Martin and Northrop Grumman stock prices rose nearly 20% after the Russian invasion of Ukraine in February of 2022, most of these gains were lost in the following six months (Goodkind 2023). To the extent that the business of war provides a source of profitable investment amidst accumulation crisis, sustained profitability requires either more sustained commitments of states like the US to war spending (defense budget increases), or for global conflicts to increase significantly in size and frequency. This creates terrifying incentives for the unending increase in what become permanent war budgets, and for increasingly hawkish, militarized approaches to international relations.

The defense industry has seen these interests translated into policy realities in the US by spending over $100 million per year ($128 million in 2022) on an army of over 800 lobbyists at the federal level alone (Opensecrets.org 2023). They also spent $18.9 million on Congressional campaign contributions in 2022, over $5.8 million of which went to members of the House and Senate Armed Services Committees, who lead the creation of defense budgets (Giorno 2023). Beyond lobbying and campaign contributions, the relationship between actors in the RSA (such as military brass or DOD executives in charge of purchasing weapons), private defense firms in search for contracts (such as Lockheed Martin or RTX), and policy makers (such as Congressional members of the House Armed Services Committee) is that of a "revolving door" where one's public service in favor of industry interests is rewarded in later employment and other perks from the private sector.

To wit, a report from Senator Elizabeth Warren's office in 2023 (Warren 2023) found that almost 700 formerly high-ranking US military and government officials went on to work for private corporate defense contractors, 91% of whom became Pentagon lobbyists. The confluence of interest between the three major nodes of the transnational military industrial complex comes together in such a way that while legal, presents obvious opportunities for corruption, theft, and mismanagement. The DOD is still the only federal agency in the US to have never passed an audit, and in 2023 could not fully account for 63% of its over $3.8 trillion in assets (Gledhill 2023). To this point, a 2023 CBS News/60 Minutes report revealed widespread price gauging for products across the Pentagon budget, including Lockheed Martin and subcontractor Boeing's overcharging for Patriot PAC-3 missiles by hundreds of millions of dollars at a profit rate of 40% (Chasan 2023). Experts explained that widespread profiteering was due to the consolidation of defense contractors into the five transnational giants since the 1980's and the neoliberal policies of the defense department since, in minimizing government oversight of their activities (Chasan 2023).

Journalist Andrew Cockburn (2021) documents how defense budgets are continually expanded by the pursuit of new, high tech, expensive weapons systems regardless of their actual effectiveness or need in actual conflicts. They're pursued without proof of effectiveness because of "the military services' eagerness for ever more money, shared with the corporations that feed off them, and the officers who will cash in with high-paid employment with these same corporations when they retire" (Cockburn 2021:xii).

The reckless pursuit of advanced but unproven weapons systems includes the most expensive US defense project in history—the F-35 fighter jet program, contracted with Lockheed Martin (who also sell the warplanes to Canada, Germany, Japan, Israel, and Australia) that is now on track to cost over $1.7 trillion over the course of the program, and that is already over a decade behind schedule and $183 million over original budget estimates (Wolf 2023). To date, the F-35 has been unable to reach its "full operational capability," and depends on seemingly endless updates—even a new engine design—to function. In fact, the Pentagon's independent testing office found "more than 800 unresolved software and hardware deficiencies" in 2021 (Capaccio 2021), and experts now claim that the plane's design has been so unreliable that, "every F-35 built until now has been a very expensive prototype," at approximately $100 million apiece (Wolf 2023). Often for such advanced weapons systems, the US government owns the weapon, but not the data needed to repair them or produce spare parts. In the case of the F-35, the creation of spare parts is monopolized by a single subcontractor (TransDigm), whose CEO (Nick Howley) was called to testify for the second time in 2022 for price gauging after a review found the company charged the US government $119 million for parts worth $28 million—an upcharge of 425% (Chasan 2023).

Though some of the most expensive US weapons programs are never proven effective on the battlefield (Cockburn 2021), their production is often constructed by lobbyists and policy makers as successful domestic jobs programs. Though Lockheed Martin claims the F-35 program created almost 300,000 jobs in 48 states, data suggest that only half of those jobs actually materialized (Hartung and Freeman 2023). Systematic analysis of job creation in the US from the weapons industry reveals that defense spending creates far fewer job opportunities than other potential investments. Specifically, "education and healthcare create more than twice as many jobs as defense for the same level of spending, while clean energy and infrastructure create over 40 percent more jobs" (Garrett-Peltier 2017). It is fairly clear that what we see as a persistent growth in the US RSA and broader global police state is significantly driven by the objective thrust of capital accumulation rather than by the functional or cost effectiveness of defense industry products or the benefits of domestic job creation. Again, the global police state is big business, and the transnational military industrial complex serves as a remaining site of capital accumulation in the context of overaccumulation crisis and deepening global insecurity (Robinson 2020, 2022a). And while the US is positioned at the center of the global police state, integrated with other powerful state RSAs through treaties and security agreements, there is additional connective tissue between the US and even geopolitical rivals such as China, and indeed among all members of the TCC in their relationships to the most powerful nexus of transnational capital that, again, includes transnational finance capital, the major transnational CIT firms, and the transnational military industrial complex.

US Centrality and the Strong Connective Tissues of the Global Police State

Perhaps no other international relationship demonstrates the strong connective tissues between powerful RSAs at the center of the global police state like that between the US, NATO members in the EU, and Israel. The US provides Israel with at least $3.8 billion per year for military spending and missile defense systems (Sharp 2023), and has given Israel more in cumulative direct foreign assistance than any other country since WWII (Nasaw 2023). Moreover, the US is reportedly building a secret $35.8 military facility ("Site 512") on Mt. Har Qeren in the Negev desert designed to detect Iranian mid-range missiles and house up to 1,000 US military personnel (Klippenstein and Boguslaw 2023). The facility is only 20 miles from Gaza and is in the same local region as the Negev Nuclear Research Center that reportedly houses plutonium processing facilities and other "weapons-related infrastructure" (Atomic Archive 2023).[15]

Weeks into Israel's assault on Gaza in 2023, when the war crimes of the Israeli IDF had already become apparent to anyone with an internet connection, the Biden Administration approved a $320 million deal to provide precision-guided bomb equipment to Israel in partnership with Rafael Advanced Tactical Industries—an Israeli based weapons firm that equips the Iron Dome missile defense system and operates in the US (Rafael USA)—and the US based C4 Advanced Tactical Systems (Brewster 2023; US State

Department 2023). This is on top of an additional $14.5 billion in military aid the Biden Administration requested to help the Israeli war effort (Mascaro 2023). The outpouring of weapons and other military assistance to Israel came less than a year after the Administration declared its "Conventional Arms Transfer Policy" that restricts providing weapons to any nation where it is "more likely than not" that the weapons will be used on civilians, critical civilian infrastructure, or to commit "serious acts of violence against children" (Brewster 2023). *This demonstrates the deep hypocrisy of American exceptionalism, and the tendency for global hegemons—in our period, the US—to pose the greatest challenges to the very human rights philosophies and legal standards they construct to legitimate a world order under their imperial authority.* In addition to claiming that US-ratified international human rights and humanitarian legal instruments are "not self-executing" and secondary to US sovereign interests, the US is willing to contradict many of its own laws regarding human rights and humanitarian law whenever transnational capital accumulation or perceived geopolitical interests (again, structurally imbricated to accumulation) are at stake.

As illustrated thus far, Israel receives most of its arms from the US and US headquartered TNCs in the military industrial complex. However, since the start of the most recent war with Hamas, weapons sales/transfers from EU nations in partnership with Western based transnational firms skyrocketed. For example, Germany approved the export of approximately $343 million in weapons to Israel in November of 2023—ten times more than what the German government approved for the entire year of 2022 (Gaal 2023). Though the RSA of the US is at the center of the global police state, it absolutely includes the RSAs of other nations—particularly powerful EU nations like the German industrial powerhouse, tied through treaties (NATO) and the transnational military industrial complex.

In addition to typical arms sales, the US and Israel have signed several bilateral security agreements, engage in intelligence and military technology sharing, and participate in regular joint military exercises. For instance, Israel provides military logistical assistance to US forces in the region and vice-versa. Soon following the Hamas attacks the US moved two powerful aircraft carrier groups into the region in a stated attempt to thwart the intervention of other regional powers (namely Iran and Iranian backed groups like Hezbollah in Lebanon and the Houthis in Yemen) and provide support in the case of an evacuation (Copp and Baldor 2023a). Though not committing combat troops, the US sent special forces units who specialize in the retrieval of hostages and has committed another 2,000 troops who could be deployed as logistical support to the IDF (Copp and Baldor 2023a). By November of 2023, the US even announced the deployment of an Ohio class nuclear submarine to the region in an effort to intimidate other nations or armed proxies from jumping into the fray against Israel (Brennan 2023), noting its capacity to launch high-explosive ballistic and cruise missiles. The building of US naval forces in the region has first been to counter these various, semi-autonomous proxy groups, funded and armed to some extent by other state powers—namely Iran. But it has also been to police critical Red Sea shipping lanes in an attempt to protect transnational capital interests—including but not limited to fossil fuel companies. Indeed, due to drone and rocket attacks on shipping vessels and the US fleet by Houthi forces in Yemen, some of the most powerful shipping companies in the world (including CMA CGM, MSC, Ocean Network Express, and OOCL) suspended all activity in the Red Sea indefinitely by December of 2023 (Laudani, Niemiec, and Calero 2023). Following this, the US announced that it would lead a "naval protection force" along with the UK, Bahrain, Canada, France, Italy, the Netherlands, Norway, the Seychelles, and Spain to protect Red Sea shipping lanes and military assets in what's being called "Operation Prosperity Guardian" (Copp and Baldor 2023b). In response to continued strikes on shipping vessels that the Houthis claimed were aimed at forcing a ceasefire in Gaza, the US and UK carried out over a dozen of airstrikes in Yemen (notably without legislative approval) in January of 2024, further risking escalation to regional war (Stewart, Ali, and Ghobari 2024).

The Gang's All Here: Secondary Connective Tissues in the Global Police State

The RSAs of Israel, the US, and many EU countries are intertwined through a strong connective tissue of treaties and security agreements, but they are connected to each other and many more nations through the most powerful nexus of transnational capital—that of technology TNCs, big finance, and the transnational military industrial complex. This forms a secondary connective tissue where the US and states such as Israel also play crucial, central roles. Australian researcher Antony Loewenstein (2023) discusses Israel's role in supplying military and surveillance technologies to nations and despotic regimes all over the world with little to no regard for the rights record or intention of their customers. For instance, phone hacking software such as Pegasus (a product of the Israeli firm, NSO Group) was sold to governments such as Mexico, who then used the tool to spy on (and target) journalists investigating narco-state corruption. Drone technologies, such as the Heron drone sold to the EU or the Hermes drones sold to the US, have been used to militarize border security and control the flow of migrants (Loewenstein 2023). Despite their commendable calls for a cease fire and peace negotiations in both Israel and Ukraine, China was a significant recipient of Israeli military technology since the 1980s—even before recognizing the state of Israel (Gal 2019). Though the US has pressured Israel to limit the sale of Israeli or US technologies to China in the past 10 years of heightened trade and military tensions, trade in related commercial technologies (semiconductors) grew in that time (Gal 2019). In the same period, Israeli arms and technologies were sold to Myanmar in the brutal repression of Rohingya minorities, and to India for use in the territorial disputes over Kashmir.

Loewenstein (2023) convincingly argues that the basis of Israeli arms distribution is that they have been "battle tested" in the "laboratory" of repression and conflict in the middle east.

The exchange of such "battle tested" technologies and techniques extend to that of increasingly militarized police forces. For instance, law enforcement officers and executives from over 100 different agencies in the US and elsewhere have attended the National Counter-Terrorism Seminar, organized in part by the Anti-Defamation League in Israel since 2004 (Speri 2017), "to share best practices and lessons learned from international law enforcement counterparts in fighting extremism" (Blades 2018). Second, the relationship between US and Israeli police and military forces has yielded similar patterns of human rights abuses in the Israeli policing of Palestinians and US policing of BIPOC and poor people in the US. A US Department of Justice report (2016) on the Baltimore Police Department in the wake of public rebellion over the murder of Freddie Grey by their officers in 2015 found "widespread constitutional violations, discriminatory enforcement, and a culture of retaliation." Soon after, Amnesty International reported (Garwood 2016) that Baltimore law enforcement officials, along with "hundreds of others" from at least 11 other states and the District of Columbia had traveled to Israel for trainings, while "thousands of others have received training from Israeli officials" in the US. Justified as part of counterterrorism efforts, the NYPD opened a branch in Israel "to learn from foreign authorities and situations that arise overseas," according to one participating detective (Hartmann 2012), and continues to exchange information, training, and techniques with Israeli counterparts.

In the big picture, the Israeli police state or RSA—along with many others—is part of a much larger security structure understood conceptually as a global police state. Israel is one place where the technologies of repression are developed as a source of militarized accumulation and as tools for accumulation by dispossession and the forceful distinction between exploitable and expropriable labor in that process. These tools are then sold and made available for deployment elsewhere through global trade in arms and technologies through the transnational military industrial complex. Indeed, the transnational military industrial complex and the powerful nexus of capital of which it is a part provide the secondary connective tissues of the global police state that now intertwine nearly *all* state RSAs across the geopolitical spectrum.

Some of the most confounding aspects of contemporary geopolitics have to do with the extent to which a) the RSAs of even competing states or imperial powers are heavily integrated in and through the transnational military industrial complex; and b) the owning and ruling class—the TCC and global power elite—all share economic interests through their investments in the transnational military industrial complex and the larger nexus of transnational capital of which it is a part. This is most relevant and apparent in the relationship between the US and China, in which geopolitical tensions are present while the two countries and their contingents of the TCC are locked into many of the same transnational circuits of accumulation.

Rising geopolitical tensions between the two countries have given rise to talk in the US of "decoupling" with China, but it is not so easy to un-ring the bell of economic globalization. In response to these calls, US Treasury Secretary Janet Yellen remarked that efforts to decouple would be "destabilizing for the global economy" and "virtually impossible to undertake" from a practical perspective (Rappeport 2023). For this reason, many US politicians and business leaders have chosen a discourse of "de-risking" or "diversifying" supply chains to reduce dependence on Chinese productive capacities (Rappeport 2023). Both countries have pursued diversification strategies when it comes to points of contention like microchip production or the sourcing of REEs. But this has been complicated, and it has become even more difficult to imagine how military conflict between the two powers would play out, given the integration of both militaries through a transnational military industrial complex.

Corporate leaders of defense industry TNCs have also been quite clear about the delusions of immediately decoupling ties. Even before committing additional resources to the war in Israel, the US had considerably drawn down its own weapons stocks to supply the Ukrainians in their war with Russia (Lipton 2023a). With military and trade tensions with China rising at the same time, many in the Western press asked whether the US would be capable of fighting a war with China given the drain from conflicts in Ukraine and Israel and the lack of a robust, independent supply chain for US ammunition and weapons systems (Ashford and Kroenig 2023). In an interview with the Financial Times (Pfeifer 2023), Chairman and CEO of RTX, Greg Hayes asserted that it would be "impossible" for his and many other companies to completely decouple from China, noting that RTX had "several thousand suppliers in China" and that firms still rely on China for a majority of processed REEs. This is not unique to RTX, and it illustrates the realities of a transnational supply chain to arm an increasingly integrated global police state. Not unlike the major, trillion dollar+ CIT firms such as Apple Inc. or Alphabet (parent company of Google) discussed in Chapter 1, the operational and ownership structures of transnational defense contractors demonstrate how "global financial circuits are so thoroughly integrated and entangled that it becomes nearly impossible to separate out national circuits in an analysis of militarized accumulation" (Robinson 2020:75–6).

In terms of ownership structure, the connective tissue between the RSAs of the US and China, and between the US and Chinese contingents of the owning and ruling class appear in their overlapping investments, and thus, relatively congruent economic interests. Robinson (2020:75–6, 2022a, 2022b) goes to great length in his work to illustrate these entanglements:

Chinese transnational capitalists and the state-party elite are deeply integrated into global financial circuits and invested in global banking conglomerates that in turn are interlocked with the US-led military-industrial-complex.... Blackrock, for instance, holds major investments in Lockheed Martin, Northop Grumman, and Boeing and also in the Bank of China, China Communications Construction Corp, China Construction Bank, China Rail Engineering, PetroChina, and so on.

This is not unique to the Chinese contingent of the TCC, in that all of transnational capital has become dependent to some considerable extent on militarized accumulation in the context of overaccumulation crisis. The TCC and global power elite are "not just heavily invested in [the] global police state but they are cross- and mutually invested in it" (Robinson 2020:20).

Arguments that the US can or should decouple from China seem to be rooted in an outdated understanding of capitalism and its relationship to geopolitics and international relations. Assumptions about inevitable conflict between the great powers in imperial competition are complicated (but certainly not prevented) by their mutual, cross-investment in the same transnational circuits of accumulation that also finance and equip the global police state. Perhaps the most critical point here is that, through this integration and cross-investment in pursuit of militarized accumulation, the material interests of the TCC across the geopolitical spectrum combine with existing structural pressures (previously discussed) to expand the global police state and its deployment around the world, presenting direct and indirect threats to human civilization as we know it.

The Global Police State and OTHS

Much of this chapter has been dedicated to describing the roles of and reasons behind the global police state in contemporary capitalist society, and how its growth and deployment often spell disaster for human rights practice. But the expansion of the global police state in its capacity to discipline the global working class, police the forceful distinctions between exploitable and expropriable labor, and provide for militarized accumulation in the context of overaccumulation crisis also manifest as OTHS—representing what should be the greatest, most fundamental concerns of the human rights enterprise.

Nuclear War, Weapons Proliferation, Forced Migration

The growth and deployment of a global police state manifests as a direct threat to human civilization through: a) the increased chances of nuclear apocalypse from the proliferation of nuclear weapons, the weakening of nuclear arms treaties and diplomatic safeguards, and increased tensions between armed powers; b) the destabilizing effects of conventional weapons proliferation; and c) the destabilizing effects of massive forced migration due to overlapping crises of conflict and climate.

Recall that the Bulletin of Atomic Scientists set their "doomsday clock" to 90 seconds before midnight, indicating that the world is closer to catastrophic nuclear conflict than ever before (Mecklin 2023)—even more so than during the Cuban Missile Crisis or following the first tests of thermonuclear weapons. This is partly due to the fact that there are very few remaining treaties to limit the production or use of nuclear weapons between the largest nuclear powers—the US, Russia, and now China. The application of strong arms control agreements was the primary strategy in successfully reducing the global nuclear stockpile from a climax of over 70,000 warheads in 1986 to the current count of approximately 12,500, with the vast majority of them held by Russia (5,899 warheads) and the US (5,244 warheads) (*The Economist* 2023a).

The US has done a great deal to undermine these prior norms and agreements, first by pulling out of the Anti-Ballistic Missile Treaty in 2002, and then the Intermediate-Range Nuclear Forces Treaty in 2019 (*The Economist* 2023a). What remains is the New START treaty that went into effect in 2021 and will expire in 2026, at which point there would be no nuclear arms control agreements between the two nations without renewal. Though New START limits each nation's larger, long distance "strategic" nuclear weapons, these limits do not apply to the smaller, so-called "tactical" nuclear weapons that are more likely to be used on a live battlefield. New START established safeguards such as a direct link and line of communication between the Nuclear Risk Reduction Centers (NRRCs) of the US and Russia and 6-month updates on each country's nuclear stockpiles (*The Economist* 2023a)—both of which have come to an end following Russia's invasion of Ukraine. In February of 2023 Russia suspended their participation in New START, ending notifications between NRRCs. The US followed suit soon after in March and June of the same year. Though there are some remaining channels of communication between them, such as the announcement of ballistic missile tests and the use of direct communication between the US State Department and the Russian Ministry of Defense (*The Economist* 2023a), the ability for communication between the two state powers to divert nuclear escalation has been severely constrained.

The need for such safeguards has been made abundantly clear throughout the war in Ukraine, where Russian leadership has repeatedly threatened to use nuclear force. In July of 2023, former President Medvedev argued that they "would have to use nuclear weapons" if Russian annexed territories in Ukraine were under threat from a successful Ukrainian advance. This followed a statement by President Putin in September 2022, declaring Russia's willingness to use "all means at its disposal" to defend territorial gains (Lieber and Press 2023). Such statements were accompanied by a move to position nuclear weapons to Belarus, marking the first time since 1991 (then the USSR) that Russia deployed warheads in a foreign country.

Though not making explicit threats of nuclear attack, the US and allied NATO forces are also engaged in risky, escalatory provocations. For example, in fall of 2023 combined NATO forces engaged in their largest military exercises since the Cold War, deploying over 50 naval ships, 40,000 military personnel and countless air combat simulations in Germany and Poland (Hancock 2023). This is in the context of considerable expansion of the NATO alliance, broadening and further integrating the primary military forces of the global police state in service of capital accumulation and the structurally imbricated drive to maintain the American hegemonic world order. According to analysts and even Putin himself (Benjamin and Davies 2022), the continued expansion of NATO closer and closer to Russian borders was a major factor, along with bolstering the Putin Administration against internal crises of legitimacy, in the Russian decision to forcefully annex Crimea in 2014 and invade further into Ukraine in 2022. To address both, Russian leadership has repeatedly called out what they see as a betrayal of US promises apparently made in the 1990 negotiations for German unification that NATO would move "not one inch" east of Berlin (Benjamin and Davies 2022). Since then, NATO expanded to 14 additional nations further into Europe and the former Soviet empire under Democratic and Republican Presidential administrations alike (Hancock 2023). Rather than stop this expansion, the 2022 Russian invasion actually spurred the acceptance of Finland to the alliance in 2023, considerable increases in military spending among NATO members, and the inclusion of Sweden in 2024. Rather than cause for increased efforts toward peaceful diplomacy or the respect for international law, the conflict in Ukraine—arguably a proxy war between Russia and NATO in many respects—has predictably yielded an expansion of NATO forces, increased military spending and militarization across Europe and the former Soviet empire, and considerable insecurity when it comes to the possibilities of greater regional or nuclear conflict.

Insecurity of this kind is also the result of what is now trilateral competition among US/NATO, Russia, and China on nuclear and other weapons technologies. In November of 2023 Russia withdrew its ratification of the Comprehensive Nuclear Test Ban Treaty (CTBT), arguing that the move would bring them in line with the US and China, who never ratified the treaty (Osborn 2023). There is currently no nuclear arms control agreement that includes China—the world's most quickly rising military power when it comes to both conventional and nuclear weapons. China now has some of the most advanced military technologies available, and has built the world's largest naval fleet, with over 340 warships that now provide the ability to project military power beyond territorial waters (Lenden and McCarthy 2023). Though current Chinese nuclear stockpiles are estimated at 410 warheads, China is on track to more than triple that supply to 1,500 warheads by 2035 (*The Economist* 2023a). Previously limited to land-based missile silos, China is now developing a nuclear triad system similar to those of the US and Russia, including a new long range strategic bomber and at least six nuclear powered ballistic missile submarines. This is in addition to relatively novel delivery technologies, such as a hypersonic fractional orbital bombardment system with an unlimited range and ability to travel and deliver a strike from above the Earth's atmosphere (Brookes 2023).

Russia is also modernizing their nuclear arsenals through the development of nuclear-powered cruise missile technology (Mellen 2023) and the successful development and deployment (in Ukraine, though not with a nuclear warhead) of hypersonic missiles (Kelly 2023). Not to be outdone, the US is modernizing its nuclear triad system at an estimated cost of over $1.5 trillion, replacing older weapons, advancing new technologies, and investing in mining and processing the plutonium necessary for modern warheads (Streep 2023). For instance, the US will replace its Minuteman III intercontinental ballistic missiles (ICBMs) with the new Sentinel missile system developed by Northrop Grumman for $100 billion, that can operate beyond Earth's atmosphere (Streep 2023; Bugos 2022). By sea, the US will supplement its Ohio class nuclear sub fleet with new Columbia class nuclear subs at a projected cost of over $127 billion. And by air, the US is purchasing new strategic bombers (dubbed the B-21 Raider, also by Northrop Grumman) for $203 billion that will replace previous B-1 and B-2 aircraft (Bugos 2022).

The proliferation and modernization of nuclear arms is not limited to these top three nations. Taking a lesson from the fates of Saddam Hussain in Iraq and Muammar Gaddafi in Libya, many nations have turned to nuclear deterrence against the chances of US military intervention. North Korea has an estimated 20–30 nuclear warheads and is very close to successful development of ICBMs capable of reaching the Western Hemisphere, while Iran is now believed to have enough nuclear fuel to build a nuclear warhead after there was a failure over multiple US Administrations to revive the Iran nuclear deal (Lieber and Press 2023; Center for Arms Control and Non-Proliferation 2022). Further, much of the expansion and modernization of nuclear arsenals involve smaller, "tactical" weapons with reduced payload that are intended for what is called "coercive nuclear escalation," where tactical warheads are deployed on the battlefield to shock and deter an aggressing opponent with significant conventional military might. This has been the strategy of NATO against Russia for some time, and is now the strategy of other nuclear players such as Pakistan against a larger, more powerful foe like that of the Indian military (Lieber and Press 2023). Though the use of smaller warheads might appear to reduce the chances of planetary annihilation, they actually serve to increase the chances that nuclear weapons will be used at all, thus boosting the chances of escalation to full-scale nuclear conflict.

Short of nuclear apocalypse, the world is being destabilized by a proliferation of conventional weapons and their use in conflicts, crime, and interpersonal violence. According to research by the Armed Conflict Location and Event Data Project (ACLED), cases of armed political violence increased by over 27% over the course of 2023, such that one out of six people on the planet are directly exposed to armed conflict (ACLED 2023). Even before Israel's assaults on Gaza in response to Hamas attacks in 2023, data revealed that 84% of casualties in the world's many conflicts were civilians (22% more than during the Cold War), and that attacks on health care facilities were up an incredible 90% (Miliband 2023), signaling a failure of humanitarian law to safeguard against the toll of war on innocent civilians. Scholar Samuel Moyn (2021) argues that the choice of those in the US and the international legal community to center their focus on the rules of warfare and somehow more humane forms of warfighting has displaced international efforts to avoid war altogether, and has not actually prevented the greatest potential tragedies of war. Not interpreted as an assertion that humanitarian law is completely irrelevant, it is hard to argue with Moyn's central point, as the US continues to undermine directly and indirectly both efforts at peace and at abiding to international humanitarian and human rights law during periods of conflict. This is abundantly evident in the US and allied invasion of Iraq and in the ongoing US and EU backed Israeli bombardment of Gaza and settlement of the West Bank, but also evident in less discussed regions of US military activity and geopolitical competition for 21st century resources.

Journalist Nick Turse, who has covered the often-ignored US "forever war" against terror across the African Continent, documents the nearly 20+ year effort by the US to

> provide copious amounts of security assistance, train many thousands of African military officers, set up dozens of outposts, dispatch its own commandos on all manner of missions, create proxy forces, launch drone strikes, and even engage in direct ground combat with militants in Africa.
> (Turse 2023)

Much of this activity has been done with the relative ignorance of the American public and much of Congress. This is in part due to the fact that several US interventions in African nations have often been carried out through secretive programs such as those operating under what's called 127e ("127-echo") authority. Under 127e, "the US arms, trains, and provides intelligence to foreign forces," who are then "dispatched on US directed missions, targeting US enemies to achieve US aims" (Turse and Speri 2022b). It follows with a strategy of training and arming local forces against those deemed a threat to US and broader capital interests in nations already grappling with incredible economic, social, and political challenges.

The decades of US and allied military counterterrorism efforts in Africa can only be described as a catastrophic failure on the numbers. As Turse (2023) points out, there were only nine recorded terrorist attacks in all of Africa at the start of the war on terror (2002–03), yet the Pentagon counted 6,756 terrorist attacks across the Continent by militant Islamic groups in 2023 alone, amounting to a dizzying 75,000% spike in annual attacks. Not only did the arming and training of more and more military forces not prevent terrorist attacks, it in some cases may have empowered those committing international crimes, such as the continued arming of the Cameroonian Rapid Intervention Battalion in 2019, long after evidence had surfaced of their committing mass atrocities, "including extrajudicial killings" (Turse and Speri 2022a). In fact, it is exceedingly difficult to find any region in the world where the approach of military intervention and the arming of proxy forces through the war on terror has succeeded in reducing terrorist attacks, or improving security or stability anywhere it was deployed. The expansion and deployment of the US RSA and the larger global police state has instead done a great deal to destabilize and militarize societies to the detriment of human rights and the central thrusts of the UN Charter to bring about a more peaceful world.

The effects of flooding regions with weapons are also readily apparent in former and current warzones. When the US finally ended its 20-year war in Afghanistan, more than $7.1 billion in equipment was left behind, including combat vehicles, over 316,000 weapons, and countless stores of ammunition (Kathju 2023). These weapons first bolstered the military power of the Taliban, who have since re-established hyper fundamentalist rule over the country, committing crimes against humanity in their persecution of women, girls, and religious/ethnic minorities (HRW 2023a). Second, it was not long before the US weapons were then sold to other armed groups, many of whom are engaged in conflicts of their own, such as Pakistan-based separatists in the disputed Kashmir region on the border with India (Kathju 2023).

In the case of Ukraine, the tidal wave of weapons and financial military support from the US and NATO allies provided opportunity for corruption and war profiteering. For instance, at one point in 2023, "about $980 million in weapons contracts missed their delivery dates… and some prepayments for weapons had vanished into overseas accounts of weapons dealers" (Kramer 2023). In fact, even before the Russian invasion, the Ukrainian military and many other state agencies were struggling with long-standing problems of corruption, and soon after the war began multiple Ukrainian officials were fired, arrested, and/or investigated for overpaying for basic supplies (like eggs) or taking $10,000 bribes to avoid military recruitment (Kramer 2023). Aside from war profiteering, officials at Interpol point to the inevitability that many of the weapons deployed in the Ukraine war will ultimately resurface on the international black market, where they can be sold to non-state militias and criminal organizations (Willsher 2022). According to Interpol Chief Stock, "Once the guns fall silent [in Ukraine], the illegal weapons will come" (Willsher 2022). In other words, once you flood the zone with weapons they don't suddenly disappear when conflicts cease—they remain, or are sold off for use elsewhere.

The destabilizing effects of weapons proliferation are even more obvious in the case of mines and unexploded ordinance that can leave generations of carnage, long after wars officially end. This has been the case in Vietnam and Cambodia following the US-Vietnam war, and is shaping up to be the case in Ukraine—now the most heavily mined country in the world. Land mines now saturate an area of Ukraine approximately the size of Florida, and experts say that it could take over a hundred years after combat ends to safely clear the area, given current conditions and equipment (Beale 2023). In addition to land mines, Ukraine is littered with unexploded ordnance, such as from internationally banned (the US, Ukraine, and Russia are not party) "cluster bombs" deployed by both Russia and Ukraine (provided by the US) in the conflict. As a result of their use in the Ukrainian war, civilian and other deaths from cluster bombs were higher in 2022 than in any other year since monitoring began with their banning in 2008 (Farge 2023). Finally, as were used with long-lasting effects on civilians and military personnel in Iraq and Afghanistan, the US has been providing Ukraine with armor-piercing, depleted uranium shells. During and long after their use, their radioactive and toxic residues cause death, cancer, and birth defects, as they fill the air and pollute the soil and groundwater (Stone 2023).

But the reach of contemporary weapons proliferation goes well beyond that of active warzones, and has served to significantly destabilize civil society in the US and elsewhere. For example, the Lake City Army Ammunition Plant was built in Independence, MO during WWII, and has since provided almost all rifle cartridges for the US military. However, operating as a private firm with the freedom to sell for profit in commercial markets, Lake City has also become one of the largest providers of military grade rifle ammunition to private gun owners in the US and overseas (Dooley and Rhyne 2023). Though a great deal of this ammunition was presumably sold to law abiding gun owners, one impact of proliferating the ammunition used in popular assault rifles like the AR-15 platform has been to fuel the incredible epidemic of gun violence in the US. According to a New York Times Investigation in 2023 (Dooley and Rhyne 2023), Lake City ammunition was used in at least a dozen mass shootings in the US, including the 2012 movie theater massacre of 12 people in Aurora, CO, and the high-profile shootings at the Tree of Life synagogue in Pittsburgh (the deadliest anti-Semitic attack in US history), the Marjory Stoneman Douglas High School in Florida, and the Robb Elementary School in Uvalde, TX. The ammunition is popular among law abiding and more nefarious consumers alike for their reliability and effectiveness. In fact, the white supremacist who murdered Black and other customers in a Buffalo supermarket previously discussed in this book, mentioned the use of Lake City ammunition in his written manifesto as "the best barrier penetration ammo" he could get (Dooley and Rhyne 2023). But the impacts of saturating commercial markets with military grade ammunition for military grade assault rifles has also been to arm organized criminal activity. According to the report, "Lake City rounds have been seized from drug dealers, violent felons, antigovernment groups, rioters at the US. Capitol, and smugglers for Mexican cartels" (Dooley and Rhyne 2023). On the whole, the Lake City plant serves as an example of the accumulation drive behind weapons production and the destabilizing effects of weapons proliferation from their commercial sale.

Finally, global weapons proliferation and the conflicts and criminal activities putting such weapons to use have contributed to the global migration crisis mentioned in prior chapters, and that will be explored in further detail in Chapter 5. That being said, signs of this crisis, driven almost entirely by the overlapping impacts of war and climate change illustrated throughout this book, are all around us. According to the UN Refugee Agency (UNHCR) Global Trends Report (2023), more people (108.4 million, or 1 in every 74 people on Earth) were internally or externally displaced in 2022 than at any time in recent history, marking a record breaking increase of over 19 million since 2021. Some of this increase was due to the 5.7 million people who attempted to flee conflict zones and military conscription in Ukraine following the Russian invasion. That said, 2023 is likely to top this record, as the war in Ukraine continued, conflict in Israel displaced over 1.6 million Palestinian residents of Gaza (OHCHR 2023b), and civil wars raged in impoverished countries awash in weapons rather than the resources needed for human flourishing. In Sudan, where half of its 46 million inhabitants already require international aid to survive, civil war has resurfaced in the Darfur and Khartoum regions, where "people are dying like insects" according to aid workers (the count at seven months of fighting was over 10,400 casualties), and just under 5 million people have been internally displaced, with another 1.2 million forced to migrate to bordering Chad, South Sudan, and Egypt (Walsh and Latif Dahir 2023). In the impoverished and civil war-torn DRC, a record 6.9 million people have been internally displaced, and "conflict has been reported as the primary reason" according to the UN International Organization for Migration (VOA 2023).

A growing global police state, including but not limited to the US RSA and allied forces at its center, poses a direct threat to human rights and survival through the terrifying potential of nuclear war and the incredibly destabilizing effect of weapons proliferation on any efforts toward lasting peace and security for civilian populations. Beyond this, the expanding US RSA and global police state pose indirect, overlapping threats to human rights and survival, such as the consumption of fossil fuels, the emission of greenhouse gasses contributing to climate change, and destruction of the ecosphere through forms of pollution.

Greenhouse Gas Emissions and Ecological Destruction

If species survival is dependent on ending the use of fossil fuels to achieve "net zero" carbon emissions, two significant barriers to this goal will be the continued dependence of the US military and other RSAs on hydrocarbons, and the tendency of war itself to invite ecological disaster. To the later point, in just the first year of fighting in Ukraine, 120 million tons of greenhouse gasses (equal to the annual output of Belgium) were released from military operations, related forest and other fires, gas leaks from (for example) the sabotage of the Nord Stream pipeline, and as projected for the necessary rebuilding efforts once the fighting is over (Mcfarlane and Volcovici 2023). This is to say nothing of the polluting effects of military operations and spent ordinance on Ukrainian air, soil, and water, or the potential ecological catastrophe that could accompany an accident at facilities like the Zaporizhzhia Nuclear Power Plant, which has repeatedly come under threat throughout the war according to the International Atomic Energy Agency (IAEA) (Kullab 2023). Data suggests similar climate consequences from Israel's war in the Gaza Strip, where the first two months of fighting produced emissions equal to the burning of over 150,000 tons of coal or the total emissions of more than 20 of the world's most climate-vulnerable nations (Lakhani 2024a). Given the ecological impacts of modern warfare and the levels of cooperation required to tackle climate change as an OTHS, the path to avoiding general systems crisis must be one of peace.

Second, the US military is the largest single consumer of oil (Lewis 2021) and one of the largest single institutional sources of greenhouse gas emissions in the world. In fact, "if the US military were a nation state, it would be the 47th largest emitter of greenhouse gasses" (Lewis 2021). According to research by Professor Neta Crawford with the Brown University Costs of War project, (Crawford 2019), between the start of the war on terror in 2001 and 2017, the US military produced 1.2 billion metric tons of greenhouse gasses, equivalent to the annual emissions of 257 million passenger cars (twice the number on the road today in the US). In her book on the subject, Crawford explores (2022) what she describes a "deep cycle" of American economic and military policy, where endless economic growth and military supremacy have traditionally been pursued through ensuring US industrial and military access to fuel (oil and other hydrocarbons since the 20th century), and attempting to deny access to perceived enemies. This was part of the geopolitical calculus behind the disastrous US and allied invasion of Iraq, and continues to frame US national security strategies. However, that approach is now being confronted by the complications of climate change and changes in what are understood as the critical strategic resources of the 21st century. In response, the US national security sector is actively focusing on "their own vulnerability to the effects of climate change, how climate change may affect the capacities of other states and increase conflict, and more recently, their own strategies for reducing their own emissions" (Crawford 2022:17). This has meant changing geopolitical analyses such that climate change is taken into account as a potential "threat multiplier," analyzing the impacts of climate change such as heat and ocean level rise on existing military installations, and reducing emissions through increased fuel efficiency for military vehicles (also a strategic advantage) and increased energy efficiency for buildings and bases under DOD control (Crawford 2022).

However, Crawford (2022) points out that the US military has accepted the greatest impacts of climate change as unavoidable, and has focused on adaptation rather than a fundamental rethink of US national security strategy or reduction in US military footprint. This has meant a prioritizing of "maintaining and expanding military capability that it believes is essential to preserving US superiority" (Crawford 2022:20). Here a doom loop of sorts materializes, in which the world becomes more unstable due to climate change, which leads to further growth of the US RSA and global police state to ensure capital accumulation and the American hegemonic world order, and that growth contributes further to climate change, ecological destruction, and global insecurity from the continued reliance on fossil fuels and the proliferation of weapons and conflict. We ultimately agree with Crawford's (2022) argument that for all of these reasons and more, the US RSA and global police state will need to be fundamentally scaled back and restructured in such a way limited to self-defense, and that replaces geopolitical domination with efforts at international cooperation and mutual aid to address OTHS and provide a path to universal human rights practice.

Unfortunately, the ecological impacts of the US military and larger global police state are not limited to fossil fuel dependence and greenhouse gas emissions. From the impacts of activities such as nuclear testing or the mining and processing of nuclear materials, and from the toxic materials found on military installations like jet fuel, US military bases are some of the most polluted places in the world (Lewis 2021). The problem of toxic contamination of soil, water, and air at US military bases is so extreme that nearly 75% (900) of the 1,200 superfund sites in the US are abandoned military bases and properties (Lewis 2021). The pollution of fresh water sources has been a particular problem, citing recent examples such as the spill of 84,000 gallons of jet fuel into waterways around the US Naval Air Station Oceana in Norfolk, VA, or dumping of toxic solvents into groundwater around the Tuscon International Airport for nearly 30 years, causing cancers and other health problems for surrounding communities (Lewis 2021). In 2021, the US Navy released jet fuel and other toxic chemicals from the Red Hill Bulk Fuel Facility in Hawaii that contaminated the drinking water affecting over 93,000 people living on or around the Joint Base Pearl Harbor-Hickam (Jowers 2023). Whether through the consumption of fossil fuels and release of greenhouse gas emissions, or through the incredible pollution that seems to follow wherever the global police state sets up shop, the militarization of the world represents an indirect, overlapping threat to human rights and survival in its contributions to climate change and ecological destruction. Through pursing a militarized approach to ensuring capital accumulation under a waning American hegemonic world order, the sustainable ecology that serves as a condition of possibility for both capital and life itself is effectively cannibalized and sacrificed in the process.

But the global police state poses a third threat to human survival in serving to repress resistance and social movements perceived as a threat to capital accumulation, the current world order, the legitimacy of states within that order, or the global police state itself. This appears in the form of sprawling surveillance programs, the violent targeting of journalists, the curtailment of rights to speech, assembly, and protest, and in some cases levels of repression amounting to what Robinson (2022a, 2022b) calls twenty-first century fascism.

Repression, Authoritarianism, and 21st Century Fascism

The structural functions of RSAs and the global police state translate into yet another OTHS, in that they serve to repress social movements (to address climate change or end wars, for example) that seek not just to secure and protect human rights, but to ensure our very survival. State repression tends to be strongest when resistance is perceived to challenge the accumulation interests of capital (class struggle and the material relations of society), the background relations of capitalist society (e.g., boundary struggles against racism, patriarchy, or colonial exploitation), or the power of RSAs and the broader global police state in the violent maintenance of these material and background relations.

One of the starkest examples of this state repression is the targeting of journalists who seek to reveal the human rights abuses of capital, empire, and the state RSAs and global police state in their service. Without journalists to cover war zones, jails and prisons, military branches, intelligence, and law enforcement agencies, or the excesses of state surveillance, effective human rights advocacy and political resistance to human rights abuses become nearly impossible, as they depend on accurate, shared understandings of realities on the ground. According to the Committee to Protect Journalists (CPJ), 2022 set a new record for the number of journalists who were incarcerated for their professional activities, up 20% from the prior year's record (Getz 2022). In Iran, where the number of jailed journalists (61)—women in particular—was highest, the state attempted to mute coverage of protests against the morality police killing of Mahsa Amini (Getz 2022). At least another 41 journalists were jailed in China, many of whom were reporting on the repression of Muslim ethnic minorities, democratic movements in Hong Kong, and the impacts of China's zero COVID policies (Getz 2022). However, perhaps nothing has been so deadly and dangerous for journalists than in the coverage of contemporary conflicts. In fact, three quarters of the 99 journalists killed all over the world in 2023 were killed covering the conflict in Israel and the occupied Palestinian territories, on top repeated total media and informational blackouts preventing accurate information from being released (CPJ 2023; Jones 2024). The first month of the conflict (October to November of 2023) was the deadliest for journalists since CPJ began documentation in 1992. Yet unlike in the early 90's, audiences online and on social media were able to witness the horrific targeting of journalists live, in real time (CPJ 2023).

In addition to the targeting of journalists, international human rights organizations point to heightening crackdowns on public protest in recent years. According to a new tracking tool by Amnesty International (AI UK

2023), the police and military forces in at least 86 of the 156 countries under monitoring used unlawful force (and in 37 of those countries used unlawful deadly force) against protesters in 2022. Crackdowns included other forms of civil and criminal penalties as well, such as forced eviction in India or the loss of rights to education or housing in China (AI UK 2023). In the same year, the UN Special Rapporteur on the Right to Peaceful Assembly (Clement N. Voule) presented a report to the Human Rights Council, arguing also in social media posts that "states are increasingly using military tactics to quash peaceful protests and military courts to prosecute protesters, leading to an escalation of tensions, violence, impunity, and human rights abuses" (UN News 2022). The report emphasized the particular impact militarized repression has on women, and the fact that sexual violence is often employed as a common tool to intimidate and silence them (UN News 2022). The militarization of policing protest in the US was made manifest to the international human rights community when the efforts to repress protests over the police murder of Michael Brown in Ferguson, MO in 2014 were streamed online and in news coverage for all to see. This helped to inspire the first phase of the BLM movement and significant international condemnation, such as in a scathing review of the US criminal legal system under the Convention Against Torture in Geneva (Hansford and Jagannath 2015). The militarization of policing in general has continued relatively unabated in the US since, but represents only one way that the right to peaceful assembly is being effectively curtailed.

To get the full picture one must look to the many state bills curtailing the rights of public protest following the record-breaking protests in 2020 of BLM's second phase, that sought to confront racist police violence and significantly reduce the power and funding of police and prisons in the American criminal legal system. In the following year, the state legislatures in 34 states introduced 81 anti-protest bills—twice as many as in any other year under observation by watchdog organizations such as the International Center for Not-For-Profit Law (ICNL) (Epstein and Mazzei 2021). According to the ICNL Protest Law Tracker, since 2017, 45 states have introduced 270 bills restricting the Constitutional and human rights to peaceful assembly, and while many have been defeated, 42 have been enacted and another 15 were pending by the end of 2023 (ICNL 2023). Despite the widely covered murder of protesters like 32-year-old Heather Heyer, who was killed when a self-described neo-Nazi purposely drove his car through a crowd of anti-racist protesters in Charlottesville, VA (Wamsley and Allyn 2019), several states including Oklahoma (HB 1674) and Iowa (SF 342) passed bills that would grant criminal immunity to those who strike protesters in public streets with their vehicle (Epstein and Mazzei 2021). Other bills, such as Florida's HB1, labeled an "anti-riot" bill, expands the definition of "riot" (a 3rd degree felony) to encompass "any group of three or more individuals whose shared intent to engage in disorderly and violent conduct results in 'imminent danger' of property damage or personal injury," without the need for actual disorderly or violent conduct to take place (ICNL 2023). Further, for any "riot" defined as such that consists of 25 or more people or that "endangers the safe movement of a vehicle" is automatically considered an "aggravated riot," amounting to a 2nd degree felony (ICNL 2023). This would mean that if such a group intentionally or accidentally stopped traffic—an extremely common tactic of peaceful assembly in the US and elsewhere—they could face felony convictions punishable by up to 15 years in prison (ICNL 2023). Similarly, so-called "anti-riot" legislation was passed in states such as Arkansas (HB 1508, HB 1578), and Iowa (SF 342), and are clear attempts to criminalize what have traditionally been some of the most common and effective forms of peaceful assembly in purportedly democratic societies.

Tellingly, almost half (20) of the 42 bills passed to curtail the right to public assembly since 2017 have been to criminalize protest activities specifically near oil and gas pipelines or other forms of "critical infrastructure." In fact, 12 of the 42 bills that have so far been enacted, such as HB 4615 in West Virginia or SB 58 in North Carolina, explicitly criminalize and/or increase criminal sanction of protests near pipelines. Another six bills, such as Indiana's SB 471 or HB 1243 in Mississippi, criminalize or increase criminal sanction for protest activity near "critical infrastructure" (ICNL 2023). The bills are a direct result of efforts by fossil fuel industry firms, local law enforcement agencies, and lawmakers to curtail environmental protests in the wake of the Dakota Access Pipeline protests on the Standing Rock reservation in 2016, and to "silence, discredit, and criminalize environmental activists and indigenous rights defenders opposed to polluting energy, mining and other extractive projects that are incompatible with meaningful climate action," as reported by *The Guardian* (Lakhani 2023). According to this reporting, many of the bills were based on a model from the industry-funded American Legislative Exchange Council (ALEC), and were passed thanks in great part to $5 million in contributions from 25 fossil fuel and energy firms to bill sponsors, including ExxonMobil, Koch Industries, and Canadian firms Enbridge and TransCanada Energy (Lakhani 2023). So far, these efforts seem to have been extremely effective in protecting fossil fuel companies from public challenge, in that from the 20 bills passed, approximately 60% (Lakhani 2023) of US gas and oil operations are now shielded from protest activity. This success demonstrates how the global police state (RSAs in Canada and the US) serves industry and the corporate TCC to repress social movements perceived as a threat to industry profits (accumulation), but also the extent to which the US RSA and broader global police state operate under the presumption that US national security and the American hegemonic world order depend on a deep cycle of ensuring access to fossil fuel resources, no matter the costs to human and other species survival on the longer term.

The repression of social movements to curtail the ecological destruction, and the racist, patriarchal, heteronormative class domination of an expanding US RSA is on display in the ongoing battles between protesters and police forces over the building of massive police counterinsurgency training facilities like the so-called "cop city" complex, planned for construction on the largest green space in the Atlanta metro area (Weelaunee Forest). Facilities like cop city should absolutely be considered as new infrastructure being built for the global police state in that at over 40% of the planned training activities will be for those from other states and countries—including the Israeli IDF (Rose 2023). Atlanta City Council approved plans to build the complex despite an overwhelming demonstration of public resistance in 17 hours of public comment from over 1,000 residents (70% against), and ongoing civil disobedience and peaceful protests since the decision in September 2021 (Lakhani 2023). Moreover, the denial and repression of resistance to cop city turned deadly when police raided a camp of peaceful protesters occupying parts of the Weelaunee Forest and riddled activist Manuel Esteban "Tortuguita" Paez Teran with 14 bullets while seated cross legged on the ground with their hands up (Lakhani 2023). This was the first case ever of an environmental activist being killed by police during a protest in the US, and the officers who shot them have escaped any criminal or civil accountability for the killing (Rose 2023). But this is not the only important precedent being set in the case of cop city when it comes to the repression of popular resistance and curtailment of the Constitutional and human rights to peaceful assembly. The state of Georgia has also opted to indict 61 community organizers behind the cop city protests with racketeering charges—essentially constructing protestors as participating in criminal conspiracies, as is done for the prosecution of mafia and other elements of violent organized crime (Lakhani 2023). The willingness to kill peaceful protestors in broad daylight and weaponize RICO (Racketeer Influenced and Corrupt Organizations Act) charges against peaceful community organizers is a further demonstration of the extent to which the US RSA and global police state responds most aggressively to perceived threats, and the extent to which Constitutional and human rights are quickly brushed aside in the process.

Of course, there is much more to be said about the repressive capacity of the US RSA to curtail resistance in the US and around the world through the global police state. The US maintains a wide reaching domestic and foreign surveillance infrastructure that began following 9/11 and has only expanded given technological advances in things such as facial recognition and other biometric monitoring (including attempts to monitor women's menstrual cycles and surveil their movement from state to state to secure their rights to bodily autonomy), communications and signal surveillance (through products like Pegasus), and big data storage/analysis. One controversial centerpiece of this surveillance infrastructure continues to be the Section 702 exception to the Foreign Intelligence Surveillance Act (FISA), that allows for the warrantless collection of any communication of foreign nationals, including with US citizens. Even given these powers, FISA Court documents reveal the "persistent and widespread" violations by US intelligence and law enforcement agencies who overstepped the bounds of Section 702 to conduct thousands of warrantless queries targeting journalists and protesters (Savage 2023). Despite calls from civil libertarians to end the program, the Biden Administration and US intelligence agencies pushed for a renewal of Section 702 powers, arguing that the Hamas attacks against Israel in October of 2023 provided evidence for the continued need for such high-tech security measures (Boguslaw 2023). This is odd given that, if anything, the October 7th attacks demonstrated the *inability* of such high-tech approaches to what the Costs of War Project calls "total Informational awareness" (Katzenstein 2023) to smother resistance or predict terrorist attacks. This approach to "total informational awareness" depends on significant cooperation among private TNCs in CIT, government intelligence and law enforcement agencies, and legal authorities. That is, mass surveillance capacities—whether in the US, China, Israel, or the EU—are provided through the most powerful nexus of transnational capital, CIT TNCs and the transnational military industrial complex specifically (Robinson 2020, 2022a).

Chinese police agencies and state authorities have invested considerable resources in an attempt to achieve total informational awareness domestically through a vast network of cameras and spyware (mostly aimed at phones and internet activity) used to gather biometric data and track the movement and the economic, political, and other activities of its population of 1.4 billion people (Mozur, Xiao, and Liu 2022). The bulk data collection and monitoring of nearly every aspect of citizens' daily lives was honed during China's zero COVID policies, and has emerged since as what experts at Human Rights Watch have called a giant "invisible cage" and others have labeled as a sort of techno-authoritarianism meant to quash dissent within the country in its earliest possible stages (Mozur, Xiao, and Liu 2022). Though the ability of current algorithmic and artificial intelligence assisted data analysis tools to predict protest, crime, and acts of terrorism have yet to be proven, the ability for the state to use its vast network to repress populations viewed as dangerous to the political status quo in the name of anti-terrorism has been clearly demonstrated.

In 2021 Amnesty International released a report on the "draconian" repression of Uyghurs, Kazakhs and other Muslim ethnic minorities in Xinjiang province. The report (Amnesty International 2021) details how the sprawling Chinese surveillance infrastructure was used to track and identify targeted minority populations, hundreds of thousands of whom where then taken from their homes or off of the streets to be interrogated by police (including the collection of biometrics), and detained without due process in prisons or a complex of "transformation-through-education" centers that amount to internment camps. Throughout their detention, those targeted have been subjected to systematic "brainwashing, torture, and other degrading treatment," and even after being released from detention are subject to "near-constant electronic and in-person surveillance, including invasive 'homestays' by government cadres who monitor them and report 'suspicious' behavior" (Amnesty International 2021). In sum, the Amnesty International report finds that the systematic mass incarceration, torture, forced labor, and religious/cultural persecution of Muslim ethnic minorities likely amount to crimes against humanity. A 2022 report from the OHCHR to the United Nations agreed,[16] despite attempts by the Chinese government to deny these activities and stop the report's release (Farge 2022). China's techno-authoritarianism exemplifies the capacity of powerful RSAs, in close partnership with CIT firms who provide many of the necessary software and tools, to monitor and repress forms of resistance. It further illustrates the role of RSAs and the global police state to forcefully differentiate expropriable populations in the disciplining of the global working class—even outside of Western settler colonialism and the orbit of NATO.

To this point, a great deal has been written in Western media and scholarship on the rise of right-wing populism and even 21st century fascism, pointing to the characteristics and policies of the former Trump Administration and so-called "MAGA" movement in the US, the rise of authoritarian strong men such as Viktor Orbán in Hungary, the election of cartoonish right populists such as the "anarcho capitalist" Javier Milei in Argentina, or the relative success of right-wing parties elsewhere in Western Europe since the great recession of 2008 (Robinson 2022a, 2022b). However, the rise of state repression and authoritarianism bordering on fascism is perhaps most notable and impactful in the case of India, given that India is the second most populous country, is the largest purported democracy, has significant trade and security relations with the West and with its fellow members of BRICS+, and is now ruled by the Hindu nationalist ("Hindutva"), and arguably ethno-fascist Bharatiya Janata Party (BJP) under the leadership of Shri Narendra Modi. According to documentary evidence from the BBC and a report by the British Foreign Office (*BBC* 2023), months after Modi was appointed Chief Minister of the state of Gujarat, he was complicit in a pogrom of Muslim minorities that killed over 2,000 people as an act of revenge for the death of 59 Hindu travelers in a rail car that was blamed on the Muslim community (Roy 2023). The evidence of Modi and BJP involvement in the pogrom, part of widening violence and repression against Muslim minorities and women across the country, was cause for his US visa to be revoked until he was then elected Prime Minister in 2014. A 2019 Human Rights Watch report documented that 44 people had been killed between 2015 and 2018, and that 90% of religious hate crimes between 2008 and 2018 had been committed since Modi's 2014 election (HRW 2019). Widespread attacks against non-Hindu minorities and Dalit ("untouchables" in the Hindu caste system) have included lynchings, gang rapes, the burning and mutilating of victims' bodies (Schultz 2019), the destruction and seizing of mosques (Ellis-Petersen 2022), and state backed segregation and ghettoization of religious minority communities (Roy 2023; Zwanenberg 2022; Saaliq 2023). Though India's 200 million Muslims represent nearly 15% of the population, they have only 5% of the seats in parliament (Saaliq 2023).

Beyond blatant ethno-nationalism, India is a deeply unequal society, in which, similar to the US, the richest 10% holds 77% of the collective wealth (Oxfam 2023). And though extreme poverty has dropped in India since, in 2017 the richest 1% took 70% of the wealth created in 2017, while the bottom 50% took only 1% of generated wealth (Oxfam 2023). In terms of health care, over 63 million Indians are pushed into poverty due to health care costs, and due to the unequal access to health care and other material supports, India accounts for 21% of child deaths (five years old or less) and 17% of maternal deaths globally (Oxfam 2023). The Modi and the BJP regime, not unlike other fascist regimes, gains much of its power from a tight relationship with the country's TCC contingency—namely that of the powerful and corrupt[17] Adani Group, headed by billionaire industrialist Gautam Adani—who grew to be one of the richest people in the world since Modi became Prime Minister. The Adani Group controls shipping ports that handle 30% of India's freight, seven airports that service 23% of India's airline passengers, and warehouses that store 30% of the country's grain (Roy 2023). And similar to the impact of the Citizens United decision in the US, electoral finance reform led by the BJP in 2017 allowed corporations to fund Indian political parties without limit or public transparency through "electoral bonds," the removal of caps on donations, and other measures (Ahmed and Ulmer 2019). The BJP enjoys the most corporate funding among the parties, and the Indian corporate owning class enjoys considerable sway over Indian elections. Finally, in terms of state repression of media and speech, India now ranks near the bottom (161 out of 180 countries) of the world press freedom index (RSF 2023), due to the concentration of media ownership in the hands of oligarchs close to the BJP and prevalence of partisan misinformation across the Indian media landscape.

Indian ethno-nationalism under the BJP represents a significant challenge to democracy and human rights that, along with the techno-authoritarianism of the Peoples Republic of China and state repression in the US, illustrates the extent to which the RSAs of the most populous and powerful countries in the world function as part of a broader global police state to prevent resistance or challenge to the political economic status quo. This political repression translates into an OTHS to the extent that it succeeds in preventing the kinds of social movements (e.g., to address climate change, fight for peace, or demand denuclearization) that might otherwise steer the course of human history away from certain disaster. In the following chapter we will explore how political economic domination by a corporate owning class has affected electoral politics in the US, and how the expanding power and "rights" of corporations and financial firms continue to have the effect of shrinking the rights and political voice of everyday people. Overcoming the greatest overlapping threats to human rights and survival—all with roots in the material and background relations of capitalist society, and confronting the destructive and repressive potentials of the global police state as argued here, will demand a reversal of these trends in the political state apparatus (part of the ISA), and a relative capture of state and transnational state political structures by civil society and global working-class interests.

Notes

1 The tendency expressed here toward a state-centered strategic vision should not be misinterpreted for a dismissal of libertarian or other socialisms, or for an uncritical endorsement of electoral politics or the contemporary nation-state. Rather, it is an estimation of the most achievable path to some survivable, and assuredly imperfect form of collectivism given the immediacy of OTHS, current (geo)political realities (including the insufficient organized power of the left at present, albeit hopeful), and given the institutional infrastructures required to address OTHS.

2 Beyond the human carnage caused by the conflicts and sanctions, consider, for example, the assassination ("targeted killing") of US citizens Anwar Al-Awlaki and his 16-year-old son Abdulrahman Al-Awlaqi via drone strikes without charge or due process in a foreign sovereign territory (Yemen) (ABC News 2011), or the CIA program to systematically kidnap ("extraordinary rendition"), torture, and interrogate ("enhanced interrogation") foreign nationals, as documented in the Senate Intelligence Committee report (2014) on its failure.

3 See the Water Conflict Chronology data set and interactive map here: http://www.worldwater.org/conflict/map/

4 Originally estimated at over 1,400, Israeli officials revised these estimates to just over 1,200 in November of 2023 (Chacar 2023).

5 The "right to resist" exists relative to the international human right to self-determination, though there is less legal clarity on when, how, and under what conditions the right can be exercised and what forms of resistance are protected.

6 Article 51(2) of the Additional Protocol to the Geneva Conventions (UN 1977) reads: "The Civilian population as such, as well as individual civilians, shall not be the object of attack. Acts or threats of violence, the primary purpose of which is to spread terror among the civilian population, are prohibited."

7 There was a significant increase in illegal settlements on Palestinian land, and this involved a spike in the demolition of Palestinian homes, the arming of many Israeli settlers, and in some cases the extrajudicial murder of Palestinian civilians (Nashed 2024; Sinmaz and Taha 2024).

8 According to the report, 9 of 10 households in northern Gaza and 2 of 3 in southern Gaza had spent at least one full day and night without food. Further, the report notes that according to the Rome statute of the ICC, depriving civilians "of objects indispensable to their survival, including willfully impeding relief supplies," is an international war crime (HRW 2023b).

9 From the Leviathan gas field near the coast of Israel/Gaza.

10 See, for example: Davis 2003; Gilmore 2007; Murakawa 2014; Cazenave 2018; Alexander 2020; Taylor 2021; Vitale 2017; Rios 2011; Wacquant 2009; Kaba and Kaepernick 2021; Davis, Dent, Meiners, and Richie 2022.

11 A crime is considered "cleared" when at least one person has been arrested, charged with the crime, and that charge was referred to the courts for prosecution. It should be noted that a crime being cleared does not mean anyone was necessarily convicted of the crime, calling further into question the regularity with which crimes are truly "solved."

12 See here: https://www.documentcloud.org/documents/24099626-peterson-letter-to-judges

13 From Robinson (2020:75): "As one senior US government official put it, US military forces and intelligence agencies are deployed around the world to ensure 'the viability and stability of major global systems: trade, financial markets, supplies of energy, and climate. In theoretical terms, the US state becomes the point of condensation for pressures from dominant groups around the world to resolve the intractable problems of global capitalism."

14 These arms sales can occur as a "direct commercial sale" from a TNC to a state military, or "foreign military sale," where the US acts as an intermediary to purchase the weapons from private firms and then distribute them to the intended state military recipient. In either case, the US must approve of the sale (Semler 2023).
15 It should be noted that Israel will neither confirm or deny possessing nuclear weapons, though experts suggest they've had them since the 1960's, and that they possess an estimated 90 nuclear warheads and 3 Dolphin and Dolphin II class submarines capable of delivering nuclear missiles (NTI 2023).
16 From the report (OHCHR 2022:44): "the extent of arbitrary and discriminatory detention of member of Uyghur and other predominantly Muslim groups, pursuant to law and policy, in context of restrictions and deprivation more generally of fundamental rights enjoyed individually and collectively, may constitute international crimes, in particular crimes against humanity."
17 According to a two year investigation by Hindenburg Research (2023), the Adani Group "has engaged in a brazen stock manipulation and accounting fraud scheme over the course of decades."

References

ABC News. 2011. "Awlaki Family Protests US Killing of Anwar Awlaki's Teen Son." *ABC News*, October 18. Retrieved 10/20/23 from https://abcnews.go.com/Blotter/a wlaki-family-protests-us-killing-anwar-awlakis-teen/story?id=14765076

Abdel-Baqui, Omar. 2023. "Israeli Air Force Says it Has Dropped 6,000 Bombs on Gaza." *The Wall Street Journal*, October 14. Retrieved 10/14/23 from www.wsj. com/livecoverage/israel-hamas-war-gaza-strip/card/israeli-air-force-says-it-has-drop ped-6-000-bombs-on-gaza-QK1aSnupiGqytMVO86PU

AghaKouchak, Amir, A. Mirchi, K. Madani, et al. 2021. "Anthropogenic Drought: Definition, Challenges, and Opportunities." *Reviews of Geophysics*, 59 (7). https// doi.org/10/1029/2019RG000683

Ahmed, Aftab and Aleandra Ulmer. 2019. "India's Elections: Rules on Campaign Financing and Spending." *Reuters*, May 1. Retrieved 11/10/23 from www.reuters. com/article/india-election-spending/indias-elections-rules-on-campaign-financing-a nd-spending-idUSKCN1S7397/

Akkerman, Mark. 2023. "Global Spending on Immigration Enforcement is Higher than Ever and Rising." *Migration Policy Institute*, May 31. Retrieved 09/20/23 from www.migrationpolicy.org/article/immigration-enforcement-spending-rising

Al-Mughrabi, Nidal. 2024. "More than 100 Killed While Seeking Aid in Gaza, Overall Death Toll Passes 30,000." *Reuters*, February 29. Retrieved 02/29/24 from www.reuters.com/world/middle-east/dozens-killed-gaza-aid-queue-overall-death-toll-passes-30000-2024-02-29/#:~:text=PALESTINIAN%20DEATH%20TOLL%20TOP S%2030%2C000,1%2C200%20people%20and%20abducted%20253

Alexander, Michelle. 2020. *The New Jim Crow*. New York: The New Press.

Althusser, Louis. 2001 [1971]. "Ideology and Ideological State Apparatuses: Notes Towards an Investigation." In *Lenin and Philosophy and Other Essays*, pp. 85–126 edited by L. Althusser. New York: Monthly Review Press.

Amnesty International. 2017. "Occupation of Water." *Amnesty International*, November 29. Retrieved 09/12/23 from www.amnesty.org/en/latest/campaigns/2017/11/the-occupation-of-water/

Amnesty International. 2021. "'Like We Were Enemies in a War': China's Mass Internment, Torture and Persecution of Muslims in Xinjiang." *Amnesty International*. Retrieved on 11/14/23 from https://xinjiang.amnesty.org/

Amnesty International. 2022. "Israel's Apartheid Against Palestinians: Cruel System of Domination and Crime Against Humanity." *Amnesty International*. Retrieved on 09/12/23 from www.amnesty.org/en/documents/mde15/5141/2022/en/

Amnesty International. 2023. "Israel/OPT: Identifying the Israeli Army's Use of White Phosphorus in Gaza." *Amnesty International*, October 13. Retrieved on 10/13/23 from https://amnesty.ca/human-rights-news/israel-opt-identifying-the-israeli-armys-use-of-white-phosphorus-in-gaza/

Amnesty International. 2024. "Israel Defying ICJ Ruling to Prevent Genocide by Failing to Allow Adequate Humanitarian Aid to Reach Gaza." *Amnesty International*, February 26. Retrieved 02/26/24 from www.amnesty.org/en/latest/news/2024/02/israel-defying-icj-ruling-to-prevent-genocide-by-failing-to-allow-adequate-humanitarian-aid-to-reach-gaza/

Amnesty International (AI) UK2023. "Global: Interactive Map Reveals a 'Blistering Attack' on Peaceful Protests Across the World." *AI UK*, September 19. Retrieved 11/10/23 from www.amnesty.org.uk/press-releases/global-interactive-map-reveals-blistering-attack-peaceful-protests-across-world

Armaline, William, Claudio Vera Sanchez and Mark Correia. 2014. "'The Biggest Gang in Oakland': Re-Thinking Police Legitimacy." *Contemporary Justice Review*. doi:10.1080/10282580.2014.944795

Armaline, William and Davita Silfen Glasberg. 2009. "What Will States Really Do for Us? The Human Rights Enterprise and Pressure from Below." *Societies Without Borders*, 4 (3): 430–451.

Armed Conflict Location and Event Data Project (ACLED). 2023. "ACLED Conflict Index: Ranking Violent Conflict Levels Across the World." *ACLED*. Retrieved 12/02/23 from https://acleddata.com/acled-conflict-index-mid-year-update/

Ashford, Emma and Matthew Kroenig. 2023. "How Many Wars Can America Fight at the Same Time?" *Foreign Policy*, October 27. Retrieved 11/02/23 from https://foreignpolicy.com/2023/10/27/united-states-middle-east-wars-asia-europe-same-time/

Atomic Archive. 2023. "Israel's Nuclear Facilities." *AtomicArchive.com*. Retrieved 10/30/23 from www.atomicarchive.com/almanac/facilities/israeli-facilities.html#:~:text=Negev%20Nuclear%20Research%20Center%2C%20Dimona

Baldwin, Robert III. 2022. "Losing a Pregnancy Could Land You in Jail in Post-Roe America." *NPR*, July 3. Retrieved 11/20/23 from www.npr.org/2022/07/03/1109015302/abortion-prosecuting-pregnancy-loss

Bales, Kevin. 2016. *Blood and Earth: Modern Slavery, Ecocide, and the Secret to Saving the World*. New York: Random House.

Baron, Jason. 2022. "The Foster Care-to-Prison Pipeline." *Vox EU*, June 12. Retrieved 10/15/23 from https://cepr.org/voxeu/columns/foster-care-prison-pipeline#:~:text=For%20example%2C%20close%20to%20one,age%2026%20(Courtney%20et%20al

Baughman, Shima Baradaran. 2021. "Crime and the Mythology of Police." *Washington University Law Review* 99 (65): 1–67.

Baumgartner, Frank and Tim Lyman. 2016. "Louisiana Death Sentenced Cases and Their Reversals, 1976–2015." *The Southern University Law Center Journal of Race, Gender, and Poverty* 7: 58–75.

Bazilian, Morgan, E. Holland and J. Busby. 2023. "America's Military Depends on Minerals That China Controls." *Foreign Policy*, March 16. Retrieved 09/08/23 from https://foreignpolicy.com/2023/03/16/us-military-china-minerals-supply-chain/

BBC. 2023. "India Government Criticizes BBC's Modi Documentary." *BBC*, January 20. Retrieved 11/18/23 from www.bbc.com/news/world-asia-india-64342679

Beale, Jonathan. 2023. "Ukraine War: Training to Clear the World's Most Heavily Mined Country." *BBC News*, September 25. Retrieved 11/16/2023 from www.bbc.com/news/world-europe-66879485

Belcher, Oliver, P. Bigger, B. Neimark and C. Kennelly. 2019. "Hidden Carbon Costs of the 'Every-Where War': Logistics, Geopolitical Ecology, and the Carbon Bootprint of the US Military." *Transactions of the Institute of British Geographers*. doi:10.1111/tran.12319

Benjamin, Medea and Nicolas J. S. Davies. 2022. *War in Ukraine: Making Sense of a Senseless Conflict*. UK: OR Books.

Besteman, Catherine. 2019. "Militarized Global Apartheid." *Current Anthropology*, 60: S19. https://doi.org/10.1086/699280

Bigg, Matthew Mpoke and Gaya Gupta. 2024. "What to Know About the UN Court's Initial Ruling in the Genocide Case Against Israel." *The New York Times*, January 25. Retrieved 02/26/24 from www.nytimes.com/2024/01/25/world/middleeast/icj-israel-genocide-ruling.html#:~:text=On%20Friday%2C%20the%20court%20ruled,physical%20destruction%20in%20whole%20or

Blades, Lincoln Anthony. 2018. "How Policing in the US and Security in Israel are Connected." *Teen Vogue*, July 25. Retrieved 10/13/23 from www.teenvogue.com/story/how-policing-in-the-us-and-security-in-israel-are-connected

Blakinger, Keri. 2022. "Why So Many Jails Are in a 'State of Complete Meltdown.' *The Marshall Project*. Retrieved 02/08/23 from www.themarshallproject.org/2022/11/04/why-so-many-jails-are-in-a-state-of-complete-meltdown

Blakinger, Keri. 2023. "Fights, Beatings, and a Birth: Videos Smuggled Out of L.A. Jails Reveal Violence, Neglect." *Los Angeles Times*, June 24. Retrieved 10/15/23 from www.latimes.com/california/story/2023-06-24/fights-beatings-and-a-birth-videos-smuggled-out-of-la-jails-reveal-violence-neglect

Boguslaw, Daniel. 2023. "Counterterror Director Used Hamas Attack to Justify Mass Surveillance Program Renewal." *The Intercept*, November 6. Retrieved 11/17/23 from https://theintercept.com/2023/11/06/hamas-counterterrorism-mass-surveillance-section-702/?utm_campaign=theintercept&utm_source=twitter&utm_medium=social

Borger, Julian. 2020. "US Dropped Record Number of Bombs on Afghanistan Last Year." *The Guardian*, January 28. Retrieved 10/16/23 from www.theguardian.com/us-news/2020/jan/28/us-afghanistan-war-bombs-2019

Borger, Julian. 2024. "Claims of Israeli Sexual Assault of Palestinian Women are Credible, UN Panel Says." *The Guardian*, February 22. Retrieved 02/25/24 from www.theguardian.com/world/2024/feb/22/claims-of-israeli-sexual-assault-of-palestinian-women-are-credible-un-panel-says

Bradsher, Keith. 2023a. "Why China Has a Giant Pile of Debt." *The New York Times*, July 8. Retrieved 07/10/23 from www.nytimes.com/2023/07/08/business/china-debt-explained.html?smid=nytcore-ios-share&referringSource=articleShare

Bradsher, Keith. 2023b. "China is Lending Billions to Countries in Financial Trouble." *The New York Times*, November 6. Retrieved 11/07/23 from www.nytimes.com/2023/11/06/business/china-bri-aiddata.html

Brennan, David. 2023. "US Ohio-Class Nuclear Submarine Deployed to Middle East Amid Tensions." *Newsweek*, November 6. Retrieved 11/07/23 from www. newsweek.com/us-ohio-class-nuclear-submarine-deployed-middle-east-tensions-is rael-hamas-1841053

Brewster, Freddy. 2023. "Biden Approves Israel Arms Deal Despite His Own Security Order." *The Lever*, November 9. Retrieved 11/11/23 from www.levernews.com/ biden-approves-israel-arms-deal-despite-his-own-security-order/?utm_source=news letter-email&utm_medium=link&utm_campaign=newsletter-article

Brookes, Peter. 2023. "China's Nuclear Weapons Buildup." *Geopolitical Intelligence Services (GIS)*, July 14. Retrieved 11/10/23 from www.gisreportsonline.com/r/china s-nuclear-weapons-buildup/

Bugos, Shannon. 2022. "US Nuclear Modernization Programs: Fact Sheets & Briefs." *Arms Control Association*. Retrieved 11/10/23 from www.armscontrol.org/fa ctsheets/USNuclearModernization

Burke, Marshall, S. Hsiang and E. Miguel. 2015. "Climate and Conflict." *Annual Review of Economics* 7: 577–617. https://doi.org/10.1146/annurev-econom ics-080614-115430

Bush, G. W. 2003. "President Discusses Beginning of Operation Iraqi Freedom: President's Radio Address." *White House Office of the Press Secretary*, March 22. Retrieved 09/10/23 from https://georgewbush-whitehouse.archives.gov/news/relea ses/2003/03/20030322.html

Callamard, Agnés. 2024. "Gaza and the End of the Rules-Based Order." *Foreign Affairs*, February 15. Retrieved 02/24/26 from www.foreignaffairs.com/israel/gaza -and-end-rules-based-order?utm_medium=newsletters&utm_source=twofa&utm_ campaign=Why%20America%20Can%E2%80%99t%20Have%20It%20All&utm_ content=20240216&utm_term=FA%20This%20Week%20-%20112017

Capaccio, Anthony. 2021. "Lockheed F-35's Tally of Flaws Tops 800 as 'New Issues' Surface." *Bloomberg*, July 13. Retrieved 10/29/23 from www.bloomberg.com/news/a rticles/2021-07-13/lockheed-f-35-s-tally-of-flaws-tops-800-as-new-issues-surface?leadS ource=uverify%20wall#xj4y7vzkg

Caselli, F., Morelli, M., & Rohner, D. 2015. "The Geography of Inter-state Resource Wars." The Quarterly Journal of Economics 130 (1): 267–316.

Cazenave, N. 2018. *Killing African Americans: Police and Vigilante Violence as a Racial Control Mechanism*. New York: Routledge.

Center for Arms Control and Non-Proliferation. 2022. "Fact Sheet: North Korea's Nuclear Inventory." *Center for Arms Control and Non-Proliferation*. Retrieved 11/ 10/23 from https://armscontrolcenter.org/fact-sheet-north-koreas-nuclear-inventory/

Center for Arms Control and Non-Proliferation. 2023. "Fiscal Year 2024 Defense Budget Request Briefing Book." *Center for Arms Control and Non-Proliferation*. Retrieved   10/30/23   from   https://armscontrolcenter.org/fiscal-yea r-2024-defense-budget-request-briefing-book/

Center for Constitutional Rights (CCR). 2023a. "Israel's Unfolding Crime of Genocide of the Palestinian People & US Failure to Prevent and Complicity in Genocide." *CCR*, October 18. Retrieved 10/20/23 from https://ccrjustice-org.webpkgca che.com/doc/-/s/ccrjustice.org/sites/default/files/attach/2023/10/Israels-Unfolding-Crime_ww.pdf

Center for Constitutional Rights (CCR). 2023b. "UN Human Rights Committee Calls for Moratorium on Life Without Parole in US." (Press release) *CCR*,

November 3. Retrieved 11/04/23 from https://ccrjustice.org/home/press-center/p ress-releases/un-human-rights-committee-calls-moratorium-life-without-parole-us

Chacar, Henriette. 2023. "Israel Revises Hamas Attack Death Toll to 'Around 1,200.'" *Reuters*, November 10. Retrieved 11/12/23 from www.reuters.com/world/middle-ea st/israel-revises-death-toll-oct-7-hamas-attack-around-1200-2023-11-10/#:~:text= Israel%20revises%20Hamas%20attack%20death%20toll%20to%20'around%201% 2C200',-Reuters&text=JERUSALEM%2C%20Nov%2010%20(Reuters),previous% 20government%20estimate%20of%201%2C400

Chasan, Aliza. 2023. "How the Pentagon Falls Victim to Price Gouging by Military Conractors." *CBS News*, May 21. Retrieved 11/02/23 from www.cbsnews.com/ news/pentagon-budget-price-gouging-military-contractors-60-minutes-2023-05-21/

Chotiner, Isaac. 2023. "How Hamas Used Sexual Violence on October 7th." *The New Yorker*, December 10. Retrieved 12/15/23 from www.newyorker.com/news/ q-and-a/how-hamas-used-sexual-violence-on-october-7th#:~:text=She%20was% 20naked.,pelvises%20from%20%E2%80%9Crepetitive%20rapes.%E2%80%9D

Chisadza, Carolyn, M. Clance, R. Gupta and M. Wohar. 2023. "Giant Oil Dis-coveries and Conflicts." *Environment, Development, and Sustainability*. Retrieved 09/01/23 from https://doi.org/10.1007/s10668-023-03270-5

Cleary, Claire. 2023. "10 Years After Landmark Stop-and-Frisk Ruling, the NYPD Practice Continues to Target West Harlem and Other Predominantly Black and Latino Precincts." *Columbia Spectator*, October 30. Retrieved 10/30/23 from www. columbiaspectator.com/city-news/2023/10/30/10-years-after-landmark-stop-and-frisk-ruling-the-nypd-practice-continues-to-target-west-harlem-and-other-predominantly-black-and-latino-precincts/

Cockburn, Andrew. 2021. *The Spoils of War: Power, Profit and the American War Machine*. Brooklyn, NY: Verso.

Colgan, Jeff. 2013. "Fueling the Fire: Pathways from Oil to War." *Quarterly Journal: International Security* 38 (2): 147–180. Retrieved 09/01/23 from www.belfercenter. org/publication/fueling-fire-pathways-oil-war

Committee to Protect Journalists (CPJ). 2023. "More than 50 Journalists Killed in Israel–Gaza War." *CPJ*. Retrieved 11/22/23 from https://cpj.org/

Conklin, Audrey. 2023. "Georgia Inmate Eaten Alive by Bugs in Conditions 'Not Fit for a Deceased Animal,' Family Attorney Says." *Fox News*, April 13. Retrieved 10/ 15/23 from www.foxnews.com/us/georgia-inmate-eaten-alive-by-bugs-condi tions-not-fit-deceased-animal-family-attorney-says

Contreras, Russell. 2023. "Rate of Latinos Killed by Police Skyrockets." *Axios*, May 30. Retrieved 10/15/23 from www.axios.com/2023/05/30/police-brutality-la tino-george-floyd

Copp, Tara and Lolita Baldor. 2023a. "More US Ships Head Toward Israel and 2,000 Troops are on Heightened Alert. A Look at US Assistance." *Associated Press*, October 17. Retrieved 10/19/23 from https://apnews.com/article/united-sta tes-israel-military-aid-2211b0c7bc27e13175d179a53fde3ac5

Copp, Tara and Lolita Baldor. 2023b. "Pentagon Announces New International Mission to Counter Attacks on Commercial Vessels in Red Sea." *AP*, December 19. Retrieved 12/20/23 from https://apnews.com/article/attacks-red-sea-navy-m ission-missiles-286d51bfd65e741e839e185f0f4a455b

Crawford, Neta. 2019. "Pentagon Fuel Use, Climate Change, and the Costs of War." *Watson Institute of International and Public Affairs at Brown University, Costs of*

War Project. Retrieved 11/15/23 from https://watson.brown.edu/costsofwar/pap ers/ClimateChangeandCostofWar

Crawford, Neta. 2022. *The Pentagon, Climate Change, and War: Charting the Rise and Fall of US Military Emissions*. Cambridge, MA: MIT Press.

Crawford, Neta, C. Lutz, K. Rubaii, et al. 2023. "Iraqi Civilians." *Costs of War* (Watson Institute, Brown University). Retrieved 09/01/23 from https://watson. brown.edu/costsofwar/costs/human/civilians/iraqi

Crisp, Wil. 2022. "Chinese win 87% of Iraq Energy Contracts." *MEED: Middle East Business Intelligence*, November 7. Retrieved 09/13/23 from www.meed.com/chi nese-win-87-per-cent-of-iraq-energy-contracts

Crowley, Michael. 2023. "Biden Taps Penny Pritzker to Drive Ukraine's Economic Revival." *The New York Times*, September 14. Retrieved 10/28/23 from www. nytimes.com/2023/09/14/us/politics/biden-ukraine-penny-pritzker-economy.html

Cumming-Bruce, Nick. 2023. "UN Says Israel-Gaza War is Deadliest Ever for Its Personnel." *The New York Times*, November 6. Retrieved 02/26/24 from www. nytimes.com/2023/11/06/world/middleeast/un-unrwa-death-toll.html

Davis, Angela. 2003. *Are Prisons Obsolete?* New York: Seven Stories Press.

Davis, Angela, G. Dent, E. Meiners and B. Richie. 2022. *Abolition. Feminism. Now.* Chicago, IL: Haymarket Books.

Debre, Isabel. 2023. "As Israeli Settlements Thrive, Palestinian Taps Run Dry. The Water Crisis Reflects a Broader Battle." *Associated Press (AP)*, August 16. Retrieved 09/12/23 from https://apnews.com/article/water-climate-change-drought-occupation-israel-palestinians-30cb8949bdb45cf90ed14b6b992b5b42

Dholakia, Nazish. 2023. "The Difference Between Jail and Prison." *The Vera Institute*, February 21. Retrieved 10/15/23 from www.vera.org/news/u-s-jails-and-p risons-explained#:~:text=And%20while%20jails%20may%20hold,been%20con victed%20of%20a%20crime

Ditmars, Hadani. 2023. "Historic Greek Orthodox Church in Gaza Hit by Deadly Missile Strikes." *The Art Newspaper*, October 20. Retrieved 10/20/23 from www. theartnewspaper.com/2023/10/20/third-oldest-church-in-the-world-struck-by-missiles -in-gaza

Dooley, Ben and Emily Rhyne. 2023. "Army Ammunition Plant is Tied to Mass Shootings Across the US." *The New York Times*, November 11. Retrieved 11/16/23 from www.nytimes.com/2023/11/11/us/army-ammunition-factory-shootings.html

Eckert, Cambrie. 2023. "US Can't Dig Itself Out of Critical Minerals Hole, Experts Say." *National Defense*, July 26. Retrieved 09/05/23 from www.nationaldefensema gazine.org/articles/2023/7/26/web-exclusive-us-cant-dig-itself-out-of-critical-minera ls-hole-experts-say

Edwards, F., H. Lee and M. Esposito. 2019. "Risk of Being Killed by Police Use of Force in the United States by Age, Race-Ethnicity, and Sex." *Proc. National Academy of Sciences* 116: 16793–16798.

Ellis-Petersen, Hannah. 2022. "Thousands of Mosques Targeted as Hindu National-ists Try to Rewrite India's History." *The Guardian*, October 30. Retrieved 11/16/ 23 from www.theguardian.com/world/2022/oct/30/thousands-of-mosques-targe ted-as-hindu-nationalists-try-to-rewrite-indias-history

Epstein, Reid and Patricia Mazzei. 2021. "G.O.P. Bills Target Protesters (and Absolve Motorists Who Hit Them)." *The New York Times*, April 21. Retrieved 11/15/23 from www.nytimes.com/2021/04/21/us/politics/republican-anti-protest-la ws.html

Fabian, Emanuel. 2023. "Defense Minister Announces 'Complete Siege' of Gaza: No Power, Food or Fuel." *The Times of Israel*, October 9. Retrieved 02/26/24 from www.timesofisrael.com/liveblog_entry/defense-minister-announces-complete-siege-of -gaza-no-power-food-or-fuel/

Fabian, Emanuel. 2024. "Two Soldiers Killed in Gaza; IDF Says Gunman Found Hiding Among Civilians." *The Times of Israel*, February 25. Retrieved 02/26/24 from www.timesofisrael.com/two-soldiers-killed-in-gaza-idf-says-gunmen-found-hi ding-among-fleeing-civilians/

Farge, Emma. 2022. "China Seeks to Stop UN Rights Chief from Releasing Xinjiang Report – Document." *Reuters*, July 19. Retrieved 11/17/23 from www.reuters.com/ world/china/exclusive-china-seeks-stop-un-rights-chief-releasing-xinjiang-report-do cument-2022-07-19/

Farge, Emma. 2023. "Ukraine War Brings Surge in Global Use of Cluster Bombs." *Reuters*, September 5. Retrieved 11/15/23 from www.reuters.com/world/europe/ cluster-bomb-use-surges-amid-ukraine-war-2023-09-05/

Fassihi, Farnaz and Isabel Kershner. 2024. "UN Team Finds Grounds to Support Reports of Sexual Violence in Hamas Attack." *The New York Times*, March 4. Retrieved 03/04/24 from www.nytimes.com/2024/03/04/world/middleeast/isra el-hamas-un-report-sexual-violence.html

Fraser, Nancy. 2016. "Expropriation and Exploitation in Racialized Capitalism: A Reply to Michael Dawson." *Critical Historical Studies* 3 (1): 163–178. https://doi.org/10.1086/685814

Fraser, Nancy. 2022. *Cannibal Capitalism: How Our System is Devouring Democracy, Care, and the Planet—and What We Can Do About It.* London: Verso.

Friedman, Barry. 2021. "Disaggregating the Policing Function." *University of Pennsylvania Law Review* 169 (925): 1–61.

Gaal, Ferenc. 2023. "German Military Exports to Israel Up Nearly 10-Fold as Berlin Fast-Tracks Permits." *Reuters*, November 8. Retrieved 11/10/23 from www.reuters.com/ world/europe/german-military-exports-israel-up-nearly-10-fold-berlin-fast-tracks-perm its-2023-11-08/#:~:text=As%20of%20Nov.,approved%20in%20all%20of%202022

Gabbatt, Adam. 2023. "Billion Dollar Prisons: Why the US is Pouring Money Into New Construction." *The Guardian*, September 28. Retrieved 10/30/23 from www. theguardian.com/us-news/2023/oct/28/states-spending-money-build-prison-republican

Gal, Danit. 2019. "The US–China–Israel Technology Triangle." *Council on Foreign Relations*, July 30. Retrieved 10/13/23 from www.cfr.org/blog/us-china-israel-tech nology-triangle

Ganeva, Tana. 2023. "Indiana Jail Let Man With Schizophrenia Starve to Death in Solitary, Lawsuit Alleges." *The Appeal*, April 12. Retrieved 10/15/23 from https:// theappeal.org/joshua-mclemore-died-solitary-jackson-county-jail-indiana/

Garrett-Peltier, Heidi. 2017. "Job Opportunity Costs of War." *Watson Institute of International and Public Affairs at Brown University, Costs of War Project.* Retrieved 05/12/24 from https://watson.brown.edu/costsofwar/files/cow/imce/papers/2017/Job %20Opportunity%20Cost%20of%20War%20-%20HGP%20-%20FINAL.pdf

Garwood, Edith. 2016. "With Whom are Many US Police Departments Training? With a Chronic Human Rights Violator—Israel." *Amnesty International*, August 25. Retrieved 10/12/23 from www.amnestyusa.org/updates/with-whom-are-ma ny-u-s-police-departments-training-with-a-chronic-human-rights-violator-israel/

Geneva International Center for Justice (GICJ). 2017. "Razing the Truth About Sanctions Against Iraq." *GICJ*. Retrieved 09/10/23 from www.gicj.org/positions-opinons/gicj-p ositions-and-opinions/1188-razing-the-truth-about-sanctions-against-iraq

Getz, Arlene. 2022. "Number of Jailed Journalists Spikes to New Global Record." *CPJ*, December 14. Retrieved 11/21/23 from https://cpj.org/reports/2022/12/num ber-of-jailed-journalists-spikes-to-new-global-record/

Gilmore, Ruth Wilson. 2007. *Golden Gulag: Prisons, Surplus, Crisis, and Opposition in Globalizing California*. Berkeley, CA: University of California Press.

Giorno, Taylor. 2023. "Armed Services Committee Members Received $5.8 Million from Defense Sector During 2022 Election Cycle." *OpenSecrets.org*, March 3. Retrieved 11/02/23 from www.opensecrets.org/news/2023/03/armed-services-comm ittee-members-received-5-8-million-from-defense-sector-during-2022-election-cycle/

Gledhill, Julia. 2023. "Pentagon Can't Account for 63% of Nearly $4 Trillion in Assets." *Responsible Statecraft*, December 4. Retrieved 12/04/23 from https://resp onsiblestatecraft.org/pentagon-audit-2666415734/

Goodkind, Nicole. 2023. "What the Israel-Hamas War Means for Defense Stocks." *CNN*, October 18. Retrieved 10/29/23 from www.cnn.com/2023/10/18/investing/p remarket-stocks-trading/index.html

Gramsci, Antonio. 1971. *Selections from the Prison Notebooks* (Quintin Hoare, Ed.). New York: International Publishers Co.

Gross, Samuel. 2017. "What We Think, What We Know, and What We Think We Know About False Convictions." *The Ohio State Journal of Criminal Law* 14 (2): 753–786.

Hagopian, Amy, A. Flaxman, T. Takaro, et al. 2013. "Mortality in Iraq Associated with the 2003–2011 War and Occupation: Findings from a National Cluster Sample Survey by the University Collaborative Iraq Mortality Study." *PLOS Medicine*. Retrieved 09/01/23 from https://doi.org/10.1371/journal.pmed.1001533

Hammel, Paul. 2023. "Mother Who Helped Teen Daughter Abort Fetus is Sentenced to Two Years in Prison." *Louisiana Illuminator*, September 25. Retrieved 11/21/23 from https://lailluminator.com/2023/09/25/abort-prison/#:~:text=The%20daughter %2C%20Celeste%20Burgess%2C%20was,a%20%E2%80%9Clack%20of%20fundi ng.%E2%80%9D

Hancock, Alice. 2023. "NATO to Launch Biggest Military Exercise Since Cold War." *Financial Times*, September 10. Retrieved 11/15/23 from www.ft.com/content/6c7a 6941-2e0c-46d0-baf5-f53b681d2936

Hansford, Justin and Meena Jagannath. 2015. "Ferguson to Geneva: Using the Human Rights Framework to Push Forward a Vision for Racial Justice in the United States After Ferguson." *Hastings Race and Poverty Law Journal*, 12 (2): 121–154.

Harari, Mariaflavia and E. La Ferrara. 2018. "Conflict, Climate, and Cells: A Dis-aggregated Analysis." *The Review of Economics and Statistics* 100 (4): 594–608. https://doi.org/101162/rest_a_00730

Harlow, Caroline W. 2003. "Education and Correctional Populations." *US DOJ Bureau of Justice Statistics*. Retrieved 10/15/23 from https://bjs.ojp.gov/content/p ub/pdf/ecp.pdf

Hartmann, Margaret. 2012. "NYPD Now Has an Israel Branch." *New York Magazine*, September 6. Retrieved 10/12/23 from https://nymag.com/intelligencer/2012/09/nyp d-now-has-an-israel-branch.html#:~:text=As%20part%20of%20the%20NYPD,and %20situations%20that%20arise%20overseas

Hartung, William. 2021. "Profits of War: Corporate Beneficiaries of the Post-9/11 Pentagon Spending Surge." *Watson Institute of International and Public Affairs at Brown University and the Center for International Policy*. Retrieved 10/30/23 from https://watson.brown.edu/costsofwar/papers/2021/ProfitsOfWar

Hartung, William. 2022. "Promoting Stability or Fueling Conflict? The Impact of US Arms Sales on National and Global Security." *Quincy Institute for Responsible Statecraft*, October 20. Retrieved 11/04/23 from https://quincyinst.org/report/prom oting-stability-or-fueling-conflict-the-impact-of-u-s-arms-sales-on-national-and-globa l-security/

Hartung, William and Benjamin Freeman. 2023. "The Military Industrial Complex is More Powerful Than Ever." *The Nation*, May 9. Retrieved 10/30/23 from www. thenation.com/article/world/military-industrial-complex-defense/

Harvey, D. 2005. *The New Imperialism* (revised edition). New York: Oxford University Press.

Harvey, D. 2007. *A Brief History of Neoliberalism*. New York: Oxford University Press.

Harvey, D. 2018. *Marx, Capital, and the Madness of Economic Reason*. New York: Oxford University Press.

Hassan, Fatima, S. Manjra and L. London. 2024. "Israel's Unrelenting War on Gaza Healthcare Requires Urgent Action." *Al Jazeera*, February 14. Retrieved 02/26/24 from www.aljazeera.com/opinions/2024/2/14/israels-unrelenting-war-on-gaza-hea lthcare-requires-urgent-action

Hendrix, Cullen. 2022. "How to Avoid a New Cold War Over Critical Minerals." *Foreign Policy*. Retrieved 09/02/23 from https://foreignpolicy.com/2022/11/22/cri tical-minerals-resources-us-china-competition-cold-war-supply-chains/#cookie_m essage_anchor

Hindenburg Research. 2023. "Adani Group: How the World's 3rd Richest Man is Pulling the Largest Con in Corporate History." *Hindenburg Research*, January 24. Retrieved 11/18/23 from https://hindenburgresearch.com/adani/

Hira, Elizabeth. 2021. "The Government Has a Long History of Controlling Women—One That Never Ended." *Brennan Center for Justice*, November 9. Retrieved 11/22/23 from www.brennancenter.org/our-work/analysis-opinion/gov ernment-has-long-history-controlling-women-one-never-ended

Hsiang, Solomon, M. Burke and E. Miguel. 2013. "Quantifying the Influence of Climate on Human Conflict." *Science* 341 (6151). Retrieved 09/09/23 from www.sci ence.org/doi/full/10.1126/science.1235367

Human Rights Watch (HRW). 2019. "Violent Cow Protection in India: Vigilante Groups Attack Minorities." *HRW*, February 18. Retrieved 11/15/23 from www.hrw. org/report/2019/02/19/violent-cow-protection-india/vigilante-groups-attack-minorities

Human Rights Watch (HRW). 2021. "A Threshold Crossed: Israeli Authorities and the Crimes of Apartheid and Persecution." *HRW*, April 27. Retrieved on 09/12/23 from www.hrw.org/report/2021/04/27/threshold-crossed/israeli-authorities-and-crim es-apartheid-and-persecution

Human Rights Watch (HRW). 2023a. "Afghanistan: Taliban's Gender Crimes Against Humanity." *HRW*. Retrieved 11/12/23 from www.hrw.org/news/2023/09/08/afgha nistan-talibans-gender-crimes-against-humanity#:~:text=Human%20Rights%20Wa tch%20research%20on,various%20written%20or%20announced%20decrees

Human Rights Watch (HRW). 2023b. "Israel: Starvation Used as Weapon of War in Gaza." *HRW*. Retrieved 12/18/23 from www.hrw.org/news/2023/12/18/israel-sta rvation-used-weapon-war-gaza

Huntington, Thomas. 2006. "Evidence for Intensification of the Global Water Cycle: Review and Synthesis." *Journal of Hydrology*, 319 (1-4): 83–95. https://doi.org/10/ 1016/j.jhydrol.2005.07.003

Hussein, Mohammed and Mohammed Haddad. 2021. "Infographic: US Military Presence Around the World." *Al Jazeera*, September 10. Retrieved 10/30/23 from www.aljazeera.com/news/2021/9/10/infographic-us-military-presence-around-the-world-interactive#:~:text=Upwards%20of%20750%20US%20bases,is%20publis hed%20by%20the%20Pentagon

International Center for Not-for-Profit Law (ICNL). 2023. "US Protest Law Tracker." *ICNL*. Retrieved 11/17/23 from www.icnl.org/usprotestlawtracker/?loca tion=&status=enacted&issue=&date=&type=legislative#

International Energy Agency (IEA). 2022. "The Role of Critical Minerals in Clean Energy Transitions." *IEA*. Retrieved 09/14/23 from www.iea.org/reports/the-r ole-of-critical-minerals-in-clean-energy-transitions/reliable-supply-of-minerals

Jackson, Jon. 2022. "Watch: Madeleine Albright Saying Iraqi Kids' Deaths 'Worth It' Resurfaces." *Newsweek*, March 23. Retrieved 09/12/23 from www.newsweek.com/ watch-madeleine-albright-saying-iraqi-kids-deaths-worth-it-resurfaces-1691193

Jobain, Najib, S. Kullab and R. Nessman. 2023. "Gaza Awaits Aid from Egypt as Israel Readies Troops for Ground Assault." *Associated Press (AP)*, October 19. Retrieved 10/19/23 from https://apnews.com/article/israel-palestinians-gaza-hama s-war-b084e9c453cc99f7bec6f66d7b5913d9

Jones, Kathy. 2024. "Israel-Gaza War Brings 2023 Journalist Killings to Devastating High." *Committee To Protect Journalists*. Retrieved 02/26/24 from https://cpj.org/ reports/2024/02/israel-gaza-war-brings-2023-journalist-killings-to-devastating-high/

Jowers, Karen. 2023. "More Families File Claims Against Navy for Hawaii Water Contamination." *Military Times*, June 21. Retrieved 11/15/23 from www.milita rytimes.com/pay-benefits/military-benefits/health-care/2023/06/21/more-families-file -claims-against-navy-for-hawaii-water-contamination/

Juhasz, Antonia. 2023. "Why the War in Iraq was Fought for Big Oil." *CNN*, March 19. Retrieved 09/12/23 from www.cnn.com/2013/03/19/opinion/iraq-war-oil-juhasz/ index.html

Kaba, Mariame and Colin Kaepernick. 2021. *Abolition for the People: The Movement for a Future Without Policing or Prisons*. New York: Kaepernick Publishing.

Kaiser Family Foundation (KFF). 2019. "Abortions Later in Pregnancy." *KFF*, December 5. Retrieved 11/22/23 from www.kff.org/womens-health-policy/fa ct-sheet/abortions-later-in-pregnancy/

Kanu, Hassan. 2022. "Police Are Not Primarily Crime Fighters, According to the Data." *Reuters*, November 2. Retrieved 10/25/23 from www.reuters.com/legal/ government/police-are-not-primarily-crime-fighters-according-data-2022-11-02/#: ~:text=Police%20%E2%80%9Chave%20never%20successfully%20solved,anoth er%202021%20law%20review%20article%2C

Kathju, Junaid. 2023. "US Arms Left in Afghanistan Are Turning Up in a Different Conflict." *NBC News*, January 30. Retrieved 11/10/23 from www.nbcnews.com/ news/world/us-weapons-afghanistan-taliban-kashmir-rcna67134

Katz, Jonathan. 2022. *Gangsters of Capitalism: Smedley Butler, the Marines, and the Making and Breaking of America's Empire*. New York: St. Martin's Press.

Katzenstein, Jessica. 2023. "Total Information Awareness: The High Costs of Post-9/ 11 US Mass Surveillance." *Watson Institute of International and Public Affairs at Brown University, Costs of War Project*, September 26. Retrieved 11/15/23 from https://watson.brown.edu/costsofwar/papers/2023/surveillance

Kelly, Linda. 2023. "Russia Recognizes First Crew to Use Hypersonic Missile in Ukraine, TASS Reports." *Reuters*, September 3. Retrieved 11/05/23 from www.reu

ters.com/world/europe/russia-recognises-first-crew-use-hypersonic-missile-ukraine-ta
ss-2023-09-04/#:~:text=Russia%20recognises%20first%20crew%20to%20use%20hy
personic%20missile%20in%20Ukraine%2C%20TASS%20reports,-Reuters&text=
Sept%204%20(Reuters)%20%2D%20The,news%20agency%20reported%20on%
20Monday

Klein, Naomi. 2010. *The Shock Doctrine: The Rise of Disaster Capitalism.* New York: Metropolitan Books.

Klippenstein, Ken and Daniel Boguslaw. 2023. "US Quietly Expands Secret Military Base in Israel." *The Intercept*, October 27. Retrieved 10/30/23 from https://thein tercept.com/2023/10/27/secret-military-base-israel-gaza-site-512/

Koshgarian, Lindsay, A. Siddique and A. Lusuego. 2023. "Tax Day 2023: Where Your 2022 Tax Dollars Went." *Institute for Policy Studies*, April 17. Retrieved 10/30/23 from https://ips-dc.org/report-2023-tax-day-receipt/

Koshgarian, Lindsay, A. Lusuego and A. Siddique. 2023. "The Warfare State: How Funding for Militarism Compromises Our Welfare." *Institute for Policy Studies* and *National Priorities Project*. Retrieved 10/30/23 from https://ips-dc.org/rep ort-warfare-state-how-funding-militarism-compromises-welfare/

Kramer, Andrew. 2011. "US Companies Get Slice of Iraq's Oil Pie." *The New York Times*, June 4. Retrieved 09/13/23 from www.nytimes.com/2011/06/15/business/ener gy-environment/15iht-srerussia15.html#:~:text=The%20oil%20services%20compani es%20Halliburton,is%20not%20the%20oil%20majors

Kramer, Andrew. 2023. "'Where Is the Money?' Military Graft Becomes a Headache for Ukraine." *The New York Times*, September 4. Retrieved 11/15/23 from www. nytimes.com/2023/09/04/world/europe/ukraine-military-spending-corruption.html

Kullab, Samya. 2023. "IAEA Warns of Nuclear Threat as Combat Spikes Near Ukraine Power Plant." *PBS Newshour*, September 9. Retrieved 11/14/23 from www.pbs.org/newshour/world/iaea-warns-of-nuclear-safety-threat-as-combat-sp ikes-near-ukraine-power-plant

Kummerer, Samantha. 2022. "A Majority of Police Agencies Across the US Increased Budgets Despite 'Defund' Movement." *ABC 11 News*, October 14. Retrieved 10/30/23 from https://abc11.com/defund-the-police-budgets-crime-safety/12324529/

Lai, Olivia. 2022. "Water Shortage: Causes and Effects." *Earth.org*, June 22. Retrieved 09/09/23 from https://earth.org/causes-and-effects-of-water-shortage/

Lakhani, Nina. 2023. "Fossil Fuel Firms Spent Millions on US Lawmakers Who Sponsored Anti-Protest Bills." *The Guardian*, October 25. Retrieved 11/15/23 from www.theguardian.com/us-news/2023/oct/25/fossil-fuel-company-donate-lawmakers-a nti-protest-exxon-koch

Lakhani, Nina. 2024a. "Emissions from Israel's War in Gaza Have 'Immense' Effect on Climate Catastrophe." *The Guardian*, January 9. Retrieved 01/09/24 from www.theguardian.com/world/2024/jan/09/emissions-gaza-israel-hamas-war-clima te-change

Lakhani, Nina. 2024b. "Israel is Deliberately Starving Palestinians, UN Rights Expert Says." *The Guardian*, February 27. Retrieved 02/27/24 from www.nytimes.com/ 2024/01/25/world/middleeast/icj-israel-genocide-ruling.html#:~:text=On%20Friday %2C%20the%20court%20ruled,physical%20destruction%20in%20whole%20or

Laudani, Paolo, Izabela Niemiec and Jesus Calero. 2023. "Shipping Firms Avoid Red Sea as Houthi Attacks Increase." *Reuters*, December 19. Retrieved 12/19/23 from www.reuters.com/world/middle-east/shipping-firms-avoid-red-sea-houthi-attacks-in crease-2023-12-18/

Lauer, Katie. 2023. "'Police Playground': Opposition Grows to $44 Million Regional Training Facility and HQ in San Pablo." *East Bay Times*, September 30. Retrieved 10/30/23 from www.eastbaytimes.com/2023/09/30/police-playground-opposition-grows-to-44-million-regional-training-facility-and-hq-in-san-pablo/

Laufer, William and Robert Hughes. 2021. "Justice Undone." *American Criminal Law Review*, 58 (155): 156–203.

Lederer, Edith. 2024. "A UN Envoy Says There Are 'Reasonable Grounds' to Believe Hamas Committed Sexual Violence on Oct. 7." *AP*, March 4. Retrieved on 03/04/24 from https://apnews.com/article/israel-palestinians-un-rape-oct7-hamas-gaza-fe1a35767a63666fe4dc1c97e397177e

Lee, Yong Jei, J. Eck and N. Corsaro. 2016. "Conclusions from the History of Research into the Effects of Police Force Size on Crime—1968 through 2013: A Historical Systematic Review." *Journal of Experimental Criminology* 12: 431–451.

Lenden, Brad and Simone McCarthy. 2023. "Blue-Water Ambitions: Is China Looking Beyond its Neighborhood Now it Has the World's Largest Navy?" *CNN World*, September 2. Retrieved 11/16/23 from www.cnn.com/2023/09/01/asia/china-navy-overseas-military-bases-intl-hnk-ml/index.html#:~:text=China%20has%20built%20the%20world's,mostly%20near%20the%20country's%20shores

Lennard, Natasha. 2023. "The Crackdown on Cop City Protesters is So Brutal Because of the Movement's Success." *The Intercept*, January 27. Retrieved 10/30/23 from https://theintercept.com/2023/01/27/cop-city-atlanta-forest/

Levin, S. 2024. "2023 Saw Record Killings by US Police. Who is Most Affected?" *The Guardian*. Retrieved 01/08/24 from www.theguardian.com/us-news/2024/jan/08/2023-us-police-violence-increase-record-deadliest-year-decade

Lewis, Jangira. 2021. "US Military Pollution: The World's Biggest Climate Change Enabler." *Earth.org*, November 12. Retrieved 11/15/23 from https://earth.org/us-military-pollution/#:~:text=US%20military%20pollution%20is%20a,consideration%20to%20protect%20our%20planet

Lieber, Keir and Daryl Press. 2023. "How America's Adversaries Have Hijacked it's Old Deterrence Strategy." *Foreign Affairs*, October 24. Retrieved 01/15/24 from www.foreignaffairs.com/united-states/return-nuclear-escalation

Lipton, Eric, 2023a. "From Rockets to Ball Bearings, Pentagon Struggles to Feed War Machine." *The New York Times*, March 24. Retrieved 11/14/23 from www.nytimes.com/2023/03/24/us/politics/military-weapons-ukraine-war.html?campaign_id=9&emc=edit_nn_20230324&instance_id=88540&nl=the-morning&regi_id=138697150&segment_id=128630&te=1&user_id=1ceda8aa3bbd02cbe08de642e72d8593

Lipton, Eric, 2023b. "Middle East War Adds to Surge in International Arms Sales." *The New York Times*, October 18. Retrieved 10/25/23 from www.nytimes.com/2023/10/17/us/politics/israel-gaza-global-arms-sales.html

Loewenstein, Antony. 2015. *Disaster Capitalism: Making a Killing Out of Catastrophe*. New York: Verso.

Loewenstein, Antony. 2023. *The Palestine Laboratory: How Israel Exports the Technology of Occupation Around the World*. Brooklyn, NY: Verso.

MacKinnon, Catherine. 1991. *Toward a Feminist Theory of the State*. Cambridge, MA: Harvard University Press.

Mansoor, Sanya. 2023. "What Nebraska's Sentencing of a Teen Who Used Abortion Pills Might Mean in Post-*Roe* America." *Time*, July 26. Retrieved 11/19/23 from https://time.com/6298166/nebraska-abortion-pill-case-legal-experts/

Manthey, Grace, F. Esposito and Amanda Hernandez. 2022. "Despite 'Defunding' Claims, Police Funding Has Increased in Many US Cities." *ABC News*, October 16. Retrieved 06/15/23 from https://abcnews.go.com/US/defunding-claims-police-funding-increased-us-cities/story?id=91511971

Mapping Police Violence. 2023. "Mapping Police Violence." Retrieved 10/15/23 from https://mappingpoliceviolence.org/

Marcetic, Branko. 2022. "NATO Expansion and the Origins of Russia's Invasion of Ukraine." *Responsible Statecraft*, November 18. Retrieved 07/15/23 from https://responsiblestatecraft.org/2022/11/18/nato-expansion-and-the-origins-of-russias-invasion-of-ukraine//

Marcetic, Branko. 2023. "Ukraine's Postwar Reconstruction Has Big Business Licking Its Lips." *Jacobin*, January 19. Retrieved 10/28/23 from https://jacobin.com/2023/01/ukraine-postwar-reconstruction-western-capital-blackrock-neoliberalism

Marlow, Iain. 2023. "US Says it Can't Cut China Out of Critical-Minerals Supply Chain." *Bloomberg*, September 22. Retrieved 09/27/23 from www.bloomberg.com/news/articles/2023-09-22/us-says-it-can-t-cut-china-out-of-critical-minerals-supply-chain#xj4y7vzkg

Mascaro, Lisa. 2023. "House Approves $14.5 Billion in Assistance for Israel as Biden Vows to Veto the GOP Plan." *PBS News Hour*, November 2. Retrieved 11/12/23 from www.pbs.org/newshour/politics/house-approves-14-5-billion-in-assistance-for-israel-as-biden-vows-to-veto-the-gop-plan

Masters, Brooke. 2023. "BlackRock and JPMorgan Help Set Up Ukraine Reconstruction Bank." *Financial Times*, June 18. Retrieved 10/25/23 from www.ft.com/content/3d6041fb-5747-4564-9874-691742aa52a2

Mcfarlane, Sarah and Valerie Volcovici. 2023. "Exclusive: Accounting for War—Ukraine's Climate Fallout." *Reuters*, June 5. Retrieved 11/15/23 from www.reuters.com/world/accounting-war-ukraines-climate-fallout-2023-06-06/

McQuaid, Julia, L. Hanson, D. Jackson, M. D. King and C. Thuringer. 2017. "The Role of Water Stress in Instability and Conflict," Final Report (CRM-2017-U-016532). *Center for Naval Analysis* (CNA). Retrieved 09/02/23 from www.cna.org/CNA_files/pdf/CRM-2017-U-016532-Final.pdf

Mecklin, John. 2023. "A Time of Unprecedented Danger: It is 90 Seconds to Midnight." *Bulletin of the Atomic Scientists*, January 25. Retrieved 07/10/23 from https://thebulletin.org/doomsday-clock/current-time/nuclear-risk/

Mellen, Riley. 2023. "Russia May Be Planning to Test a Nuclear-Powered Missile." *The New York Times*, October 2. Retrieved 11/05/23 from www.nytimes.com/2023/10/02/video/russia-nuclear-missile.html

Miliband, David. 2023. "Our Age of Impunity." *The New York Times*, February 17. Retrieved 11/12/23 from www.nytimes.com/2023/02/17/opinion/ukraine-corruption-human-rights.html

Milne, Sandy. 2022. "How Water Shortages Are Brewing Wars." *BBC*, May 3. Retrieved 10/05/23 from www.bbc.com/future/article/20210816-how-water-shortages-are-brewing-wars

Moyn, Samuel. 2021. *Humane: How the United States Abandoned Peace and Reinvented War*. New York: Farrar, Straus and Giroux.

Mozur, Paul, Muri Xiao and John Liu. 2022. "'An Invisible Cage': How China is Policing the Future." *The New York Times*, June 25. Retrieved 11/13/23 from www.nytimes.com/2022/06/25/technology/china-surveillance-police.html

Murakawa, Naomi. 2014. *The First Civil Right: How Liberals Build Prison America.* New York: Oxford University Press.

Mystal, Elie. 2024. "Alabama's IVF Ruling is Christian Theology Masquerading as Law." *The Nation,* February 23. Retrieved 02/26/24 from www.thenation.com/a rticle/society/alabama-ivf-ruling/

Nasaw, Daniel. 2023. "US Has Given Israel Billions in Military Aid Over the Years." *The Wall Street Journal,* October 7. Retrieved 10/09/23 from www.wsj.com/live coverage/israel-hamas-gaza-rockets-attack-palestinians/card/u-s-has-given-israel-bil lions-in-military-aid-over-the-years-Gj9oQ1zVww0Fey70eV0s

Nashed, Mat. 2024. "With All Eyes on Gaza, Israel Steps up Demolitions of Palestinian Homes." *Al Jazeera,* February 25. Retrieved 02/26/24 from www.aljazeera. com/features/2024/2/25/with-all-eyes-on-gaza-israel-steps-up-demolitions-of-palesti nian-homes

Nichols, Michelle. 2024. "US Blocks Ceasefire Call with Third UN Veto in Israel-Hamas War." *Reuters,* February 20. Retrieved 02/26/24 from www.reuters.com/ world/us-casts-third-veto-un-action-since-start-israel-hamas-war-2024-02-20/

Nuclear Threat Initiative (NTI). 2023. "Country Spotlight: Israel." *NTI.* Retrieved 11/01/23 from www.nti.org/countries/israel/

Observatory of Economic Complexity (OEC). 2023. "Aluminum Ore." *OED.* Retrieved 09/13/23 from https://oec.world/en/profile/hs/aluminium-ore

OHCHR. 2022. "OHCHR Assessment of Human Rights Concerns in the Xinjiang Uyghur Autonomous Region, People's Republic of China." *OHCHR,* August 31. Retrieved 11/15/23 from www.ohchr.org/en/documents/country-reports/ohchr-a ssessment-human-rights-concerns-xinjiang-uyghur-autonomous-region

OHCHR, Special Rapporteur on the Human Right to Safe Drinking Water and Sanitation. 2023. "Frequently Asked Questions." *OHCHR.* Retrieved 10/19/23 from https://sr-watersanitation.ohchr.org/en/rightstowater_5.html

Omi, Michael and Howard Winant. 2014 [1986]. *Racial Formation in the United States* (3rd edition). New York, NY: Routledge.

Open Secrets. 2023. "Defense Lobbying 2022." *Opensecrets.org.* Retrieved 10/31/23 from www.opensecrets.org/industries/lobbying.php?cycle=2022&ind=D

Osborn, Andrew. 2023. "Putin Revokes Russian Ratification of Global Nuclear Test Ban Treaty." *Reuters,* November 2. www.reuters.com/world/europe/putin-revo kes-russias-ratification-nuclear-test-ban-treaty-2023-11-02/#:~:text=Nov%202%20 (Reuters)%20%2D%20President,the%20landmark%20arms%20control%20pact

Oxfam International. 2023. "India: Extreme Inequality in Numbers." *Oxfam International.* Retrieved 11/18/23 from www.oxfam.org/en/india-extreme-inequality-num bers#:~:text=While%20India%20is%20one%20of,through%20crony%20capitalism %20and%20inheritance

Pacchiani, Gianluca and E. Fabian. 2023. "Israel Said to Bomb Rafah Crossing to Egypt After Telling Gazans to Flee Through It." *The Times of Israel,* October 10. Retrieved 10/12/23 from www.timesofisrael.com/israel-said-to-bomb-rafah-cross ing-to-egypt-after-telling-gazans-to-flee-through-it/

Palast, Greg. 2005. "Secret US Plans for Iraq's Oil." *BBC Two: Newsnight,* March 17. Retrieved 09/01/23 from http://news.bbc.co.uk/2/hi/programmes/newsnight/4354269. stm

Parenti, C. 2011. *Tropic of Chaos.* New York: Nation Books.

PBS Newshour. 2023. "Live Updates: What's Happening on Day 13 of the Israel-Hamas War." *PBS Newshour*, October 19. Retrieved 10/19/23 from www.pbs.org/newshour/world/live-updates-whats-happening-on-day-13-of-the-israel-hamas-war

Peltier, Heidi. 2020. "The Growth of the 'Camo Economy' and the Commercialization of the Post-9/11 Wars." *Watson Institute for International and Public Affairs at Brown University* and *The Frederick S. Pardee Center for the Study of the Longer-Range Future at Boston University*, June 30. Retrieved 10/27/23 from http s://watson.brown.edu/costsofwar/costs/social/corporate

Perez, Andrew, N. B. Campbell, J. Warner and L. D. Stockton. 2023. "Military Contractors are Framing the Israeli War on Gaza as a Win for Investors." *Jacobin*, October 28. Retrieved 10/29/23 from https://jacobin.com/2023/10/raytheon-general-dynamics-gaza-israel-war-military-industrial-complex

Pfeifer, Sylvia. 2023. "'We Can De-Risk But Not Decouple' From China, Says Raytheon Chief." *Financial Times*, June 19. Retrieved 11/02/23 from www.ft.com/content/d0b94966-d6fa-4042-a918-37e71eb7282e?accessToken=zwAF_n0pJdKokdPQuUlm1v pAQtOpGDfnHrcoLg.MEUCIE1d_NmTr4P5SftLTcNmzMh849ll6TT2tRGexjoejhe gAiEAiTspBi_mtwj6YxUr5PvOVWa0zv__uYTRJ7OhbEp4IxY&sharetype=gift&to ken=da098c09-273c-4196-b326-1d4dc0b55011

Pfeifer, Sylvia and Eri Sugiura. 2023. "Global Defense Orders Surge as Geopolitical Tensions Mount." *Financial Times*, December 27. Retrieved 12/28/23 from www. ft.com/content/001d2e1c-8e59-444b-a07b-9a62be620431

Pitney, Nico. 2011. "Abizaid: 'Of Course It's About Oil, We Can't Really Deny That.'" *Huffington Post*, May 25. Retrieved 09/10/23 from www.huffpost.com/entry/abizaid-of-course-its-abo_n_68568

Pratt, Timothy. 2023. "Real Cost of 'Cop City' Under Question After Atlanta Approves \$67M for Project." *The Guardian*, June 9. Retrieved 10/30/23 from www. theguardian.com/us-news/2023/jun/09/cop-city-cost-atlanta-city-council#:~:text=The %20city%20owns%20land%20in,the%20city%20at%20%2467m

Prison Policy Initiative (PPI). 2023a. "Race and Ethnicity." *PPI*. Retrieved 10/15/23 from www.prisonpolicy.org/research/race_and_ethnicity/

Prison Policy Initiative (PPI). 2023b. "Mental Health: Policies and Practices Surrounding Mental Health." *PPI*. Retrieved 10/15/23 from www.prisonpolicy.org/research/mental_health/

Rabuy, Bernadette and Daniel Kopf. 2015. "Prisons of Poverty: Uncovering the Pre-Incarceration Incomes of the Imprisoned." Retrieved 10/13/23 from www.prisonp olicy.org/reports/income.html

Rahman, Anjuman. 2023. "Israel's Strategic Weaponization of Water Against Palestine is a War Crime." *Middle East Monitor*, October 7. Retrieved 10/07/2023 from www.juancole.com/2023/10/strategic-weaponization-palestine.html

Rappeport, Alan. 2023. "Yellen Says Bid to Decouple From China Would Be 'Disastrous.'" *The New York Times*, June 13. Retrieved 11/02/23 from www.nytimes. com/2023/06/13/business/economy/janet-yellen-china.html

Reiman, Jeffrey and Paul Leighton. 2023 [1979]. *The Rich Get Richer and the Poor Get Prison* (13th edition). New York: Routledge.

Reporters Without Borders (RSF). 2023. "2023 World Press Freedom Index – Journalism Threatened by Fake Content Industry." *RSF*. Retrieved 11/17/23 from https://rsf.org/en/2023-world-press-freedom-index-journalism-threatened-fake-content-industry

Richards, Alan and N. Singh. 2002. "Inter-State Water Disputes in India: Institutions and Policies." *International Journal of Water Resource Development* 18 (4): 611–625.

Rios, V. 2011. *Punished: Policing the Lives of Black and Latino Boys.* New York: New York University Press.

Robinson, William. 2018a. *Into the Tempest: Essays on the New Global Capitalism.* Chicago, IL: Haymarket Books.

Robinson, William. 2018b. "Debating the Precariat: An Exchange on the Essay, 'The Precariat: Today's Transformative Class?'" *Great Transition Initiative (GTI).* Retrieved on 07/01/23 from https://greattransition.org/roundtable/precariat-william -robinson

Robinson, William. 2020. *The Global Police State.* London, England: Pluto Press.

Robinson, William. 2022a. *Global Civil War: Capitalism Post-Pandemic.* Oakland, CA: PM Press.

Robinson, William. 2022b. *Can Global Capitalism Endure?* Atlanta, GA: Clarity Press.

Robinson, William and Hoai-An Nguyen. 2024. "Gaza: A Ghastly Window Into the Crisis of Global Capitalism." *The Philosophical Salon,* January 15. Retrieved 02/ 26/24 from https://thephilosophicalsalon.com/gaza-a-ghastly-window-into-the-crisis-of-global-capitalism/

Rose, Akira. 2023. "5 Things You Need to Know about Cop City." *American Friends Service Committee (AFSC),* September 15. Retrieved 11/17/23 from https://afsc.org/ news/5-things-you-need-know-about-cop-city

Roy, Arundhati. 2023. "Arundhati Roy: The Dismantling of Democracy in India Will Affect the Whole World." *Scoll.In,* September 14. Retrieved 11/16/23 from https:// scroll.in/article/1055943/arundhati-roy-the-dismantling-of-democracy-in-india-will-a ffect-the-whole-world

Rubin, Anat. 2023. "The Scandal That Never Happened." *ProPublica,* November 4. Retrieved 11/04/23 from www.propublica.org/article/louisiana-judges-ignored-p risoners-petitions-without-review-fifth-circuit

Runde, Daniel and A. Hardman. 2023. "Elevating the Role of Critical Materials for Development and Security." *Center for Strategic and International Studies (CSIS).* Retrieved 09/02/23 from www.csis.org/analysis/elevating-role-critical-minerals-de velopment-and-security

Saaliq, Sheikh. 2023. "1 City, 2 People—and India's Widening Religious Divide." *AP,* April 19. Retrieved 11/17/23 from https://apnews.com/article/india-population-a yodhya-religion-muslims-hindus-070ec1e8ec6fbd0ad2b54ab485ef9531

Savage, Charlie. 2023. "F.B.I. Violated Surveillance Program Rules After George Floyd Protests and Jan. 6 Attack." *The New York Times,* May 19. Retrieved 11/15/23 from www.nytimes.com/2023/05/19/us/politics/fbi-violated-surveillance-program-rules.html

Save the Children. 2023. "Save the Children Calls for a Ceasefire in Gaza as Casualties Soar and Water Runs Out." (press release). *Relief Web/OCHA,* October 17. Retrieved 10/17/23 from https://reliefweb.int/report/occupied-palestinian-territory/sa ve-children-calls-ceasefire-gaza-casualties-soar-and-water-runs-out#:~:text=RAMAL LAH%2C%2017%20Oct%202023%20%2D%20More,calling%20for%20an% 20immediate%20ceasefire

Sawyer, Wendy and Peter Wagner. 2023. "Mass Incarceration: The Whole Pie 2023." *Prison Policy Institute.* Retrieved 06/15/23 from www.prisonpolicy.org/reports/p ie2023.html#bigpicture

Scahill, Jeremy, R. Grim and D. Boguslaw. 2024. "'Between the Hammer and the Anvil': The Story Behind the New York Times October Exposé." *The Intercept,*

February 28. Retrieved 02/28/24 from https://theintercept.com/2024/02/28/new-york-times-anat-schwartz-october-7/

Scauzillo, Steve. 2023. "L.A. County to Treat Severely Mentally Ill Inmates in the Twin Towers Jail." *Los Angeles Daily News*, May 16. Retrieved 10/15/23 from www.dailynews.com/2023/05/16/la-county-to-treat-severely-mentally-ill-inmates-in-the-twin-towers-jail/

Schultz, Kai. 2019. "Murders of Religious Minorities in India Go Unpunished, Report Finds." *The New York Times*, February 18. Retrieved 11/16/23 from www.nytimes.com/2019/02/18/world/asia/india-cow-religious-attacks.html

Schwarz, Jon. 2018. "Lie After Lie: What Colin Powell Knew About Iraq 15 Years Ago and What He Told the UN." *The Intercept*, February 6. Retrieved 09/10/23 from https://theintercept.com/2018/02/06/lie-after-lie-what-colin-powell-knew-about-iraq-fifteen-years-ago-and-what-he-told-the-un/

Segal, Raz. 2023. "A Textbook Case for Genocide." *Jewish Currents*, October 13. Retrieved 10/13/23 from https://jewishcurrents.org/a-textbook-case-of-genocide

Semler, Stephen. 2022. "How Much Did the US Spend on Police, Prisons in FY 2021?" Speaking Security. *Substack*, January 20. Retrieved 11/04/23 from https://stephensemler.substack.com/p/how-much-did-the-us-spend-on-police#:~:text=The%20US%20spends%20at%20least,than%20China's%202020%20military%20budget

Semler, Stephen. 2023. "Biden is Selling Weapons to the Majority of the World's Autocracies." *The Intercept*, May 11. Retrieved 11/03/23 from https://theintercept.com/2023/05/11/united-states-foreign-weapons-sales/

Sharara, F., E. Wool, et al. 2021. "Fatal Police Violence by Race and State in the USA, 1980–2019: A Network Meta-Regression." *The Lancet*, 398 (0307): 1239–1255. https://doi.org/10.1016/S0140-6736(21)01609–01603

Sharp, Jeremy. 2023. "US Foreign Aid to Israel." *Congressional Research Service (CRS)*, March 1. Retrieved 10/01/23 from https://sgp.fas.org/crs/mideast/RL33222.pdf

Singh, Nikhil Pal. 2017. *Race and America's Long War*. Oakland, CA: University of California Press.

Sinmaz, Emine and Sufian Taha. 2024. "'It Was an Execution': Family Mourns Boy Shot Dead by Israeli Forces." *The Guardian*, February 22. Retrieved 02/26/24 from www.theguardian.com/world/2024/feb/22/family-mourns-nihal-abu-ayashboy-shot-dead-israeli-forces-west-bank?utm_term=65d826638bb183a1f5d72001c0b914f9&utm_campaign=GuardianTodayUK&utm_source=esp&utm_medium=Email&CMP=GTUK_email

Skliris, Nikolaos, J. Zika, G. Nurser, S. Josey and R. Marsh. 2016. "Global Water Cycle Amplifying at Less than the Clausius-Clapeyron Rate." *Scientific Reports*, 6 (38752). https://doi.org/10.1038/srep38752

Smith, Chauncee, E. M. Graves, J. Guerrero, M. Ochoa, E. Bitran. 2022. "Reimagining Community Safety in California: From Deadly and Expensive Sheriffs to Equity and Care-Centered Wellbeing." *Catalyst California* and *ACLU of Southern California*. Retrieved 10/25/23 from www.aclusocal.org/sites/default/files/catalyst_ca_aclu_-_reimagining_community_safety_2022.pdf

Speri, Alice. 2017. "Israel Security Forces Are Training American Cops Despite History of Rights Abuses." *The Intercept*, September 15. Retrieved 10/12/23 from https://theintercept.com/2017/09/15/police-israel-cops-training-adl-human-rights-abuses-dc-washington/

Speri, Alice. 2023. "Going All-In for Israel May Make Biden Complicit in Genocide." *The Intercept*, October 19. Retrieved 10/19/23 from https://theintercept.com/2023/10/19/israel-gaza-biden-genocide-war-crimes/?utm_campaign=theintercept&utm_source=twitter&utm_medium=social

Statista Market Insights. 2023a. "Security – Worldwide (Revenue)." *Statista*. Retrieved 10/31/23 from www.statista.com/outlook/dmo/smart-home/security/worldwide#revenue

Statista Market Insights. 2023b. "Cybersecurity – Worldwide (Revenue)." *Statista*. Retrieved 10/31/23 from www.statista.com/outlook/tmo/cybersecurity/worldwide#revenue

Stemen, Dan. 2017. "The Prison Paradox: More Incarceration Will Not Make Us Safer." *Vera Institute of Justice*. Retrieved 10/30/23 from www.vera.org/downloads/publications/for-the-record-prison-paradox_02.pdf

Stewart, Phil, I. Ali and M. Ghobari. 2024. "US and Britain Strike Yemen in Reprisal for Houthi Attacks on Shipping." *Reuters*, January 12. Retrieved 01/12/24 from www.reuters.com/world/us-britain-carry-out-strikes-against-houthis-yemen-officials-2024-01-11/

Stone, Mike. 2023. "Exclusive: US to Send Depleted-Uranium Munitions to Ukraine." *Reuters*, September 5. Retrieved 09/05/23 from www.reuters.com/world/us-send-its-first-depleted-uranium-rounds-ukraine-sources-2023-09-01/#:~:text=WASHINGTON%2C%20Sept%201%20(Reuters),confirmed%20by%20two%20U.S.%20officials

Streep, Abe. 2023. "Inside the $1.5-Trillion Nuclear Weapons Program You've Never Heard Of." *Scientific American*. Retrieved 11/16/23 from www.scientificamerican.com/article/inside-the-1-5-trillion-nuclear-weapons-program-youve-never-heard-of/?utm_source=promotion&utm_medium=email&utm_campaign=december-sa-alert&utm_content=article&utm_term=SA-20231201_CVP_v1_s1

Suter, Margaret. 2017. "Running Out of Water: Conflict and Water Scarcity in Yemen and Syria." *The Atlantic Council*, September 12. Retrieved 09/12/23 from www.atlanticcouncil.org/blogs/menasource/running-out-of-water-conflict-and-water-scarcity-in-yemen-and-syria/

Syed, Armani. 2024. "At World's Top Court, Palestinians Seek an End to Israeli Occupation." *Time Magazine*, February 19. Retrieved 02/26/24 from https://time.com/6696453/icj-case-occupation-israel-palestine/

Taylor, Keeanga Yamahtta. 2021. *From #BlackLivesMatter to Black Liberation* (2nd edition). Chicago, IL: Haymarket Books.

The Economist. 2023a. "Taiwan's Dominance of the Chip Industry Makes it More Important." *The Economist*, March 6. Retrieved 09/20/23 from www.economist.com/special-report/2023/03/06/taiwans-dominance-of-the-chip-industry-makes-it-more-important

The Economist. 2023b. "A New Nuclear Arms Race Looms." *The Economist*, August 29. Retrieved 11/10/23 from www.economist.com/international/2023/08/29/a-new-nuclear-arms-race-looms

The Washington Post. 2023. "Fatal Force." *The Washington Post*. Retrieved 10/15/23 from www.washingtonpost.com/graphics/investigations/police-shootings-database/

The White House. 2022. "FACT SHEET: President Biden's Safer America Plan." *The White House*, August 1. Retrieved 10/30/23 from www.whitehouse.gov/briefing-room/statements-releases/2022/08/01/fact-sheet-president-bidens-safer-america-plan-2/

Tian, Nan, D. L. Da Silva, X. Liang, et al. 2023. "Trends in World Military Expenditure, 2022." *SIPRI*. Retrieved 10/30/23 from www.sipri.org/sites/default/files/2023-04/2304_fs_milex_2022.pdf

Turse, Nick. 2023. "The Pentagon Proclaims Failure in its War on Terror in Africa." *TomDispatch*, November 14. Retrieved 11/17/23 from https://tomdispatch.com/the-pentagon-proclaims-failure-in-its-war-on-terror-in-africa/

Turse, Nick and Alice Speri. 2022a. "Even After Acknowledging Abuses, the US Continued to Employ Notorious Proxy Forces in Camaroon." *The Intercept*, March 9. Retrieved 11/12/23 from https://theintercept.com/2022/03/09/cameroon-military-abuses-bir-127e/

Turse, Nick and Alice Speri. 2022b. "How the Pentagon Uses Secretive Program to Wage Proxy Wars." *The Intercept*, July 1. Retrieved 11/12/23 from https://theintercept.com/2022/07/01/pentagon-127e-proxy-wars/

Unfried, Kerstin, K. Kis-Katos and T. Poser. 2022. "Water Scarcity and Social Conflict." *Journal of Environmental Economics and Management*, 113. https//doi.org/10.1016/j.jeem.2022.102633

UN. 1977. "Protocol Additional to the Geneva Conventions of August 12, 1949, and Relating to the Protection of Victims of International Armed Conflicts (Protocol I)." Retrieved 11/02/23 from www.unhchr.ch/html/menu3/b/93.htm

UNHCR (The UN Refugee Agency). 2023. "Global Trends: Forced Displacement in 2022." *UNHCR*. Retrieved 11/15/23 from www.unhcr.org/global-trends-report-2022

UN General Assembly (UNGA). 2015. "Resolution Adopted by the General Assembly: 70/169. The Human Rights to Safe Drinking Water and Sanitation." *UNGA*, December 17. Retrieved 07/15/23 from https://digitallibrary.un.org/record/821067

UN News. 2022. "'Militarized Approach' to Policing Peaceful Protests, Only Increases Risk of Violence: UN Human Rights Expert." *UN News*, June 20. Retrieved 11/15/23 from https://news.un.org/en/story/2022/06/1120852

UN Office of the High Commissioner for Human Rights (OHCHR). 2023a. "Gaza: UN Experts Decry Bombing of Hospitals and Schools as Crimes Against Humanity, Call for Prevention of Genocide." *OHCHR*, October 17. Retrieved 10/19/23 from www.ohchr.org/en/press-releases/2023/10/gaza-un-experts-decry-bombing-hospitals-and-schools-crimes-against-humanity

UN Office of the High Commissioner for Human Rights (OHCHR). 2023b. "Gaza: UN Experts Call on International Community to Prevent Genocide Against the Palestinian People." *OHCHR*, November 16. Retrieved 11/17/23 from www.ohchr.org/en/press-releases/2023/11/gaza-un-experts-call-international-community-prevent-genocide-against#:~:text=The%20bombardment%20and%20siege%20of,and%2025%20per cent%20are%20women

UN Water Supply and Sanitation Collaborative Council (WSSCC). 2015. "The Human Right to Water and Sanitation: Media Brief." *United Nations*. Retrieved on 09/13/23 from www.un.org/waterforlifedecade/pdf/human_right_to_water_and_sanitation_media_brief.pdf

US Department of Justice (DOJ) Office of Public Affairs. 2016. "Justice Department Announces Findings of Investigation into Baltimore Police Department." *US DOJ*, August 10. Retrieved 10/13/23 from www.justice.gov/opa/pr/justice-department-announces-findings-investigation-baltimore-police-department

US Department of State. 2023. "Transmittal No. DDTC 23–023 Certification of Proposed Issuance of an Export License Pursuant to Section 36(C) of the Arms Export Control Act." *US Department of State*, October 31. Retrieved 11/12/23 from https://static01.nyt.com/newsgraphics/documenttools/5b66fdb955baeecd/5608873d-full.pdf

US Energy Information Administration (EIA). 2021. "Iraq." *USEIA*. Retrieved 09/10/23 from www.eia.gov/international/overview/country/IRQ

US Geological Survey (USGS). 2022. "US Geological Survey Releases 2022 List of Critical Minerals." *USGS*. Retrieved 09/13/23 from www.usgs.gov/news/nationa l-news-release/us-geological-survey-releases-2022-list-critical-minerals

US Senate Select Committee on Intelligence. 2014. "Report of the Senate Select Committee Study of the Central Intelligence Agency's Detention and Interrogation Program." *US Senate*, December 9. Retrieved 10/19/23 from www.intelligence.sena te.gov/sites/default/files/publications/CRPT-113srpt288.pdf

Urban Institute. 2023. "Criminal Justice Expenditures: Police Corrections, and Courts." *Urban Institute*. Retrieved 10/30/23 from www.urban.org/policy-centers/ cross-center-initiatives/state-and-local-finance-initiative/state-and-local-background ers/criminal-justice-police-corrections-courts-expenditures#:~:text=From%201977 %20to%202020%2C%20in,an%20increase%20of%20189%20percent

Vallet, Elisabeth. 2022. "The World Is Witnessing a Rapid Proliferation of Border Walls." *Migration Policy Institute*, March 2. www.migrationpolicy.org/article/rap id-proliferation-number-border-walls

Vitale, Alex. 2017. *The End of Policing*. New York: Verso Books.

Voice of America (VOA). 2023. "UN: Record 6.9 Million Internally Displaced in DR Congo." *VOA*, October 30. Retrieved 11/10/23 from www.voanews.com/a/un-rec ord-6-9-million-internally-displaced-in-dr-congo/7332597.html#:~:text=30%2C% 202023.&text=The%20number%20of%20internally%20displaced,the%20United %20Nations%20said%20Monday

Wacquant, Loic. 2009. *Punishing the Poor: The Neoliberal Government of Social Insecurity*. Durham, NC: Duke University Press.

Walsh, Declan and Abdi Latif Dahir. 2023. "Seizing Darfur Region, Paramilitary Forces Are Accused of Atrocities." *The New York Times*, November 16. Retrieved 11/17/23 from www.nytimes.com/2023/11/16/world/africa/sudan-darfur-fighting.html?campaign_id=9&emc=edit_nn_20231116&instance_id=107853&nl= the-morning&regi_id=138697150&segment_id=150182&te=1&user_id=1ceda8aa 3bbd02cbe08de642e72d8593

Wamsley, Laurel and Bobby Allyn. 2019. "Neo-Nazi Who Killed Charlottesville Protester is Sentenced to Life in Prison." *NPR*, June 28. Retrieved 11/15/23 from www.npr.org/2019/06/28/736915323/neo-nazi-who-killed-charlottesville-protester-is-sentenced-to-life-in-prison

Wang, Leah. 2021. "The US Criminal Justice System Disproportionately Hurts Native People: The Data, Visualized." *PPI*. Retrieved 10/15/23 from www.prisonp olicy.org/blog/2021/10/08/indigenouspeoplesday/

Wang, Leah, W. Sawyer, T. Herring and E. Widra. 2022. "Beyond the Count: A Deep Dive into State Prison Populations." *PPI*. Retrieved 10/16/23 from www. prisonpolicy.org/reports/beyondthecount.html#childhood

Warren, Elizabeth. 2023. "Pentagon Alchemy: How Defense Officials Pass Through the Revolving Door and Peddle Brass for Gold." *United States Senate*. Retrieved 10/30/23 from www.warren.senate.gov/oversight/reports/new-report-from-sena tor-warren-uncovers-defense-industrys-abuse-of-revolving-door-hiring-practices#: ~:text=%E2%80%9CWhen%20government%20officials%20cash%20in,contractin g%2C%E2%80%9D%20wrote%20Senator%20Warren

Willsher, Kim. 2022. "Arms Sent to Ukraine Will End Up in Criminal Hands Says Interpol Chief." *The Guardian*, June 2. Retrieved 11/15/23 from www. theguardian.com/world/2022/jun/02/ukraine-weapons-end-up-criminal-hands-says-in terpol-chief-jurgen-stock

Wolf, Zachary. 2023. "That Jet the Marines Lost? Taxpayers Will Pay $1.7 Trillion for the F-35 Program." *CNN*, September 18. Retrieved 10/29/23 from www.cnn.com/2023/09/18/politics/f-35-missing-jet-what-matters/index.html#:~: text='Failure%20at%20the%20conceptual%20level'&text=The%20jet%20has% 20never%20reached,prototype%2C%E2%80%9D%20Grazier%20told%20me

World Bank. 2022. "Water in Agriculture." *The World Bank*. Retrieved 09/12/23 from www.worldbank.org/en/topic/water-in-agriculture#:~:text=Currently%2C% 20agriculture%20accounts%20(on%20average,to%20the%20evapotranspiration% 20of%20crops)

World Bank. 2023. "Updated Ukraine Recovery and Reconstruction Needs Assessment." *The World Bank*. Retrieved 10/25/23 from www.worldbank.org/en/news/press-release/ 2023/03/23/updated-ukraine-recovery-and-reconstruction-needs-assessment

Zraick, Karen and A. Harouda. 2023. "Israeli Airstrike Hits Greek Orthodox Church Compound in Gaza City." *The New York Times*, October 20. Retrieved 10/20/23 from www.nytimes.com/2023/10/20/world/middleeast/israel-airstrike-gaza-city.html

Zwanenberg, Roger van. 2022. "Hindu Nationalism: BJP in Historical and Comparative Perspective of Fascism." *Policy Perspectives*, 19 (1): 95–109. www.jstor. org/stable/48676297

4 Political Human Rights

Voter Suppression and Undermining Democracy in the US

The US has long cherished its self-designation as the global beacon of democracy and the gold standard to which other countries could and should aspire. This belief lies at the very core of American exceptionalism, where the global hegemon stands somehow outside the reach of its own rules-based international order as the embodiment of rights protective democracy. But democratic processes in the US have always been corrupted by an outsized influence of owning class interests and by forms of popular disenfranchisement levied against those other than White, male, property holding citizens. This is overwhelmingly due to the instrumental and structural influence of capital over the state, the structural imbrication of the state to racist/(neo)colonial systems of expropriation, and a similar imbrication to patriarchal modes of social reproduction—all of which drive state policy to expand the political voice and "rights" of capital while constraining the enfranchisement, political rights, and voice of the diverse working class and general public.

As should be expected, owning class capture of electoral politics and especially attempts to completely exclude or disenfranchise entire swaths of the public—such as for women or people of color—have always been met with resistance from below in a manifestation of the human rights enterprise in action. The right to participate in government—including but not limited to the right to vote—is a clearly articulated, first generation international human right that, at least for the West, stems both from classic antiquity (Hayden 2001) and later from the political theories and social struggles that would climax in the American and French revolutions of the 18th century (Ishay 2008).[1] Specifically, Article 25 of the International Covenant on Civil and Political Rights (ICCPR) demands that all citizens have the right to the following without discrimination, distinction, or "unreasonable restrictions" (ICCPR 2021):

a   To take part in the conduct of public affairs, directly or through freely chosen representatives;

DOI: 10.4324/9781003323556-5

b   To vote and to be elected at genuine periodic elections which shall be by universal and equal suffrage and shall be held by secret ballot, guaranteeing the free expression of the will of the electors;

c   To have access, on general terms of equality to public service in his (sic.) country.

However, the notion of universal voting rights has always been a highly, and often violently contested terrain across US history; noting most obviously the women's suffrage movement of the 19th and 20th centuries and the enduring struggles of African American and other allied populations during the Reconstruction period, and again in the "second Reconstruction," or modern civil rights movement culminating in the civil rights acts and urban rebellions of the 1960s (Blackmon 2009; Taylor 2021a).

The point of this chapter is not to survey this well documented history, but to illustrate how voting rights in purportedly emblematic democratic states like the US are anything but resolved. Instead, the hypocrisy that characterized US and European colonial powers' claims to common humanity in the creation of the United Nations and Universal Declaration in the face of violent colonial repression, apartheid, and Jim Crow segregation in the post-WWII period (Ishay 2008; Blackmon 2009) absolutely continues. This is not only a problem for the US democratic experiment, *but it points to a persistently questionable assumption built into the foundation of international law—that state governments viably represent the interests of their people.*

In what follows, we illustrate how the human right to "universal and equal suffrage" is in crisis for populations of color, immigrants, the poor, the young, the elderly, and those with disabilities in the US, largely through voter suppression bills and redistricting processes (gerrymandering) in states with conservative legislatures. After decades of advances in the voting rights and political power of workers, women, people of color, immigrants, LGBTQ+, and people with disabilities, the tumultuous US 2020 election cycle ushered in a return to rampant political disenfranchisement with a particular focus on voter suppression and gerrymandering. The 2020 election itself presented a number of glaring indications that disenfranchisement is still fundamental to American electoral politics, including constant challenges to mail-in ballots in various states (even after elections were certified in states), the removal of post office drop boxes, the installation of fake ballot drop boxes around city streets, vote nullification schemes, and forms of voter intimidation through the deployment of "poll watchers" to patrol public polling sites. Since the 2020 election and in the run up to 2024, several states have passed policies to suppress the popular vote and reconfigure voting districts (gerrymandering) to eliminate the ability of marginalized populations to gain representation in legislative bodies.[2]

To illustrate, according to research by the Brennan Center for Justice (2023) over 150 bills were introduced in 32 states in state legislative sessions across the US as of January 2023, from which at least 18 states enacted over 30 such laws. Not since the "great betrayal" of former slaves following Civil War Reconstruction in 1877 have there been so many voter restriction bills introduced at one time in the US. The bills passed so far restrict access to voting (by mail, for example), impose stringent voter identification (ID) requirements, and initiate voter purges in search of voter fraud, despite a lack of supporting evidence for such suspicion. They include several large "omnibus" voter restriction bills, such as Texas' SB 1 (see more below), that was so politically divisive that democratic legislators fled the state in an ultimately unsuccessful attempt to deny quorum to the conservative majority and block the bill. In sum, this wave of voter restrictions in conservative states violate the human rights of many Americans in the form of systematic discrimination and a minefield of "unreasonable restrictions" to political participation.

However, efforts at voter suppression and disenfranchisement continue to face significant resistance from below, and voter restrictions are not being applied evenly across the country. In addition to grassroots movements in conservative states like the Poor People's Campaign who are directly confronting voter suppression and pressuring for federal legislative reform around the country, 32 states introduced or enacted 399 laws in 2021 to expand voting access and restore voting rights to some populations, including those with prior criminal convictions (Brennan Center for Justice 2022; Lewis 2022). And by 2023, 34 states introduced at least 274 bills that would expand voting rights (Brennan Center for Justice 2023). But these reforms are mostly occurring in states where comparatively few voting restrictions exist, and the political consequences of an expanding electorate would not affect a considerable political or party shift at the state or national level. Indeed, by 2023 at least 27 states had introduced or enacted more than 250 bills that restrict voter access (Brennan Center for Justice 2022). As such, the expansion of some voting access in already liberal states will not have the effect of cancelling out the drastic curtailment of voting (and other) rights across so-called "red" (conservative leaning) states. Further, and most importantly, it will ultimately be harder for the most marginalized populations (poor people, people of color, immigrants, the elderly, and so forth) to exercise their rights in much of the country. As is now the case for women's reproductive rights since the overturning of *Roe v. Wade*, whether you have the right to vote will largely be determined by the resources available to you and where you happen to live in the US.[3] While this balkanization of rights by individual states is possible in a Federalist system, this does not comport with international law or the international legal obligations of the US under the ICCPR. International law does not make exceptions for the American notion of "state's rights," and constructs current voting restrictions as clear violations.

To wit, the 2018 "Report of the Special Rapporteur on extreme poverty and human rights on his mission to the United States of America" dedicated an entire section to the "undermining of democracy" for America's poor—over represented among the nation's women, children, Black, Latinx, and indigenous populations. The report makes several explicit points on already existing US violations of ICCPR article 25 including (Alston 2018):

- The overt disenfranchisement of nearly 6 million Americans serving felony convictions and millions more ex-felons in the US struggling under their life-long civil penalties, disproportionately affecting African Americans (see also: The Sentencing Project 2022; Eberstadt 2019).
- Other forms of "covert disenfranchisement" in the US, which include "the dramatic gerrymandering of electoral districts to privilege particular groups of voters, the imposition of artificial and unnecessary voter identification requirements, the blatant manipulation of polling station locations, the relocation of the Department of Motor Vehicles' offices to make it more difficult for certain groups to obtain identification, and the general ramping up of obstacles to voting, especially for those without resources" (Alston 2018). As a result, "people living in poverty, minorities and other disfavored groups are being systematically deprived of their right to vote" (Alston 2018).
- Some of the lowest voter turnout rates for elections among all industrialized and post-industrialized countries (approximately 60% in national elections), and the lowest percentage of eligible registered voters (about 64%) among all OECD nations (see also Desilver 2021).
- The absence of meaningful political rights for American citizen residents of Puerto Rico, due to its colonial past and current realities as an annexed American "territory."
- Clearly, "universal and equal suffrage" is far from being realized in the US, and we expect political rights will remain a highly contested terrain for the foreseeable future. But how are we to understand the particularly drastic curtailment of political rights in current contexts? How should we understand the struggle for political rights as a contemporary form of human rights praxis?

Here we recognize the tendency described in our previous work (Armaline, Glasberg, and Purkayastha 2015) that the expanding economic power and "rights" (as people, for instance) of transnational corporations and banks (i.e., transnational capital and the TCC) would be mirrored by shrinking rights for the masses. This relationship between the rights/reach/power of corporations and the rights/voice/power of everyday people in a context where only one of them is to be allotted human rights by the state according to international law, is a thread from our previous work that we expand on here. Moreover, we argue that political repression accompanies the global police state, with the US still firmly at the center of its development and deployment, as power relations are less easily maintained through hegemonic consent, and more people are rendered superfluous to transnational circuits of capital accumulation. In this sense, the US RSA and ISA (of which the political ideological apparatus is a part) work in relative concert with one another as critical state theory would predict.

But the case of the US presents more than a singular (voting) rights crisis—it poses a problem for the formal international legal regime that presumes the legitimacy of state governments in representing the interests of the governed. In fact, this philosophical assumption is made clear in the language of the Universal Declaration of Human Rights (UDHR) (Article 21), where the right to political participation also asserts that, "the will of the people shall be the basis of the authority of government; [and] this will shall be expressed in periodic and genuine elections which shall be by universal and equal suffrage" (UDHR 2021). It is rather dangerous and aspirational to suggest that state governments represent the real, expressed interests of their public—an assumption that in fact undergirds the very notion of defining human rights via treaties between sovereign states.

It goes without saying that many member states to the United Nations are expressly not democracies of any sort. Further, even in liberal democratic states like the US, voting rights are a constantly contested terrain, and their status depend on very real power struggles. Like all human rights, voting and other political rights are not guaranteed simply because of their articulation in formal Constitutional or international law. This is a painfully obvious lesson learned in the history of Reconstruction Era Constitutional legislation like the 14th Amendment or the Civil Rights Acts of 1866 or 1875 that would all wait until the rebellions of the Second Reconstruction to be realized in a lasting, meaningful way (Blackmon 2009, Taylor 2021a). Still, the United States branded itself as a global beacon of democracy in the modern era, and continues to set itself apart as a paragon of freedom and political participation in the world. Further, there is a hegemonic notion expressed in and through international law and US international relations—that a measure of state legitimacy is democratic representation, and that the United States is exceptional in forging that governing principle. The legitimacy of US state authority, and its legitimacy as a global hegemon relative to international law and the "rules based international order" rely on the dominance of these assumptions.

But there is considerable evidence that the democratic legitimacy of the US government is on extremely shaky ground. A well-known study (2014) from researchers Martin Gilens and Benjamin Page examined nearly 1,800 policy issues over 20+ years spanning from the 1980s to the 2000s to test the notion that US operates as a pluralistic democracy as often claimed. Instead, they found overwhelming evidence of "Economic-Elite Domination," finding that "economic elites [the wealthiest 10%] and organized groups representing business interests have substantial independent impacts on US government policy, while mass-based interest groups and average citizens [the remaining 90%] have little or no independent influence" (Gilens and Page 2014:1).

Public opinion polling suggests that the American people agree with this assessment. According to an AP-NORC poll in 2023, only 1 in 10 Americans ranked the US highly on its democratic representation of the constituent public, while over half said the political system in the US does poorly representing Americans' interests on major policy issues (Riccardi and Sanders 2023). Pew Research Center polling (2023b) from the same year suggested that the American public continues to lose faith in the democratic representation and general performance of all three branches of government. Specifically, data suggests that in 2018 only half of adults in the US believed that members of Congress "care about the people they represent *at all*," and by 2023 that number dropped to 38% (Pew Research Center 2023b, emphasis added). Similarly, in 2018, 47% of American adults believed that members of Congress promoted law and policy in the public interest "at least some of the time," and only five years later this number dropped to 36% (Pew Research Center 2023b). Taken together, just under two thirds of adults in the US don't believe that Congress represents the interest of their constituents in any meaningful way. International legal observers also apparently agree. In a 2021 interview, former UN independent expert on the promotion of a democratic and equitable international order Alfred-Maurice de Zayas asserted that the US is not a "functional democracy," claiming that the US "may call itself democratic, but in essence, it's an oligarchy" (*XinhuaNet* 2021; *Daily News Egypt* 2021). He pointed specifically to the overwhelming influence of the transnational military industrial complex over US policy, and decried endless weapons spending in the face of "millions of people dying of hunger" and "extreme poverty" across the world (*XinhuaNet* 2021; *Daily News Egypt* 2021).

In turn, there is considerable pressure on the US to create the appearance of democracy to avoid legitimacy crisis, while simultaneously subverting and warping that very "democratic" process. As discussed in Chapter 1, this is not unique to the US, or even to liberal electoral democracies—but instead reflects the crisis of state legitimacy created as states fulfill their role to secure transnational capital accumulation and maintain the foreground and background relations of capitalist society. Today, two primary tools for subverting the political rights of everyday people in the US are voter suppression and redistricting (gerrymandering), which together ensure the disenfranchisement of populations whose interests are likely to challenge or be inconsistent with those of the TCC or the entrenched privileges of (for example) patriarchy, white supremacy, or heteronormativity.

Further, as will be discussed in the following chapter (Chapter 5), questions of political enfranchisement—in the US and all over the world—are complicated by exploding migration. The UN has long predicted (McAuliffe and Khadria 2020) and we have already discussed massive increases in human migration resulting from a mix of rising conflicts, resource and care needs in parts of the aging worlds, climate change, and a global economic system relegating more and more people to increasingly precarious labor and living conditions (see also Apostolidis 2019; Chacko and Price 2020; Jordan 2017). The status and experiences of migrants provide a lens into assessing the actual universality of political human rights and the growing processes of politically, socially, and economically disenfranchising migrants who would have been able to claim some types of political, social, economic or cultural rights during previous phases in the 20th century. Moreover, the case of migrants starkly reveals the dynamic balance powerful states like the US maintain between economic needs for cheap labor—including care labor—and the historical reluctance of states dependent on migrant labor to grant them political rights.

The restriction of political rights exacerbates other structured inequalities as well. Illustrated by the rollback of bodily autonomy and reproductive rights in the US, political disenfranchisement and the empowerment of capital accumulation interests undermine the rights of women and other (trans or gender non-conforming) people capable of pregnancy. The curtailment of reproductive rights can push women and girls once again toward subservient, expropriable positions in the process of social reproduction, making them more vulnerable to the imperatives of transnational capital accumulation. Similarly, continued political disenfranchisement of people of color in the US reinforces systemic racism in an attempt to constrain their historically won rights and subjugate a population whose expropriated labor has always served as a backbone of capital accumulation and the building of the American hegemonic world order (as discussed in Chapter 2). As we've argued previously, institutional and legal contexts complicate the ability to achieve rights in practice, particularly for already marginalized populations (Armaline, Glasberg and Purkayastha 2015; see also Bonilla-Silva and Mayorga 2009; Falcon 2009; Libal and Hertel 2011; Rosino 2017). While we are discussing political rights here, and racial and gendered justice by implication, the ability of the human rights enterprise to thoroughly accomplish either or both of those goals is compromised by the systemic imperatives of capitalist society. That is, the goals of racial and gendered justice and universal enfranchisement confront the background relations of capitalist society, and their ability to divide and discipline the diverse working class.

Corporations, financial firms, and the TCC that own and run them are well aware of the need to influence or capture political institutions for the purposes of capital accumulation and maintaining the background relations of capitalist society, as evidenced by the history of US corporate case law (Bakan 2004, 2020) and the 2010 *Citizens United v. Federal Elections Commission* Supreme Court decision that awarded corporations "rights" to political speech, translating in part to nearly unrestricted spending on campaign funding in US elections. It isn't surprising that such decisions have vastly increased the political influence and power of corporations, banks, and the owning class in the US, as they have unleashed the concentrated wealth and power of national and transnational capital on the US political system (see also Evers-Hillstrom, Arke and Robinson, 2019; Lao, 2019;

Shiribman, 2020). This growth of corporate owning class power has been accompanied by accelerating attempts by capital and conservative political groups (think tanks, lobbying firms, and so forth) to disenfranchise marginalized populations that have in previous decades gained greater access to rights (Berman, 2016, 2017; Levinson-King, 2020). As we will find, conservative think tanks and dark money groups have been the central drivers of expanding corporate "rights" and the curtailment of political and other rights—such as those to reproductive health care—for the public masses in recent years through a decades long effort to politicize and transform state and federal courts in the US.

The systemic, cannibalistic imperatives of capitalism's foreground and background relations, discussed in Chapters 1 and 2, are absolutely antagonistic to human rights and survival, including the kinds of political rights through which common people can effectively change conditions and systems. The shrinking of political and other rights in step with expanding "rights" for corporations and their owners/managers in the TCC continues to present a formidable challenge for the human rights enterprise. Though electoral political rights are not always the best or only form of political action for realizing social change in the relations of power, it remains useful to examine the struggle for universal suffrage as political right with great bearing on the legitimacy of states and of US hegemony in particular. This is especially important considering the stakes of upcoming US elections and their implications for global stability (remembering the role of the US, for instance, at the center of the global police state) or action on climate change at the international level, and issues of economic justice, racial justice, LGBTQ+ rights, the rights of migrants, and the rights of women (e.g., reproductive rights) within the US.

Setting the Stage: What Do Voting Participation Patterns Look Like in the US?

Though popular electoral participation spiked in 2020 (at approximately 66%), voting participation in the US is typically low (rarely over 60%), and is lowest among industrialized and post-industrial nations (Schlozman, Brady, and Verba 2018). The strongest participation rates occur in the US during presidential elections, and drop dramatically for elections at all levels (federal, state, local) in the midterms. However, a demographic breakdown of electoral participation reveals an even more troubling pattern: underrepresented populations, younger voters, and lower-income voters have tended to participate in the lowest proportions; and while voting by women in the US has surged in recent years, they too have lagged behind the participation rates of Whites and men. There is a myriad of explanations for these patterns (see Silfen Glasberg and Shannon 2011), including social psychological factors stemming from individuals' political socialization (Lipset 1960; Schwadel 2002); structural and institutional obstacles created by the rules of voting (Piven and Cloward 2000); and political apathy resulting from the sense that it makes no difference who wins (Bay and Blekesaune 2002; Docherty, Goodland and Paddison 2001). However, none of these explanations address the effect of political alienation (the belief that voting simply doesn't or can't address individuals' needs—an understandable assumption given current data previously discussed), or the deliberate impediments created by practices and policies that pose roadblocks to participation, particularly for traditionally disenfranchised populations (women, people of color, the poor, the incarcerated, etc.). Many existing explanations for low political participation ignore the deliberate political restructuring of voting rights primarily gerrymandering and voter suppression in the case of the US—that subvert the democratic process and undermine political rights. But how are voter suppression and gerrymandering best understood or defined in the US, and how does a critical sociological framework help us understand their deployment and implications for human rights and survival?

Voter Suppression in the US

Voter suppression is the practice of creating policies and practices that systematically reduce or eliminate access to voting rights to particular populations. According to the Voting Rights Alliance (Arnwine, 2011), there are at least 61 identifiable types of voter suppression across US history. The introduction of voter suppression policies accelerated following the 2020 Presidential election that saw the highest participation rate of marginalized populations and younger voters than ever before, ushering in the election of President Joseph Biden and prompting cries of "voter fraud" and a "rigged election" by former President Trump and right populist, so-called "MAGA Republicans" (a claim that has been resoundingly rejected repeatedly at every level of the judicial system and by states' own Secretaries of State, including Republicans, after several recounts).

Generally speaking, high voter turnout rates tend to produce greater support for more progressive candidates and policies that favor the poor, underrepresented, and relatively disempowered populations (Avery and Peffley 2005; DeNardo 1980). It should be no surprise that tactics have evolved since to suppress their vote. Voter suppression policies and practices are not new, dating back to the mid-19th century during the development of municipal and federal government in the US, and to efforts to deny formerly enslaved populations the fruits of newly won civil and political rights following the Civil War (Wang 2012). Contemporary use of these practices, combined with modern technology, has accelerated disenfranchisement of voters who are poor, young, or racialized people of color. Of late in the US, disenfranchisement schemes have primarily targeted three main groups in ways that mirror those of the Jim Crow Era: convicted felons (who are disproportionately poor, Black, and Brown), the homeless, and immigrants (Manza and Uggen 2008; Ruth, Matusitz, and Simi 2017; Minnite and Piven 2012).

Convicted Felons

No other representative democracy in the world besides the US permanently strips convicted felons of their right to vote through the application of "civil penalties" (Alexander 2020), even after they have completed their prison sentences, probation, and/or parole. But voting eligibility is to a large degree a state-controlled issue, so it varies across the country. For example, people convicted of felonies are stripped of their right to vote while incarcerated in all states except Maine and Vermont, (Spates and Mathis 2014). Convicted felons in Kentucky, and Virginia are disenfranchised forever, even after completing their so-called "debt to society" (ACLU, 2022; Gray 2014). Further, in 15 states those on probation are ineligible to vote, and those on parole are barred from voting in 17 states (ProCon.Org, 2022).

This is no small matter. Nearly 1.3 million people in the US are currently serving prison sentences (note, this does *not* include those in jail or immigrant detention), and approximately 20 million Americans have felony convictions—up from less than two million in 1948 (Sawyer and Wagner 2023; Eberstadt 2019). Notably, Black and Brown people, especially men, are disproportionately represented in the prison population. The Sentencing Project (2022) has estimated that over 5.2 million people in the US have lost their right to vote, temporarily or permanently, because they are currently under sanction for felony convictions. More than one fourth of these are Black men, representing about one out of 16 Black males in the US (compared with one in 59 non-Black males) (Uggen et al. 2020). Indeed, while the Constitution provided full voting rights to all citizens after the Civil War, states like Florida found a way to confront the perceived demographic threat by disproportionately policing and sanctioning Black communities while passing lifetime voting bans on convicted felons. This strategy became commonplace around the country, as the "wars" on drugs and crime in the late 20th and early 21st centuries targeted the poor and Black, Latinx, and indigenous populations (Elfrink 2018) and the US committed to its long, arguably failed experiment with mass incarceration.

It is difficult to overstate the racist political consequences of this widespread disenfranchisement of Black men in the US. In Wyoming and Tennessee, the felony disenfranchisement of Black men now exceeds 20% (one in five), and nine additional states (including Virginia and Kentucky, where disenfranchisement is permanent) are quickly approaching the same rate (Uggen et al. 2020). Alexander (2020) referred to the implications of such "civil penalties" (including but not limited to felon disenfranchisement) as part of "the New Jim Crow," referring to the various mechanisms developed in the wake of the 20th century civil rights movement to deny Black people the right to vote under a colorblind crime-fighting discourse rather than an overtly racial discourse of segregation or apartheid.

The Homeless

Although every state in the US formally allows the homeless the right to vote, the very circumstances of homelessness pose severe obstacles to voting, given the practices and policies in most states regarding voter eligibility and the distribution and casting of ballots. For example, most, if not all states have residency requirements to establish an individual's rightful voting district and supposedly deter fraudulent votes. For someone who is homeless, establishing residency (typically defined as a permanent or long-term residency in a permanent structure such as a house or apartment) is at the very least difficult if not impossible, since most homeless people are transient by necessity or definition. The Supreme Court had previously stepped in to address this: in *Pitts v. Black* (1984) the Court instructed states to broaden their definitions of residence so that any location, such as a park, street corner, or shelter such as a tent, intended as a living space for an indefinite period of time would be construed as legitimate. Nearly a decade later, in *National Coalition for the Homeless v. Jenson* (1992), the Court determined that it is unconstitutional to disenfranchise the homeless by requiring the establishment of residency in a more conventional residence.

In addition to residency requirements, federal law requires an identification (ID) such as a valid driver's license or Social Security number to register to vote. Securing such documents can be a monumental obstacle for someone who is homeless, because such IDs are also complicated by the need for a verifiable address. Federal law establishes that individuals who do not have these IDs can get a voter ID card that theoretically would allow them to vote. However, when they show up at the polls in most states, they are often required to present a valid form of ID along with their voter ID, thereby making the solution moot (Ruth, Matusitz, and Simi 2017; Keyssar 2013; Bentele and O'Brien 2013; Minnite and Piven 2012; Keyes, Millhiser, Van Oster, and White 2012). Although they may be issued a provisional ballot to vote, which requires validation before being counted, this acts as a humiliating discouragement to voting for the homeless (National Coalition for the Homeless 2010), and for other populations, such as the elderly, who may not have need for or access to a driver's license or state ID.

It became painfully clear during the COVID pandemic that structural inequalities in the labor and housing markets (see also Taylor 2021b) are heavily racialized, throwing millions of people, particularly Black and Brown people, into unemployment and eviction. As discussed in the Introduction, the homeless population in the US has grown to record highs amidst a massive housing crisis, and the people most likely to be disenfranchised and otherwise affected are traditionally disempowered populations—such as the young, the elderly, those with disabilities, the poor, people of color, and immigrants.

Immigrants

Again, the history of political rights and citizenship in the US has been heavily intertwined and shaped by the state's relation to capitalism, geopolitics (empire), and the background relations of capitalist society, where voting rights were most consistently reserved for White male property owners. The framing of suffrage was at first explicitly based on class in addition to race or gender (property ownership was viewed to provide independence of thinking, and was originally a requirement to vote or hold office in many states). The political exclusion of those without property, women, people of color, and the indigenous gave White male elites electoral dominance in the country. While the Fifteenth Amendment, which passed in 1870 during the Reconstruction period, granted Black men the right to vote, it sparked an almost instant backlash—particularly but not exclusively in the south, where paramilitary forces (the Ku Klux Klan), poll taxes, literacy requirements, and other so-called "black codes" under Jim Crow laws effectively nullified that right for another century (Lalami 2020).

The US has a spotty and often clumsy history of extending and then restricting voting rights of immigrants, sometimes allowing them to vote in state and local elections if not federal elections. In fact, while individual states and municipalities may allow non-citizens to vote, federal law bars non-citizens from voting in federal elections. The process is complicated because significant delays in the immigration system—for some it can be up to a decade—prevent immigrants from achieving citizenship and the right to vote in federal elections. Finally, the treatment of White European origin immigrants in the Northeast—variably considered "White" or "non-White," but eventually constructed as legitimate political subjects—vary from (for example) the treatment of Mexican, Central American, and indigenous populations in the west and southwest, who were made "immigrants" through forced displacement or national boundary changes and subjugated to extrajudicial violence (such as lynching) and social, political, and economic exclusion similar to that of the formerly enslaved (Grandin 2020).

The extension of such limited enfranchisement of immigrants since the 1970s has become more front-and-center in US politics (see Ruth, Matusitz and Simi 2017). Indeed, the struggle over immigrants' enfranchisement have been central in the battles over broader immigration policy since the late 1990's that re-emerged in the Trump/MAGA movement of 2016 and 2020. Estimates suggest that the US is now home to the highest proportion of documented and undocumented immigrants in the last hundred years. The result is a significantly depressed voting participation rate of Latinx and Asian people, who remain the dominant immigrant populations attempting to enter the US (Passel and Krogstad 2023; Budiman, Tamir, Mora, and Noe-Bustamante 2020; Parkin and Zlotnik 2014).

It is hard to ignore the implications of this suppression. Given the increasing numbers of Asian and Latinx immigrants over the past decade, there is strong potential for substantial immigrant voting blocks in state and local elections. This is something that conservatives, nativists, and white supremacists in the US have long decried as a demographic threat to the "American way of life" (in so-called theories of "replacement" or "white genocide," see Hayduk 2006). Demographers' predictions that Whites are likely to represent a statistical minority nationwide by 2030 has fueled such fears, along with the propagandizing of any number of right-wing pundits and social media personalities.

The suppression of immigrants' voting rights results in the significant loss of potential political power for millions of residents who are essential to the functioning of American society. The indispensability of immigrant labor was made abundantly clear during the COVID pandemic, where even at the height of the emergency, immigrants in agricultural labor—overwhelmingly immigrants of color—were forced to continue working in the fields and slaughterhouses that continued to feed the American public. This was accomplished through the Trump Administration's application of the Defense Production Act (DPA) that required workers in US meat processing facilities (slaughterhouses and meat packing plants) to stay on the job while protecting companies (such as Tyson Foods) from legal liability for the predictable infections and deaths that followed for their workers (Laughland and Holpuch 2020). The disenfranchisement of immigrants, including but not by any means limited to agricultural labor, contributes to the construction and treatment of immigrant lives and labor as expropriable by corporate capital and the state, and limits their political options to challenge that construction.

Renewed Voter Suppression in the Twenty-First Century

The unique circumstances of the 2020 presidential election, in the context of a global pandemic, created great potential for increasing voter access, but also unfortunately saw widespread attempts to further suppress participation, particularly among underrepresented populations. While states all around the US tried to develop safe voting protocols to minimize the spread of the COVID-19 (that ramped up considerably as election day approached), efforts to undermine these efforts and nullify votes quickly followed. The creativity and variety of these efforts were impressive to say the least.

Most if not all states allowed early voting, "no-excuse" mail-in ballots, and special drop boxes for ballots in an effort to reduce long lines, avoid crowded polling places, encourage social distancing, and enable people who couldn't afford to take time off from work to vote. Election observers in the US have long argued that increased participation rates in voting tend to favor more progressive policies, parties (typically the Democratic Party), and politics (Pew Research Center 2023a). This is one of several reasons why voter registration drives, voting rights efforts, and "get-out-the-vote" drives have often been central strategies of the civil rights and other progressive movements.

Conservative opponents to increasing voter participation in the 2020 election launched several strategies to subvert the rights of voters and thereby depress voter turnout. For example, there were widespread, multimedia disinformation campaigns to inspire disruptions in the democratic process while confusing and intimidating voters (particularly immigrant voters, who were made to fear deportation because voting might call attention to ICE) in battleground states. For instance, during the campaign Trump himself used Twitter (now "X") to encourage supporters to "liberate" Michigan, Minnesota, and Virginia from their Democratic governors, inciting large and belligerent protests (for example, an armed militia entered the Michigan statehouse looking for its Governor in an attempt to remove her) (Miller and Sedensky, 2020). He also used social media to instigate "Trump's army" of poll watchers to show up at polling places, often openly carrying long guns and other weapons to interrogate, challenge the legitimacy of, and otherwise intimidate people waiting in line to vote (Liu, Rhyne, Tabrizy, Laffin, and Sarhan 2020).

In addition, conservatives in several states sought to nullify the legitimacy of more liberal or progressive voters between 2016 and the 2020 election. For example, Nevada labeled 90,000 otherwise legitimate voters to an "inactive" status, Indiana canceled nearly half a million registrations, Georgia delayed 53,000 registrations (70% of which were African American, despite the fact that African Americans were only one-third of the Georgia population) (Brater, Morris, Perez, and Deluzio 2018), and Florida placed 27,000 re-enfranchisement applications on hold. Meanwhile, North Dakota disenfranchised 70,000 voters under a street address voter ID law (Mayer and DeCrescenzo 2017), Texas rejected thousands of online registrations; and Ohio purged registered voters who failed to vote in two federal elections—a practice upheld by the Supreme Court (Weindling 2018; NPR 2018; Hughey 2020). Many states saw well-organized challenges in the courts and in state legislatures to same-day registration, early voting, and mail-in ballots (it is noteworthy that mail-in ballots have traditionally been used without challenge by military personnel stationed abroad). Other states saw the installation of fraudulent ballot drop boxes that could capture the ballots of unsuspecting voters so that they would never be counted (Thrush and Medina 2023). In many Black and Brown voting districts drop boxes were simply removed and/or polling places were closed. In fact, in the six years following the 2013 *Shelby v. Holder* Supreme Court decision to strike down key provisions of the Voting Rights Act, local districts around the country previously covered by the Act in 13 states shut down 1,688 polling places (The Leadership Conference on Civil and Human Rights 2019). The closing of polling places posed considerable challenges for those attempting to assert their rights. In Georgia, for example, voters trying to cast their ballots in the 2018 midterms waited for more than four hours to vote in polling places where some voting machines were inoperable. (Gardner and Reinhard 2018).

Some voter suppression efforts during this period were targeted at indigenous and immigrant populations. During the same midterm elections of

2018, Native Americans in North Dakota were denied the right to vote because poll workers rejected IDs that had been issued by tribal officials. In Texas, there were complaints that voters with limited command of the English language were barred from bringing interpreters with them, because the ballots were not bilingual (Gardner and Reinhard 2018).

Even after the 2020 election was over, voter suppression attempts led by Trump and his Republican supporters continued. Trump himself engaged in attempts to nullify ballots already cast and recounted in Georgia with a phone call to the Secretary of State, pressuring him to falsify the count in his favor, and filing more than 60 lawsuits seeking to overturn the election results. Significantly, many of these lawsuits targeted the results in Milwaukee, Detroit, Philadelphia and Atlanta, "all of them cities with significant Black populations in states that he lost" (Cobb 2021:30). These lawsuits were denied by the courts, including the Supreme Court, prompting a refusal by Trump to concede the election to Biden or to engage in a peaceful transfer of power. Ultimately, he incited insurrectionists to try to stop the vote count by violently storming the Capitol in Washington, DC while Congress was attempting to certify the Electoral College votes. And although court cases filed by Trump and his supporters denied their claims of widespread voter fraud, Republican supporters continued that spurious narrative, insisting that legal solutions to the non-problem were necessary: at least 43 states had more than 250 new laws proposed that would limit mail-in ballots, early in-person voting, and pose stricter ID laws, limited polling hours, and far more stringent absentee ballot rationales (Gardner, Rabinowitz, and Stevens 2021; Izaguirre and Coronado 2021; Nadler and Yoganathan 2021). Following the 2020 election, six states established "election integrity units" to criminally investigate cases of voter fraud. According to a December 2023 investigation by *The Washington Post* (Jouvenal 2023), these units were only able to secure 47 convictions (in Florida, Texas, and Ohio) with another 42 cases dropped or dismissed, where the violations were almost entirely single cases of human error rather than some widespread pattern of fraud. Perhaps most tellingly, the election integrity units overwhelmingly targeted Black and Latinx voters (76%) in their pursuit (Jouvenal 2023).

In 2021 efforts continued full-steam-ahead in conservative states to severely curtail voting rights in ways that would impact marginalized populations of all party affiliations. By the end of 2021, 19 states had passed 34 laws designed to hinder or obstruct access to voting (Wilder and Baum 2022). Among these included Florida Senate Bill 90, which implemented wide-ranging restrictions on mail voting, which millions of voters successfully used during the pandemic. Georgia Senate Bill 202, described by some analysts as a form of "Jim Crow in the 21st century" (Amy 2021:3), criminalized the provision of water or food to voters standing on long lines waiting to vote (Georgia has long suffered an infamous reputation of limiting polling places in largely black voting districts, causing huge lines in extreme heat). Iowa Senate File 413 made it a crime for election officials to protect voters from voter roll purges. Montana House Bill 176 eliminated Election Day registration (one Republican state representative asserted that same-day registration enfranchised younger voters who tended not to be sympathetic to conservatives).

Moreover, Texas State Bill 1 was an aggressive, broad bill designed for voter suppression. It restricted mail-in ballots, threatened poll workers and election officials with criminal charges if they so much as encouraged eligible voters to request them, and required voters who were approved to use mail-in ballots to put their Social Security numbers on the ballot in a potentially serious breach of privacy rights (Wilder and Baum 2022). When introduced, the Texas bill even borrowed a phrase from southern US House Democrats pursuing the end of Black Reconstruction in 1893, calling for measures to "purify the ballot"—presumably from the stain of Black suffrage. Though this phrase was eventually struck from the bill, and Democratic Texas congressmembers—many of them Black and Latinx—went to extremes to stop the bill's passage, including fleeing the state to deny quorum to the Texas legislature at risk of arrest and censure (Johnstone and Grumbach 2021).

Despite resistance, on September 7th 2021, Texas Governor Greg Abbott signed the controversial SB1—an "omnibus" voting restriction bill that conservatives argued was necessary to address "voter fraud" and protect the legitimacy of elections in the state. This was despite the fact that there was no evidence of significant voter fraud in Texas, or anywhere else in the country for that matter. A study by the Texas Attorney General's office found only 16 cases of incorrect addresses out of over 17 million voter registration applications; and since 2010, only two cases of (in person) voter impersonation were tried to conviction (Weinberg 2021). It is also important to note that even before SB 1, Texas was the hardest state in the country to cast a ballot according to research by Northern Illinois and Jacksonville Universities that provide a "cost of voting index" nationwide (Schraufnagel, Pomante, and Li 2020). This is further born out in voter participation statistics, where Texas ranks near the bottom of the US at 45.6% of the eligible electorate (Ramsey 2020). In addition to existing barriers, Texas Senate Bill 1 banned drive-thru and 24-hour voting, further restricted early voting, made it more difficult for those with disabilities or who speak English as a second language to receive assistance, prohibited sending mail ballot applications to eligible voters, required hand signatures and identification numbers on all mail-in ballots, expanded the possible number and reach of so-called "poll watchers" at polling sites, and restricted the ability of Texas courts to make accommodations to voters during natural disasters or pandemic conditions (Weinberg 2021). Finally, there were early indications that these restrictions had the most negative impacts on the voting rights of the poor, elderly, young, disabled, and populations of color (Latinx, Black, and indigenous people in particular) in Texas for many of the reasons already discussed (Weinberg 2021).

But as illustrated throughout this chapter, suffrage is a constantly contested terrain in the US, and such voter suppression policies like Texas's SB 1 have not enjoyed unwavering support, and continue to face court and legislative challenge. For example, in April 2022, Chief US District Court Judge Mark Walker ruled that Florida's voter suppression strategies were intolerable, noting the state's increasingly racist history. His nearly-300-page ruling determined that Florida's laws increasingly made voting inaccessible to Black voters because of their propensity to favor Democratic candidates (Romance 2022). He continued, "in summation, Florida has a horrendous history of racial discrimination in voting, noting that at some point … this court can no longer accept that the effect is incidental (Romance 2022).

However, despite this pointed judicial repudiation of Florida's draconian policies to suppress the vote of marginalized populations, most voter suppression initiatives in the state remain.

The continued curtailment of political rights for those most marginalized in the US—the poor and people of color in particular—should be understood as an explicit strategy of the American owning class to suppress public political participation as capitalism faces crisis and humanity faces OTHS. Made clear in a leaked video (Berman and Surgey 2021; Corasaniti and Epstein 2021), Heritage Action for America—a "dark money"[4] offshoot of the conservative think tank, The Heritage Foundation—continues to lead "a massive campaign to draft and pass model legislation restricting voting access, which was been swiftly adopted (in 2021) in the battleground states of Georgia, Florida, Arizona, and Iowa [and now Texas]" (Berman and Surgey 2021). In their own words, Heritage Action America spent over $24 million by 2021 to "create this echo chamber" about the need for voter restrictions (Corasaniti and Epstein 2021). While there was some resistance (a single letter/statement) to the Texas voting restrictions by TNCs in the state such as Microsoft and Patagonia, this was not the broad response of corporate or finance capital in the state—noting the particular silence of fossil fuel companies.

The important point here is that the wave of voter suppression bills across the country has been financed and directed by big business through the now common mechanism of the think tank (e.g, the Heritage Foundation) and Political Action Committee (e.g., Heritage Action for America). Contemporary voter suppression cannot be accurately described as the result of "right wing populism," or even purely partisan party politics, but must be understood in the context of a broader class and boundary struggles in a capitalist society. Shortly, we will find the same forces, funded and administered by the same or similar organizations and capital interests, have been behind the regression of reproductive rights in the US—another impact of the expanding power of the corporate owning class, rather than simply a religious conservative or right populist project. But first, we will briefly discuss the use of "gerrymandered" Congressional districts as one of the most common forms of contemporary voter suppression in the US, as it is likely to remain an issue of contention for election cycles to come.

Gerrymandering

While voter suppression tactics commonly employ extra-legal practices (such as voter intimidation) and the manipulation of policies and procedures for casting ballots, gerrymandering involves legally manipulating the Congressional redistricting process for political gain. The Constitution calls for redrawing Congressional voting district lines that define representation in the House of Representatives to reflect shifts in population documented by the Census every ten years; where states with population declines should lose the number of representatives they can send to Congress, while states with increasing populations should gain representatives. This constitutional provision vests the power of legislative reapportionment in state legislatures and governors (Forgette and Winkle 2006). Although the regular redrawing of voting district boundaries was originally designed to create representative balance in Congress based on population, this process also became subject to political weaponization by political parties in competition for Congressional seats.

For conservative leaning states, this has often led to the suppression of representation by poor, Black, Brown, and indigenous populations. Indeed, Okonta (2018) refers to the blatant racism of gerrymandering districts in this way as a "badge of slavery," echoing the Post-Reconstructionist Jim Crow laws designed to deny Blacks the right to vote and other political rights. In effect, gerrymandering is the practice of redrawing legislative voting district boundaries to advantage one group over another, frequently advantaging White and traditionally empowered (such as the wealthy) voters. In cases where diverse representation is being restricted, gerrymandering ultimately serves as a mechanism for subverting the Voting Rights Act of 1965 that enfranchises underrepresented populations by prohibiting redistricting that eliminates or minimizes the effectiveness of minority votes.

For example, in North Carolina gerrymandering was used to break apart largely African American districts and splinter Black neighborhoods and households into several White districts where their votes were diluted (Ingraham 2018). In 2022, the state's Supreme Court ruled the state's gerrymandered districts as unconstitutional under a liberal Court majority along party lines. However, in 2023, when the state's Supreme Court flipped to a Conservative majority, it reversed its 2022 decision (suggesting it had no authority to act), helping to solidify Republican control of the state legislature (Wines 2023). In the end, conservatives in the North Carolina Supreme Court and legislature have been able to effectively curtail the Constitutional and human political rights of Black and other affected constituents through gerrymandering formerly Black Congressional districts.

The Voting Rights Act of 1965 introduced the possibility of using redistricting as an opportunity to empower and enfranchise underrepresented populations, with race as a criterion. But historically, several states challenged or subverted this intent. The US Supreme Court attempted to address the conflict by identifying appropriate criteria for drawing the lines of voting districts through several cases. In *Thornburg v. Gingles* (1986) for example, the Court determined three criteria for states to redraw the boundaries of voting districts in the creation of majority-minority districts: the new districts must be geographically compact, they must be politically cohesive, and there must be evidence of a White majority that could defeat candidates of color.

Legislatures in several states, notably North Carolina, Georgia, Texas, Illinois, Florida, Maryland, and Ohio, have found strategies to navigate these criteria to develop meandering and oddly shaped congressional districts that in fact guaranteed minimal representation of minorities. They used a practice sometimes referred to as "stacking and cracking" (Bazelon 2017): "stacking" districts so that Whites vastly outnumbered Black, Brown and indigenous voters, and "cracking" apart districts where underrepresented populations were the majority. So odd were these district shapes that *The Washington Post* referred to them as resembling "a Rorschach test" (Petri 2021). Contemporary gerrymandering practices result in part from previous case law on the subject. For instance, decades ago, battles over the use of race in defining voting districts resulted in a 2001 decision that using race to develop minority-majority voting districts was unconstitutional, but that legislative reapportionment to maintain the political power of a party was legitimate and Constitutional. This provided states a useful loophole to continue gerrymandering districts to suppress the vote of Black and other constituents under the color-blind discourse of preserving the political power of a party rather than the overtly racist discourse employed under Jim Crow segregation (Forgette and Winkler 2006).

All of that said, federal courts have ruled in several cases to rein in gerrymandering that obviously resulted in the suppression or denial of voting rights for underrepresented populations. For example, a federal judge ruled in 2019 that Ohio's congressional districts were unconstitutional, arguing that "the GOP-controlled Ohio Legislature put the Democrats at a disadvantage by packing lots of them into four districts and scattering the reset across the remaining twelve" (Sewell 2019: A5). The judge ordered the state to redraw its districts ahead of the 2020 elections. It is telling that the ruling in no way recognizes the powerful intersection of race and party: Black, Brown and indigenous voters are far more likely to be registered and to vote Democrat than Republican. Focusing on party rather than race allowed the judge to sidestep the uglier racist intentions of gerrymandering. In fact, similarly color-blind discourse concerning party politics rather than racism emerged in the state Supreme Court rulings of North Carolina's gerrymandering.

Although the Supreme Court has on occasion recognized the racist implications and ramifications of gerrymandering and voter suppression, it has also ruled to reinforce it. For example, in *Shelby County v. Holder* (2013), the Court substantially undermined the Voting Rights Act of 1965 by determining that changes in voting laws to prevent "fraud" was in fact allowable and not unconstitutional. That decision allows states to simply claim concerns of preventing voter fraud, even where none exists, to redraw district lines that make voting rights increasingly inaccessible to under-represented populations. Notably, such laws were "overwhelmingly passed in state legislatures controlled by Republicans" (Cobb 2021:29) since the controversial Court decision. The Supreme Court notably ignored the persistent lack of evidence of widespread voting fraud in their ruling. Even more to the point, in cases challenging the congressional district boundaries in North Carolina and Maryland the Supreme Court ruled in *Rucho v Common Cause* (2019) that, "federal courts have no role to play in policing political districts for partisan gain" (Sherman 2019:1). That ruling overturned decisions by lower federal courts that ordered redrawn maps in Maryland, Michigan, North Carolina, and Ohio, and opened the way for blatantly racist gerrymandering and the subversion of the Voting Rights Act without fear of running afoul of the Constitution. And in 2022, the Supreme Court stopped attempts in Alabama to create a second primarily black Congressional district, raising alarms that the court was undermining the Voting Rights Act in much the same way that it was about to erode reproductive rights in the overturning of *Roe v. Wade* (Mascaro 2022).

Why do these machinations at the state level matter in national politics? Since congressional district boundaries and the consequent representation in Congress are decided by state legislatures, those legislators are granted significant control over the terms (and ultimately the legitimacy) of democratic representation in the state. As such, "control of Congress in many ways is decided by rules put together in state legislatures" (Elliott 2019:45). Yet data clearly indicate that participation rates are lowest at the local and state level compared to presidential elections. Republicans, with a largely White base, have long appreciated that opportunity to skew national politics and power through state legislative processes while disenfranchising Black, Brown, indigenous and poor populations.

A question emerges here: given the clear historical efforts to build structures, policies and practices that dilute or eliminate the right to vote of underrepresented populations, how have people chosen to fight back to regain their Constitutional and human political rights? As it has been since the nation's founding, the notion of universal enfranchisement remains a deeply contested terrain and an illustration of the human rights enterprise, where resistance from below serves as the primary force to define and realize rights in the lives of everyday people.

Why Does Voting Matter?

A seductive argument is often made on the left that voting is not a relevant source of political power. Given the data on and history of electoral politics in the US, and the long history of the human rights enterprise (rooted in forms of resistance and political action "from below") discussed throughout this book, we have considerable sympathy for that position. Voting is only one of many fundamental political human rights, and is often not the only or best vehicle through which to wage material/class or boundary (anti-racist, feminist, etc.) struggles in the US or any other country. As will be discussed in the concluding chapter, a much wider variety of political action will need to be employed to ensure any chance at human rights and survival in the face of OTHS. However, as demonstrated by centuries of struggle, the vote is an important tool for the public to affect social change via the state (through changes in policy and representation), as an (albeit often weak) check on the domination of states by capital and other elite interests, and as an expression of the ostensibly "democratic" state—which is the basis of legitimacy for the US government and American hegemony over the inter-national rules-based order.

In fact, voting and other political rights are vital tools in the arsenal of marginalized populations to define and realize other Constitutional and human rights—now clearly demonstrated in the battles over reproductive rights and bodily autonomy taking place in public referendums and state legislatures all over the US. The 1973 *Roe v. Wade* decision of the US Supreme Court established 50 years of access to abortion rights for women across the country, actionable until the point of fetal viability. Over those 50 years, fights ensued at the state and federal levels over attempts by con-servative and capital interests to restrict that access. These restrictions typi-cally took the form of shortening the time during pregnancy when abortions could be legally performed (ranging from six weeks to the first two terms of pregnancy); redefining the circumstances under which pregnancies could be ended (for example, in cases of rape and incest, miscarriages, fatal fetal conditions, potential death of the woman carrying the fetus, parental per-mission for minors seeking abortions, "late term" abortions, and, in some states, elimination of all acceptable circumstances); limiting the conditions under which abortions could be legally performed (for example, only in hospitals, only in clinics such as Planned Parenthood that are affiliated with hospitals); and limiting the legal methods of abortive services (such as the elimination of dilation and curettage (D&C) abortions or restrictions on access to medical abortive drugs such as mifepristone) (Center for Repro-ductive Rights 2023). Though contested, these efforts succeeded such that state policies governing access to abortion differed across the country, even while federal protections under *Roe* were technically still in effect.

Efforts to curtail reproductive rights through state legislatures and the federal court system accelerated considerably leading up to and during the Trump Administration. However, these efforts should not be understood as an outcome of rightwing fundamentalist populism so much as the outcome of a deliberate campaign on the part of concentrated capital interests. Not unlike for voter suppression, conservative think tanks like the Federalist Society and any number of "dark money" groups have worked for several decades to stack state legislatures and federal courts—including the Supreme

Court—with pro-life, so-called Constitutional "originalists." According to investigative reporting from outlets like ProPublica and The Lever, a key figure in this deliberate campaign is Leonard Leo, who joined the Federalist Society in 1991 and later served as its executive director (Perez, Kroll, and Elliot 2022; Perez 2023). More recently, Leo came to serve as co-chair of the Federalist Society Board of Directors while running a number of dark money groups including the Marble Freedom Trust, which received the largest known contribution to a political advocacy group in US history at approximately $1.6 billion (from manufacturing billionaire Barre Seid, who avoided over $400 million in taxes in the process) in 2022 (Perez, Kroll, and Elliot 2022). Entities like the Marble Freedom Trust have a great deal of flexibility, and can spend on elections, advocacy groups, think tanks, religious institutions/organizations, universities, and direct organizing campaigns—all without public financial transparency. This flexibility is in part thanks to the 2010 Citizens United decision that awarded capital "rights" to political speech, and allowed corporations and the TCC unlimited spending (through such trusts and super-PACs) to support political candidates or causes of their choosing.

According to reporting, in 2005 Leo joined others in organizing support and fundraising for the nominations of Supreme Court Justices John Roberts and Samuel Alito, before scaling up to raise upwards of $460 million through a network of dark money groups between 2005 and 2021, which was then funneled to rightwing campaigns and political groups like the Judicial Crisis Network (now the Concord Fund) to support electing pro-life conservatives to Congress and state legislatures, and flooding the federal courts with similarly minded appointees (Perez, Kroll, and Elliot 2022). By 2016, Leo was serving as a direct judicial advisor to President Trump, and "helped the President appoint and confirm more than 200 nominees to the federal bench, most famously Supreme Court Justices Neil Gorsuch, Brett Kavanaugh, and Amy Coney Barrett." (Perez, Kroll, and Elliot 2022). Leo and his colleagues were able to effectively stack the courts and legislatures in such a way to set the stage for the 2022 *Dobbs v. Jackson Women's Health Organization* decision by the Supreme Court that overturned *Roe v. Wade*. Following *Dobbs*, questions of abortion access were essentially kicked back to individual states, making state and local elections all the more significant (Temme 2022). Access to reproductive rights is now significantly different from state to state, and many of the most pitched battles over reproduction rights are being fought at the state level. By the end of 2023, 14 states enacted a "full ban" on abortive services, two enacted bans after six weeks of pregnancy, another two enacted bans after 12 weeks, and three more enacted bans after 15–18 weeks (*The New York Times* 2023). Further, over 66 clinics across 15 states had discontinued abortion care, and many closed entirely (Fuentes 2023).

Some states, such as Texas, have sought and established expansive approaches that criminalize any and all attempts to cross state lines to seek abortions elsewhere, and to make it a criminal felony to "aid and abet" such activity. In the first test of this policy, Texas resident Marcus Silva sued three women in 2023 for "wrongful death" because they helped his wife obtain the medications necessary to achieve an abortion. Though the suit failed, the women stood to be charged with a felony of homicide if he won his case, and would have established abortion as akin to murder, to which the friends would be criminal accomplices (Klibanoff 2023). Further, as noted by reporters and analysts since the case, "not every man will be as dumb as Marcus Silva," and it seems to be a matter of time before the criminal ban in Texas is confirmed in case law (Donegan and Stern 2023).

Texas is also home to a lawsuit filed in a federal court to block access to mifepristone (one of two drugs most commonly used for medical abortions—the most common type of abortive procedure) on the grounds that it is not safe and that the Federal Drug Administration (FDA), which studies and approves drugs, did not do its due diligence to establish its safety. This claim defies the fact that the drug has been safely in use for over two decades, and is one of the only cases in US history where a court sought to supplant the FDA in its role to make such determinations (Christensen 2023). If this case is upheld, it stands to eliminate the most widely-used method by which most abortions are achieved in every single state in the US. It wasn't coincidental that this case was first brought before the Texas federal court. The presiding judge, a staunch anti-abortion activist, was appointed by Trump and supported by Leo and the Federalist Society. The case has since been appealed to the same Supreme Court whose conservative majority—including Trump appointees Gorsuch, Kavanaugh, and Coney Barrett along with long-time Federalist Society darling (Cole 2023) Samuel Alito (who wrote the majority opinion in *Dobbs v. Jackson*)—overturned *Roe v. Wade*.

Moreover, the ramifications of the post-*Roe* era ushered in by the *Dobbs* decision stand to accelerate existing structural inequalities. Although the Dobbs decision and individual state restrictive laws and bans on abortion clearly affect anyone who becomes pregnant (along with their friends, families, and communities), and deepen the patriarchal and heteronormative background relations of reproduction, they also deepen the repression and restrict the rights of the poor and people of color, who suffer exploitation and expropriation in capitalist society. Women of color, indigenous women, poor women, adolescents, trans men and gender non-conforming people, and immigrants are most likely to be affected by restrictions in reproductive rights. This is because income/wealth, access to health insurance, vulnerability to health care providers' bias, and existing abortion restrictions remain significant determining factors for one's options for reproductive health care from state to state. For example, among women between the ages of 15 and 49, nearly one-quarter of Latinas, 13% of Black women, and 22% of women living below the poverty threshold have no health care insurance, compared to 8% of White women and 11% of those living above the poverty threshold (Fuentes 2023). The drivers behind these figures are far less about choice and much more about policy determining reproductive and other Constitutional and human rights. For example, some states in the US have refused to expand their Medicaid programs under opportunities made available through the Obama-care reforms of the 2000s or COVID policies of recent years, leaving thousands of impoverished women ineligible for Medicaid—almost two-thirds of whom are women of color (Fuentes 2023). For immigrants, federal law bans non-citizens from eligibility for their first five years in the US (Fuentes 2023). Further, and perhaps most importantly, while Medicaid does provide for other critical forms of reproductive health care, the 40+ year old "Hyde Amendment" does not allow those who are covered by Medicaid—or any federally funded health care recipient for that matter—to cover abortions under their federal insurance plans. Thus, the reproductive rights of marginalized populations in the US are much narrower than those of White, cisgender, middle-class and affluent women, making access to reproductive rights yet one more place where existing structural inequalities—inseparable from the background relations of capitalist society—are enhanced and further entrenched. These are the very same populations most likely to be targeted by voter suppression and gerrymandering, and whose political Constitutional and human rights are systematically curtailed.

However, as with universal suffrage, reproductive rights are a vigorously contested terrain in the US, and resistance has seen some significant success—even in battleground, conservative ("red") leaning states. In conservative Kansas, voters shocked many political observers in killing a statewide abortion ban in August of 2022, less than two months following the *Dobbs* decision. In Ohio, voters overwhelmingly passed an amendment to the state constitution that overturned a previous six week ban and enshrined abortion rights into law—also by public referendum. This was despite at least $16 million in spending by the Concord Fund, headed by Leonard Leo, which amounted to approximately 60% of the money raised to oppose the amendment (Perez 2023). Further, since *Dobbs*, 20 states and the District of Columbia have actually added additional protections for abortion rights in affirming their legality (*The New York Times* 2023). In sum, the battle over reproductive rights continues to unfold as one largely between popular interests and those of conservative contingents of concentrated corporate capital. Such popular interests are represented by public referendums (as a form of direct democracy, unlike legislative debate) such as in Kansas or Ohio, and by public polls indicating that over 61% of the American public oppose the *Dobbs* decision (Gallup 2023). The interests of conservative contingents of corporate capital and the TCC are represented by political organizations like the Federalist Society and dark money groups like the Concord Fund or Marble Freedom Trust who have been most active and effective in walking back reproductive rights while maximizing the political power and voice of corporations, business, and property owners.

This is not to say that there is no popular "pro-life" movement, or that cultural or religious differences do not help to frame the political debate over reproductive rights. Instead, it is to suggest that the conscious, deliberate campaign of concentrated capital remains the primary force behind the relatively effective conservative movement to curtail abortion access in the US. Further, it is to suggest that, like voting rights, reproductive rights are the result of popular resistance from below as part of the ongoing human rights enterprise, and this resistance must be understood within the context of material and boundary struggles (e.g., on the relations of social reproduction) in capitalist society, where the political power and rights of concentrated corporate capital square off against the collective power of everyday people.

Human Rights from Below: Pushing Back in the 2020 Election and the Ebb and Flow of Protest

As noted earlier, voter participation rates are typically relatively low in the US, where the highest participation is seen in presidential elections and state and local elections typically draw lower turnout. Yet the 2020 election notably defied that pattern. According to the United States Election Project, the 2020 election elicited the highest voter participation rate ever in a presidential race, at 66.3% of the eligible population. Moreover, there were significant increases in the participation rates of underrepresented populations who more commonly lag substantially behind the rates for White voters. In fact, the only election cycles when Black voters participated at higher rates than Whites were in 2008 and 2012, when Obama won the presidency. In 2020, Black participation rates were nearly the same as that of Whites. And while Latinx participation rates are normally among the lowest of racialized and ethnic groups, in 2020 that participation rate was similar to the rate in 2012. In addition, women and younger voters also turned out in record numbers for the 2020 elections (Dorman 2020).

Why does this record demographic turnout matter? For one, after the 2020 election, the 117th Congress was more diverse than ever, showing never-before seen representation of underrepresented populations. For example, 28% of the new Congress were people of color: there were 57 Black members (five more than the 116th Congress), 43 Latinx members (three more than before), and five Native American members (two more than before). There were also a record number of women in the 117th Congress, with 141 women, or more than one fourth of the total number of the total members; a record 51 members were women of color. And a record 11 LGBTQ members were elected to the 117th Congress (Lindsay 2020). This shift was important in the narrow passage of the most expensive and comprehensive economic rescue and support bill (American Rescue Plan) within weeks of the new Congress, at $1.9 billion, that required Vice President Kamala Harris' vote to break the tie in the Senate. Without the shift producing a more diverse set of voices and perspectives in Congress, the bill, which will provide much-needed economic support and aid to the poor and working class (where a disproportionate of underrepresented populations languish) amidst the COVID pandemic, would arguably never have passed.

How do we understand this significant departure from the more typical voter participation patterns in previous elections going back to 1932? We argue that using the framework of the human rights enterprise illuminates the relationships, processes and practices that were key in producing that departure.

While public protests were growing under the Obama Administration—from the first manifestation of BLM on the progressive left to the astroturfed right-wing populism of the Tea Party, the four years under the Trump Administration were accompanied by an explosion of public protests and popular political activity. Massive marches on Washington by over a million women in pink "pussy hats" protested what they viewed as growing misogyny ushered in by the Trump Presidency and MAGA movement. The renewed BLM movement erupted in record breaking protests across the country, galvanized by new, viral cases of racist police violence against unarmed Black people and by Trump's constant berating and dehumanizing of immigrants, political opponents, and people of color. These movements coalesced, even if often begrudgingly (noting the heated Democratic primary race where the Bernie Sanders campaign was effectively kneecapped by the Democratic party establishment who circled the wagons around then Vice President Biden) in the 2020 election in a move to mobilize voter participation that echoed in some ways the civil rights voter registration drives of the 1960s. In particular, organizations like Fair Fight 2020 aggressively sought to register voters of color in Georgia, encouraged voters to follow through by casting ballots, and later continued to resist attempts to suppress Georgia voters. Organizations like Fair Fight 2020 did not just focus on Georgia—they organized a voter protection initiative in several key battleground states around the country to ensure the right to vote for all citizens (*The Hartford Courant* 2019). As a result of these and similar efforts by liberals and progressive organizations across the country, both Senate seat runoffs in Georgia went to the Democratic challengers (Jon Ossoff and Raphael Warnock) of two Trump Republicans whose racism was no secret, and other battleground states shifted away from GOP support to elect Democrat Joe Biden in 2020.

In addition, Emily's List, which raises money in support of women and underrepresented candidates running for office, opened a second flank by 2016 in the fight against voter suppression with its focus on down-ballot races in state legislatures. To support this fight in the 2020 election they increased their organizational staff by 300% and their fundraising target to $50 million, up from its previous $10 million (Elliott 2019). This is significant, given the power of state legislatures to set the redistricted boundaries in processes of gerrymandering. Their efforts helped to convert 283 state legislative seats to Democrats, resulting in gains in six chambers by the end of the Trump Presidency (Elliott 2019).

These down-ballot efforts by organizations like Emily's List were joined by the National Democratic Redistricting Committee, which devotes its attention to challenging the gerrymandering of districts by the GOP (but is also in support of gerrymandering districts in favor of Democrats). In addition to this largely conventional party organization, Flippable, a grassroots Democratic organization dedicated to winning state legislative elections, poured $125 million into Virginia's races, and sent similar support to legislative races in eight other states (Elliott 2019).

That same pressure from below resulted in the introduction of two significant bills in Congress to increase voting rights: The John Lewis Voting Rights Advancement Act (HR-4/S-4253) and For the People Act of 2019 (HR-1). The John Lewis Voting Rights Advancement Act, named for the voting rights activist and Congressman John Lewis, emerged from an examination of 25 years of voter suppression and would establish "a targeted process for reviewing voting changes in jurisdictions nationwide, focused on measures that have historically been used to discriminate against voters," including voter ID laws and the elimination of multilingual voting materials, practices long known to suppress voting rights access (Johnson 2022). The bill would also increase access to voting for indigenous populations. And though it was passed by the House in 2021, it has yet to pass the Senate.

Similarly, Rep. John P. Sarbanes introduced HR-1, For the People Act, in 2019. It was designed to address voter suppression by expanding voter access (particularly expansion of voter registration and strict limits on removal of voters from lists of registered voters), election security and integrity. Further, it proposed limits on campaign financing that underwrites misinformation and disinformation campaigns by limiting campaign spending, expanding the restrictions on foreign contributions to campaigns, expanding rules of spending disclosures by organizations (like Super PACs) that spend money on political advertisements (including online ads and social media), and enhances the financial power and amplifies the voices from below by proposing a campaign finance reform initiative that provides federal matching of small contributions to qualified candidates in federal elections. And it would address gerrymandering by proposing to establish an independent, nonpartisan commission for redistricting. But like the John Lewis Voting Rights bill, HR-1 passed the House in 2019 but never passed the Senate, even despite a slim Democratic majority (with Vice President Harris as a tie-breaking vote).

While the introduction of the John Lewis Voting Rights Advancement Act and the For the People Act illustrate the power of popular resistance to voter suppression, their failure to pass (not unlike federal bills introduced to address racist police violence following the BLM protest movement of 2020) demonstrates the entrenched interests of concentrated capital in both parties of Congress and the need for sustained political action from below to realize expanded political Constitutional and human rights.

Human Rights Praxis and Political Human Rights in the US: What Can We Learn and Why Does it Matter?

The legitimacy of liberal democratic states like the US hinges on the extent to which people believe they have a voice in governance—centrally including but not limited to the right to vote. In this sense, "suffrage is the embodiment of individual sovereignty" (Ruth, Matusitz and Simi 2016:58) from which state sovereignty is then constructed. In the US and elsewhere in the world, the notion of universal suffrage is a primary political mechanism through which the equal political rights of all people under a state (regardless of gender, race, ethnicity, sexuality, and so forth) is actually employed. However, that principle, and the legitimacy of the US as a democratic state and global hegemon at the head of the "rules based international order" is compromised by the persistent outsized influence of capital and other elite interests over the state, and through two key political strategies to undermine universal suffrage: voter suppression and gerrymandering—both disproportionately affecting populations of color, the poor, and migrants. Indeed, in an editorial, *The Washington Post* (2017) referred to voter suppression as the "civil rights issue of this era." And, in the absence of salient power from below through access to voting rights, disenfranchised voters are increasingly turning up the heat on political and organizational elites by organizing on the ground, protesting, and pressuring political leaders to address these twin strategies for disenfranchisement. Finally, the cases of voter suppression and reproductive rights in the US both demonstrate the tendency of capitalists and other elites to expand the political power and "rights" of corporate capital while walking back, weakening, or completely eliminating the political voice, power, and rights of the very diverse working and unemployed public.

The right to vote and other political human rights will be an issue of concern in the US, but also in elections around the world by the fall of 2024, where decisions concerning conflict, climate change, and economic policy vis-à-vis transnational capital and shifting geopolitics will be up for debate. In fact, 2024 will see what *The New York Times* has called a "wave of national elections" in about 50 countries including India, Indonesia, Mexico, South Africa, and all 27 members of the European Union—together representing over 60% of global economic output (Cohen 2023). Human rights praxis will be necessary to ensure political rights protections in the 2024 election season, and to bolster efforts to make sure that global working-class interests are powerfully represented. This, as we've mentioned before, will require building meaningful bases for national and international solidarity between a) traditionally "doubly-free" exploited citizen-workers, b) growing ranks of expropriable-and-exploitable citizen-workers (Fraser 2022), including but not limited to the so-called "global precariat," and c) deeply insecure populations of migrants, prisoners, coerced/trafficked labor (including some forms of military conscription and sex trafficking), women, children, and "modern day" slaves (Bales 2016) whose lives, labor, property, and popular sovereignty are deemed fully expropriable. In the following chapter we will explore the political and other rights of migrants of all sorts amidst an ever-increasing global migration crisis, thanks to the many conflicts, economic precarity, and ecological challenges characteristic to the current regime of accumulation.

Notes

1 These limited conceptions of political rights, typically granted to land owning White men, were only expanded as the result of massive social struggles, such as in the Haitian Revolution of the 19th century, the women's suffrage movements of the 19th and 20th centuries, and the civil rights movements of the 19th and 20th centuries.
2 Political rights, like the right to vote, are contested terrains in the US at the state and federal level, and are subject to constant change and challenge. We've done our best here to contextualize and present the nature of this contestation as a manifestation of the human rights enterprise and certain forms of human rights praxis in action. That being said, it is impossible for us to encapsulate or anticipate all of the specific changes in voting rights that will inevitably continue to evolve and emerge as the US approaches the 2024 elections and beyond.
3 Current court challenges that seek a nationwide elimination of access to mifepristone and other drugs for "medical abortions" threatens to curtail abortion rights even in states that maintain the right to abortion, ultimately subjecting women to the decisions of more conservative states and of the conservative majority of the Supreme Court (Hurley and Jarrett 2023).
4 Now well known, the fundraising powers of such "dark money" groups (read: zero public transparency) and political action committees [PAC] were unleashed on the US political system following the Citizens United (2010) case.

References

Alexander, Michelle. 2020. *The New Jim Crow*. New York: The New Press.
Alston, P. 2018. "Report of the Special Rappporteur on Extreme Poverty and Human Rights on his Mission to the United States of America." *United Nations Human Rights Council*. Retrieved 09/01/21 from https://digitallibrary.un.org/record/1629536?ln=en#record-files-collapse-header
American Civil Liberties Union (ACLU). 2022. "Map of Convicted Felon Rights." *ACLU*. Retrieved 09/02/23 from www.aclu.org/issues/voting-rights/voter-restoration/felony-disenfranchisement-laws-map
Amy, Jeff. 2021. "GA voting law called Jim Crow in the 21st century." *The Hartford Courant*. March.
Apostolidis, P. 2019. *The Fight for Time: Migrant Day Laborers and the Politics of Precarity*. New York, NY: Oxford University Press.
Armaline, William T., Davita Silfen Glasberg and Bandana Purkayastha (Eds). 2011. *Human Rights in Our Own Back Yard: Injustice and Resistance in the United States*. Philadelphia: University of Pennsylvania Press.
Armaline, William T., Davita Silfen Glasberg and Bandana Purkayastha (Eds). 2015. *The Human Rights Enterprise: Political Sociology, State Power and Social Movements*. Malden, MA: Polity Press.

Arnwine, Barbara R. 2011. "61 forms of voter suppression." Voting Rights Alliance. Retrieved 09/03/23 from www.votingrightsalliance.org

Avery, James M. and Mark Peffley. 2005. "Voter Registration Requirements, Voter Turnout, and Welfare Eligibility Policy: Class Bias Matters." *State Politics and Policy Quarterly* 5 (1): 47–67.

Bakan, Joel. 2004. *The Corporation: The Pathological Pursuit of Profit and Power.* New York, NY: Free Press.

Bakan, Joel. 2020. *The New Corporation: How "Good" Corporations Are Bad for Democracy.* New York: Vintage.

Bales, Kevin. 2016. *Blood and Earth: Modern Slavery, Ecocide, and the Secret to Saving the World.* New York: Random House.

Bay, Ann-Helen and Morten Blekesaune. 2002. "Youth, Unemployment and Political Marginalization." *International Journal of Social Welfare* 11 (2): 132–139.

Bazelon, Emily. 2017. "The New Front in the Gerrymandering Wars: Democracy vs. Math." *The New York Times Magazine*, August 29. Retrieved 09/02/23 from www.nytimes.com/2017/08/29/magazine/the-new-front-in-the-gerrymandering-wars-democracy-vs-math.html

Bentele, Keith G. and Erin E. O'Brien. 2013. "Jim Crow 2.0? Why States Consider and Adopt Restrictive Voter Access Policies." *Perspectives on Politics* 11 (4): 1088–1116.

Berman, Ari. 2016. *Give Us the Ballot: The Modern Struggle for Voting Rights in America.* New York: Picador.

Berman, Ari. 2017. "American Democracy is Now Under Siege by Both Cyber-Espionage and GOP Voter Suppression," *The Nation.* Retrieved 11/01/20 from www.thenation.com/article/archive/american-democracy-is-now-under-siege-by-both-cyber-espionage-and-gop-voter-suppression/

Berman, Ari. 2021. "Jim Crow Killed Voting Rights for Generations. Now the GOP is Repeating History." *Mother Jones*, June 2. Retrieved 09/01/23 from www.motherjones.com/politics/2021/06/jim-crow-killed-voting-rights-for-generations-now-the-gop-is-repeating-history/

Berman, A. and N. Surgey. 2021. "Leaked Video: Dark Money Group Brags About Writing GOP Voter Suppression Bills Across the Country." *Mother Jones*, May 13. Retrieved 09/01/21 from www.motherjones.com/politics/2021/05/heritage-foundation-dark-money-voter-suppression-laws/

Blackmon, D. 2009. *Slavery by Another Name: The Re-Enslavement of Black Americans from the Civil War to WWII.* New York: Anchor Books.

Bonilla-Silva, Eduardo and Sarah Mayorga. 2009. "Si Me Permiten Hablar: Limitations of the Human Rights Tradition to Address Racial Inequality." *Societies Without Borders* 4 (3): 366–382.

Brater, Jonathan, Kevin Morris, Myrna Perez and Christopher Deluzio. 2018. "Purges: A Growing Threat to the Right to Vote." *Brennan Center for Justice.* Retrieved 08/01/21 from www.brennancenter.org/sites/default/files/publications/Purges_Growing_Threat_2018.1.pdf

Brennan Center for Justice. 2021. "Voting Laws Roundup: July 2021." *Brennan Center for Justice*, July 22. Retrieved 09/01/21 from www.brennancenter.org/our-work/research-reports/voting-laws-roundup-july-2021

Brennan Center for Justice. 2022. "Voting Laws Roundup: February, 2022." *Brennan Center for Justice.* Retrieved 09/04/23 from www.brennancenter.org/our-work/research-reports/voting-laws-roundup-February-2022

Brennan Center for Justice. 2023. "Voting Laws Roundup: February, 2023." *Brennan Center for Justice.* Retrieved 09/02/23 from www.brennancenter.org/our-work/research-reports/voting-laws-roundup-february-2023

Budiman, Abby, C. Tamir, L. Mora and L. Noe-Bustamante. 2020. "Facts on US Immigrants, 2018." *Pew Research Center,* August 20. Retrieved 12/10/23 from www.pewresearch.org/hispanic/2020/08/20/facts-on-u-s-immigrants/

Center for Reproductive Rights. 2023. "After Roe Fell: Abortion Rights Laws by State." *Center for Reproductive Rights.* Retrieved 11/18/23 from https://reproduc tiverights.org/maps/abortion-laws-by-state/

Chacko, E. and M. Price. 2020. "(Un)settled Sojourners in Cities: The Scalar and Temporal Dimensions of Migrant Precarity." *Journal of Ethnic and Migration Studies,* doi:10.1080/1369183X.2020.1731060.

Christensen, Jen. 2023. "What is Mifepristone, the Drug at the Heart of the Texas Medication Abortion Lawsuit." *CNN.* Retrieved 10/01/23 from https://www.cnn.com/2024/03/25/health/mifepristone-abortion-pill-explained/index.html

Cobb, Jelani. 2021. "What is Happening to the Republicans?" *The New Yorker,* March 8. Retrieved 09/02/23 from www.newyorker.com/magazine/2021/03/15/wha t-is-happening-to-the-republicans

Cohen, Donald and Allen Mikaelian. 2023. *The Privatization of Everything.* New York: The New Press.

Cohen, Patricia. 2023. "Two Wars, 50 Elections: The Economy Faces Rising Geo-political Risks." *The New York Times,* December 24. Retrieved 12/24/23 from www.nytimes.com/2023/12/24/business/economy/global-economic-risks-red-sea.html?smid=nytcore-ios-share&referringSource=articleShare

Cole, Devan. 2023. "4 Supreme Court Justices Who Voted to Reverses Roe Get Warm Reception at Federalist Society Dinner." *CNN Politics,* November 11. Retrieved 12/02/23 from www.cnn.com/2022/11/11/politics/supreme-court-justi ces-dobbs-decision-federalist-society/index.html

Collins, P. H. 1999. *Black Feminist Thought: Knowledge, Consciousness, and the Politics of Empowerment* (2nd edition). New York: Routledge.

Corasaniti, N. and R. Epstein. 2021. "GOP and Allies Draft 'Best Practices' for Restricting Voting," *The New York Times,* March 23. Retrieved 09/01/21 from www.nytimes.com/2021/03/23/us/politics/republican-voter-laws.html

Daily News Egypt. 2021. "Interview: Disgrace for America to Spend so Much on Wars, Arms, Says Former UN Independent Expert." *Daily News Egypt,* December 8. Retrieved 12/02/23 from www.dailynewsegypt.com/2021/12/08/interview-disgra ce-for-america-to-spend-so-much-on-wars-arms-says-former-un-independent-expert/

DeNardo, James. 1980. "Turnout and the Vote: The Joke's on the Democrats." *American Political Science Review* 74 (2): 406–420.

Desilver, D. 2021. "Turnout Soared in 2020 as Nearly Two-Thirds of Eligible US Voters Cast Ballots for President." *Pew Research Center.* Retrieved 09/01/21 from www.pewresearch.org/fact-tank/2021/01/28/turnout-soared-in-2020-as-nearly-two-thirds-of-eligible-u-s-voters-cast-ballots-for-president/

Docherty, Iain, Robina Goodland and Ronan Paddison. 2001. "Civic Culture, Com-munity and Citizen Participation in Contrasting Neighborhoods." *Urban Studies* 38 (12): 2225–2250.

Donegan, Moira and Mark Joseph Stern. 2023. "Not Every Man Will Be as Dumb as Marcus Silva." *Slate,* May 4. Retrieved 11/10/23 from https://slate.com/news-and-p olitics/2023/05/texas-man-medication-abortion-lawsuit-backfired-explained.html

Dorman, John L. 2020. "Young Voters in the US Turned Out in Record Numbers in 2020, Powering Biden's Presidential Victory." *Business Insider*, November 22. Retrieved 11/10/23 from www.businessinsider.com/youg-voters-record-voting-turnout-biden-trump-presidential-election-2020-11

Eberstadt, Nicholas. 2019. "America's Invisible Felon Population: A Blind Spot in US National Statistics." *American Enterprise Institute (AEI)*. Retrieved 12/02/23 from www.jec.senate.gov/public/_cache/files/b23fea23-8e98-4bcd-aeed-edcc061a4bc0/testimony-eberstadt-final.pdf

Elfrink, Tim. 2018. "Florida's Racist History on Voting Rights." *The Hartford Courant*, November 11: A6.

Elliott, Phillip. 2019. "The Battle to Draw the Battle Lines: State Races Starting this Fall Will Shape Congress for the Next Decade." *Time*, September 16. Retrieved 11/02/23 from www.magzter.com/stories/News/Time/The-Battle-To-Draw-The-Battle-Lines

Evers-Hillstrom, Karl, R. Arke and L. Robinson. 2019. "A Look at the Impact of Citizens United on its 9th Anniversary." OpenSecrets.org. Retrieved 11/01/20 from www.opensecrets.org/news/2019/01/citizens-united/

Falcon, Sylvanna M. 2009. "Invoking Human Rights and Transnational Activism in Racial Justice Struggles at Home: US Antiracist Activists and the UN Committee to Eliminate Racial Discrimination." *Societies Without Borders* 4 (3): 295–316.

Forgette, Richard and John W. Winkle III. 2006. "Partisan Gerrymandering and the Voting Rights Act." *Social Science Quarterly* 87 (1): 155–173.

Fraser, Nancy. 2022. *Cannibal Capitalism: How Our System is Devouring Democracy, Care, and the Planet—and What We Can Do About It*. London: Verso.

Fuentes, Liza. 2023. "Inequity in US Abortion Rights and Access: The End of Roe is Deepening Existing Divides." *Guttmacher Institute*. Retrieved 12/02/23 from www.guttmacher.org/2023/01/inequity-us-abortion-rights-and-access-end-roe-deepening-existing-divides

Gallup. 2023. "Where Do Americans Stand on Abortion?" *Gallup*, July 7. Retrieved 12/15/23 from https://news.gallup.com/poll/321143/americans-stand-abortion.aspx

Gardner, Amy and Beth Reinhard. 2018. "Voting Problems Spring Up Across the Country, Groups Say." *The Hartford Courant*, November 7: A7.

Gardner, Amy, Kate Rabinowitz and Harry Stevens. 2021. "How GOP-Backed Voting Measures Could Create Hurdles for Tens of Millions of Voters." *The Washington Post*, March 11. Retrieved 11/15/23 from www.washingtonpost.com/politics/interactive/2021/voting-restrictions-republicans-states/

Gilens, Martin and Benjamin Page. 2014. "Testing Theories of American Politics: Elites, Interest Groups, and Average Citizens." *Perspectives on Politics* 12 (3): 564–581.

Glasberg, Davita Silfen and Deric Shannon. 2011. *Political Sociology: Oppression, Resistance, and the State*. Thousand Oaks, CA: Sage/Pine Forge.

Grandin, G. 2020. *The End of the Myth: From the Frontier to the Border Wall in the Mind of America*. New York: Metropolitan Books.

Gray, Anthony 2014. "Securing Felons' Voting Rights in America." *Berkeley Journal of African American Law and Policy* 16 (1): 3–31.

Hayden, P. 2001. *The Philosophy of Human Rights*. St. Paul, MN: Paragon House Pub.

Hayduk, Ronald. 2006. *Democracy for All: Restoring Immigrant Voting Rights in the United States*. New York: Routledge.

Hughey, Matthew W. 2020. "Gender and Race in American Elections: From the Pathos of Prediction to the Power of Possibility." *Sociological Forum* 35 (51): 877–897.

Hurley, Lawrence and Laura Jarrett. 2023. "Justice Department Asks Supreme Court to End Abortion Pill Legal Challenge That Threatens Widespread Access." *NBC News*, September 9. Retrieved 12/03/23 from www.nbcnews.com/politics/supreme-court/jus tice-department-asks-supreme-court-maintain-abortion-pill-access-rcna104115

Ingraham, Christopher. 2018. "One State Fixed its Gerrymandered Districts, the Other Didn't. Here's How the Election Played Out in Both." *The Washington Post*, November 9. Retrieved 09/10/23 from www.washingtonpost.com/business/2018/11/09/one-state-fixed-its-gerrymandered-districts-other-didnt-heres-how-elec tion-played-out-both/

Ishay, M. 2008. *The History of Human Rights from Ancient Times to the Globalization Era.* Berkeley, CA: University of California Press.

Izaguirre, Anthony and Acadia Coronado. 2021. "GOP Lawmakers Looking to Make Voting Tougher." *The Hartford Courant*, February 1: 3.

Jacobs, Rose. 2022. "Rising Corporate Concentration Continues a 100-Year Trend." *Chicago Booth Review*, November 15. Retrieved 11/14/23 from www.chicagobooth. edu/review/rising-corporate-concentration-continues-100-year-trend; www.promarket. org/2022/04/21/new-data-shows-the-rise-of-corporate-concentration-in-the-us-in-the-past-100-years/

Johnson, Kenyatta. 2022. "Council Member Kenyatta Johnson Calls on the US Senate to Pass the John Lewis Voting Rights Advancement Act and the Freedom to Vote Act." Retrieved 01/20/23 from https://phlcouncil.com/councilmember-kenyatta-johnson-ca lls-on-the-u-s-senate-to-pass-the-john-lewis-voting-rights-advancement-act-and-the-fr eedom-to-vote-act/

Johnstone, L. and G. Grumbach. 2021. "Texas Democrats Stage Walkout Over Restrictive Voting Bill, Killing it For Now." *NBC News*, May 30. Retrieved 09/01/22 from www.nbcnews.com/politics/elections/texas-democrats-stage-walkout-stop -debate-restrictive-voting-bill-delaying-n1269079

Jordan, L. 2017. "Introduction: Understanding Migrants' Economic Precarity in Global Cities." *Urban Geography* 38 (10): 1455–1458.

Jouvenal, Justin. 2023. "GOP Voter-Fraud Crackdown Overwhelmingly Targets Minorities, Democrats." *The Washington Post*, December 20. Retrieved 12/20/23 from www.washingtonpost.com/dc-md-va/2023/12/20/voter-fraud-prosecutions-2020/

Keyes, Scott, Ian Millhiser, Tobin Van Oster and Abraham White. 2012. "Voter Suppression Disenfranchises Millions." *Race, Poverty and the Environment* 19 (1): 11–12.

Keyssar, Alexander. 2013. "Barriers to Voting in the Twenty-First Century." In *Representation: Elections and Beyond*, pp. 39–58, Jack H. Nagel and Roger M. Smith (Eds). Philadelphia: University of Pennsylvania Press.

Klibanoff, Eleanor. 2023. "Three Texas Women Are Sued for Wrongful Death After Allegedly Helping Friend Obtain Abortion Medication." *Texas Tribune*, March 10. Retrieved 11/10/23 from www.texastribune.org/2023/03/10/texas-abortion-lawsuit

Lalami, Laila. 2020. *Conditional Citizens: On Belonging in America.* New York: Pantheon Books.

Lao, Tim. 2019. "The Citizens United Decision Explained," *Brennan Center for Justice*. Retrieved 11/01/22 from www.brennancenter.org/our-work/research-rep orts/citizens-united-explained

Laughland, Oliver and Amanda Holpuch. 2020. "'We're Modern Slaves': How Meat Plant Workers Became the New Frontline in Covid-19 War." *The Guardian*, May

2. Retrieved 12/01/23 from www.theguardian.com/world/2020/may/02/meat-pla nt-workers-us-coronavirus-war

Levinson-King, Robin. 2020. "US Election 2020: Why it Can Be Hard to Vote in the US." *BBC News.* Retrieved 11/01/20 from www.bbc.com/news/election-us-2020-54240651

Lewis, Megan. 2022. "The State of Election Law: A Review of 2021–22 and a First Look at 2023." Retrieved 11/12/23 from https://votingrightslab.org/wp-content/up loads/2022/12/VotingRightsLab_TheStateofStateElectionLaw2021_2022-1.pdf

Libal, Kathryn and Shareen Hertel. 2011. "Paradoxes and Possibilities: Domestic Human Rights Policy in Context." In *Human Rights in the United States: Beyond Exceptionalism*, pp. 1–22, Shareen Hertel and Kathryn Libal (Eds). New York: Cambridge University Press.

Lindsay, James M. 2020. "The 2020 Election by the Numbers," *Council on Foreign Relations.* Retrieved 09/01/21 from www.cfr.org/blog/2020-election-numbers

Lipset, Seymour Martin. 1960. *Political Man: The Social Bases of Politics.* Garden City, NY: Doubleday.

Liu, Isabelle, Emily Rhyne, Nilo Tabrizy, Ben Laffin and Hanaan Sarhan. 2020. "Trump's Campaign is Building an Army of Poll Watchers. What Can They Actually Do?" *New York Times*, October 30. Retrieved 09/03/23 from www.nytim es.com/video/us/elections/100000007399774/1982-consent-decree.html

Manza, Jeff and Christopher Uggen. 2008. *Locked Out: Felon Disenfranchisement and American Democracy.* New York: Oxford University Press.

Mascaro, Lisa. 2022. "High Court Ruling on Alabama Voting Maps Sparks Alarm." *The Hartford Courant*, February 9: 4.

Mayer, Kenneth R. and Michael G. DeCrescenzo. 2017. "Supporting Information: Estimating the Effect of Voter ID on Nonvoters in Wisconsin in the 2016 Pre- sidential Election." Retrieved 09/01/22 from https://elections.wisc.edu/wp-content/ uploads/sites/483/2018/02/Voter-ID-Study-Supporting-Info.pdf

McAuliffe, Marie and B. Khadria. 2020. "World Migration Report 2020." United Nations, International Organization for Migration. Retrieved 11/15/20 from www. un.org/sites/un2.un.org/files/wmr_2020.pdf

Miller, Zeke and Matt Sedensky. 2020. "President Tweets Support for Protestors." *The Hartford Courant*, April 18: 1.

Minnite, Lorraine C. and Frances Fox Piven. 2012. "The Other Campaign: Who Gets to Vote?" *New Labor Forum* 21 (2): 34–40.

Nadler, Ben and Anila Yoganathan. 2021. "Georgia House Passes Voting Restric- tions Bill." *The Hartford Courant*, March 2: 3.

National Coalition for the Homeless. 2010. "Voter Rights/Registration Packet." *National Coalition for the Homeless.* Retrieved 09/03/23 from https://nationalhom eless.org/voting/

National Coalition for the Homeless v. Jensen. 1992. 187 A.D. 2d 582 (N.Y. App. Div).

National Public Radio. 2018. "Supreme Court Upholds Ohio's Use-It-or-Lose-It Voting Law." *NPR's Morning Edition*, June 12. Retrieved 09/01/21 from www.npr.org/ 2018/06/12/619109646/supreme-court-upholds-ohios-use-it-or-lose-it-voting-law

Okonta, Patricia. 2018. "Race-Based Political Exclusion and Social Subjugation: Racial Gerrymandering as a Badge of Slavery." *Columbia Human Rights Law Review* 49 (2): 254–296.

Parkin, Michael and Frances Zlotnick. 2014. "The Voting Rights Act and Latino Voter Registration: Symbolic Assistance for English-Speaking Latinos." *Hispanic Journal of Behavioral Sciences* 36 (1): 48–63.

Passel, Jeffrey and Jens Manuel Krogstad. 2023. "What We Know About Unauthorized Immigrants Living in the US." *Pew Research Center*, November 16. Retrieved 12/05/23 from www.pewresearch.org/short-reads/2023/11/16/what-we-know-abou t-unauthorized-immigrants-living-in-the-us/

Perez, Andrew. 2023. "Leonard Leo's Fight Against Abortion Access." *The Lever*, October 27. Retrieved 12/10/23 from www.levernews.com/leonard-leos-fight-aga inst-abortion-access/?utm_source=newsletter-email&utm_medium=link&utm_ campaign=newsletter-article

Perez, Andrew, Andy Kroll and Justin Elliot. 2022. "How a Secretive Billionaire Handed His Fortune the Architect of the Right-Wing Takeover of the Courts." *ProPublica*, October 22. Retrieved 12/10/23 from www.levernews.com/leona rd-leos-fight-against-abortion-access/?utm_source=newsletter-email&utm_mediu m=link&utm_campaign=newsletter-article

Perez, Chris. 2014. "US Has Highest Percentage of Immigrants in 93 Years." *New York Post*. Retrieved 11/10/23 from https://nypost.com/2014/09/26/us-has-highest-p ercentage-of-immigrants-in-93-years/

Petri, Alexandra. 2021. "The Nation's Ten Most Gerrymandered Districts: A Rorschach Test." *Washington Post*, May 19. Retrieved 09/01/21 from www.wa shingtonpost.com/blogs.compost/wp/2014/05/19/the-nations-ten-most-gerrymand ered-districts-a-rorschach-test/

Pew Research Center. 2023a. "Voting Patterns in the 2022 Elections." *Pew Research Center*, July 12. Retrieved 12/02/23 from www.pewresearch.org/politics/2023/07/ 12/voting-patterns-in-the-2022-elections/

Pew Research Center. 2023b. "Evaluations of Members of Congress and the Biggest Problem with Elected Officials Today." *Pew Research Center*, September 19. Retrieved 12/02/23 from www.pewresearch.org/politics/2023/09/19/evaluations-of-m embers-of-congress-and-the-biggest-problem-with-elected-officials-today/

Pitts v. Black. 1984. 608 F. Supp. 696 (S.D.N.Y.).

Piven, Frances Fox and Richard A. Cloward. 2000. *Why Americans Still Don't Vote: And Why Politicians Want It That Way*. Boston: Beacon Press.

ProCon.Org. 2022. "State Voting Laws & Policies for People with Felony Convictions." Retrieved 11/11/23 from https://felonvoting.procon.org/state-felon-voting-laws/

Ramsey, R. 2020. "Analysis: It's Harder to Vote in Texas than in Any Other State," *Texas Tribune*, October 19. Retrieved 09/01/21 from www.texastribune.org/2020/ 10/19/texas-voting-elections/

Riccardi, Nicholas and Linley Sanders. 2023. "Americans Are Widely Pessimistic About the State of Democracy in the US, AP-NORC Poll Finds." *PBS Newshour*, July 14. Retrieved 12/02/23 from www.pbs.org/newshour/politics/americans-a re-widely-pessimistic-about-the-state-of-democracy-in-the-u-s-ap-norc-poll-finds

Romance, Jeff. 2022. "Voter Suppression Gets Deserved Jolt in Judge's Ruling." *The Palm Beach Post*. Retrieved 11/14/23 from www.palmbeachpost.com

Romm, Tony and Isaac Stanley-Becker. 2019. "Pro-Trump Super PACs Draw Scrutiny for Facebook Ads Seeking Voter Registration Data." *The Washington Post*, October 28. Retrieved 11/10/23 from www.washingtonpost.com/technology/2019/10/28/p ro-trump-super-pacs-draw-scrutiny-facebook-ads-seeking-voter-registration-data/

Rosino, Michael L. 2017. "A Problem of Humanity: The Human Rights Framework and the Struggle for Racial Justice." *Sociology of Race and Ethnicity* 7 (1): 338–352.

Ruth, Terrence, Jonathan Matusitz and Demi Simi. 2017. "Ethics of Disenfranchisement and Voting Rights in the US: Convicted Felons, the Homeless, and Immigrants." *American Journal of Criminal Justice*, 42: 56–68.

Sawyer, Wendy and Peter Wagner. 2023. "Mass Incarceration: The Whole Pie 2023." *Prison Policy Institute (PPI)*, March 14. Retrieved 12/02/23 from www.prisonp olicy.org/reports/pie2023.html

Schlozman, Kay Lehman, Henry E. Brady and Sidney Verba. 2018. *Unequal and Unrepresented: Political Inequality and the People's Voice in the New Gilded Age.* Princeton, NJ: Princeton University Press.

Schraufnagel, S., M. Pomante II and Q. Li. 2020. "Cost of Voting in the American States: 2020." *Election Law Journal*, 19 (4). https://doi.org/10.1089/elj.2020.0666

Schwadel, Philip. 2002. "Testing the Promise of the Churches: Income Inequality in the Opportunity to Learn Civic Skills in Christian Congregations." *Journal for the Scientific Study of Religion* 41 (3): 565–575.

Sewell, Dan. 2019. "Federal Judges Strike Down Congressional Map in Ohio." *The Hartford Courant*, May 4: A5.

?>Sherman, Mark. 2019. "Supreme Court Says Federal Courts Have No Role in Policing Partisan Redistricting." *Boston Globe*, June 27. Retrieved 09/01/21 from www. bostonglobe.com/news/politics/2019/06/27/supreme-court-says-federal-courts-have-role-policing-partisan-redistricting/mFeBGridoCIBMS

Shiribman, David. 2020. "Ten Years On, Citizens United Ruling Has Changed US Politics—But Not in the Way Many Feared," *Los Angeles Times*. Retrieved 11/01/22 from www.latimes.com/world-nation/story/2020-01-12/citizens-united-ruling-a nniversary-how-it-changed-american-politics

Singh, N. P. 2019. *Race and America's Long War*. Berkeley, CA: University of California Press.

Spates, Kamesha and Carlton Mathis. 2014. "Preserving Dignity: Rethinking Voting Rights for US Prisoners, Lesson from South Africa." *The Journal of Pan African Studies* 7 (6): 84–105.

Taylor, Keeanga Yamahtta. 2021a. *From #BlackLivesMatter to Black Liberation* (2nd edition). Chicago, IL: Haymarket Books.

Taylor, Keeanga Yamahtta. 2021b. *Race for Profit: How Banks and the Real Estate Industry Undermined Black Homeownership*. Chapel Hill, NC: University of North Carolina Press.

Temme, Laura. 2022. "Why Was Roe v. Wade Overturned?" *FindLaw*. Retrieved 11/12/23 from https://supreme.findlaw.com/supreme-court-insights/could-roe-v-wa de-be-overturned-.html

The Leadership Conference on Civil and Human Rights. 2019. "Democracy Diverted: Polling Place Closures and the Right to Vote." *The Leadership Conference on Civil and Human Rights*. Retrieved 12/01/23 from https://civilrights.org/democra cy-diverted/

The Hartford Courant. 2019. "Voter Initiative." August 14: A3.

The New York Times. 2023. "Tracking Abortion Bans Across the Country." *The New York Times*, December 8. Retrieved 12/15/23 from www.nytimes.com/intera ctive/2022/us/abortion-laws-roe-v-wade.html?smid=tw-nytimes&smtyp=cur

The Sentencing Project. 2022. "Voting Rights." Retrieved 09/03/23 from www.sen tencingproject.org/issues/voting-rights/

The Washington Post (editorial board). 2017. "Voter Suppression is the Civil Rights Issue of This Era." *The Washington Post*, September 19. Retrieved 09/03/23 from

www.washingtonpost.com/opinions/voter-suppression-is-the-civil-rights-issue-of-this
-era/2017/08/19/926c8b58-81f3-11e7-902a-2a9f2d808496_story.html

Thrush, Glenn and Jennifer Medina. 2023. "California Republican Party Admits It Placed Misleading Ballot Boxes Around State." *The New York Times*, October 12. Retrieved 12/02/23 from www.nytimes.com/2020/10/12/us/politics/california -gop-drop-boxes.html

Uggen, Chris, Ryan Larson, Sarah Shannon and Arleth Pulido-Nava. 2020. "Locked out 2020: Estimates of People Denied Voting Rights Due to a Felony Conviction." Retrieved 11/10/23 from www.sentencingproject.org/publications/lock ed-out-2020-estimates-of-people-denied-voting-rights-due-to-a-felony-conviction/

Wang, Tova Andrea. 2012. *The Politics of Voter Suppression: Defending and Expanding Americans' Right to Vote*. Ithaca, NY: Cornell University Press.

Weinberg, D. 2021. "Texas's Proposed Voter Suppression Law." *Brennan Center for Justice*, October 23. Retrieved 09/01/22 from www.brennancenter.org/our-work/a nalysis-opinion/texass-proposed-voter-suppression-law

Weindling, Jacob. 2018. "Your State-By-State Guide to GOP Voter Suppression," *Paste Magazine*, October 16. Retrieved 09/01/21 from www.pastemagazine.com/p olitics/2018-elections/your-state-by-state-guide-to-gop-voter-suppression/

Wilder, Will and Stuart Baum. 2022. "5 Egregious Voter Suppression Laws From 2021." *Brennan Center for Justice*. Retrieved 11/08/23 from www.brennancenter. org/our-work/analysis-opinion/5-egregious-voter-suppression-laws-2021

Wines, Michael. 2023. "North Carolina Gerrymander Ruling Reflects Politization of Judiciary Nationally." *The New York Times*, April 28. Retrieved 11/10/23 from www.nytimes.com/2023/04/28/us/north-carolina-supreme-court-gerrymander.html

XinhuaNet. 2021. "US Democracy Run by Oligarchy, Says Former UN Independent Expert." *XinhuaNet*, December 9. Retrieved 12/02/23 from www.news.cn/english/ 2021-12/09/c_1310360338.htm

Zinn, Maxine Baca and Bonnie Thornton Dill. 1996. "Theorizing Difference from Multiracial Feminism." *Feminist Studies*, 66 (2): 321–331.

5   Migrants, Legitimated Instability, and Human Rights[*]

In her 1993 book on Asian Americans, sociologist Yen Espiritu pointed out that US policy toward migrants of color has always reflected a dynamic between consistent eagerness for their labor and persistent unwillingness to offer rights (see Golash Boza 2015 for a similar study on Latinx populations). This statement remains true for most migrant populations today, and demonstrates the legitimacy crisis that emerges when the objective drive of the state to secure capital accumulation runs headlong into state responsibilities to respect, protect, and fulfill its international human rights obligations.

We start here, even though scholars and activists have described structured migrant precarity since the 1990s. Over the last few decades, the US has institutionalized such precarity (also see Goldring, Bernstein and Bernhard 2009), even as it projects a rhetoric of welcoming people with much-needed skills (Garip, Gleeson, and Hall 2019; Banerjee and Rincón 2019). While we will discuss the eroding rights of migrants in the US due to US policy and barriers to accessing rights due to the actions of locally dominant groups later in the chapter, we must also consider migrants in the US from a global perspective, and identify the industries and enterprises that profit from repelling, detaining, and managing migrants. To understand the mechanisms through which human rights are eroded, we continue to analyze the impediments that affect migrants' quest for human security.

As we discussed in previous chapters, increasing global migration and refugee crises are current and future implications of the overlapping threats of proliferating conflict, ecological destruction, and climate change throughout the world, stemming from the legitimacy crisis of states and general crises that plague capitalist society in the current regime of accumulation. Research from the Migration Policy Institute confers on the connection of migration crises to these overlapping threats, arguing that the massive increases in migration to wealthy nations in the global North— including but not limited to the US—should be understood relative to, for example, "the Russian invasion of Ukraine; the Taliban takeover in Afghanistan; and a mixture of authoritarian government and collapsing economy in countries like Venezuela, Nicaragua, Cuba, and Haiti;" adding that, "climate change has further exacerbated migration from some traditional

DOI: 10.4324/9781003323556-6

sending countries—in Central America and the Caribbean—that are experiencing significant changes in weather patterns" (Selee 2023). To demonstrate the scale of migration coming from and/or through Central and South America alone (also noting upticks in Chinese, Indian, and other international migration through Latin American routes), over 10,000 migrants per day arrived at the southern US border seeking asylum at multiple points in December of 2023, over 40% of whom were families or unaccompanied children, bringing the US border and migration system to what officials and observing journalists agreed was an apparent "breaking point" (Isacson 2023). Though the number of migrants arriving at the southern border dropped by 50% in January of 2024 (Aleaziz and Jordan 2024), migration patterns over the last several years have tended to spike in waves. And overall, the number of people crossing the southern border "illegally" more than doubled during the Biden Administration, even despite the US Border Patrol taking the highest number of migrants into custody (approximately 2 million people per year) in its entire 100-year history (Shear, Aleaziz, and Kanno-Youngs 2024; Miroff, Sacchetti, and Frostenson 2024).

Growing migrant populations will continue to find themselves the targets of a global police state (with the US at its center), that works to forcibly differentiate migrants as partially (global precariat) or fully expropriable (chiefly via the enforcement of systemic racism, ethno-nationalism, patriarchy, and so forth), and discipline them as part of the growing population simultaneously deemed superfluous and dangerous to capital. Further, the control of migrant populations is an industry, and the global police state itself will continue to become a source for "accumulation by repression" as capital searches for a return on their investment amidst crisis in the militarization of borders and border policy—described by some (see Chapter 3) as a form of "global apartheid." Human rights praxis in the US, if it is to take on the challenges posed by OTHS, must examine some of the conditions that prevent migrants—especially those who are least protected by political and civil rights within countries—from accessing other (economic, social, and cultural) rights to build lives of dignity, free from constant threats of coercion and insecurity. This is not simply a moral or international legal obligation, but a recognition that, as will be discussed in Chapter 6, global working-class solidarity must embrace migrant and populations otherwise constructed as expropriable to address OTHS.

Despite a long history of being in the US, and acquiring citizenship[1] whenever they were allowed to do so, the ideology and structure of contemporary systemic racism and other background relations of capitalist society (such as patriarchal, heteronormative relations of reproduction) ensure that many populations of color—such as members of Asian American, many Muslim, and Latinx communities—continue to be viewed as dangerous "foreigners" or "aliens"[2] in the US regardless of their legal status. These background relations and social systems remain relevant for human rights praxis with regard to migrants in the US and elsewhere.

As we discussed in Chapters 2 and 3, one role of state RSAs and the broader global police state is to enforce the border politics of nationalism that determine citizens from non-citizens, often including racialized and dehumanized populations constructed as "aliens," "enemies," or somehow criminally dangerous. This is necessary in the processes of both "race making" and "war making" (Singh 2017), and in differentiating between rights-holding exploitable workers and otherwise expropriable populations. One must remain mindful of these attempts to "guard the golden doors," so to speak (Daniels 2005), through policy and political rhetoric which often includes attempts to vilify migrants. Simon and Alexander (1993), among others, have documented a long history of the vilification of migrants in the West. The persistent political rhetoric in the US about two classes of migrants—illegal or legal—reflects earlier discursive constructions of the 1990's (Romero 2018) that erase the culpability of US policy in driving that migration (through the "pull" of inviting workers and the "push" of destabilizing their home countries through foreign policy). The construction of more or less desirable migrant populations tends to focus on what immigrants can contribute, while deflecting attention from the structural classifications and policies that continue to shape lives of migrants in different ways.

As we will discuss later in the chapter, while the Biden Administration has refrained from the overtly racist and anti-immigrant rhetoric of the former Trump Administration, the so called MAGA movement, and affiliated political movements like that for Christian Nationalism, many of the most repressive policies toward migrants and immigrant communities persisted regardless (in effect, if not in form). But the explicitly racist and ethno-nationalist discourse of the American right wing is seeing a resurgence as the US struggles to deal with increasing numbers of migrants at the border—many forcefully displaced asylum seekers—without anything resembling comprehensive immigration reform from Congress. In what seems like a redux to his 2016 and 2020 campaigns, former President Trump offered up classically fascist discourse to preview his 2024 run, claiming in multiple public speeches and interviews that migrants attempting to enter the US were "poisoning the blood of our country" (Layne 2023). It would be a mistake to think of this as an off-color remark rather than a statement of the current, nationalist, right wing position in the US (and arguably on the right in many other countries around the world, as an element of 21st century fascism). At the time of these comments Trump was the clear frontrunner for the GOP nomination, despite countless ongoing criminal and civil cases against him. According to polls among likely GOP Iowa caucus voters following his statements, over 42% said they were more likely to support Trump for his comments, and another 29% said they didn't care (Trautmann 2023). To this point, scholars such as Sökefeld (2020) have argued that the refusal or deportation of migrants "is today much less a result of legal procedure, conforming with the international law of refugee protection, than of political imperatives intended for the fulfillment of various pursuits such as to placate right-wing anti-refugee demands" (Sökefeld 2020:13).

All of that said, it would be a mistake to approach the emergent internal and external migration crisis based on narrow, isolationist and/or nationalist politics alone—noting the extreme difficulty in actually achieving isolationism in the age of transnational capital accumulation. We have already discussed in some detail how transnational capital accumulation, represented by powerful MNCs, TNCs, financial firms, and the global power elite that own and manage them, reorganize the world in ways that lead to the cannibalization of humanity's conditions of possibility and the "churning of the Earth," to borrow a phrase from Shrivastava and Kothari (2012), that forces so many people to relocate and drives what some have called global apartheid. Thus, our conceptualization of migrants reflects a more fully transnational or global understanding of migration, migrants, and their treatment when it comes to human and other (i.e., Constitutional) rights (Purkayastha 2018). Specifically, we draw on two aspects of this expanded international conversation on migration and migrants. First, we bring into focus the conditions of migrants prior to, during, and after migration. For instance, to understand the desperation of Afghans seeking to flee their country following the pull-out of US troops and a return of the Taliban regime (reminiscent of the chaotic US exit from Vietnam), we need to understand their condition as centrally related to the seemingly endless US war on terror, and the geopolitical quest to secure strategic resources in Asia for transnational capital. Instead of considering human rights and human security issues as somehow mutually exclusive, we attempt to situate the accounts of migrants and struggles to realize their human rights in proper socio-historical context. Such an approach enables us to understand efforts to define and realize human rights for migrant populations as power struggles, and engage them through effective human rights praxis.

For instance, examining refugees and migrants together, and paying attention to the legal classifications of each, brings into view the structures of marginalization (including but not limited to state and vigilante violence), before and after migration, through which human rights have been and are likely to be undermined (Menjívar and Abrego 2012; Glenn 2002; Del Real 2022). Thinking of migration and migrants before, during, and after migration enables us to think about refugee camps, forced migrant enclosures— such as internment camps—and allows us to draw attention to the rapidly growing industries that have sprung up to control and detain migrants for profit (accumulation by repression).

Second, we use this transnational or global perspective on migrants to disrupt the traditionally nation-centered approaches that separate (through policy, practice, and political rhetoric) internal and external migration, whereas they are the result of similar systemic drives, and should not differ in their access to fundamental human rights. Other typical legal categorizations must also be challenged in such a transnational analysis. For instance, while we understand there are vast differences between those who are trafficked, or forced (through coercion or condition) into migration, and those who migrate "voluntarily" (for improved employment opportunities, for example)—these are not always clearly distinct categories. Many so-called "voluntary" economic migrants are structurally placed in conditions of precarious, expropriated, and/or indentured labor, in conditions of migration and work that closely resemble the definitions of trafficked victims.

Similarly, those who lack the requisite documents, and are labeled "illegal" might be constructed as such due to logistical delays in processing systems and other problems rather than some willful criminality as extreme political rhetoric would often suggest. To wit, as part of an effort to more efficiently process overwhelming numbers of asylum seekers at the southern border, the US employed the CBPOne smartphone application in January of 2023. But the system was plagued with problems and glitches, where many could not log in, others had their interview appointments inexplicably dropped, darker complected migrants could not have their headshots accepted, and many had no way to decipher the application, since it was only operable in English and Spanish (Spagat 2023). The lives of migrant populations are often subject to the coherence of immigration policies, and the ability and willingness of states to provide for due process (in asylum claims, for example) and abide by human rights and humanitarian law.

Scholars have long discussed the impacts of racist immigration and asylum laws (Kibria, Bowman, and O'Leary 2014) and the blurring line between legality and illegality (Gonzales and Raphael 2017) that contribute to the differential categorization and treatment of migrant populations and their resulting insecurity. To this point, all International Global Compacts and the International Bill of Human Rights require that Nation-states not make distinctions among migrants that lead to forms of legal precarity and stratified access to rights, other legal protections, and resources. Yet, the practice continues as commonplace in most states around the world, and there is considerable variation in how migrant rights are understood and dealt with on the ground in different states at different times, under different contexts.

Our focus on migrants and migration in this chapter not only highlights the repression of migrant populations and their construction and treatment as expropriable (particularly for those who are not White Christians from the global North [Joshi 2020]), but it reveals how the human rights of migrants (and the diverse global working class) are undermined through the construction of what we will call legitimated instability: the creation of laws and policies designed to keep many migrants caught in ambiguous legal statuses and in conditions of extreme precarity, where their lives and labor are subject to expropriation (see also Menjívar 2006 on "legal liminality" and Banerjee 2022 on the liminality of highly skilled migrants). Ghassan Moussawi (2020) has described this state as "al-awad," or that of constant insecurity and turbulence. Such instability includes distancing, and explicit processes of placing migrants outside the sphere of established political-economic structures, and includes a temporal dimension, where constant changes of policies and practices put the onus on migrants to constantly keep up with these frequent changes to achieve a favorable (e.g., legal immigrant or refugee) legal status granting rights protections.

This chapter is divided into three sections. The first section discusses legitimated instability using Asian Americans and Latinx groups' histories and experiences as examples. It includes discussions of guest workers— including those who are trafficked—as well as internally displaced people. The second section focuses on the practices and industry that repel and detain migrants, as part of the expanding and increasingly privatized global police state. We offer a critique of the increasingly common "refugee camp" as well as the rapid growth in the private industry of migrant detention. While the question of human rights is woven through these first sections, the third section focuses on the efforts to define and realize human rights— human rights praxis—as power struggles against the material and background relations of capitalist society that pose major impediments to the universal enjoyment of basic human dignity for migrants and other members of the global working class. Ultimately, as the history of the human rights enterprise suggests, migrant struggles for human rights and survival on the ground tend to put them at odds with the states charged with their protection and humane treatment in the first place. Effective human rights praxis should reflect a sophisticated understanding of these struggles of global migrant populations, and must be waged against the forces of capital and the global police state that seek to differentiate and control migrants through institutionalized violence, coercion, and surveillance, thus undermining any global compact that would otherwise ensure their international human rights.

Legitimated Instability: State Sanctioned Precarity and the Racialized, Gendered, Heteronormative Differentiation of Migrants as Expropriable in the US

Previously discussed in Chapters 2 and 3, forced displacement and other forms of global migration continues to climb. By the end of 2022 there were over 281 million migrants[3] worldwide (UN 2023). By mid-year 2023, this included over 110 million people subject to forced displacement,[4] 36.4 million refugees, 6.1 million asylum seekers, and 62.5 million internally displaced peoples (UNHCR 2023). Though the US is the leading destination as a single country (there were 51 million migrants in the US in 2022 (IOM 2022), the EU is currently the top regional destination (with 87 million migrants, or 30.9% of the international migrant population) followed by Asia (86 million, 30.5%). According to reporting from the Migration Data Portal (2021) on remittances, the US also tops the list of countries from which most migrant remittances (money sent back to their home country) originate.[5] At one level, these statistics can be read as an affirmation of the attractive conditions for migrants to the US—often referred to as "pull" factors. Still, we argue such assumptions about the reasons for migration flows tend to downplay the role of other "push" factors and the forms of legitimated instability in host countries that contribute to migrant precarity. Data on migration also tends to obfuscate important differences between migrants, which are key to understanding the constellation of human rights abuses and other challenges they face.

For instance, consider the twenty-year US led war in Afghanistan that caused the displacement of over 5.9 million civilians since 2001[6] (Bilmes and Intriligator 2013). As Lalami (2021) reminds us, "the deaths of some 800,000 people, including 335,000 civilians; and the displacement of an estimated 38 million people" are tied to US attacks on other countries, justified as part of the "war on terror." These implications of US led militarism all preceded the departure of US forces from Afghanistan in September 2021, which has since caused another wave of internal and external migration in response to Taliban rule. According to a report by the Costs of War Project (Coburn, Noah, N. Crawford, N. Niland, et al. 2023), 38 million people have been displaced by the US led war on terror since 2001—in Afghanistan, Iraq, Pakistan, Yemen, Somalia, the Philippines, Libya, and Syria. Yet the US often refuses to offer refuge to most of those displaced by its military interventions, and is not among the top five refugee hosting countries. With the partial exception of Germany, refugees of the US and allied war on terror have been housed outside the EU or North America in countries such as Turkey, Colombia, Pakistan and Uganda (UNHCR 2023). Further, more recent refugee populations such as those from Afghanistan are being admitted to the US as "parolees"—a term borrowed from the criminal justice system—in that their access to many of the supports available to refugees are delayed, typically for three months (Dalmia 2021). A similar political rhetoric labeling all migrants as suspect or potentially dangerous—also erasing distinctions between asylum seekers, undocumented border crossers, refugees, and international migrants from countries that are not favored by the US—has the effect of criminalizing migrants and even legal immigrant communities. In reality, most migrants have to go through extreme vetting processes examining their health, political opinions, possible criminal background, and their motivations to immigrate. Following such checks, they arrive on a variety of visas that differentiate their access to rights protection.

This widely varying access to human rights is a form of legitimated instability (or as Menjívar has argued, legitimated liminality), especially for migrants who are forcefully displaced and for a considerable number of those migrating "voluntarily," recalling our questioning of their mutual exclusivity. By "legitimated," we mean that the conditions of migrant insecurity are often backed by state policy and other state discourse. Legitimated instability is a way to describe the differentiation of migrants (through racism and criminalization, for example) as expropriable and undeserving of rights protections (in part through a thicket of rules and bureaucratic processes), despite their contributing often essential labor (legally and in black or grey markets), paying taxes, and paying into other programs to which they have no access to benefits (such as social security). In other words, states such as the US both lure and forcefully differentiate migrants as partially or fully expropriable through state policy and legal discourse. This leaves migrants of all sorts in variably precarious, insecure positions, whose treatment is legitimated through state policies and international laws that differentiate between migrants of different sorts. To be clear, we are not arguing that legal or sociological differentiation between types of migrants is somehow unnecessary or irrelevant. We simply wish to point out that human rights are to apply equally to all people regardless of citizenship or nationality, yet in the assignment of responsibility for the protection and fulfillment of these rights, states employ legal and other categorizations to offer the stratified access to rights prohibited by international human rights law (Purkayastha and Roy 2023).

Specifically, US immigration policy continues to yield unequal freedoms and rights protections for Latinx, Asian American and African migrants[7] to the US, placing them in a condition of liminality, or a kind of legal limbo. To illustrate the migrant experience of liminality, we look to the interplay between laws, policies, and experiences and conditions on the ground. Overall, the US—like many other countries in the global North—employs something akin to an international caste system to determine who can migrate and under which conditions (Velitchkova 2021). However, this hierarchical categorization of more or less desirable migrant populations varies over time depending on political economic and geopolitical conditions. For instance, 1965 marked the beginning of a brief period when people from countries outside Europe could migrate to the US, though this was a limited invite of sorts, encouraging the immigration of those highly educated in the fields of science, medicine, and technology, and those who would be willing to provide manual labor in the fields and factories. Earlier periods of immigration law reflected the explicit racism already exacted on African Americans and indigenous populations under Jim Crow and genocidal western expansion. Notable examples include the Chinese Exclusion Act 1882—which was the first act of immigration law targeting a specific ethnic group, the Page Laws of 1885—which required Chinese female migrants to prove they were not prostitutes before they would be allowed into the US, the blocking of migrants from the "Asiatic barred zone," extending from Turkey to Polynesia in 1917, or the National Origins Act 1922 that restricted all migration and exacerbated the impacts of earlier noted exclusions—overwhelmingly affecting migrants from Latin America and Asia (especially Asian women (Purkayastha 2020)).

The apparent racism and xenophobia employed to determine who is or is not allowed into the US and under what conditions is well illustrated by Golash Boza's (2015) study of those migrating from Latin America. As

Golash Boza argues, the relationship of immigration policy to the construction of migrants of color as criminal, dangerous, and expropriable is apparent in the history of US border policies:

> Operations Wetback, Hold-the-Line, Gatekeeper, and Safeguard all focused on US-Mexico border enforcement, while the US-Canadian border did not experience this level of vigilance. During these operations, millions of would-be migrants were sent back at the southern border. In the first decade of the 21st century, immigration law enforcement shifted. In addition to returning large numbers of people at the border, immigration agents began to remove immigrants from the interior. While continuing to remove Mexicans, immigration law enforcement began to target other Latin American as well as Caribbean immigrants.
>
> (2012, xiii)

As we will explore in the next section, the US has gone further to extend these policies beyond its own borders, providing funding to and applying diplomatic pressure on neighbors like Mexico to stop all migrants from reaching US borders. In any case, border enforcement initiatives such as Operation Wetback in the 1950s (that removed migrants and citizens of Latinx origin and deported them to Mexico) and other national and local law enforcement policies function to control immigration flows while differentiating migrant labor as up for expropriation in the service of transnational capital and US imperial hegemony (Gonzales 1990).[8] Menjívar and others (see Menjívar and Kanstroom 2014) have written about this multi-layered enforcement regime that affects migrants in the short and long term, and how it varies across and within Nation-states.

In addition to laws and local policies that place migrants in states of liminality, informal vigilante and formal state violence—such as in the repression of Chicano "Zoot Suit" riots in the 1940s or forced migration and internment of Japanese Americans during WWII (two thirds of whom were American citizens), have historically functioned to keep migrants and immigrant communities of color in a state of relatively constant fear and uncertainty (Ramon 2019; Esquivel 2019). Interestingly, many of the Japanese internment camps were constructed on Native American territory—such as on the Gila Reservation outside Phoenix—as extensions of ongoing settler colonialism that affected the sovereignty of indigenous tribes.

Explicitly racist immigration policies remained in place in the US until the civil rights movement and civil rights acts of the 1960's led to the prohibition of formal segregation or apartheid (Purkayastha and Subramaniam 2004; Torres, Purkayastha and Berdahl 2005). However, systemic racism continued to impact the conceptualization of immigrants and immigration policy in the post-civil rights era. Consider, for example, the racism and xenophobia accompanying the wave of killings, attacks, and hateful propaganda against Asian Americans in the US during the COVID pandemic, as part of a long-established pattern of forceful differentiation between rights holding American citizens and the dangerous, criminal, or otherwise undesirable racial and ethnic "other" or "foreigner." Or consider the mistreatment and increased deportation of Black Haitian refugees at the southern US Border in 2021 after the assassination of President Moise, collapse of Haitian government institutions, and rise of violent gangs that attempted to fill the country's power vacuum. In fact, nearly 1 in every 500 Haitians living on the island nation in 2022 had been on a deportation flight from the US in the previous year (Isacson 2022). By summer of 2023, the US continued to deport Haitian migrants and asylum seekers at record numbers, despite several warnings from human rights organizations, and even despite the fact that the US was at the same time ordering its own citizens to evacuate due to worsening conditions of violence and insecurity (Hesson, Erol, and Morland 2023).

US immigration law (especially the laws determining who can or cannot immigrate to the US and under what conditions) has also been historically gendered and heteronormative—in the prioritization of nuclear family reunification, for example. Coupled with caps on visas for those from particular countries, and severe delays in issuing these visas for reunification, women attempting to migrate are disproportionately affected. Scholar Margaret Abraham (2000) wrote about the ways in which women who are spouses of green-card holders (visa holders who are officially labeled "resident aliens," with access to all rights except the right to vote) are placed under conditions of coverture until they are able to prove they are married within a certain period of time. One overarching effect of such immigration policies is a selection pattern that facilitates a migrant stream favorable to men. In addition, COVID pandemic restrictions on travel brought into focus the challenges of reunifying families beyond the nuclear unit (spouse and children). Indeed, such restrictions can be imposed due to health security, along with other ongoing restrictions based on the other countries' relationship with the US. Romero (2018) has pointed out that even despite the need for care workers in the US (mostly women, recruited into professions like nursing), existing law restricts the ability of migrant women to fill those positions while maintaining their own families or exercising labor protections afforded by human and other rights frameworks.

Since the 1990s, a series of political measures enhanced legitimated instability in general and created legal categories for migrants whose lives and labor could be partially or fully expropriated in the US (Gonzales and Raphael 2017). A variety of temporary worker visas—ranging from H1 visas for skilled professionals, to those for seasonal agricultural labor—essentially hold workers in states of indenture to employers that include some of the most powerful TNCs in the world (Banerjee 2022). The path to more permanent visa statuses (and to possible citizenship) for these workers has numerous barriers including long waiting periods, excessive fees, the inability to access state and federal welfare benefits, and the constant threat of deportation. Indeed, eroding the distinction between the criminal legal and immigration systems within the RSA, "crimmigration" processes have made it easier to detain and deport people, including those brought to the US as accompanied or unaccompanied children of refugees (Aranda and Vaquera 2015; Bibler Coutin, Ashar, Chacon, and Lee 2017). While most White migrants from (for example) Ukraine, Canada, the EU, or Australia are not subject to anything near the same level of criminalization as those of color, the thicket of rules, policies, and practices place all immigrants in a state of liminality. This state of legal limbo or "al-awad" is accompanied by the threat of detention and deportation, and helps to define the conditions of temporary migrant and even more permanent immigrant populations in the US.

The possibility of deportation comes into play when the legal status of migrant populations is put in question or direct jeopardy. This can be due to a variety of reasons, such as the shutting down of immigration service portals as happened during the COVID pandemic in 2020 (Purkayastha and Roy 2023). Further, constantly shifting immigration policies with regard to people from countries that fall in or out of favor with the US, and the need for migrants to keep up and comply with episodic, unique requirements contribute to this state of constant insecurity. This was the case for migrants from majority-Muslim countries following the September 11th attacks of 2001, who were forced to register with the National Security Entry-Exit Registration System (NSEERS), otherwise called "Special Registration." This and other measures to surveil Muslim migration in the US led to the increased criminal scrutiny of Muslim American communities, causing "widespread fear, stress and alienation" and increased deportations of Muslim migrants (Sherer 2004). Research on NSEERS and its impacts revealed that:

> The rules and deadlines of NSEERS were complex, confusing and poorly publicized. NSEERS has provided many opportunities for people to unintentionally violate regulations and therefore become subject to deportation. The confusion was complicated by missing, incomplete or incorrect instructions given out by immigration officials at registration.
> (Sherer 2004)

Additionally, new rules, introduced in the US during the period of (gutting) welfare reform in the 1990s, added draconian measures for immigrants. For instance, sponsors had to show they could economically support whoever they were sponsoring for a visa—a near-impossibility for those who are poor or low income. Additional rules required refugees to find jobs to pay for any US support for their resettlement, creating more economic pressure and insecurity for migrants (Westcott 2015; American Immigration Council 2021). In fact, even trafficked persons who qualify for "T-visas" face the lack of sufficient support to build stable lives in the US (see Purkayastha and Yousaf 2018).[9]

Indeed, the lives of all migrants to the US, regardless of classification, are, in part, defined by precarity. As we indicate above, even citizenship does not protect immigrant communities from formal (state) and informal (vigilante) repression. That said, the working and living conditions for workers on temporary visas are particularly precarious. Holmes's book (2013) documents the suffering of migrant labor who work the fields and farms of US agribusiness to produce the American food supply—a population of absolutely "essential" workers, many of whom were forced to work at threat of deadly disease during the COVID pandemic. At the other end of the temporary visa migrant continuum, the case of "skilled"[10] guest workers (migrants on "H-visas") is also instructive for understanding the state liminality common to all migrants. H1-B visa holders must be highly educated/credentialed, and are often recruited into US TNCs that are part of the most powerful nexus of transnational capital (finance, CIT firms, and the military industrial complex).[11] However, as Banerjee (2022) writes, these "highly skilled" laborers are indentured in ways very similar to their "deskilled" counterparts. Their right to work (and presence in the US) is predicated in employer satisfaction. And since the Trump Administration, their spouses (H-4 visa holders) are not allowed to work, putting even more economic pressure on migrant families. Using the case of highly educated Indian guest workers, Banerjee and Rincón (2019) argue:

> Highly skilled immigrants are rarely viewed as legally vulnerable or as facing limited social and economic opportunities.... Highly skilled workers are uncertain and anxious about the stability and prospects of their jobs and immigration statuses because of their temporary work visas.... [T]he legal stipulations of H-1B visas and the backlogs associated with their legal status adjustment—from H-1B to Legal Permanent Residence [LPR]—are amplifying the vulnerability experienced by workers.... [W]orkers experience exploitation, downward economic and occupational mobilities, and workplace marginalization.... [T]he laws associated with these temporary visas negatively affect their spouses and families. In some cases, *the stress and panic associated with having only temporary legal status stems from their sense that they could be deported at any time* [emphasis added].

In sum, the accounts of both "skilled" and "low" or "unskilled" migrants and their families document how legitimated instability serves to facilitate the hyper-exploitation and expropriation of their lives and labor by limiting their rights protections. Guest workers essentially represent the face of modern indenture (Samaddar 2020), as they provide essential labor for the nation without the relative security, rights, or entitlements of citizenship. This reality is further complicated by the fact that migrant and immigrant families/households often include a mix of people with different legal statuses.

Legitimated Instability and Accumulation by Repression

In Chapter 3 we discussed the militarization of borders all over the world as a development of RSAs and the global police state in the context of migration crisis and an increasingly insecure, precarious, and diverse global working class. Here we extend that conversation in looking in more detail at how migrants are "managed" by deportation or detention, and how that management provides opportunities for accumulation by repression.

US foreign policy in Central and South American countries for well over a century has been incredibly destabilizing in its effects, and remains a root cause of the contemporary migration crisis in Mexico and at the southern US border. Consider the colonial relations forcefully established in Central America on behalf of US corporations (e.g., the United Fruit Company), the failed drug war in Columbia or Mexico, or late cold-war (covert and overt) military and economic interventions in Nicaragua, Guatemala, and El Salvador (including the deployment of paramilitary death squads on civilian and indigenous communities) in the 20th century for obvious examples. The poverty and insecurity in the wake of US foreign policy, including crippling economic sanctions on countries such as Cuba or Venezuela, continue to serve as some of the greatest "push" factors for those migrating north from these countries (Ballvé and McSweeney 2020).

However, US immigration policy has sought to repel or detain migrants from these regions who seek to escape such conditions and apply for asylum in the US (Purkayastha 2021). In a discussion of Central American refugees and asylum seekers, Musalo and Lee (2017) point out that by 2016 the US raised the total number of refugees the country would receive per year from 85,000 to 110,000. At the same time, the Obama Administration began to bolster and militarize border enforcement, and requested $3.7 billion specifically to address the women and children who were showing up at the southern border in growing numbers from Central America (Cohen 2014). This funding went primarily to border and law enforcement agencies like Customs and Border Protection (CBP), and to create 6,300 new beds for the detention of migrant families (LIRS 2014). The budget request also included money for State Department officials to develop messages and diplomatic means of detouring migrants from seeking asylum or opportunity in the US. In total, the Obama Administration removed over 2.5 million people from the US through immigration orders between 2009 and 2015—more than any other President in history at that point, and more than all of the other US Presidential administrations in the 20th century combined. For this, Obama earned the nickname "deporter in chief" from progressives and immigrant rights advocates (ABC News 2016).

Not to be outdone, the Trump Administration came to power in an overtly anti-immigrant campaign to criminalize, marginalize, and discourage migrants (particularly migrants of color and those from the global South, including nations President Trump referred to as "shithole countries") from seeking asylum in the US (Fram and Lemire 2018). The Trump Administration reduced the number of refugees that the US would receive to 50,000 in 2017, and referencing a now infamous campaign promise to "build the wall," the Trump Administration also facilitated (re-)building sections of a southern border wall in an effort to further harden and militarize border security. The discourse and policies of the Trump Administration criminalized migrants coming to the border, making little to no distinction between those seeking asylum or opportunity, through often racially charged political rhetoric that described them as inherently dangerous to Americans and American society, repeatedly referring to Latin American migrants as "rapists," for example (Wolf 2018). Practices of repelling migrants during and since the Trump Administration have included (illegally) firing tear gas at migrant "caravans" (Cheslow 2019) gathering to apply for asylum over the Mexican border and firing rubber bullets and pepper balls at Venezuelan migrants protesting their denial to entry under "Title 42" (Vera, Flores, Alvarez, and Valdes 2022).

During the COVID pandemic, countries all over the world were faced with the challenge of mitigating the spread of mutating viral strains over their borders. In the US, the Trump Administration and Center for Disease Control and Prevention (CDC) applied a section of the Public Health Service Act of 1944, called "Title 42." This allowed federal agencies to take necessary measures to "stop the introduction of communicable diseases," and was employed to deny any asylum seeker at the US border as a public health risk (Ellis and Kuhn 2023). To wit, between 2020 and 2023 over 2 million people were turned away by CBP under Title 42—a practice continued by the Biden Administration until the COVID pandemic health emergency was formally lifted in May of 2023 (Selee 2023). Once Title 42 was lifted, immigration policy fell back to the standards of "Title 8," where the international right to apply for asylum in the US was restored, but migrants could be detained and expelled if they didn't have qualifying conditions or originate from a qualifying country, or if they attempted to re-apply within a five-year period. It was at this point the Biden Administration employed the CBPOne smartphone application to aid in processing such asylum claims—a program that got off to an incredibly rocky start, as previously mentioned.

Throughout and since the pandemic, the US government pursued additional strategies to prevent migrants from reaching the southern border. This included funding and encouraging the governments of Mexico, Guatemala, and Honduras to repel Central American asylum seekers (Frelick, Kysel, and Podkul 2016). Similarly, the "remain in Mexico policy" that ran officially from 2019 to 2022 required that asylum seekers stay in Mexico as their asylum applications were processed and to await their asylum hearings (Miroff 2022). Third, the Biden Administration announced plans to open regional processing centers along migratory routes through Latin America to provide some level of humanitarian protection and to process asylum claims at greater distance from the US border (Selee 2023). For asylum seekers forced to wait in Mexico since 2019 when these strategies (such as "remain in Mexico") began, media accounts report that most were forced to sleep on the streets in border communities, at the mercy of charitable organizations, or in temporary refugee camps that were constantly being torn down and hastily rebuilt (Jordan 2021). This is on top of the threats of violence, sexual abuse, abduction/trafficking, and extortion that migrants to the southern US border now describe as commonplace in their journey. Doctors Without Borders reported that the number of sexual assaults their organization treated in the Darién Gap more than doubled (from 180 cases to 397 cases) between 2022 and 2023—when a record-breaking half million people attempted to traverse the dangerous jungle pass in Panama (Fabregas 2023). They note this is likely a considerable undercount of the actual frequency of sexual violence experienced by migrants, given what is assumed to be an extremely low reporting rate.

The US has also chosen to mitigate the influx of migrants through expanded detention—a manifestation of the global police state and widespread militarization of borders as part of global apartheid, and an opportunity for accumulation by repression. In 2018, the US DOJ implemented a "zero tolerance" policy, where anyone crossing the border without permission, including asylum seekers, would be detained and referred to the DOJ for criminal prosecution. As a result,

> Undocumented asylum seekers were imprisoned, and any accompanying children under the age of 18 were handed over to the US Department of Health and Human Services (HHS), which shipped them miles away from their parents and scattered them among 100 Office of Refugee Resettlement (ORR) shelters and other care arrangements across the country. Hundreds of these children, including infants and toddlers, were under the age of 5.
>
> (SPLC 2022)

Migrants, including unaccompanied children, who have fled explicit violence and severe insecurities in Central and South America, and having reached the US to exercise their international right to apply for asylum, have ended up in state-run and private detention centers, where overcrowding, draconian rules, and abuse are commonplace (Cheatham and Roy 2023). Detainees are under constant surveillance by cameras and uniformed guards, subject to repeated searches, in a facility with centrally controlled locked doors, and surrounded by fences topped with razor wire. Men and women are held in separate wings, with a special section for children detained with their mothers. Personal effects are confiscated. Movement from one area to another within the center is prohibited unless escorted by a guard. The rules for children—including unaccompanied migrant children, children in families (including young infants), asylum seeking and refugee children, and children whose parents are seeking asylum or are refugees—are similarly draconian. According to *The Independent*, children in US detention centers are expected to follow strict rules about sleeping, eating, sitting, using nicknames, and even crying—but are also expected to make their beds, and mop, scrub, and clean bathrooms.[12] The profit motive also drives these companies to charge detainees—including unaccompanied children and families—for everything, including underwear, food, books and family visits (Mastropasqua 2020). Though there are protocols for children's rights protections in detention facilities (see Gran 2021), reporting on migrant detention revealed a harsh reality for children and families desperate to be released and reunified (Sullivan 2021; Dickerson 2019). Moreover, López and Park (2018) report that neither the US immigration service, nor the management of private prison companies are effective in stopping sexual assault in their facilities. This has been particularly disturbing given the number of accompanied and unaccompanied children held in detention. Finally, in one of the most startling accounts of abuse and medical malpractice reported thus far, several migrant women came forward with proof they had received unwanted hysterectomies during or in lieu of other medical procedures provided in detention centers during the "zero tolerance" crackdown (Dickerson, Wessler, and Jordan 2020; Dickerson 2020).

Generally speaking, migrant detention is perhaps one of the most severe and obvious examples of contemporary "crimmigration" seeing as those held in immigration detention centers have typically not committed any actual crimes besides (in some cases) attempting to cross the border or through the simple status offense of being undocumented (for those detained by Immigration and Customs Enforcement (ICE)). Feminist scholars have certainly begun to reject the state construction of "criminal" (vs. legal) migration, and consider forced detention and separation/departure as *the* salient criteria for understanding the ubiquity of force and violence during migration (Purkayastha 2021, Romero 2018, 2020). And though the Trump Administration's "zero tolerance" policy was rescinded by the Biden Administration in January of 2021, this did not mean the end of "family separation" or migrant detention (Debusmann 2023). In fact, the detention of migrants and undocumented immigrants in the US continues to be a fertile area of growth for the private prison industry and transnational capital accumulation by repression.

Even before the "zero tolerance" orders, in 2016 approximately 353,000 immigrants identified for detention or removal by the US Immigration and Customs Enforcement (ICE) passed through one of more than 200 immigration detention facilities, up from 209,000 in 2001 (Luan 2018). By August 2016, nearly three quarters of the average daily immigration detainee population were held in private prison facilities—a sharp contrast from a decade prior, when the majority were held in local (public) jail and state prison spaces contracted out for that purpose. While both of these approaches served to criminalize and sanction migrant populations, private prison facilities subject detainees more directly to the profit maximizing forces of the modern corporation and the transnational accumulation drive.

These private detention centers hold men, women, and children in austere states of liminality—seemingly absent meaningful rights protections, while distancing them from systems of redress. At the same time, the business of detaining migrants is highly profitable. Recall, the market for worldwide border militarization is already worth over $48 billion and is on track for $81 billion by 2030 (Akkerman 2023). Companies such as the GEO Group, CoreCivic, LaSalle Corrections and the Management Training Corporation are among the firms who've made billions in profit from detention contracts with the federal government over the last 20 years (Cho 2023). For example, US immigration services paid GEO Group (the largest of these firms) $32 million a year to house, feed and provide medical care for a thousand detainees during the "zero tolerance" period. In a further blurring of boundaries, so called charities, such as Southwest Key, received millions of dollars from the US government to house children of migrants in "shelters" that have subsequently been sharply criticized for harsh, inhumane conditions that reduced overhead costs while company management profited through greatly enhanced salaries (Dickerson 2019). According to Burnett (2017), forced labor is also a constant at these private sector detention centers. For instance, multiple lawsuits alleged people were forced to work for a dollar a day in centers run by GEO Group—an accusation the company does not deny, but blames on ICE for setting its pay rates (Burnett 2017).

Though the Biden Administration began to phase out DOJ contracts with private prison companies in 2021, the phase out did not include contracts with ICE. In turn, ICE detention skyrocketed from a daily average of 15,444 detainees in 2021 to over 30,000 in 2023—over 90% of whom are held in private prison facilities, and private prison profits from such contracts have continued to climb (Cho 2023). By the start of 2024 these averages rose to 35,000, and according to research by Physicians for Human Rights and Harvard University (Wilson 2024), conditions in these facilities continued to be extremely punitive, including the widespread use of solitary confinement for even minor infractions in violation of international standards and even internal ICE policy promising to limit the practice back in 2013. In any case, undocumented immigrants and migrants attempting to enter the country have become the fodder for accumulation by repression as the US fails to meet its clear international human rights obligations to migrant populations whose precarity is typically rooted in US foreign policy decisions and terribly outdated and dysfunctional immigration policy (a thicket of incoherent rules and bureaucratic processes) that yield conditions of legitimated insecurity.

According to UNHCR's 2012 guidelines, seeking asylum is not an unlawful act, and asylum seekers and refugees are supposed to be protected by a series of rights. Edwards (2013) points out that states flagrantly violate these guidelines, which are supposed to protect migrants. Much of migrant detention in the US is taking place in private prisons, so that asylum seekers, *like trafficked persons*, are dehumanized and treated as commodities for profit making. This traffic in migrants violates every global compact and human rights instrument, and it occurs with the participation of states. We deliberately use the term "trafficking" because the conditions in these detention centers—violent coercion, family separation, dislocation, isolation, indenture, sexual violence, and so forth—actually fit some of the legal definitions of human trafficking under international and US law.[13]

Further, the enormity of human rights violations related to detention extends to those fleeing or being relocated from warzones. For instance, many airlifts of people from Afghanistan following the US withdrawal brought them—not to the US—but to other "third country" centers for processing and holding in often hastily constructed places. Many of the migrants forcefully displaced by US military involvement in the region have been designated as refugees by UNHCR, and are in camps elsewhere in the global South. These camps act as containers for migrants in places distant from their intended destination. Conditions in camps reflect chronic shortages and continuing human insecurities.[14] And at the international level, many of the tasks of providing relief and rehabilitation for these migrants have been given over to non–state actors, especially NGOs and international entities, that balance—sometimes problematically—their own institutional resource needs with the needs of populations they're meant to serve.[15]

Roth (2015) has argued that the rise of the big humanitarian nongovernmental organizations pursuing their brand identities to secure donations from individuals as well as government support, can be understood as a corporatization of activism that results in constraining the advocacy of groups concerned with global social justice. Similarly, Sari Hanafi (2008) affirms that the approaches of some humanitarian organizations can have the effect of depoliticizing refugees: refugees are reduced to bodies (biopower) to be fed and sheltered without political existence. Even outsourcing governance to the UN and/or NGOs in the absence of mechanisms through which migrants can access rights leads them to a state of liminal instability. NGOs, through their selective interactions with state governments, can contribute to the distancing practices at the expense of refugees' rights. Confining refugees to camps, and restricting their ability to advocate for themselves according to the terms set out by migrant and refugee conventions, are now established mechanisms through which NGOs and humanitarian organizations can govern the life of migrants in these camps.

Migrants are increasingly detained and interned around the world, suffering not only deprivation of liberty, but also other abuses of their fundamental human rights. The Global Compact for Migration (2018; see Appendix A) repeatedly calls for upholding the human rights and human security of migrants at all stages, "in all of its dimensions." Even the brief overview we provide here shows that global compacts on migration have had little impact on US policy, keeping with dominant notions of American exceptionalism in regard to international law and standards.

Human Rights Praxis and Rights Protections for Migrants

The current US approach to migrants and the growing global migration crisis is to a) continue destabilizing foreign policy practices (military interventions, economic sanctions, and so forth) that "push" populations into migration, b) "pull" migrant labor through temporary and other visa programs while mounting a thicket of rules, categorization, and bureaucratic processes that place them in conditions of legitimated instability when they arrive, and c) feed national and transnational accumulation drives by partially or fully expropriating migrant labor while privatizing their coercion, surveillance, and detention as sources of accumulation by repression. For those who reach US borders, as Espiritu (2003) argued, the appetite for cheap labor has not diminished, while the provision of political and other human rights continues to be a bitterly contested terrain.

As we indicated in Chapter 1, the accumulation drive places the state in a sort of legitimation crisis, where the human rights of migrants arriving at the border and established immigrant communities alike are secondary to the need to differentiate and discipline migrants (via the global police state) as partially or fully expropriable segments of the global working class. This is starkly evident from the accounts of migrant insecurity and turbulence described throughout this chapter. Taking the approach articulated here (looking at migration as transnational/global, and at every stage of the migratory process) allows us to examine accounts of exploitation and violence, as well as US histories of war, extraordinary rendition, torture, and other related practices that undermine human security over vast swaths of the world (push factors), while contributing to OTHS like environmental destruction/climate change and the global proliferation of weapons and conflict.

International human rights mechanisms currently present small opportunities for changing the conditions of migrants attempting to reach the US and other wealthy nations in the global North and other quickly developing economies. The 2018 Global Compact (see Appendix A) is far from being able to address the realities migrants experience in current contexts, and powerful states such as the US largely ignore the Compact's insistence to respect, protect, and fulfill their international legal obligations.

But is a better global compact possible? Perhaps. The 2018 Kolkata Declaration, developed by academics and practitioners[16] who are mostly located in the global South and who work with refugees and stateless people, aligns more closely to addressing the human rights challenges faced by migrants in current contexts. Apart from noting the rights of all migrants—migrants, refugees, and stateless people—the Kolkata Declaration insists that migrant protection frameworks must deal with discrimination based on race, religion, caste, ability, sexuality, gender and class that affect the rights and dignity of all human beings. Perhaps most importantly, it calls for redesigning global compacts to require *accountability* for "perpetrators of violence and displacement." If this were followed, the US and other state parties could be brought within its scope for its destabilizing foreign policy and relatively incoherent, repressive immigration policies. Further, the Kolkata Declaration insists that all migrants are entitled to social and economic rights, regardless of whether they work in legal or grey/black labor markets—helping to deconstruct the criminalization of migrants and immigrant communities. In sum, and in comparison to the 2018 Global Compact adopted by the UN, the Kolkata Declaration pushes back against the construction of "crimmigration," and sets the stage for working class solidarity among migrant populations and between expropriated migrants and other sectors of exploited and expropriated citizen-workers. As we will insist in the concluding chapter to follow, this kind of broad national and international solidarity and cooperation will be absolutely necessary to address OTHS and increase the potential for human rights practice around the world.

All of that said, the Kolkata Declaration is not being used by any state, and even the adopted Global Compact lacks the sufficient binding force or enforcement mechanisms to compel action from the US or other powerful states. As with any other rights, the definition and realization of rights protections for migrant populations will ultimately be determined through social movement strategies—grassroots organizing, struggle, resistance and so forth as forms of human rights praxis that may employ the frameworks of (for instance) the Kolkata Declaration in their work.

Migrants attempting to enter the US and American immigrant communities have continued to raise consciousness, find allies, protest, and seek legal recourse to address these human rights abuses. Over time, this resistance has included lawsuits, rallies, protests, lobbying for legislative redress, and seeking sanctuary.

Looking at historical cases for instance, one might note *US vs. Ozawa*—a case brought to the Supreme Court in 1921. Similar to the status of the young people with temporary reprieve under DACA (Liptak 2020), Ozawa's parents—of Japanese origin—were not allowed to become citizens. He had been brought to the US when he was two years old, and filed suit to challenge his citizenship status, but lost his plea. In 1922, Bhagat Singh Thind filed a lawsuit challenging the race-based assumption used to keep Indian-origin migrants from citizenship on the grounds that only "Aryan origin" people were allowed to be citizens. He lost this legal challenge as well, and the judge defined "Whiteness" according to a subjective test (as there is no effective objective measure to this social construction) as to how an everyday US citizen might define or interpret "Whiteness." Similarly, protesting forced curfew and forced removal of Japanese Americans to internment camps, Korematsu and Hirabayashi filed lawsuits in 1943 and 1944 as US citizens. They lost their cases at that time, but their suits are now considered defining caselaw for the rights of citizens and migrants to the US (see Muller 2020). Mostly forgotten by history, Mitsuye Endo filed a successful lawsuit that ultimately ended the Japanese internment camps;[17] and some of her arguments in that case could provide new legal arguments against current migrant detention. Yet the unfortunate reality is that not only are current migrants rarely able to file suit, most are left entirely indigent, without legal representation as they navigate the maze of US immigration law (ACLU 2018; Lee 2017).

Much like Ozawa's quest for legal recognition, many young members of immigrant families who have lived most of their lives in the US have been attempting to change their liminal status through activism to maintain protections under the Obama-era Deferred Action for Childhood Arrivals (DACA) program. Often ignoring the legal risks, they have held rallies, marched to draw attention to their cause, lobbied senators and other political allies (Wides-Muñoz 2018). Much like the social media activism of refugees (Nikunen 2019), young people in liminal statuses have attempted to change how people see them—as valuable members of American society rather than dangerous or foreign criminals. Bibler Coutin et al. (2017) point out however that with DACA related struggles, the transitory status of DACA, and the discretionary power of the state has led to some gains, but DACA itself remains buffeted by constant political challenges and changes in federal administrations.

Migrants and undocumented immigrants facing deportation have also attempted forms of organized resistance (Das Gupta 2014). Some have sought sanctuary in churches (Flores-González and Gomburg-Muñoz 2013), which have acted on social justice principles to offer such help. One man who spent an incredible two years in a church basement, which acted as sanctuary for him, was granted a reprieve from federal courts (Altimari 2021). Still, ICE has been fining activists to prevent such sanctuary appeals and practices (see Saxon 2020). Of course, these efforts are joined by the declaration of several "sanctuary cities" on the basis of organizing by local activists (Vaughan and Griffith 2023). However, the topic of sanctuary cities remains one of great contestation in local and national politics. Most recently, this debate has been exacerbated by the practice of border states such as Texas or Florida transporting migrant arrivals—many who are asylum seekers—to cities like New York or Los Angeles to challenge the sanctuary city model and draw attention to what is being constructed as a crisis at the southern US border (Jordan and Sandoval 2023).

A final aspect of migrants' struggle to realize human rights protections has been through the stream of activism to stop violence against migrant women and girls. Initially, the Violence Against Women Act (VAWA) was passed in the US at the behest of White women who refused to include the coverture status of recent migrants as a significant condition that increased the vulnerability of women to violence within families and communities (Das Gupta 2007). Organizing by migrant women of color led to a correction to the next iterations of VAWA, and migrant women are now able to advocate for themselves under VAWA protections as a result. But, the process to do so remains onerous, particularly for those without resources or assistance with the burden of paperwork and evidence necessary to prove their cases.

Despite this legacy of resistance, continuing human rights praxis is absolutely necessary to address the rights conditions experienced by migrant populations at US borders and around the world. As we will discuss in the following chapter, this can be and is partially being achieved through a diverse, organized international labor movement of the global working class that includes "doubly free" exploited workers with the protections of citizenship, hyper-exploited or partially expropriated citizen-workers and immigrants as part of the global precariat, and expropriable populations of undocumented migrants, prisoners, and modern-day slaves. Admittedly, labor unions in the US have not had the best track record when it comes to solidarity with migrant workers, and immigrant rights movements in the US have had some trouble in capturing the interests of the country's considerably diverse (im)migrant population (in terms of race/ethnicity, country of origin, immigration/VISA status, etc.) (see Roy 2022). However, we argue that there are signs of hope that the contemporary labor movement in the US can engage in forms of international organizing, and is now finding ways to flex organized labor power with regard to issues of foreign policy, including those of immigration reform and a just transition away from an economy still grounded in things like fossil fuel extraction and militarized accumulation.

Notes

* This chapter was completed with contributions from Bandana Purkayastha.
1 Acquiring citizenship does not ensure human rights, but it does provide a relatively better chance to seek legal redress. As part of the praxis of struggle migrants have fought for their rights through cases such as *US vs. Thind* (1922), *Ozawa vs. US* (1921), *Korematsu* (1944), and *Hirabayashi* (1943) (for a discussion, see Muller 2020).
2 Since the 1990s, the most secure non-citizen status—those holding permanent residency visas which allow all activities except voting—were renamed as "resident aliens" by the government.
3 The definition of migrants in many databases vary. These figures, for instance, are not intended to show the number of people on the move now. These are cumulative statistics gathered from different sources.
4 According to UN Refugee Agency, the rise in forcibly displaced peoples is due to "persecution, conflict, violence, human rights violations or events seriously disturbing public order" (UNHCR 2023).
5 According to Migration Data Portal (2021) "Remittances exceed official development aid but are private funds."
6 Laila Lalami (2021) describes the wars in this way: "In the United States, Sept. 11 led directly to the creation of the Department of Homeland Security, the passing of the Patriot Act, the Authorization for Use of Military Force, the use of warrantless surveillance programs, and special registration of immigrants and foreign students from Muslim countries. Outside the United States, the attacks served as justification for the 20-year war in Afghanistan; the invasion and occupation of Iraq; the indefinite detention of prisoners at Guantánamo Bay; the use of torture at Abu Ghraib and elsewhere; the killing of thousands of US and foreign service members; the periodic bombing of Pakistan, Yemen, Syria and Somalia; the deaths of some 800,000 people, including 335,000 civilians; and the displacement of an estimated 38 million people. At each step in this parade of horrors, we

were reminded that the United States was attacked on Sept. 11. The terrible wound of that day was left open, causing pain and anger that lasted for years. In that continually grieving state, the public was perhaps more willing to accept what it might not have otherwise—security theater at our airports, constant surveillance, bombs being dropped on wedding parties in Afghanistan."

7 When we examine the construction of liminality historically, the roots extend to the forced migration of Native Americans and forced migration and enslavement of people from African countries (Feagin and Ducey 2019), arguably until the late early 20th century—noting the wounded knee massacre in 1890 or the Battle of Bear Valley in 1918 for example, and the long struggle for civil and human rights that followed (Anderson 2003). In the interest of brevity, we focus here on current migrants and those still constructed as "foreign."

8 Gonzales (1990) among others has provided many details about each of these groups, illustrating how the national laws intersected with state and local policies and ordnances. These laws remained in place till after 1965 when the Civil Rights movement led to rethinking of race-based laws.

9 The case of trafficking victims is complicated. They have to prove they did not enter the country illegally. That is, they must prove not to have paid third parties to assist in their entering the country, and prove that they encountered violent coercion, fraud, intimidation, or related conditions outlined in the US trafficking protocols to force their migration (see Purkayastha and Yousaf 2018).

10 The language of "skilled" and "deskilled" labor in this context is incredibly misleading, as (for example) agricultural labor requires considerable skill and physical capabilities.

11 As part of outsourcing work the US and other countries have also set up workplaces in economic enterprise zones in other countries, where the companies enjoy significant tax breaks and freedom from the laws of that nation, while holding workers to the rules and work times in the US (Aneesh 2015; Mirchandani 2019). Highly skilled workers on H1-B visas represent a different variation of this phenomenon since they are in the US on temporary visas, beholden to the companies, for their political right to stay and work.

12 For slight variations in conditions, which do not yet meet human rights standards, see Sullivan, Kanno-Youngs, and Broadwater 2021.

13 For the UN definition see OHCHR 2000. For the US definition see US Dept. of State N.d.

14 Writing about camps housing the internally displaced people, Njiru and Purkayastha (2017; see also Purkayastha 2018) pointed out the vulnerable position of women and children to sexual assaults and even a growing sense that providing sex might be a way of earning money for essentials to survive; this insight remains true in refugee camps, as media accounts of camps where asylum seekers to the US or refugees are held, testify.

15 One stated rationale for this shift is that civil society organizations, rather than governments, are most effective (and efficient) in providing solutions to people in conditions of distress. Despite these claims, the efforts are partial at best. Samaddar (2017) describes the endeavor as "gigantic humanitarian machines which would liken to the transnational corporations (TNCs) ... managing societies, which produce the obdurate refugees and migrants to stop them from leaving the shores, to keep them within the national territorial confines."

16 Most were located in the global South. See York University Center for Refugee Studies 2018 for the full text of the Declaration. The 2018 Declaration was followed by a specific "Kolkata Declaration on the Need for a Coherent Protection Policy and Justice for Refugees and Migrants of Afghanistan" in 2021 that applied the original Declaration to the conditions of Afghans fleeing Taliban control in the aftermath of US war and withdrawal (Refugee Watch Online 2021).

17 For an account of the internment and subsequent struggles, see Weglyn 1996. For an account of the struggle over reparations see Maki et al. 1999. For a review of *Korematsu* and *Hirabayashi* and their most recent iterations, see Muller 2020.

References

ABC News. 2016. "Obama Has Deported More People Than Any Other President." *ABC News*, August 29. Retrieved 12/10/23 from https://abcnews.go.com/Politics/obamas-deportation-policy-numbers/story?id=41715661

Abraham, Margaret. 2000. *Speaking the Unspeakable*. New Brunswick, NJ: Rutgers University Press.

ACLU. 2018. "Lawsuit: Ice Detention Centers Deny Detainees Contact with Attorneys." *ACLU*. Retrieved 09/05/23 from www.aclusocal.org/en/press-releases/lawsuit-ice-detention-centers-deny-detainees-contact-attorneys

Akkerman, Mark. 2023. "Global Spending on Immigration Enforcement is Higher than Ever and Rising." *Migration Policy Institute*, May 31. Retrieved 09/20/23 from www.migrationpolicy.org/article/immigration-enforcement-spending-rising

Aleaziz, Hamed and Miriam Jordan. 2024. "Illegal Border Crossings Plummeted in January." *The New York Times*, February 13. Retrieved 02/26/24 from www.nytimes.com/2024/02/13/us/politics/illegal-border-crossings-january.html?campaign_id=9&emc=edit_nn_20240214&instance_id=115133&nl=the-morning&regi_id=138697150&segment_id=158153&te=1&user_id=1ceda8aa3bbd02cbe08de642e72d8593

Altimari, Daniela. 2021. "After 2 Years Living in a Church Basement, a New Haven Man Gets a Stay of Deportation and a Chance to Move on With His Life." *Hartford Courant*, July 30. Retrieved 09/09/23 from www.courant.com/politics/hc-pol-nelson-pinos-church-sanctuary-20210730-b3qlzul5hrbtzdkkns5tqgdhse-story.html

American Immigration Council. 2021. "An Overview of US Refugee Law and Policy." *American Immigration Council.* Retrieved 09/15/23 from www.americanimmigrationcouncil.org/research/overview-us-refugee-law-and-policy

Anderson, Carol. 2003. *Eyes Off the Prize: The United Nations and the African American Struggle for Human Rights, 1944–1955.* Cambridge University Press.

Aneesh, A. 2015. *Neutral Accent: How Language, Labour, and Life Became Global.* Duke University Press.

Aranda, Elizabeth and Elizabeth Vaquera. 2015. "Racism, the Immigration Enforcement Regime, and the Implications for Racial Inequality in the Lives of Undocumented Young Adults." *Sociology of Race and Ethnicity* 1 (1): 88–104.

Ballvé, Teo and McSweeney, Kendra. 2020. "The 'Colombianisation' of Central America: Misconceptions, Mischaracterizations and the Military-Agroindustrial Complex." *Journal of Latin American Studies* (52) 4: 805–829.

Banerjee, Pallavi, 2022. *The Opportunity Trap.* New York: New York University Press.

Banerjee, Pallavi and Lina Rincón. 2019. "Trouble in Tech Paradise." *Contexts* 18 (2): 24–29.

Bibler Coutin, Susan, S. Ashar, J. Chacon and S. Lee. 2017. "Deferred Action and the Discretionary State: Migration, Precarity and Resistance." *Citizenship Studies* 21 (8): 1–17.

Bilmes, Linda J. and Michael D. Intriligator. 2013. "How Many Wars is US Fighting Today?" *Peace Economics, Peace Science and Public Policy* 19 (1): 8–16.

Burnett, John. 2017. "Big Money as Private Immigrant Jails Boom." *National Public Radio*, November 21. Retrieved 09/09/23 from www.npr.org/2017/11/21/565318778/big-money-as-private-immigrant-jails-boom

Cheatham, Amelia and Diana Roy. 2023. "US Detention of Child Migrants." *Council on Foreign Relations*, March 27. Retrieved 09/14/23 from www.cfr.org/backgroun der/us-detention-child-migrants

Cheslow, Daniella. 2019. "US Agents Fire Tear Gas at Migrants Trying to Cross Mexico Border." *NPR*, January 2. Retrieved 12/10/23 from www.npr.org/2019/01/02/681513362/us-agents-fire-tear-gas-at-migrants-trying-to-cross-mexico-border

Cho, Eunice. 2023. "Unchecked Growth: Private Prison Corporations and Immigration Detention, Three Years into the Biden Administration." *ACLU*, August 7. Retrieved 12/17/23 from www.aclu.org/news/immigrants-rights/unchecked-growth-private-prison-corporations-and-immigration-detention-three-years-into-the-biden-administration

Coburn, Noah, N. Crawford, N. Niland, et al. 2023. "Afghan Refugees." *Watson Institute of International and Public Affairs at Brown University, Costs of War Project.* Retrieved 11/15/23 from https://watson.brown.edu/costsofwar/costs/huma n/refugees/afghan

Cohen, Tom. 2014. "Obama Seeks Emergency Immigration Funds, More Authority." *CNN Politics*, July 8. Retrieved 09/02/23 from www.cnn.com/2014/07/08/politics/immigration/index.html

Dalmia, Aoushka. 2021. "Community Effort: Mayor Says Worcester Ready to Welcome More Than 300 Refugees from Afghanistan." *Worcester Telegram and Gazette*, September 2. Retrieved 09/01/23 from www.telegram.com/story/news/2021/09/02/afghanistan-worcester-mayor-joe-petty-united-state-refugees/5698164001/

Daniels, Roger. 2005. *Guarding the Golden Door. American Immigration Policy and Immigrants since 1882.* New York: Hill and Wang.

Das Gupta, Shamita. 2007. *Body Evidence: Intimate Violence Against South Asian Women in America.* New Brunswick: Rutgers University Press.

Das Gupta, Monisha. 2014. "'Don't Deport Our Daddies': Gendering State Deportation Practices and Immigrant Organizing." *Gender and Society* 28 (1): 83–109.

Debusmann, Bernd. 2023. "How Joe Biden and Donald Trump's Border Policies Compare." *BBC News*, May 7. Retrieved 09/15/23 from www.bbc.com/news/worl d-us-canada-65574725

Del Real, D. 2022. "Seemingly Inclusive Liminal Legality: The Fragility and Illegality Production of Colombia's Legalization Programs for Venezuelan Migrants." *Journal of Ethnic and Migration Studies*, 48 (15): 3580–3601.

Dickerson, Caitlin. 2019. "'There Is a Stench': Soiled Clothes and No Baths for Migrant Children at a Texas Center." *The New York Times*, June 21. Retrieved 09/16/23 from www.nytimes.com/2019/06/21/us/migrant-children-border-soap.html

Dickerson, Caitlin. 2020. "Inquiry Ordered Into Claims Immigrants Had Unwanted Gynecology Procedures." *The New York Times*, September 16. Retrieved 09/13/23 from www.nytimes.com/2020/09/16/us/ICE-hysterectomies-whistleblower-georgia.html

Dickerson, Caitlin, S. Wessler and M. Jordan. 2020. "Immigrants Say They Were Pressured Into Unneeded Surgeries." *The New York Times*, September 29. Retrieved 09/12/23 from www.nytimes.com/2020/09/29/us/ice-hysterectomies-sur geries-georgia.html

Edwards, Alice. 2013. "Detention Under Scrutiny." *Forced Migration Review* 44: 4–6.

Ellis, Nicole and Casey Kuhn. 2023. "What is Title 42 and What Does it Mean for Immigration at the Southern Border?" *PBS News*, January 13. Retrieved 12/10/23 from www.pbs.org/newshour/nation/what-is-title-42-and-what-does-it-mean-for-im migration-at-the-southern-border

Espiritu, Yen. 1993. *Asian American Panethnicity: Bridging Institutions and Identities.* Philadelphia, PA: Temple University Press.

Espiritu, Yen. 2003. *Asian American Women and Men: Love, Labor, and Laws.* New York: Rowman & Littlefield.

Esquivel, Paloma. 2019. "El Paso Massacre Was Just the Latest in Long Line of Anti-Latino Violence in the US." *Los Angeles Times*, August 16. Retrieved 11/20/23 from www.latimes.com/california/story/2019-08-16/el-paso-massacre-timeline-of-a nti-latino-violence-in-united-states

Fabregas, Alicia. 2023. "As Migration to the US Border Rises, Experts Fear Surge in Sexual Violence." *Al Jazeera*, December 21. Retrieved 12/22/23 from www.aljazeera. com/news/2023/12/21/as-migration-to-the-us-border-rises-experts-fear-surge-in-sexual-violence

Feagin, Joe and Kimberly Ducey. 2019. *Racist America: Roots, Current Realities, and Future Reparations* (4th edition). New York: Routledge.

Flores-González, Nilda and Ruth Gomberg-Muñoz. 2013. "FLOResiste: Transnational Labor, Motherhood, and Activism." In *Immigrant Women Workers in the Neoliberal Age*, edited by Nilda Flores-Gonzalez, pp. 262–276. University of Illinois Press.

Fram, Alan and Jonathan Lemire. 2018. "Trump: Why Allow Immigrants From 'Shithole Countries'?" *AP*, January 11. Retrieved 12/09/23 from https://apnews. com/article/immigration-north-america-donald-trump-ap-top-news-international-news-fdda2ff0b877416c8ae1c1a77a3cc425

Frelick, Bill, I. Kysel and J. Podkul. 2016. "The Impact of Externalization of Migration Controls on the Rights of Asylum Seekers and Other Migrants." *Journal on Migration and Human Security* (JMHS) 4 (4): 190–220.

Garip, Feliz, Shannon Gleeson and Matthew Hall. 2019. "How the State Criminalizes Immigrants and to What Effect: A Multidisciplinary Account." *American Behavioral Scientist* 63 (9): 1159–1171.

Glenn, Evelyn Nakano. 2002. *Unequal Freedom: How Race and Gender Shaped American Citizenship and Labor.* Cambridge, MA: Harvard University Press.

Golash Boza, Tanya. 2015. *Deported: Immigrant Policing, Disposable Labor and Global Capitalism.* New York: New York University Press.

Goldring, Luin, Carolina Bernstein and Judith Bernhard. 2009. "Institutionalizing Precarious Migratory Status in Canada." *Citizenship Studies* 13 (3): 239–265.

Gonzales, Juan L. 1990. *Racial and Ethnic Groups in America.* Dubuque, IA: Kendall Hunt Publishing Company.

Gonzales, Roberto G. and Steven Raphael. 2017. "Illegality: A Contemporary Portrait of Immigration." *RSF: The Russell Sage Foundation Journal of the Social Sciences* 3 (4): 1–17. doi:10.7758/ RSF.2017.3.4.01.

Gran, Brian. 2021. *The Sociology of Children's Rights.* London: Polity.

Hanafi, Sari. 2008. "Palestinian Refugee Camps in Lebanon: Laboratory of Indocile Identity Formation." In *The Lived Reality of Palestinian Refugees in Lebanon*, edited by Mohamed Ali Khalidi, pp. 45–74. Institute of Palestine Studies.

Hesson, Ted, R. Erol and S. Morland. 2023. "US to Continue Deporting Haitians as it Evacuates its Citizens." *Reuters*, August 31. Retrieved 01/10/24 from www.reuters.com/ world/americas/us-continue-deporting-haitians-it-evacuates-its-citizens-2023-09-01/

Holmes, Seth. 2013. *Fresh Fruit, Broken Bodies: Migrant Farmworkers in the United States*. Berkeley: University of California Press.

International Organization for Migration (IOM). 2022. *World Migration Report 2022*. IOM. Retrieved 12/20/23 from https://worldmigrationreport.iom.int/wmr-2022-interactive/

International Organization for Migration (IOM). 2023. *Global Migration Trends*. IOM. Retrieved 12/20/23 from www.iom.int/global-migration-trends

Isacson, Adam. 2022. "A Tragic Milestone: 20,000[th] Immigrant Deported to Haiti Since Biden Inauguration." *Washington Office on Latin America (WOLA)*, February 17. Retrieved 01/10/24 from www.wola.org/analysis/a-tragic-milestone-20000th-migrant-deported-to-haiti-since-biden-inauguration/

Isacson, Adam. 2023. "Weekly US–Mexico Border Update: Heavy Migration, No Congress Deal, Texas Law." *Washington Office on Latin America (WOLA)*, December 21. Retrieved 12/22/23 from www.wola.org/2023/12/weekly-u-s-mexico-border-update-heavy-migration-no-congress-deal-texas-law/

Japanese American National Museum. N.d. Retrieved 09/10/23 from https://eacc.janm.org/camp/gila-river/#:~:text=The%20Gila%20River%20War%20Relocation%20Center%20was%20one%20of%20the,River%20and%20its%2013%2C348%20inmates

Jordan, Miriam. 2021. "Unauthorized Migration Across the Mexico-US Border Slips." *The New York Times*, November 15. Retrieved 09/11/23 from www.nytimes.com/2021/11/15/us/migrants-border-crossings.html

Jordan, Miriam and Edgar Sandoval. 2023. "Is Texas Busing Responsible for the Migrant Crisis Across Cities?" *The New York Times*, September 7. Retrieved 12/05/23 from www.nytimes.com/2023/09/07/us/migrant-buses-texas-nyc-los-angeles.html

Joshi, Khyati. 2020. *White Christian Privilege: The Illusion of Religious Equality in America*. New York: NYU Press.

Kibria, Nazli, Cara Bowman and Megan O'Leary. 2014. *Race and Immigration*. Malden, MA: Polity Press.

Lalami, Laila. 2021. "The Real Meaning of 'Never Forget.'" *The New York Times*, September 10. Retrieved 09/09/23 from www.nytimes.com/2021/09/10/opinion/9-11-memorial.html

Layne, Nathan. 2023. "Trump Repeats 'Poisoning the Blood' Anti-Immigrant Remark." *Reuters*, December 16. Retrieved 12/22/23 from www.reuters.com/world/us/trump-repeats-poisoning-blood-anti-immigrant-remark-2023-12-16/

Lee, Patrick G. 2017. "Immigrants in Detention Centers Are Often Hundreds of Miles from Legal Help." *ProPublica*. Retrieved 09/10/23 from www.propublica.org/article/immigrants-in-detention-centers-are-often-hundreds-of-miles-from-legal-help

Liptak, Adam. 2020. "'Dreamers' Tell Supreme Court Ending DACA During Pandemic Would Be 'Catastrophic.'" *The New York Times*, March 27. Retrieved 09/13/23 from www.nytimes.com/2020/03/27/us/dreamers-supreme-court-daca.html

López, Victoria and Sandra Park. 2018. "ICE Detention Center Says It's Not Responsible for Staff's Sexual Abuse of Detainees." *American Civil Liberties Union (ACLU)*, November 6. Retrieved 09/12/23 from www.aclu.org/blog/immigrants-rights/immigrants-rights-and-detention/ice-detention-center-says-its-not-responsible

Luan, Livia. 2018. "Profiting from Enforcement: The Role of Private Prisons in U.S." *Immigration Policy Institute*, May 2. Retrieved 10/15/23 from www.migrationpolicy.org/article/profiting-enforcement-role-private-prisons-us-immigration-detention

Lutheran Immigration and Refugee Service (LIRS). 2014. "Locking Up Family Values, Again." LIRS and Women's Refugee Commission (WRC). Retrieved 09/12/23 from www.womensrefugeecommission.org/wp-content/uploads/2020/04/Locking-Up-Family-Values-Again-Exec-Summ.pdf

Maki, Mitchell, et al. 1999. *Achieving the Impossible Dream: How Japanese Americans Obtained Redress.* University of Illinois Press.

Mastropasqua, Jonna. 2020. "Children Detained in America's Prisons are Charged for Underwear, Food, Books, Even Family Visits. This Has to Stop." *Newsweek,* February 19. Retrieved 09/11/23 from www.newsweek.com/i-teach-kids-prison-arizona-pay-everything-1488072

Menjívar, C. 2006. "Liminal Legality: Salvadoran and Guatemalan Immigrants' Lives in the United States." *American Journal of Sociology,* 111 (4): 999–1037.

Menjívar, Cecilia and Daniel Kanstroom (Eds). 2014. *Constructing Immigrant 'Illegality': Critiques, Experiences, and Responses.* Cambridge University Press.

Menjívar, Cecilia and Leisy J. Abrego. 2012. "Legal Violence: Immigration Law and the Lives of Central American Immigrants." *American Journal of Sociology* 117 (5):1380–1421.

Migration Data Portal. 2021. "Remittances." *Migration Data Portal.* Retrieved 11/10/23 from www.migrationdataportal.org/themes/remittances

Mirchandani, Kiran. 2019. "Globality in Exceptional Spaces: Service Workers in India's Transnational Economy." In *Handbook of Indian Transnationalism,* edited by Ajaya Sahoo and Bandana Purkayastha, pp. 21–30. New York: Routledge.

Miroff, Nick. 2022. "Homeland Security Says it Will End 'Remain in Mexico' Policy and Allow Asylum-Seekers to Enter US." *The Texas Tribune*August 9. Retrieved 12/03/23 from www.texastribune.org/2022/08/09/remain-in-mexico-migrant-protection-protocols-judge-injunction/

Miroff, Nick, M. Sacchetti and S. Frostenson. 2024. "Trump vs. Biden on Immigration: 12 Charts Comparing US Border Security." *The Washington Post,* February 12. Retrieved 02/26/24 from www.washingtonpost.com/immigration/2024/02/11/trump-biden-immigration-border-compared/

Moussawi, Ghassan. 2020. *Disruptive Situations, Fractal Orientalism and Queer Strategies in Beirut.* New York: New York University Press.

Muller, Eric. 2020. "Korematsu Hirabayashi and the Second Monster." *Texas Law Review* Issue 4. Retrieved 09/15/23 from https://texaslawreview.org/korematsu-hirabayashi-and-the-second-monster/

Musalo, Karen and Eunice Lee. 2017. "Seeking a Rational Approach to a Regional Refugee Crisis: Lessons from the Summer 2014 'Surge' of Central American Women and Children at the US-Mexico Border." *JMHS* 5 (1): 137–179.

Nikunen, Kaarina. 2019. "Once a Refugee: Selfie Activism, Visualized Citizenship and the Space of Appearance." *Popular Communication* 17 (2): 154–170.

Njiru, Roseanne and Bandana Purkayastha. 2017. "'As a Woman I Cannot Just Leave the House': Gendered Spaces and HIV Vulnerability in Marriages in Kenya." *Journal of Gender Studies* 27 (8): 957–968.

Office of the United Nations High Commissioner for Human Rights (OHCHR). 2000. "Protocol to Prevent, Suppress and Punish Trafficking in Persons Especially Women and Children, Supplementing the United Nations Convention Against Transnational Organized Crime." OHCHR. Retrieved 09/12/23 from www.ohchr.org/en/professionalinterest/pages/protocoltraffickinginpersons.aspx

Physicians for Human Rights, Harvard Immigration and Refugee Clinical Program, and the Peeler Immigration Lab. 2024. "'Endless Nightmare': Torture and Inhuman Treatment in Solitary Confinement in US Immigration Detention." Physicians for Human Rights, February 6. Retrieved 03/01/24 from https://phr.org/our-work/resources/endless-nightmare-solitary-confinement-in-us-immigration-detention/

Purkayastha, Bandana. 2018. "Migration, Migrants, and Human Security." *Current Sociology* 66 (2): 167–191.

Purkayastha, Bandana. 2020. "From Suffrage to Substantive Human Rights: The Continuing Journey for Racially Marginalized Women." *Western New England Law Journal* 42 (3): 119–138.

Purkayastha, Bandana. 2021. "Distancing as Governance." In *On the Margins of Protection*, edited by Paula Banerjee. Kolkata: Orient Black Swan.

Purkayastha, Bandana and Farhan Navid Yousaf. 2018. *Human Trafficking: Trade for Sex, Labor, and Organs*. London: Polity Press.

Purkayastha, Bandana and Mangala Subramaniam (Eds). 2004. *The Power of Women's Informal Networks: Lessons in Social Change from South Asia and West Africa*. Lanham, MD: Lexington Books.

Purkayastha, Bandana and Rianka Roy. 2023. "Hidden in Plain Sight: 'Neutral' Enclosures for High-Skilled Immigrants during COVID-19." *Sociological Forum*, 38 (4) 1176–1197.

Ramon, Bettina. 2019. "White Supremacist Terrorism and the History of Anti-Latino Racism in Texas." *People for the American Way*, August 7. Retrieved 11/01/23 from www.pfaw.org/blog-posts/white-supremacist-terrorism-and-the-history-of-a nti-latino-racism-in-texas/

Refugee Watch Online. 2021. "Kolkata Declaration on the Need for a Coherent Projection Policy and Justice for Refugees and Migrants of Afghanistan, 2021." *Refugee Watch Online*. Retrieved 12/15/23 from https://refugeewatchonline.wordp ress.com/2021/12/04/kolkata-declaration-on-the-need-for-a-coherent-protection-p olicy-and-justice-for-refugees-and-migrants-of-afghanistan-2021/

Romero, Mary. 2018. "Reflections on Globalized Care Chains and Migrant Women Workers." *Critical Sociology* 44 (7-8): 1179–1189.

Romero, Mary. 2020. "Sociology Engaged in Social Justice." *American Sociological Review* 85 (1): 1–30.

Roth, Silke. 2015. *The Paradoxes of Aidwork: Passionate Professionals*. New York: Routledge.

Roy, Rianka. 2022. "Immigrant Workers' Movements in the US: Where are High-skilled 'Nonimmigrants'?" *Sociology Compass* 16 (6): https://doi.org/10. 1111/soc4. 12985C

Samaddar, Ranabir. 2017. "Histories of the Late Nineteenth to Early Twentieth Century Immigration and Our Time." *Current Sociology* 66 (2): 192–208.

Samaddar, Ranabir. 2020. *The Postcolonial Age of Migration*. New York: Sage.

Saxon, Shani. 2020. "Advocates Sue ICE for Targeting Sanctuary Leaders with Retaliatory Fines." *ColorLines*, February 27. Retrieved 09/17/23 from www.color lines.com/articles/advocates-sue-ice-targeting-sanctuary-leaders-retaliatory-fines

Selee, Andrew. 2023. "What Does the End of Title 42 Mean for US Migration Policy?" *Carnegie Corporation of New York and the Migration Policy Institute*, June 5. Retrieved 12/18/23 from www.carnegie.org/our-work/article/what-does-end-ti tle-42-mean-us-migration-policy/#:~:text=Title%2042%2C%20a%20COVID% 2D19,for%20COVID%2D19%20was%20lifted

Shear, Michael, Hamed Aleaziz and Zolan Kanno-Youngs. 2024. "How the Border Crisis Shattered Biden's Immigration Hopes." *The New York Times*, January 30. Retrieved 02/10/24 from www.nytimes.com/2024/01/30/us/politics/biden-border-cri sis-immigration.html

Sherer, Paul. 2004. "Targets of Suspicion: The Impact of Post-9/11 Policies on Muslims, Arabs and South Asians in the United States." *Immigration Policy Center*. Retrieved 12/15/23 from www.americanimmigrationcouncil.org/sites/default/files/ research/Targets%20of%20Suspicion.pdf

Shrivastava, Aseem and Ashish Kothari. 2012. *Churning of the Earth: The Making of Global India*. New Delhi, India: Penguin Global.

Simon, Rita and Susan Alexander. 1993. *The Ambivalent Welcome: The Print Media, Public Opinion and Immigration*. New York: Praeger.

Singh, Nikhil Pal. 2017. *Race and America's Long War*. Oakland, CA: University of California Press.

Sökefeld, Martin. 2020. "Forced Migration, the Other Way Round? The Politics of Deporting Afghans from Germany." In *Forced Migration and Conflict-Induced Displacement: Impacts and Prospective Responses*, edited by Muhammad Makki, Aizah Azam, Syed Ali Akach and Faryal Khan, pp. 1–20. Islamabad: NUST Press.

Southern Poverty Law Center (SPLC). 2022. "Family Separation – A Timeline." *SPLC*, March 23. Retrieved 12/10/23 from www.splcenter.org/news/2022/03/23/fam ily-separation-timeline

Spagat, Elliot. 2023. "Online System to Seek Asylum in US is Quickly Overwhelmed." *AP*, January 28. Retrieved 12/10/23 from https://apnews.com/article/technology-united-sta tes-government-caribbean-mexico-mobile-apps-49b38b18869ed3b2260fb6d774153456

Sullivan, Eileen. 2021. "For Migrant Children in Federal Care, a 'Sense of Desperation.'" *The New York Times*, May 18. Retrieved 09/16/23 from www.nytimes. com/2021/05/18/us/politics/biden-migrant-children.html

Sullivan, Eileen, Z. Kanno-Youngs and L. Broadwater. 2021. "Overcrowded Jails Give Way to Packed Migrant Child Shelters." *The New York Times*, September 6. Retrieved 09/13/23 from www.nytimes.com/2021/05/07/us/politics/migrant-chil dren-shelters.html

Torres Stone, Rosalie, B. Purkayastha and T. A. Berdahl. 2005. "Beyond Asian American: Examining Conditions and Mechanisms of Earnings Inequality for Filipina and Asian Indian Women." *Sociological Perspectives* 49 (2): 261–281.

Trautmann, Mike. 2023. "Why Does Trump Keep Saying Migrants Are 'Poisoning' America? Many GOP Caucusgoers Like It." *Des Moines Register*, December 22. Retrieved 12/23/23 from www.desmoinesregister.com/story/news/politics/iowa -poll/caucus/2023/12/22/iowa-poll-shows-depth-of-republicans-support-for-dona ld-trump-poisoning-the-blood-speech-gop/71998614007/

United Nations (UN). 2018. "Global Compact for Migration." *UN*. Retrieved 12/22/ 23 from https://refugeesmigrants.un.org/migration-compact

United Nations (UN). 2023. "International Migration." *UN*. Retrieved 12/20/23 from www.un.org/en/global-issues/migration

United Nations High Commissioner for Refugees (UNHCR). 2000. "Protocol to Prevent, Suppress, and Punish Trafficking in Persons Especially Women and Children, Supplementing the United Nations Convention Against Transnational Organized Crime." *UNHCR*. Retrieved 10/02/23 from www.ohchr.org/en/instruments-mecha nisms/instruments/protocol-prevent-suppress-and-punish-trafficking-persons

United Nations High Commissioner for Refugees (UNHCR). 2021. "Figures at a Glance." *UNHCR.* Retrieved 10/01/23 from www.unhcr.org/en-us/figures-at-a-gla nce.html

United Nations High Commissioner for Refugees (UNHCR). 2023. "Refugee Data Finder." *UNHCR.* Retrieved 12/20/23 from www.unhcr.org/refugee-statistics/

US Department of State. N.d. "International and Domestic Law: Office to Monitor and Combat Trafficking in Persons." US Department of State. Retrieved 12/20/23 from www.state.gov/international-and-domestic-law/

Vaughan, Jessica and Bryan Griffith. 2023. "Map: Sanctuary Cities, Counties, and States." *Center for Immigration Studies*, December 22. Retrieved 12/23/23 from https://cis.org/Map-Sanctuary-Cities-Counties-and-States

Velitchkova, Ana. 2021. "Citizenship as a Caste Marker: How Persons Experience Cross-National Inequality." *Current Sociology* 71 (5): 1–20.

Vera, Amir, Rosa Flores, Priscilla Alvarez and Gustavo Valdes. 2022. "US Federal Agents Fired Pepper Ball Projectiles at Venezuelan Protesters Near El Paso After Border Patrol Agent Was Injured, Officials Say." *CNN*, November 1. Retrieved 12/05/23 from www.cnn.com/2022/10/31/us/venezuela-protesters-us-customs-and-bor der-protection-pepper-balls/index.html

Weglyn, Michi Nishura. 1996. *Years of Infamy: The Untold Story of America's Concentration Camps.* University of Washington Press.

Westcott, Lucy. 2015. "A Brief History of Refugees Paying Back the US Government for Their Travel." *Newsweek*, December 12. Retrieved 09/17/23 from www.news week.com/brief-history-refugees-paying-back-us-government-their-travel-403241

Wides-Muñoz, Laura. 2018. *The Making of a Dream: How a Group of Young Undocumented Immigrants Helped Change What It Means to Be American.* Harper Collins e-book.

Wilson, Tessa. 2024. "'Endless Nightmare': Torture and Inhuman Treatment in Solitary Confinement in US Immigration Detention." *Physicians for Human Rights*, February 6. Retrieved 02/26/24 from https://phr.org/our-work/resources/endless-nightmare-solita ry-confinement-in-us-immigration-detention/?utm_campaign=1029634_FY24%20ICE %20Report%20Release%20Lift%20Note&utm_medium=email&utm_source=Physi cians%20for%20Human%20Rights&dm_i=4GV7,M2GY,1IF6Y4,2IT4G,1

Wolf, Byron. 2018. "Trump Basically Called Mexicans Rapists Again." *CNN Politics*, April 6. Retrieved 12/10/23 from www.cnn.com/2018/04/06/politics/trump -mexico-rapists/index.html

York University Centre for Refugee Studies. 2018. "Kolkata Declaration." *York University Centre for Refugee Studies*, November 30. Retrieved 12/22/23 from www.yorku.ca/crs/kolkata-declaration/

6   Conclusion

An overarching goal of this book, and of the critical sociology of human rights as a field of scholarship, has been to investigate why the international legal system continues to fall short on ensuring the survival of human civilization, let alone the achievement of universal human dignity or human rights practice. While there is no single, all-encompassing answer to a question of such scope, we ultimately join other critical scholars and human rights activists in recognizing that the primary, overlapping threats to human rights and survival are posed by capitalism as an institutionalized social order. However, to understand and illustrate this, capitalist society must be understood in its full sophistication and complexity, reflecting both its foregrounded material relations based in the exploitation of "doubly free" wage labor, and its equally fundamental background relations that provide the "conditions of possibility" for both capital accumulation and for organized human civilization and other life on Earth (Fraser 2022), recognizing that these background relations are not reducible to their role in the process of capital accumulation, or to their undeniable connections to one another.

This theoretical approach first helps one to understand the non-accidental, historically specific, co-constitutive, structural imbrication (rather than coincidental "intersection") between the material (class) relations of capitalism and: a) the form and function of national and transnational state structures; b) the patriarchal and heteronormative relations of social reproduction; c) the racist, (ethno)nationalist, (neo)colonial relations of expropriation and geopolitical competition under a specific hegemonic, imperial "world order" (McCoy 2021); and d) the cannibalistic relation between political economy and a sustainable ecology (Fraser 2022). Such an approach helps to move critical sociology forward from what are now relatively tired and unproductive debates over the "primacy" of capitalist political economy or social systems such as racism or patriarchy. Second, the theoretical framework constructed and applied here provides a framework to demonstrate that the greatest challenges to human rights conditions are posed by the exploitive, expropriative, and cannibalistic relations of capitalist society. Indeed, the critical sociology of human rights demands that we understand human rights struggles as power struggles to resist material and other

DOI: 10.4324/9781003323556-7

(gendered, racialized, etc.) relations of domination and rule. Third, our theoretical framework reveals that the most significant overlapping threats to human survival—by the proliferation of weapons and (potentially nuclear) war, and by climate change and ecological destruction—can be found in the internal and external crises that plague and define contemporary capitalist society.

Further, the inability or unwillingness of states to choose human rights protections when in conflict with the interests of capital accumulation and powerful elites can be sourced in the external legitimacy crises that constrain all national state parties. That is, states are instrumentally constrained by the concentrated power of the TCC (Robinson 2018) and its Global Power Elite (Phillips 2018), and structurally constrained by their imbrication to the material and background relations of capitalist society. As a result, states tend to act in the interests of powerful elites, to ensure national and transnational circuits of capital accumulation, and to reinforce the (racist, patriarchal, nature-commodifying, etc.) background relations of capitalist society instead of the interests of their constituent public or international legal obligations (such as to human rights or humanitarian law) when these interests clash. As a result, states face a crisis of legitimacy in the eyes of their public—and for the ostensibly emblematic democracy and global hegemon of the US—in the eyes of the world as well. Such crises can and often are mediated through repression, censorship, propaganda, or through nationalist projects of scapegoating and even warmongering against "others" (such as constructed "enemies" or growing populations of migrants, deemed dangerous "outsiders," "criminals," or "foreigners").

In order to deal with the external crisis of legitimacy and a related internal crisis of overproduction (that forces capital to search high and low for reliable return on investment and pressures states to play along), we join Robinson (2020) in observing the rise and role of a global police state. The global police state emerges not by accident, but: 1) to discipline a diverse and increasingly precarious global working class; 2) to facilitate accumulation by dispossession (Harvey 2005, 2018) and other forms of expropriation while forcefully differentiating the often racialized and/or gendered lines between exploitable and expropriable populations; and 3) to provide sites of investment as opportunities for accumulation by repression and militarized accumulation (Robinson 2020, 2022a, 2022b). The global police state is perhaps best understood as a network of repressive state apparatuses (RSAs) (Althusser 2001 [1971]), connected through what we call "strong" (formal treaties, security agreements, and so forth) and "secondary" (through the transnational military industrial complex and supply chain) connective tissues with the US at its center.

The latent functions or consequences of the global police state's rise should be understood as creating a condition of ubiquitous global surveillance, ever-ready coercion, and catastrophic military conflict that is pushing human civilization to the brink of annihilation. Specifically, the global police state first poses a direct threat to human survival in the form of devastating and potentially apocalyptic (nuclear) conflicts, as geopolitical tensions increase under waning US global hegemony, the world is flooded with weapons, and a migration crisis explodes from the combined effects of war, instability, climate change, and ecological destruction. Second, it poses an indirect, overlapping threat (with climate change), as a significant source of greenhouse gas emissions and other pollutants (Crawford 2019, 2022; Belcher, Bigger, Neimark, and Kennelly 2019). Third, the global police state poses an indirect, overlapping threat in providing the repressive apparatus deployed to suppress social movements meant to confront OTHS and other human rights crises. To this third point, we also join Robinson (2020, 2022a, 2022b) in observing the related emergence of increasingly authoritarian, anti-democratic forms of government across a globally contested terrain, including but not limited to what he calls forms of 21st century fascism.

In addition to the external crisis of legitimacy and internal crisis of overaccumulation, contemporary capitalist society faces a general crisis (Fraser 2022) rooted in the cannibalistic, commodified relation between the capital accumulation drive and a finite and sensitively balanced natural ecology upon which capitalism and all life on Earth are dependent. Indeed, as illustrated in the most recent, 28th UN Conference of Parties (COP28), climate change and related forms of ecological destruction continue to pose dire threats as the world begins to reach what have been understood as the upper limits of survivable average temperature rise, or 1.5 degrees Celsius above pre-industrial levels. In fact, only a month before the COP28 Conference in December of 2023, the UN published findings from a new study (Hansen, Sato, et al. 2023) arguing that the world is on track to surpass the 1.5 degree barrier within the next decade, providing even more evidence of the need for swift and drastic cuts to global emissions.

The COP meetings are the primary global forum for international diplomatic engagement to understand and address the threats of climate change to humans and other life on Earth. COP28 was the largest of such meetings to date, and the conference has become a flashpoint for conflicts between grassroots climate activists representing global civil society and the interests of fossil fuel companies and other related industries (transnational capital), also represented by powerful military (China, Russia, the US, etc.) and petrostates (Saudi Arabia, Russia, the United Arab Emirates (UAE), etc.). The COP28 in 2023 was no different in this regard. However, it was held in the United Arab Emirates (UAE)—a markedly anti-democratic[1] petrostate, where journalists and peaceful protesters reported being surveilled, intimidated, and otherwise excluded or repressed throughout the conference (Green 2023).

As a clear indication of the forces most influential over the international climate change debate, the conference was led by COP28 President Sultan Al Jaber—CEO of the Abu Dhabi National Oil Company (ADNOC), and the first CEO of any kind to preside over the conference (Stockton and

Westervelt 2023).[2] Further, leaked documents revealed that Al Jaber and the Emirates used the deliberations leading up to the conference to "lobby on oil and gas deals around the world," with countries like fellow BRICS+ nations Brazil and China (Tabuchi 2023). It is no exaggeration to suggest that the COP28 conference was part fossil fuel trade show, since the conference was attended by nearly 2500 fossil fuel industry lobbyists (more than any in COP history), which would amount to the third largest delegation to the conference behind the national delegations of Brazil and the UAE.

During the Conference, Al Jaber shocked many participants in claiming, inaccurately, that there is "no science" behind calls to completely phase out fossil fuels to achieve current emissions and warming targets (Carrington and Stockton 2023). And in the end, thanks to pressures from lobbyists and resistance from China and several petrostates from the Organization of the Petroleum Exporting Countries (OPEC), the final COP28 report fell short of calling for a fossil fuel "phase out"—instead simply calling for their reduction (Abnet, Dickie, and Stanway 2023). And while contingents from the US, EU, and other wealthy nations from the global North continued to call for a fossil fuel phase out as the conference's "north star," their calls were considerably disingenuous, not accompanied by their own commitment to decarbonize "first and fastest," or providing the necessary resources for less wealthy and/or developing nations to achieve an energy transition or plan for climate change mitigation. The apparent shortcomings of the COP28 conference help to illustrate the role of transnational capital and powerful states in their service to drive ecological collapse while preventing effective human rights praxis that could help steer the course of humanity away from certain disaster.

But the UAE is not simply an authoritarian petrostate, and other aspects of their foreign policy reveal the same dangerous structural imbrication to transnational capital accumulation, the proliferation of weapons and war, and the perpetuation of (neo)colonial international relations of expropriation as exist for the US and its traditional Western allies. The UAE is a regional military player with both strong and weak connective tissues to the US, Saudi Arabia, and other RSAs networked in the global police state including China, with whom the UAE has pursued greater military cooperation and companies owned by the Emirati royal family (G24) have provided AI and other technologies for the Chinese RSA (Wong, Mazzetti, and Mozur 2024). UAE's role in the global police state has been made obvious in the country's participation in a military partnership with the US and Saudi Arabia against the Houthis in Yemen—a war that at one point created the largest humanitarian crisis in the world, where in Yemen over 80% of the population was still food insecure by the end of 2023, despite having reached a peace agreement (UNFPA 2023).[3] Beyond fighting in Yemen, the UAE has also helped to arm and support the Rapid Support Forces (RSF) against the Sudanese military in Sudan's brutal, ongoing civil war that has forcefully displaced over 6 million people and "triggered waves of ethnically driven killings" in the Darfur region (Eltahir 2023; Walsh, Koettl, and Schmitt 2023) that have included beheadings, systematic weaponization of rape, the recruitment of child soldiers, and other horrific war crimes (Cumming-Bruce and Walsh 2024). Also on the African Continent, the UAE is engaged in what is now called "green neocolonialism," where through companies like Blue Carbon, petrostates and high carbon emitters buy up cheap land in the developing world (also forcing out indigenous communities) as controversial forms of "carbon offsets" that may help to protect undeveloped land, but also serve to allow for continued production and consumption of fossil fuels. To date, Blue Carbon (owned by members of the royal family in Dubai) has land rights to 10% of Liberia, 8% of Tanzania, 10% of Zambia, 20% of Zimbabwe and millions of hectares more in Kenya (Goodman and Moynihan 2023).

As a final, but very important observation from the COP28 conference before moving on, the Global Stocktake report (the major assessment of nations' progress and needed actions regarding current emissions and other targets) was gaveled in without a contingent of 39 island nations even in the room. The contingent of island nations commented that the move, and the general shortcomings of wealthy nations' commitments at the conference were "not conducive" to their literal survival. To be clear, this means that the populations most immediately and existentially threatened by the climate crisis, with the least contributions to global emissions, were excluded in the final, and most important deliberations of the conference. This is indicative of the contemporary "necropolitics" that now help to define state policy and international relations in our time. Developed by Mbembe (2019:80) from a critical revision of Foucault's concept of "bio-power," necropolitics refer to an aspect of sovereignty that grants states "the capacity to define who matters and who does not, who is *disposable* and who is not," where one's disposability is deeply informed by their racialization, (neo) colonial position, and general socio-political precarity. In the context of rapidly heightening OTHS, transnational and national state policy take on the form or effect of necropolitics—in forcefully differentiating the rights holding citizen from the precarious, expropriable, "superfluous" (Robinson 2022a, 2022b), or "disposable" global rabble. And US domestic and foreign policy are certainly no exception.

As we've argued throughout this book and in our previous work (Armaline, Glasberg, and Purkayastha 2015), the US has been both a chief architect and the most hypocritical actor when it comes to the creation and application of international human rights law and standards. This is appropriately discussed as a manifestation of American exceptionalism. However, as made clear by the work of McCoy (2021; see Chapter 2), all three imperial world orders spanning the last several centuries—each also providing the necessary scaffolding and infrastructure for the development, growth, and globalization of capitalist society across regimes of accumulation—were marked by imperial powers or hegemons who a) created and employed a specific conception of "human rights" as part of their ideological imperial legitimation, and b) eventually rendered these conceptions relatively meaningless through their own policies and practices to manage and maintain imperial rule.

There is a tendency in some circles of progressive or left politics to suggest that it is in fact American hegemony that is at the heart of overlapping threats to human survival and the perpetuation of (neo)colonial relations and conditions of global apartheid. We clearly have considerable sympathy for this position. But while the US is deserving of these critiques, it would be a mistake to assume that an end to American hegemony alone would mean an end to such problems. As illustrated above and in earlier chapters, there doesn't seem to be much evidence to suggest that a new (for example) Chinese or multi-polar world led by the rising BRICS+ nations would automatically lead to a sustainable, let alone rights protective future for human civilization, or even an end to (neo)colonial international relations. In a recent essay on the prospects for international left politics, Gidley, Mang, and Randall (2023) issue a similar warning:

Faced with this moment, a radical left that has, for years preached the view that anything that harms the hegemonic imperialism (that of the US) and its allies must necessarily be progressive (a perspective known as "campism"—siding with a geopolitical "camp" rather than pursuing a genuinely internationalist project) is highly likely to collapse into apologism for those reactionary alternatives. This campist "anti-imperialism" is blind to the fact that in supporting [for example] the "axis of resistance" it is not opposing imperialism but siding with a rival imperial pole in a "multipolar" world.

Instead, we suggest that addressing OTHS requires a complete abandonment of traditional great power competition, in favor of new international relations built on cooperation and mutual aid in a global effort to demilitarize the world and take seriously what can only be a collective, cooperative project of climate change prevention and adaptation. To remain on the path of economic and military geopolitical competition between great (nuclear armed) powers is to flirt with certain disaster with respect to the proliferation of weapons and war, and is to ensure unsustainable levels of global warming and ecological destruction. This is because the competition (even in the creation of green energy alternatives) is still running largely on the access to and use of fossil fuels (whether continued use of coal or oil, or in the use of so-called "bridge" fuels that also contribute to global greenhouse emissions), and it by definition prevents the kind of cooperation that will ultimately be necessary to meet emissions and other important targets for avoiding climate catastrophe and to move from the current multi-lateral nuclear arms race to a new direction of denuclearization and disarmament.

Addressing OTHS and ensuring even a possibility of universal human rights practice will require addressing not only American exceptionalism, but imperial great power competition in general, and of capitalism as a transnational, institutionalized social order—regardless of shifting geopolitics. While there are no easy paths to meeting such tall orders in the short time available to address climate change, and we would not be so bold as to have any all-encompassing answers to what are admittedly tough prospects for the fate of humanity, we offer some thoughts here on what could be fruitful directions for human rights praxis in our time, particularly for those of us living and working in the US. Though challenging American hegemony will not be a cure-all, there are particular opportunities and responsibilities for those of us in the US to reign in the more devastating US policies and practices, given the role of the US vis-à-vis transnational capital, the waning "rules based international order," and the global police state.

What is to be done?

For one, human rights praxis must confront anti-democratic or authoritarian politics in the US and elsewhere in the world. As discussed in Chapter 4, in the US, this involves passing significant voting rights legislation that addresses forms of voter suppression while reaffirming the notion of universal suffrage, expanded to include populations like immigrants (certainly those who are permanent residents), those incarcerated or under current/ previous felony convictions, or the homeless and working poor who are effectively silenced by barriers in voting logistics. But it also must include a fundamental reform of campaign finance law to reduce the instrumental influence of big banks, TNCs, and the TCC, including but not limited to an overturning of court decisions like *Citizens United v. FEC* (2010). To this point, we've gone through great lengths here and in previous work to demonstrate how the rising power and granted political "rights" of corporations and the TCC are met with a steady curtailment of political and other related Constitutional and human rights (reproductive rights, freedom of speech/assembly, right to apply for asylum, etc.) for everyday people. In fact, the projects of universal suffrage and reproductive rights are both terrains of praxis that confront virtually the same people and organizational entities (such as the Federalist Society or Marble Freedom Trust), representing socially conservative and even moderate arms of concentrated corporate capital. Rather than cultural or religious debates, they should be viewed through a more materialist lens, and addressed as a problem of concentrated owning class power and of patriarchal, heteronormative background relations of social reproduction as part of what we will describe as the rising, militant, diverse, labor movement in partnership with other appropriate allies (such as feminist and reproductive rights organizations).

Second, in order to begin to address what will be a growing worldwide migration crisis, human rights praxis must include a push to more aggressively protect the rights of migrant populations worldwide. Discussed in Chapter 5, efforts like those behind the Kolkata Declaration, that seek to address the inherent forms of (ethnic, racial, gendered, etc.) discrimination that undergird the immigration policies of national states while holding states accountable for their failure to respect, protect, and fulfill the human rights of migrant populations are an example of this important work.

Further, human rights praxis in the US must involve a left articulation of holistic immigration reform across the entire Western Hemisphere. Such immigration reform must reaffirm the international right to asylum, address the differential application of human rights protection to migrants of differing status with coherent pathways to asylum or citizenship (to address the phenomenon of legitimated instability), and be designed with the goal of building international worker solidarity and support. Rather than criminals, inherent dangers, or public burdens, migrant populations should be treated as genuine partners (not reduced to their raw labor or bio-power) in the very real work required in a 21st century "just transition" away from global warming and global militarization.

This cannot be done by the US alone, and reform must ensure greater security and stability in nations across the Americas and Caribbean—not simply safe passage to or opportunity in the global North. Though immigration reform in the US has seemed nearly impossible through typical party politics, there is still great potential in organizing migrant and immigrant populations to build solidarity across groups of exploited and expropriated labor and apply the appropriate political pressures to achieve reform. Fortunately, there are some signs of hope for new, cooperative international relations in the Western Hemisphere that could lay the foundation for diplomatic solutions on migration—but also on issues of security and equitable access to 21st century strategic resources and the benefits of a just transition.

Opportunities exist for progressive political actors and leftist organizations in the US to build better alliances with progressive or labor-led political parties and organizations in the Americas and Caribbean for these purposes. For instance, House Resolution (HR) 943 was introduced in the US Congress on December 19th of 2023 by House Rep. Nydia Velasquez (NY D-7), "Calling for the annulment of the Monroe Doctrine and the development of a 'New Good Neighbor' policy in order to foster improved relations and deeper, more effective cooperation between the United States and our Latin American and Caribbean Neighbors."[4] The bill is a throwback to the admittedly imperfect "good neighbor" policy under FDR that temporarily ended the period of gunboat diplomacy during the New Deal. The US born advocacy organization for global peace, Code Pink, is a major supporter of HR 943, and aptly described the legacy of the Monroe Doctrine that the policy would seek to end:

> The Monroe Doctrine—asserting US geopolitical control over the region—served as a pretext for over 100 years of military invasions,

support for military dictatorships, the financing of security forces involved in mass human rights violations, and support for coups against democratically elected governments, among other horrors that have caused many Lantin Americans and Caribbeans to flee north in search for safety and opportunity.

(Code Pink 2023)

We join supporters of the bill (Code Pink 2023) in imagining several possible outcomes of such a policy. It could open the door to 1) end unilateral economic sanctions against (for example) Cuba and Venezuela; 2) end the US proliferation of weapons and training of military, paramilitary, and insurrectionary forces throughout the region in favor of peaceful diplomacy; 3) end practices of overt and covert political interference in nations across the Western Hemisphere; 4) bring about a US (re)commitment to human rights protections in the region; 5) create collaborative and more comprehensive/ cohesive immigration policy between neighboring countries that seeks to maximize security and stability (to address forced and economic dislocation), while demilitarizing borders and reaffirming the international right to asylum; and 6) imagine mutually beneficial trade policy and plans for economic development that move away from the model of international debt dependency, while making available the 21st century strategic resources necessary for a just transition and sharing the economic and other benefits from such a transition (rather than re-establishing (neo)colonial, extractive relations). Whether or not HR 943 passes, and certainly whether or not its passage could open the door to these other desperately needed reforms and new alliances, will be a matter of effective human rights praxis from below, and whether or not stakeholders in the global working class can organize and mobilize effectively toward these ends.

In addition, given the enormity and immediacy of OTHS, human rights praxis in the US and at the international level must work to establish pathways for diplomacy, denuclearization, and disarmament that include a redistribution of the resources dedicated to the global police state for the purposes of mitigating the implications of climate change and global instability/insecurity. We agree with scholars like Neta Crawford (2019, 2022) and her colleagues at the Costs of War Project that the US can and should heavily reduce its global military footprint to a position of self-defense rather than that of projected military domination in surrounding the "world island" (McCoy 2021) landmass of Europe and Asia. These resources should instead be dedicated to building international, cooperative approaches to climate change prevention and adaptation with partners around the world. To this point, advocacy groups like the Transnational Institute argued at COP28 that, since global military activity produces over 5% of global emissions (more than that of Japan), and military spending has skyrocketed among wealthy nations who have also fallen far short of their commitments to funding a just transition, that countries should dedicate 5%

of their current military budgets to provide over $110 billion per year for climate finance (Noor 2023). This would be an important first step to meet the original $100 billion annual target set by prior COPs. However, it falls short of the nearly $1 trillion annual cost over the next decade necessary to protect those on the front lines of ecological disaster and expedite a full transition to green energy systems. Even more aggressive action will ultimately be necessary to divert more resources from military budgets to cooperative climate change solutions to achieve such a transition in time to avoid the worst possible outcomes.

Moreover, the power and wealth of the fossil fuel industry and their leverage over national and transnational state policies must be confronted. Public subsidy of fossil fuel extraction must end, and the vast resources and revenues of the fossil fuel industry must be diverted to the costs of climate change adaptation for which they are particularly responsible. As made clear throughout this book, industry players and petrostates are highly unlikely to commit to such actions (out of market pressures, for instance) on their own, which means that national and transnational state power will need to be leveraged (as it would need to be leveraged to affect military spending) to reign in and unwind fossil fuel and related industry TNCs through nationalization and other available means.

Finally, these efforts to repurpose the resources now dedicated to militarism and the (deeply connected) fossil fuel industry must be accompanied by a return to the diplomatic politics of nuclear disarmament and an immediate end to what is now a mounting, multi-lateral nuclear arms race. This will arguably require a new treaty framework between the US, Russia, and China that (for example) (re)affirms a commitment to reducing nuclear stockpiles, ends nuclear weapons development and testing, establishes more robust safeguards against nuclear escalation, and establishes grounds for great power cooperation on addressing OTHS. It will also require significant diplomatic measures to pull smaller or aspiring nuclear powers into such agreements, and provide them appropriate incentives, protections, and assurances to shift the geopolitical logic behind nuclear arms development as a safeguard against aggression or domination by regional adversaries or global military powers.

Where do we go from here? Human Rights Praxis and the Organized Labor Movement.

When it comes to the forms of politics and (human rights) praxis necessary to achieve such massive, yet necessary changes, considerable power from below must be organized and mobilized on a very aggressive time-scale. Unfortunately, we are not optimistic about the prospects of what has so far been incremental reformism to fit this bill. Instead, something approaching capture of national state power in places like the US and of TNS power in the case of the UN by civil society and diverse working-class interests will be required to affect necessary change.

While this is an "all hands on deck" situation, where multiple strategies must be vigorously pursued to address overlapping threats to human rights and survival, we suggest that human rights praxis focus primarily on the growth and political mobilization of a *militant international labor movement of the exploited and expropriated global working class.*[5] Human rights praxis in the US must prioritize building a democratic, diverse, international labor movement in solidarity with others around the world through union, political, and community organizing, with the aim of establishing forms of eco-socialism (or otherwise sustainable collectivism)[6] as an alternative to capitalism and authoritarian rule. This can and should be done through the rekindling of international anti-racist, anti-imperial, anti-patriarchal, and anti-capitalist solidarity much like the template established by DuBois, Malcolm X, and other marginalized groups from the US in the 20th century (Anderson 2003; Horne 2008), and the creation of new solidarities born from current contexts—such as those with refugees, asylum seekers, and other migrant populations. It is critical that solidarity is built 1) at the level of civil society between organizations directly representing public interest rather than between powerful state or economic actors alone; and 2) in contrast to the dominant, prescriptive, pedantic historical model of Western humanitarianism that has tended to act as an extension of hegemonic power rather than of uncorrupted human comradery or mutual aid (Roth, Purkayastha, and Denskus 2024). This will involve developing ways through which workers and civil society interests can be better and more forcefully represented in national and transnational state political structures, as well as developing new mechanisms outside of these traditional political state structures that have historically been dominated by capital. In fact, we are only bound by creativity in creating multiple, novel, and enduring bases and terrains of direct civil society engagement between nations and peoples that are not mediated by global rulers and owners at every turn.

All of that being said, the world does not need to choose between developing a socialist or collectivist mode of production and the application of liberal rights protections.[7] We share great sympathy with Marxist critiques of liberal rights as a concept or approach (demonstrated in our own scathing critique of international law as a liberal project over the last 15+ years). However, in practice, eco-socialism is absolutely compatible with and should be accompanied by a human rights framework that provides the concept of universal humanity (non-discriminatory) and the necessary tapestry of rights protections (civil, political, social, economic, cultural) for all to enjoy the freedom and material abundance made possible by collective planning and both indigenous knowledge and modern (re)productive technologies. In fact, we argue that international forms of eco-socialism are actually necessary for and compatible with human rights. Alternatives to the relations of exploitation and (racist, patriarchal, etc.) expropriation at the heart of capitalist society, such as forms of eco-socialism, will be fundamental to the provision of basic human needs and to ending the many forms of domination that manifest as human rights crises. In turn, human rights create conceptual and real grounds for international solidarity across identity and circumstance, provide protections against left (state) authoritarianism, and ensure that everyday people are not forced to choose, for example, between the economic security of collectivism and the political or religious individual liberties of expression. Fundamental human dignity requires material resources *and* the political and cultural autonomy to make decisions about how life should or could be, free from significant state and other institutional interference, surveillance, and directives.

Finally, our focus on organized labor as a mechanism for effective contemporary human rights praxis is not born out of class reductionism, but of sober practicality. Organized labor is one of few existing mechanisms through which state power can be confronted or mobilized, corporate power can be subdued, and democratic solidarity can be (and is being) built across race, ethnicity, nationality, age, gender, sexuality, and industry in tangible, collective, material pursuits. There are many signs of these struggles already underway (see the last section below), and opportunities for human rights scholars, advocates, and stakeholders to contribute to these efforts, especially for those of us in the US with the responsibility and ability to reign in the historically unprecedented (in size, scope, and destructive power) American military and transnational military industrial complex.

In an attempt to end on a hopeful note, it is worth taking a look at how this movement has been building in the US, particularly since the COVID pandemic that laid bare for many Americans the "essential" nature of labor in capital accumulation and the facilitation of daily life in American society. Since the pandemic, the American public has also begun to shift their opinion on the role of unions and organized labor to address pressing collective social problems.

It remains true that union membership is low in the US—at approximately 10% of the workforce. This is in comparison to the height of union density in the 1950s when about a third of American workers were unionized (Feiveson 2023). Perhaps unsurprisingly, this is also when income and wealth inequalities were at some of their lowest rates in American history. Still, total public and private union membership is on the rise, adding 273,000 new members in 2022. Though union density fell during this period, it was only because of a uniquely large post-pandemic increase in employment that outpaced union recruitment (Grantham-Philips 2023). In addition to growing numbers of unionized workers, unions in the US are showing signs of becoming more active and aggressive in their tactics. According to Cornell University's ILR Labor Action Tracker,[8] approximately 539,000 workers participated in 470 work stoppages (466 were strikes) in the US in 2023—higher rates of participation and frequency than in the previous two years.

The prospect for continued growth in union membership in the US is more and more evident. Over 67% of Americans now approve of unions, and public opinion is trending upward among people from all political parties. Even support among registered republicans now approaches 50% (Saad 2023). Regardless of party affiliation, approval is highest among the youngest ("generation Z") workers, even compared to older generations when they were the same age. This is largely because young workers face massive generational inequality (particularly when it comes to owning assets, like homes) and job instability, and unionization is proving to be a useful solution to these problems. Data suggests that unionized gen Z workers make over 11% more than their non-union counterparts, with the highest gains going to Black and Latinx workers (at about 14% and 20%, respectively) (Glass 2023). Further, union membership is drastically affecting young workers' access to benefits. Unionized workers between age 18–34 have seen their health care coverage increase 38% (77% for Latinx workers) and retirement benefits—a disappearing privilege in the US—rise by a staggering 90% (170% for Latinx workers) (Glass 2023).

Overall, unionized workers typically earn 10% to 20% more than their non-unionized counterparts (Dynarski 2018). And this extra pay typically comes from funds otherwise used for executive salaries and stock dividends—putting even further downward pressure on income and wealth inequality between workers and owners, keeping in mind that the wealthiest 1% of Americans own 54% of all stocks (the bottom 50% own 6%), and the top 10% own 89%. In terms of race, White Americans control about 89% of stocks (Frank 2021; Caporal 2023).

There is no shortage of wins for the labor movement in the US to celebrate, and the victories demonstrate how the labor movement can be simultaneously effective at confronting the material relations of capitalism and its racist, patriarchal, heteronormative, and cannibalistic background relations:

- Note the success of the Starbucks union, led by gen Z workers with significant participation from workers of color and trans workers, where over 336 Starbucks stores had been successfully unionized by 2023 (there were zero in November 2021, and only two in December 2021 before exploding to over 250 a year later) (Unionelections.org 2023).
- Note the success of a new, radicalized, democratized United Auto Workers (UAW) union, who effectively employed an explicit discourse of class conflict and the deployment of strategic "stand up" strikes to win record contracts including 25%+ wage increases for workers at the big three automakers in the US: GM, Ford, and Stellantis. Efforts were so successful that other automakers like Toyota, Honda, Hyundai, and Subaru followed with wage increases of 9% to 25% to try and stem the union tide (Boudette 2023; Press 2023). Unmoved, the UAW has begun organizing campaigns in these and 7 other TNCs with headquarters outside the US, in addition to three EV companies—Tesla, Lucid, and Rivian. These corporations employ an additional 150k workers across 13 states in the US, and would represent the largest increase seen by the UAW since its start in the 1930's if organization efforts succeed. The six

Japanese and Korean producers made more ($470 billion, with 40% from operations in North America) than twice that of the "big three" American car companies over the last decade, as did the German auto makers (Volkswagen, BMW, and Mercedes, at $460 billion) (Press 2023).

- Note the historic contract won by the Coalition of Kaiser Permanente Unions in the largest health care strike in US history (75K workers) in October of 2023, trending up from the previous record by Minnesota nurses in 2022. This is in the context of rising power among nurses and health care unions around the country since COVID, also pushing for important reforms like universal health care. Moreover, doctors and pharmacists are now unionizing for the first time in a push back to the financialization of health care (Scheiber 2023).

- In addition to the unionization of such workers in the "professional" class, note union expansion into previously unorganized territory in the US. In December of 2023, workers at an Albuquerque, New Mexico branch of Wells Fargo became the first to establish a union at a "modern megabank" (Eisen 2023).

- Note the success and public support for the writers (WGA) and actors (SAG-AFTRA) guild strikes of 2023 that won new contracts with a majority of public support, and began to establish new worker protections in the face of artificial intelligence (AI) technologies (Dalton and Sanders 2023).

- Last but certainly not least, note the unexpected grassroots victory of a small, independent union (Amazon Labor Union (ALU)) against corporate behemoth Amazon, with young Black and other leadership of color, where they were able to organize over 8,000 workers at the JFK8 warehouse. This was despite Amazon retaliating against union organizers and paying so-called "union avoidance" consultants who referred to organizers and union members as "thugs," according to a National Labor Relations Board (NLRB) ruling (Palmer 2023). Though they have since joined forces with larger union orgs, the ALU proved the efficacy of democratic grassroots organizing against considerable odds.

Admittedly, the organized labor movement in the US faces many challenges. Corporations are rarely held accountable for union busting practices, and when they are, action comes slow and late. When workers are successful in unionizing their workplaces, it can be very difficult to get companies to actually negotiate a contract with the workers. Though the 2021 Protecting the Right to Organize (PRO) Act would have addressed this to some extent, it died in the Senate. In the absence of such legislation, recent union gains were bolstered by a more labor friendly NLRB under the Biden Administration, that, for example, cracked down on corporate union busting tactics (Nichols 2023). But the "most union-friendly President in history" also joined most of Congress and the owners and executives of the seven big rail carriers in effectively killing railroad workers' chance to strike for the most minimal benefits and protections—including for the safety of communities who have suffered the environmental costs of countless derailments (Tormey 2022).

Though it is beyond the scope of our book or expertise to give a full diagnostic evaluation of the US and international labor movement to date, there are a few places where concentrated praxis could pay off for the US and global working class. First, many unions are still deeply divorced from their original purpose as a vehicle for class war from below, and require significant internal change to be effective. This is the story of the UAW election of Shawn Fain, that resulted from a many-years effort to enact popular elections (rather than corrupt appointments) of union leadership. Other unions can and should adopt similar models of radical democratization to decouple interests from corporate managers. Second, aggressive labor-friendly legislation must be pursued well beyond measures like the PRO Act. For instance, the prohibition of solidarity strikes in the US is one reason that labor movements cannot command the same kind of public political power as in many other nations. Workers in the US and elsewhere around the world must retain the right (or ability, if necessary to act in violation of the law—such as in wildcat strikes) to participate in solidarity actions with one another in order to mount the kinds of mass, general strikes that are effective in mobilizing worker power against that of the state and concentrated capital. Third, organized labor needs to organize nationally and internationally to confront a transnational capitalist class, and to solve what are quickly being understood as collective international challenges—to affect a just transition away from climate catastrophe and militarism while addressing the rights and needs of migrant and precarious workers in the global economy. This is exemplified by organizations like the Farm Labor Organizing Committee (FLOC) that now organizes across the Americas, EU, and African continent to take on tobacco and other transnational agribusiness interests on behalf of agricultural labor—one of the most precarious yet essential populations of typically migrant labor (FLOC 2023). On this point we ultimately agree with analysts and journalists like *Jacobin*'s Alex Press (2024), who argue that "the US labor movement's failure to exercise solidarity internationally," whether in the past or in the present, should be seen as a critical "structural weakness."

The capacity for major US labor unions to directly engage in international working-class politics is now being demonstrated by unions like the UAW who in February of 2024 "voted to establish a new solidarity project to support autoworkers in Mexico fighting for economic justice and improved working conditions." The new project is meant to "provide resources to Mexican workers and independent unions in Mexico, and aims to strengthen cross-border solidarity between US and Mexican workers" (UAW 2024). This capacity is further demonstrated by the UAW and others' statements and protest activities to stop wars and international war crimes, and through increasing participation in the movement to address climate change.

Indeed, organized labor can and must flex its power for purposes well beyond that of improving workers' wages or working conditions.

As an illustration, in December of 2023 (see Appendix A) a public letter was issued by some of the biggest and most powerful unions in the country demanding a ceasefire in the conflict between Israel and Hamas in a clearly measured defense of everyday Israeli and Palestinian civilians. The letter was sponsored by the United Food and Commercial Workers International Union (UFCW), United Auto Workers (UAW), and the United Electrical, Radio, and Machine Workers of America (UE), but included scores of others such as the American Postal Workers Union (APWU) and Chicago Teachers Union, who continue to play critical roles in the building of organized labor power in the US. Their call was accompanied by protest actions in New York City and other major metros (Corbett 2023), and were joined by many individual calls for ceasefire by other unions, such as National Nurses United (2023), who decried the killing of innocent medical staff and humanitarian workers throughout the conflict. By January of 2024, these and other unions representing over 9 million organized workers formed The National Labor Network for Ceasefire,[9] and were joined the following month by individual calls for a ceasefire in Gaza from the Service Employees International Union (SEIU) (representing over 2 million members) and the American Federation of Labor and Congress of Industrial Organizations (AFL-CIO) (representing over 12.5 million workers).

Most importantly, when the UAW voted to sponsor the initial open letter, they also created a Divestment and Just Transition Committee, which will in part "examine the size, scope, and impact of the US military-industrial complex that employs thousands of UAW members and dominates the global arms trade" (Ackerman 2023). According to UAW regional director Brandon Mancilla, the Committee will also "think about what it would mean to actually have a just transition, what used to be called a 'peace conversion,' of folks who work in the weapons and defense industry into something else" (Ackerman 2023).

The foreign policy interests of the UAW are also informed by the direct experience of many union members who fought in the US war on terror, such as Marine veteran and UAW Region 9 Director, Dan Vicente who aptly described the class component of American military interventionism from the first-person perspective:

> You get there and you realize, oh, these people are poor as shit. You get a poor shithead from Philly fighting a poor shithead from fucking, I don't know, Najaf or somewhere [else] in Iraq. It's an endless cycle of people who don't have shit being forced to fight people who don't have shit.
>
> (Ackerman 2023)

Interestingly, unions such as the UAW are figuring out ways to protect the interests of workers in the fossil fuel or weapons industries, while facilitating transitions away from pathological militarism and ecological destruction that existentially threaten all workers. In comments to author and journalist Seth Ackerman in his reporting for *The Nation* (2023), one UAW regional director commented that while he supports his members at arms-maker General Dynamics, that they "have a moral obligation to put pressure on politicians to make sure that our products are used for their intended purposes of *defense*, and not massacres." Furthermore, union leadership is aware of the fact that these unions represent workers from sometimes divergent political party alignment, but have grown disillusioned with both dominant parties in the US. To this point, a UAW regional director asserted the following in what could also be interpreted as a full-throated support for the grassroots, bottom-up struggles that characterize the kind of effective praxis that powers the human rights enterprise: "We're gonna have to do it ourselves. We're gonna have to fight for our own better working conditions and lifestyles of the middle class here, and we're gonna have to advocate for peace around the world" (Ackerman 2023).

We absolutely agree with this assessment. And human rights scholars, advocates, activists, and stakeholders have an opportunity and responsibility to join or contribute to the national and international labor movement(s) however they can. Similar efforts must be made to build solidarity between international labor and civil society organizations across the global North and South, and to heighten collective struggle for a better world in the face of the greatest overlapping threats to human rights and survival.

Notes

1 The UAE is governed by a "Supreme Council of Rulers" with executive and legislative powers, including the appointment of the President, Vice-President, and Council of Ministers (UAE Embassy to the US 2023).
2 In addition, COP29 will be held in the fossil fuel rich country of Azerbaijan, to be presided over by yet another former Oil company executive (Mukhtar Babayev) (McGrath 2024).
3 It is worth noting that the ongoing humanitarian disaster in Yemen has had "an inordinate toll on women and girls," who have been denied medical care and endured widespread abuse and sexual violence at the hands of waring parties (UNFPA 2023).
4 See the full text and legislative progress of the bill here: www.congress.gov/bill/118th-congress/house-resolution/943?s=1&r=1
5 One should keep in mind that this is a broad conception of "working class" that absolutely includes workers commonly described as "middle" class—even highly paid/skilled professionals. Stated in the last section below, even medical doctors and pharmacists are now joining nurses and other medical staff in joining the union movement to fight against (for example) the corporatization and financialization of health care.
6 By this we mean a system through which the means of production are somehow collectivized and not monopolized by private capital, and the processes of production and consumption are conducted within the survivable limits of Earth's ecosphere for humans and other species (also critical to human survival). We are

purposely not offering a specific form of eco-socialism here, in that a wide variety of models might be necessary for different contexts, and in that there needs to be room for stakeholders to deliberate the specifics.

7 This is not to say that such a combination would not require some healthy revisions of, for instance, more authoritarian models of socialism or models of liberal human and other rights that center a somewhat ambiguous "right to property" (that, without clarification, could refer to personal property and/or capital components of the means of production). In our view, this is precisely why they should be developed and deployed in tandem.

8 See https://twitter.com/ILRLaborAction

9 See www.laborforceasefire.org

References

Abnet, Kate, G. Dickie and D. Stanway. 2023. "New COP28 Draft Deal Stops Short of Fossil Fuel 'Phase Out.'" *Reuters*, December 12. Retrieved 12/20/23 from www.reuters.com/markets/commodities/new-cop28-draft-deal-stops-short-fossil-fuel-phase-out-2023-12-11/

Ackerman, Seth. 2023. "A Working-Class Foreign Policy is Coming." *The Nation*, December 18. Retrieved 12/23/23 from www.thenation.com/article/world/working-class-labor-foreign-policy-uaw/

Althusser, Louis. 2001 [1971]. "Ideology and Ideological State Apparatuses: Notes Towards an Investigation." In *Lenin and Philosophy and Other Essays*, edited by L. Althusser, pp. 85–126. New York: Monthly Review Press.

Anderson, Carol. 2003. *Eyes Off the Prize: The United Nations and the African American Struggle for Human Rights, 1944–1955.* Cambridge University Press.

Armaline, William, Davita Silfen Glasberg and Bandana Purkayastha. 2015. *The Human Rights Enterprise: Political Sociology, State Power and Social Movements.* London: Polity Press.

Belcher, Oliver, P. Bigger, B. Neimark and C. Kennelly. 2019. "Hidden Carbon Costs of the 'Every-Where War': Logistics, Geopolitical Ecology, and the Carbon Bootprint of the US Military." *Transactions of the Institute of British Geographers.* doi:10.1111/tran.12319

Boudette, Neal. 2023. "UAW Announces Drive to Organize Nonunion Plants." *The New York Times*, November 29. Retrieved 12/10/23 from www.nytimes.com/2023/11/29/business/uaw-union-organizing.html?campaign_id=9&emc=edit_nn_20231206&instance_id=109436&nl=the-morning&regi_id=138697150&segment_id=151843&te=1&user_id=1ceda8aa3bbd02cbe08de642e72d8593

Caporal, Jack. 2023. "How Many Americans Own Stock? About 158 Million—But the Wealthiest 1% Own More than Half." *The Motley Fool*, November 1. Retrieved 12/10/23 from www.fool.com/research/how-many-americans-own-stock/

Carrington, Damian and Ben Stockton. 2023. "COP28 President Says There is 'No Science' Behind Demands for Phase-Out of Fossil Fuels." *The Guardian*, December 3. Retrieved 12/20/23 from www.theguardian.com/environment/2023/dec/03/back-into-caves-cop28-president-dismisses-phase-out-of-fossil-fuels

Code Pink. 2023. "Letter to Biden Calling for a Real Good Neighbor Policy for Latin America and the Caribbean." *Code Pink*. Retrieved 12/22/23 from www.codepink.org/biden_trump_latam

Corbett, Jessica. 2023. "UAW and American Postal Workers Union Members Lead NYC March for Gaza." *Truthout*, December 22. Retrieved 12/23/23 from https://truthout.org/articles/uaw-and-american-postal-workers-union-members-lead-nyc-march-for-gaza/

Crawford, Neta. 2019. "Pentagon Fuel Use, Climate Change, and the Costs of War." *Watson Institute of International and Public Affairs at Brown University, Costs of War Project*. Retrieved 11/15/23 from https://watson.brown.edu/costsofwar/papers/ClimateChangeandCostofWar

Crawford, Neta. 2022. *The Pentagon, Climate Change, and War: Charting the Rise and Fall of US Military Emissions.* Cambridge, MA: MIT Press.

Cumming-Bruce, Nick and Declan Walsh. 2024. "Atrocities Mount in Sudan as War Spirals, UN Says." *The New York Times*, February 24. Retrieved 02/26/24 from www.nytimes.com/2024/02/24/world/africa/sudan-civil-war-atrocities-un.html?smid=nytcore-ios-share&referringSource=articleShare

Dalton, Andrew and Linley Sanders. 2023. "Hollywood Actor and Writer Strikes Have Broad Support Among Americans, AP-NORC Poll Shows." *AP*, September 21. Retrieved 12/14/23 from https://apnews.com/article/hollywood-strikes-poll-public-opinion-actors-writers-5727ed3078c4f69851c18c560670f480

Dynarski, Susan. 2018. "Fresh Proof that Strong Unions Help Reduce Income Inequality." *The New York Times*, July 6. Retrieved 12/10/23 from www.nytimes.com/2018/07/06/business/labor-unions-income-inequality.html

Eisen, Ben. 2023. "Wells Fargo Workers in Albuquerque Vote to Form a Union, a First for a Megabank." *The Wall Street Journal*, December 21. Retrieved 12/24/23 from www.wsj.com/finance/banking/wells-fargo-workers-in-albuquerque-vote-to-form-union-a-first-for-a-megabank-1ff5aafb

Eltahir, Nafisa. 2023. "Sudanese General Accuses UAE of Supplying Paramilitary RSF." *Reuters*, November 28. Retrieved on 12/20/23 from www.reuters.com/world/africa/sudanese-general-accuses-uae-supplying-paramilitary-rsf-2023-11-28/

Embassy of the United Arab Emirates, Washington D.C. 2023. "Political System and Governance." Retrieved 12/27/23 from www.uae-embassy.org/discover-uae/governance/political-system-governance

Farm Labor Organizing Committee (FLOC Media). 2023. "FLOC Leaders Go to Geneva, Cultivate Solidarity and Meet with Big Tobacco!" *FLOC Media*, June 30. Retrieved 12/23/23 from https://floc.com/floc-leaders-go-to-geneva-cultivate-solidarity-and-meet-with-big-tobacco/

Feiveson, Laura. 2023. "Labor Unions and the US Economy." US Department of Treasury, August 28. Retrieved 12/14/23 from https://home.treasury.gov/news/featured-stories/labor-unions-and-the-us-economy#:~:text=Union%20membership%20peaked%20in%20the,and%20was%20continuing%20to%20fall

Frank, Robert. 2021. "The Wealthiest 10% of Americans Own a Record 89% of All US Stocks." *CNBC*, October 18. Retrieved 12/10/23 from www.cnbc.com/2021/10/18/the-wealthiest-10percent-of-americans-own-a-record-89percent-of-all-us-stocks.html

Fraser, Nancy. 2022. *Cannibal Capitalism: How Our System is Devouring Democracy, Care, and the Planet—and What We Can Do About It.* London: Verso.

Gidley, Ben, D. Mang and D. Randall. 2023. "For a Consistent Democratic and Internationalist Left." *LeftRenewal.net*, December 10. Retrieved 12/15/23 from https://leftrenewal.net/

Glass, Aurelia. 2023. "What You Need to Know About Gen Z's Support for Unions." *Center for American Progress (CAP)*, August 9. Retrieved 12/12/23 from www.am

ericanprogress.org/article/what-you-need-to-know-about-gen-zs-support-for-unions/#:~:text=Gen%20Z%20is%20America's%20most,generations%20were%20at%20their%20age

Goodman, Amy and Dennis Moynihan. 2023. "Carbon Colonialism, COP28 and the Climate Crisis." *Democracy Now*, December 7. Retrieved 12/23/23 from www.democracynow.org/2023/12/7/carbon_colonialism_cop28_and_the_climate

Grantham-Philips, Wyatte. 2023. "Labor Movements are Seeing Historic Victories This Year. Can Unions Keep Up the Momentum?" *PBS News Hour*, October 11. Retrieved 12/14/23 from www.pbs.org/newshour/economy/labor-movements-a re-seeing-historic-victories-this-year-can-unions-keep-up-the-momentum

Green, Graeme. 2023. "Environmental Campaigners Filmed, Threatened and Harassed at COP28." *The Guardian*, December 20. Retrieved 12/21/23 from www.theguardian. com/environment/2023/dec/20/threats-intimidation-creating-climate-of-fear-un-cop-e vents#:~:text=Environmental%20campaigners%20filmed%2C%20threatened%20a nd%20harassed%20at%20Cop28,-Indigenous%20campaigners%2C%20human&te xt=Incidents%20of%20harassment%2C%20surveillance%2C%20threats,in%20Du bai%2C%20experts%20have%20said

Hansen, James, Makiko Sato, et al. 2023. "Global Warming in the Pipeline." *Oxford Open Climate Change* 3 (1). https://doi.org/10.1093/oxfclm/kgad008

Harvey, D. 2005. *The New Imperialism* (revised edition). New York: Oxford University Press.

Harvey, D. 2018. *Marx, Capital, and the Madness of Economic Reason*. New York: Oxford University Press.

Horne, Gerald. 2008. *The End of Empires: African Americans and India*. Philadelphia, PA: Temple University Press.

Lakhani, Nina. 2023. "Record Number of Fossil Fuel Lobbyists Get Access to COP28 Climate Talks." *The Guardian*, December 5. Retrieved 12/20/23 from www.thegua rdian.com/environment/2023/dec/05/record-number-of-fossil-fuel-lobbyists-get-a ccess-to-cop28-climate-talks

Mbembe, Achille. 2019. *Necropolitics*. Durham, NC: Duke University Press.

McCoy, Alfred. 2021. *To Govern the Globe: World Orders and Catastrophic Change*. Chicago, IL: Haymarket Books.

McGrath, Matt. 2024. "Climate Change: Former Oil Executive Mukhtar Babayev to Lead COP29 Talks in Azerbaijan." *BBC*, January 5. Retrieved 01/08/24 from www.bbc.com/news/science-environment-67895068?xtor=AL-72-%5Bpartner% 5D-%5Bbbc.news.twitter%5D-%5Bheadline%5D-%5Bnews%5D-%5Bbizdev% 5D-%5Bisapi%5D&at_ptr_name=twitter&at_format=link&at_bbc_team=edi torial&at_link_type=web_link&at_campaign=Social_Flow&at_link_id= F8A8E51C-ABE3-11EE-B16A-40BED0B4AF07&at_link_origin=BBCNews&at_m edium=social&at_campaign_type=owned

National Nurses United. 2023. "National Nurses United Statement on the Crisis in the Middle East." *NationalNursesUnited* (website). Retrieved 12/26/23 from www.nationa lnursesunited.org/national-nurses-united-statement-on-the-crisis-in-the-middle-east

Nichols, John. 2023. "Most Pro-Labor President in History? Joe Biden's Not There Yet." *The Nation*, September 4. Retrieved 12/08/23 from www.thenation.com/arti cle/politics/labor-president-joe-biden/

Noor, Dharna. 2023. "Divert Military Spending to Fund Climate Aid, Activists Urge COP28." *The Guardian*, December 2. Retrieved 12/23/23 from www.theguardian. com/environment/2023/dec/02/cop28-climate-change-military-funds

Palmer, Annie. 2023. "Amazon Broke Federal Labor Law by Calling Staten Island Union Organizers 'Thugs,' Interrogating Workers." *CNBC*, December 1. Retrieved 12/20/23 from www.cnbc.com/2023/12/01/amazon-broke-federal-labor-law-by-racially-disparaging-union-leaders.html

Phillips, Peter. 2018. *Giants: The Global Power Elite.* New York: Seven Stories Press.

Press, Alex. 2023. "The UAW Has Had a Big Year. They're Preparing for an Even Bigger One." *Jacobin*, December 4. Retrieved 12/22/23 from https://jacobin.com/2023/12/uaw-big-three-strike-nonunion-organizing-gaza-cease-fire

Press, Alex. 2024. "Internationalism is in Labor's Interest." *Jacobin*, January 25. Retrieved 02/10/24 from https://jacobin.com/2024/01/uaw-joe-biden-endorsement gaza-ceasefire

Robinson, William. 2018. *Into the Tempest: Essays on the New Global Capitalism.* Chicago, IL: Haymarket Books.

Robinson, William. 2020. *The Global Police State.* London, England: Pluto Press.

Robinson, William. 2022a. *Global Civil War: Capitalism Post-Pandemic.* Oakland, CA: PM Press.

Robinson, William. 2022b. *Can Global Capitalism Endure?* Atlanta, GA: Clarity Press.

Roth, Silke, B. Purkayastha and T. Denskus. 2024. *Humanitarianism and Inequality.* Northampton, MA: Edward Elgar Publishing.

Saad, Lydia. 2023. "More in US See Unions Strengthening and Want It That Way." *Gallup*, August 30. Retrieved 12/10/23 from https://news.gallup.com/poll/510281/unions-strengthening.aspx#:~:text=On%20all%20measures%20of%20public,views%20somewhere%20in%20the%20middle

Scheiber, Noam. 2023. "Why Doctors and Pharmacists Are in Revolt." *The New York Times*, December 3. Retrieved 12/20/23 from www.nytimes.com/2023/12/03/business/economy/doctors-pharmacists-labor-unions.html?action=click&pgtype=Article&state=default&module=styln-labor-movement&variant=show&region=MAIN_CONTENT_1&block=storyline_top_links_recirc

Sefeti, Sera. 2023. "'Not Conducive to Our Survival': Pacific Islands on the Climate Frontline Respond to COP28 Deal." *The Guardian*, December 19. Retrieved 12/23/23 from www.theguardian.com/environment/2023/dec/20/not-conducive-to-our-survival-pacific-islands-on-the-climate-frontline-respond-to-cop28-deal

Stockton, Ben and Amy Westervelt. 2023. "Inside the Campaign That Put an Oil Boss in Charge of a Climate Summit." *The Intercept*, October 25. Retrieved 12/20/23 from https://theintercept.com/2023/10/25/cop28-uae-oil-climate-sultan-al-jaber/

Tabuchi, Hiroko. 2023. "Files Suggest Climate Summit's Leader is Using Event to Promote Fossil Fuels." *The New York Times*, November 28. Retrieved 12/20/23 from www.nytimes.com/2023/11/28/climate/uae-cop28-documents-al-jaber.html?campaign_id=9&emc=edit_nn_20231129&instance_id=108849&nl=the-morning&regi_id=138697150&segment_id=151231&te=1&user_id=1ceda8aa3bbd02cbe08de642e72d8593

Tormey, John. 2022. "I'm a Rail Worker, and Biden Screwed Us." *The Nation*, December 13. Retrieved 12/12/23 from www.thenation.com/article/economy/rail-worker-unions-strike-biden/

Unionelections.org. 2023. "Current Starbucks Statistics." *Unionelections.org.* Retrieved 12/10/23 from https://unionelections.org/data/starbucks/

United Auto Workers (UAW). 2024. "UAW Establishes Solidarity Project to Support Mexican Autoworkers." *UAW*, February 23. Retrieved 02/26/24 from https://uaw.org/uaw-establishes-solidarity-project-to-support-mexican-autoworkers/

United Food and Commercial Workers International Union (UFCW), United Auto Workers (UAW), and the United Electrical, Radio, and Machine Workers of America (UE). 2023. "The US Labor Movement Calls for Ceasefire in Israel and Palestine." Open letter via everyaction.com. Retrieved 12/27/23 from https://secure.everya ction.com/w1qW7B3pek2rTtv9ny5bqw2?utm_source=substack&utm_medium=email

United Nations Population Fund (UNFPA). 2023. "Yemen: A Crisis for Women and Girls." *UNFPA*, December 20. Retrieved on 12/21/23 from www.unfpa.org/yem en-crisis-women-and-girls#:~:text=Yemen%20remains%20one%20of%20the,table %20and%20access%20basic%20services

Walsh, Declan, C. Koettl and E. Schmitt. 2023. "Talking Peace in Sudan, the UAE Secretly Fuels the Fight." *The New York Times*, September 29. Retrieved 12/20/23 from www. nytimes.com/2023/09/29/world/africa/sudan-war-united-arab-emirates-chad.html

Wong, Edward, M. Mazzetti and P. Mozur. 2024. "Lawmakers Push US to Consider Trade Limits with AI Giant Tied to China." *The New York Times*, January 9. Retrieved 01/09/24 from www.nytimes.com/2024/01/09/us/politics/ai-china-uae-g42. html?campaign_id=9&emc=edit_nn_20240109&instance_id=112054&nl=the-morni ng&regi_id=138697150&segment_id=154673&te=1&user_id=1ceda8aa3bbd02cbe0 8de642e72d8593

Appendix A
Unions in the US Issue Open Letter, "Calls for Ceasefire in Israel Palestine"

US Labor Movement Calls for Ceasefire in Israel Palestine

We, members of the American labor movement, mourn the loss of life in Israel and Palestine. We express our solidarity with all workers and our common desire for peace in Palestine and Israel, and we call on President Joe Biden and Congress to push for an immediate ceasefire and end to the siege of Gaza. We cannot bomb our way to peace. We also condemn any hate crimes against Muslims, Jews, or anyone else.

In issuing this call, US unions are joining the efforts of 13 Congressmembers and others who are calling for an immediate ceasefire.

The basic rights of people must be restored. Water, fuel, food, and other humanitarian aid must be allowed into Gaza, power must be restored, and foreign nationals and Palestinians requiring medical care must be allowed out of Gaza.

The Israeli hostages taken by Hamas must be immediately released. Both Hamas and Israel must adhere to standards of international law and Geneva Convention rules of warfare concerning the welfare and security of citizens.

There must be a ceasefire in Gaza. The cycle of violence must stop so that negotiations for an enduring peace proceed.

The US must act. We call on President Biden to immediately call for a ceasefire. The road to justice cannot be paved by bombs and war. The road to peace cannot be found through warfare. We commit ourselves to work in solidarity with the Palestinian and Israeli peoples to achieve peace and justice.

Union members come from diverse backgrounds, including Jews, Muslims, and Middle Eastern communities. The rising escalation of war and arms sales doesn't serve the interests of workers anywhere. In the end, we all want a place to call home and for our children to be safe. Working people around the world want and deserve to live free from the effects of violence, war, and militarization.

Thousands of Americans have joined the groundswell of global solidarity demanding a ceasefire now.

It's the labor movement's turn to make our voices heard and demand a ceasefire. Together, we can stand for peace, justice, and a better future for working people everywhere.

Appendix B
UN Global Compact for Migration

The *Global Compact for Migration* [1] is the first-ever UN global agreement on a common approach to international migration in all its dimensions. The global compact is non-legally binding. It is grounded in values of state sovereignty, responsibility-sharing, non-discrimination, and human rights, and recognizes that a cooperative approach is needed to optimize the overall benefits of migration, while addressing its risks and challenges for individuals and communities in countries of origin, transit and destination.

The global compact comprises 23 objectives for better managing migration at local, national, regional and global levels. To summarize, the compact:

- Aims to mitigate the adverse drivers and structural factors that hinder people from building and maintaining sustainable livelihoods in their countries of origin;
- Intends to reduce the risks and vulnerabilities migrants face at different stages of migration by respecting, protecting and fulfilling their human rights and providing them with care and assistance;
- Seeks to address the legitimate concerns of states and communities, while recognizing that societies are undergoing demographic, economic, social and environmental changes at different scales that may have implications for and result from migration;
- Strives to create conducive conditions that enable all migrants to enrich our societies through their human, economic and social capacities, and thus facilitate their contributions to sustainable development at the local, national, regional and global levels.

Note

1 See the 2018 Global Compact for Migration in full here: https://refugeesmigrants.un.org/migration-compact

Index

Footnotes will be denoted by the letter 'n' and Note number following the page number.

Milton Keynes UK
Ingram Content Group UK Ltd.
UKHW022032220924
448658UK00027B/532